CW00723221

CAMBRIDGE STUDIES IN EARLY MODERN HISTORY

Editors

J. H. ELLIOTT   OLWEN HUFTON   H. G. KOENIGSBERGER

Religious Toleration and Social Change in Hamburg
1529–1819

CAMBRIDGE STUDIES IN EARLY MODERN HISTORY

*Edited by Professor J. H. Elliott, The Institute for Advanced Study, Princeton,
Professor Olwen Hufton, University of Reading, and Professor H. G. Koenigsberger,
King's College, London*

The idea of an 'early modern' period of European history from the fifteenth to the late eighteenth century is now widely accepted among historians. The purpose of the Cambridge Studies in Early Modern History is to publish monographs and studies which will illuminate the character of the period as a whole, and in particular focus attention on a dominant theme within it, the interplay of continuity and change as they are represented by the continuity of medieval ideas, political and social organisation, and by the impact of new ideas, new methods and new demands on the traditional structures.

Religious Toleration and Social Change in Hamburg 1529–1819

JOACHIM WHALEY

Fellow of Robinson College, Cambridge

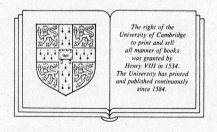

The right of the
University of Cambridge
to print and sell
all manner of books
was granted by
Henry VIII in 1534.
The University has printed
and published continuously
since 1584.

CAMBRIDGE UNIVERSITY PRESS

Cambridge

London   New York   New Rochelle

Melbourne   Sydney

Published by the Press Syndicate of the University of Cambridge
The Pitt Building, Trumpington Street, Cambridge CB2 1RP
32 East 57th Street, New York, NY 10022, USA
10 Stamford Road, Oakleigh, Melbourne 3166, Australia

© Cambridge University Press 1985

First published 1985

Printed in Great Britain by the University Press, Cambridge

Library of Congress catalogue card number: 84-29311

British Library Cataloguing in Publication Data
Whaley, Joachim
Religious toleration and social change in
Hamburg 1529–1819. – (Cambridge studies in
early modern history)
1. Religious tolerance – Germany – Hamburg –
History – 17th century   2. Religious tolerance
– Germany – Hamburg – History – 18th century
3. Religious tolerance – Germany – Hamburg –
History – 19th century
I. Title
291.1′772′0943515   BR1610

ISBN 0 521 26189 9

To my Parents

Contents

Preface

During the course of my research I have incurred debts too numerous and various to list in full. I would, however, like to record my thanks to a variety of institutions and individuals whose help has been particularly instrumental.

The work was begun while I was a Fellow of Christ's College, Cambridge, and I am grateful to the Master and Fellows for their generosity and support. In particular, they made several grants which enabled me to spend considerable time in Hamburg. I am also grateful to the Wolfson Foundation for a generous European Fellowship which allowed me to complete my archival work. The Warden and Fellows of Robinson College contributed towards the cost of typing both the original thesis and the final draft of this book.

I am also grateful to the staff of the *Staatsarchiv der Freien und Hansestadt Hamburg* for their help over a number of years. The director, Professor Dr Hans-Dieter Loose, and Dr Klaus Richter both provided me with invaluable assistance. Herr Amthor and Frau Neidhöfer in the *Lesesaal* were also particularly patient and courteous. Fräulein Eva Horthvath guided me in the *Staats- und Universitätsbibliothek*, as did Frau Eva Lembke in the *Commerzbibliothek*.

Also in Hamburg, I received much help and encouragement from Dr Franklin Kopitzsch. His encyclopedic knowledge of the bibliography and sources of Hamburg's history and his enthusiasm for any attempt to open up new avenues of enquiry was much appreciated whenever I worked in Hamburg. I have also profited from his fine study of the *Aufklärung* in Hamburg, which appeared as I was about to embark upon the final draft of this book.

Dr T. C. W. Blanning supervised my thesis; he was unfailingly generous with his time; and his support was extremely valuable on many occasions. I am also grateful to the Reverend Professor Owen Chadwick, O.M. and Dr R. J. W. Evans for their valuable comments on and criticism of my work. In addition, I have profited considerably from the criticisms and encouragement of Professors J. H. Elliott and H. G. Koenigsberger in preparing the book for publication.

More general and longer-standing is the debt of gratitude which I owe to Sir John Plumb. As a teacher, colleague and a friend, his advice and encouragement have been enduring and invaluable since I was an undergraduate. The benefit of his wisdom and generosity has enhanced my life, and hence this book, in numerous ways.

Finally, I would like to thank my parents, who gave me a 'second identity'.

Robinson College   JOACHIM WHALEY
Cambridge

Abbreviations

ADB	*Allgemeine Deutsche Biographie*
CBH	*Commerzbibliothek*, Hamburg
DRG	Deutsch-evangelisch-reformierte Gemeinde
EB	Erbgesessene Bürgerschaft
EPS	Extractus Protocolli Senatus Hamburgensis
GDHV	*Geschichtsblätter des Deutschen Hugenottenvereins*
HGH	*Hamburgische Geschichts- und Heimatsblätter*
Hss.	Handschriftensammlung
MVHG	*Mitteilungen des Vereins für Hamburgische Geschichte*
PRO	Public Record Office
RGG	*Die Religion in Geschichte und Gegenwart*
SP	State papers
StAH	*Staatsarchiv der Freien und Hansestadt Hamburg*
VSWG	*Vierteljahresschrift für Sozial- und Wirtschaftsgeschichte*
ZVHG	*Zeitschrift des Vereins für Hamburgische Geschichte*

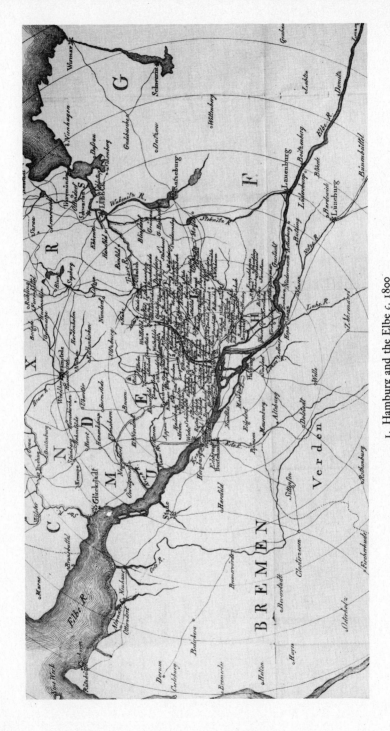

1. Hamburg and the Elbe *c.* 1800

Source: *The picture of Hamburg, or the Englishman's guide to that Free Imperial City,*
London, n.d.

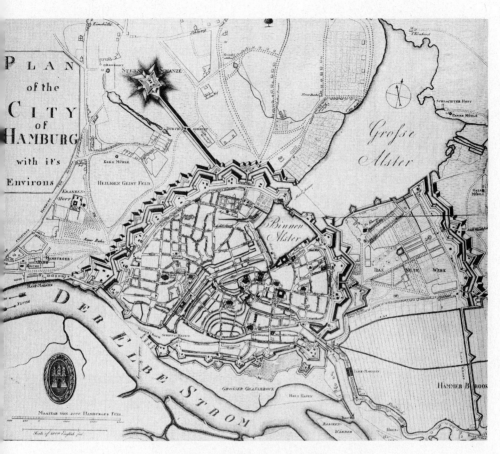

2. The city of Hamburg *c.* 1800
Source: *The picture of Hamburg, or the Englishman's guide to that Free Imperial City,*
London, n.d.

Introduction

In his *Dichtung und Wahrheit* Goethe recalled how as an aspiring young
writer he had practised his literary skills by drafting a pamphlet in the form
of a letter from a rural parson to a newly ordained colleague: 'The main
theme of this letter was the watchword of that time, namely, "Tolerance",
which prevailed among the better minds and spirits.'[1] His immediate
inspiration was the work of his uncle Johann Michael von Loen, one of
the most prominent German polemicists of religious toleration; but his
youthful exercise reflected one of the major preoccupations of the age.[2] For,
as contemporaries constantly pointed out, the eighteenth century was the
century of toleration. United in their rejection of persecution and
discrimination on grounds of faith, the *Aufklärer* saw the propagation of
mutual recognition and respect as their prime vocation.[3]

Even the most cursory survey of enlightened literature reveals just how
fundamental the idea of toleration was to the *Aufklärung*. Sermons, travel
reports, historical works, topographies, encyclopedias, studies of population
growth and the economy, plays, poems and novels, all are littered with
references to the evils of religious persecution and the beneficial results of
an irenic pacifism. The writings of Bayle, Locke and Voltaire became
the devotional literature of a new cult of humanity which condemned the
brutality of the Old Testament. Both the Orthodox guardians of the
Lutheran Church and the intolerant Jesuits became the object of passionate

Bibliographical references have been abbreviated throughout; full citations may be found in the
bibliography.
[1] Goethe, *Werke*, 9, p. 512.
[2] On Loen, see *ADB*, 19, pp. 86–8 and Goethe, *Werke*, 9, pp. 75–6. There is no good study of
his work. The most important essays, dealing with relations between Lutherans and Calvinists
in Frankfurt am Main, are collected in von Loen, *Kleine Schrifften*, esp. pp. 1–22, 295–314, 375–86.
[3] The term *Aufklärung* is the German equivalent of 'the Enlightenment'. The best surveys of the
eighteenth-century debate in Germany and its European context are: Schultze, *Lessings
Toleranzbegriff*, pp. 11–23 and Kiesel, 'Toleranz', *passim*. See also: Kopitzsch, 'Sozialgeschichte
der Aufklärung', pp. 89–95; Gay, *Enlightenment*, 2, pp. 398–407; Kantzenbach, *Protestantisches
Christentum*, pp. 81–4; Grossmann, 'Religious toleration'; François, 'De l'uniformité à la
tolérance'.

criticism. The histories of Spain and Portugal provided salutary warnings of what evils would ensue from a rigid adherence to a single truth; those of Britain, Holland, Prussia and later Joseph II's Austria, provided both confirmation of the wisdom of toleration and hope for its spread in the future.[4]

The vision of an end to the religious controversies which had marred the history of Christianity (which Voltaire characterised as the most intolerant of all religions) was, of course, neither new nor confined to Germany.[5] As Hans Guggisberg has shown, the later debate had its roots in the writings of Nicholas of Cusa, Ficino and Pico della Mirandola. Their ideas were synthesised in the work of Erasmus as he reacted to the brutal reality of the division of Christendom during the Reformation.[6] Like later apologists, Erasmus propagated a return to the fundamental texts of Christianity (the first texts of the Gospels and the works of the Church Fathers), an end to elaborate theological speculation, and the reduction of faith to a limited set of basic teachings.[7] These themes were taken up by later writers such as Castellio, Bodin, Bayle, Locke, Leibniz and Thomasius, and they provided the broad framework for the theological and philosophical discussion of the eighteenth century. Throughout, the debate transcended national frontiers and preoccupied the whole Republic of Letters. Just as bitter confessional strife embraced the whole of Europe, so the desires first for the reunion of Christendom and then for toleration were the most prominent international causes in the early modern era.[8]

The history of the idea is well known and the debate about it has been traced and analysed in great detail. Indeed, in many ways too much attention has been devoted to theology and philosophy, and this has obscured the nature of the real progress of toleration before the French Revolution. A comparison of the radical demands often made by intellectuals with the actual implementation of measures designed to establish a religious equilibrium should warn against adopting a whiggish view of the forceful march of ideas.[9] Understandably, modern scholars have been concerned to trace the provenance of principles which are fundamental to the society in which they live. They point to toleration edicts, especially in the eighteenth century, as evidence of the gradual acceptance of the concept of individual freedom of conscience first explicitly proclaimed in the Virginia Bill of Rights and the French Declaration of the Rights of Man.[10] But in doing so they confuse two fundamental issues: on the one hand the

[4] Kiesel, 'Toleranz', pp. 372–82.   [5] Voltaire, *Dictionnaire philosophique*, p. 365.
[6] Guggisberg, 'Wandel der Argumente', pp. 460–1.   [7] Ibid., pp. 461–2.
[8] Ibid., pp. 455–60, 465–81.
[9] The point is stressed by Butterfield, 'Toleration', pp. 573–4.
[10] Dickmann, 'Problem der Gleichberechtigung', p. 247.

modern development of social attitudes which accept the right of the individual to believe anything or indeed nothing at all, and on the other hand the much older establishment of the legal principle that the state has a duty to guarantee if not the equality of all Churches then at least freedom from persecution of all groups which do not subscribe to the faith of an established Church.[11]

Both principles can be traced back to the sixteenth century. But the Enlightenment was particularly significant because its debates elucidated the difference between the two more explicitly than ever before. For despite the polemical exuberance of the Enlightenment, it soon became clear that the pursuit of the claims of reason over those of revelation led into murky and potentially dangerous waters. It is true that the uncompromising stance of Voltaire was universally admired in enlightened circles.[12] Lessing became a hero in Nicolai's Berlin circle because of his outright confrontation with the Orthodox Lutheran pastor Johann Melchior Goeze.[13] The *Aufklärer* applauded Frederick the Great's robust statements on the rights of his subjects to believe whatever they liked (though many of them preferred to do so from a vantage-point outside Prussia itself).[14] But the chorus of praise for great thoughts and deeds belied a deep sense of unease about many of the principles which underpinned them. Few shared Voltaire's scepticism about any form of organised religion.[15] Nicolai and his circle did not concur in Lessing's demand for the acceptance of heretics, atheists and Jews.[16] Nor did they approve of Frederick the Great's declaration that he would build mosques and temples for Turks and heathens if they were honest in the profession of their beliefs.[17]

Such sentiments were praiseworthy enough in an intolerant world in need of provocative education. But they smacked of an indifference which many regarded as harmful both to religion and to man. It might be true that there were many paths to salvation; but most *Aufklärer* believed that it was more certainly to be found in Lutheranism, Calvinism or Catholicism. For the established Christian Churches represented more than just organised faith: they were durable pillars of state and society whose worth had been proved by history and whose indispensability remained a *sine qua non* for the future.[18] Indeed, as Locke had pointed out, heretics and atheists who

[11] Ibid., pp. 247–51.   [12] Schultze, *Lessings Toleranzbegriff*, pp. 11–12.
[13] Schultze, 'Toleranz und Orthodoxie', *passim*; Kantzenbach, *Protestantisches Christentum*, pp. 161–5.
[14] Kiesel, 'Toleranz', p. 380; Conrad, 'Religionsbann', p. 189; Kantzenbach, *Protestantisches Christentum*, pp. 142–8.
[15] Schultze, *Lessings Toleranzbegriff*, pp. 11, 19.   [16] Ibid., pp. 39–48.
[17] Quoted by Kiesel, 'Toleranz', p. 380.
[18] Wild, 'Freidenker', *passim*; Scholder, 'Grundzüge der theologischen Aufklärung', *passim*; Whaley, 'Protestant Enlightenment', pp. 107–8, 111–13.

rejected God could not be relied upon to contribute to his kingdom on earth; nor could the Jews, whose religion knew nothing of the obligations expressed in the oaths of Christians to their fellow men.[19]

Doubt and uncertainty about the degree of religious freedom permissible according to the will of God and the needs of government and society were not new. But the prominence of their discussion in Germany in the eighteenth century not only delineated the contours of the modern debate, but, more importantly, pointed to the specifically German framework which the *Aufklärer* inherited. For the prominent few, men like Thomasius and Lessing, did not themselves create the demand for a change in religious attitudes. It was rather the context, the social and political realities of German society, which generated the need for reform which they articulated.

Toleration was an international idea, but nowhere was the debate as clearly circumscribed in practical, legal and administrative terms as in the Holy Roman Empire. The *Aufklärer* eagerly debated the theological and philosophical implications of the literature they read. But on the level of action they were concerned primarily with the implementation of legal and constitutional principles – principles gradually evolved during the century after the Reformation and enshrined in the Peace of Westphalia in 1648.

In Germany the confessional conflicts of the sixteenth century posed legal and constitutional problems which demanded a political solution earlier and more acutely than anywhere else. The Reformation was preceded by and became part of a constitutional struggle between the Emperor and the princes. For many, Protestantism was a vehicle of resistance to the Emperor's claims to sovereignty over them, and its establishment during the 1530s and 1540s marked the first stage in the long and difficult process of defining his position in the amorphous *Reich*.[20] Far from resolving the situation, the first truce at Augsburg in 1555 exacerbated the dispute. It did not recognise Calvinism, while the principle of *cuius regio eius religio* gave both Catholics and Lutherans hopes of extending their powers by converting or reconverting individual rulers. The peace effectively created a machinery of conflict which ultimately precipitated the outbreak of the Thirty Years War. It did, however, embody principles which later provided the foundations of a more lasting peace. The *jus reformandi* was placed firmly in the hands of the princes and magistrates, while subjects who did not share the faith of their ruler were granted the right of emigration on the payment of compensation.[21]

The problems resulting from the ambiguities of the Augsburg settlement

[19] Guggisberg, 'Wandel der Argumente', pp. 475–8.
[20] Dickmann, 'Problem der Gleichberechtigung', pp. 203–35.
[21] Conrad, 'Religionsbann', pp. 169–75. Cf. Scheuner, 'Auswanderungsfreiheit', pp. 208–11.

were only resolved by the Treaty of Osnabrück in 1648. The Treaty placed the seal on the truce between the Emperor, the *Reichsstände* and Sweden. More than just a declaration of peace, it became the foundation of the Imperial constitution until 1806; and its most significant achievement was the construction of a complex legal code governing the relationship of the Christian Churches in Germany.[22]

Catholicism, Lutheranism and Calvinism were recognised as established religions with equal constitutional rights. The *jus reformandi* was ceded unambiguously to the sovereign princes. In all states, the privileges of those confessions which owned property or which enjoyed public worship in 1624 were guaranteed. While the right of dissenting subjects to emigrate and the *jus reformandi* of the rulers were both reinforced, the Treaty also imposed a kind of limited toleration on all rulers. They had the right to determine the dominant religion in their lands, but could neither persecute nor force into emigration members of other Churches established before 1624. Those who had no such rights could emigrate, but if they did so, they were not to be deprived of their property.[23]

Three types of religious worship emerged from this complex legislation. The dominant religion alone enjoyed the *exercitium religionis publicum*; the other recognised Churches were granted *exercitium religionis privatum*. Members of recognised religions without rights before 1624 were only allowed an *exercitium religionis domesticum*. Public worship meant churches with spires and bells; private worship meant chapels without either; domestic worship meant prayers in the family home and the right to visit churches in a neighbouring state.[24]

The Treaty's clauses were all-embracing. But it was only unambiguous and fully effective in establishing the constitutional parity between Protestants and Catholics in the Imperial Courts. At this level it served its purpose in putting an end to the kind of inter-state quarrels which had led to the Thirty Years War. But within the states themselves it soon became clear that it had merely provided a rather ambiguous set of guidelines. In practice it was difficult to maintain the distinction between *publicum* and *privatum*. The sects excluded from the Treaty did not disappear as some had hoped.[25] Above all it was never clear whether the Treaty represented a final statement of limitations or whether it merely guaranteed minimal rights which might be extended at will by the princes and magistrates.[26]

[22] Feine, 'Verfassungsentwicklung des Heil. Röm. Reiches', pp. 65–74; Vierhaus, *Deutschland*, pp. 83–4.
[23] Conrad, 'Religionsbann', pp. 175–81; Dickmann, 'Problem der Gleichberechtigung', pp. 235–43; Fürstenau, *Grundrecht der Religionsfreiheit*, pp. 49–73. See also Dietrich, 'Landeskirchenrecht und Gewissensfreiheit'.   [24] Sägmüller, 'Begriff des *exercitium religionis*'.
[25] Fürstenau, *Grundrecht der Religionsfreiheit*, p. 54.
[26] Grossmann, 'Toleration', pp. 133–4.

Disputes over the Treaty's implications punctuated the history of the *Reich* to its dissolution. It provided the legal framework for the debate about religious toleration in Germany. Those who espoused moderation claimed that the *jus reformandi* of the rulers logically implied that they might extend the liberties guaranteed by the Treaty – both with regard to members of the recognised religions and, more controversially, to the unrecognised sects. Their opponents clung to the letter of the law which apparently sanctioned discrimination and restrained official tolerance.[27] But in the last resort even those *Aufklärer* who applauded the toleration edicts of the eighteenth century were able to rationalise their distrust of sectarians and their rejection of the Jews by reference to the religious constitution of the *Reich*. A law which fostered religious peace at the level of the state simultaneously excused and justified the refusal to grant anything more than freedom from persecution to anyone who was not either a Catholic, Lutheran or Calvinist member of a community established before 1624.

Even at the time, the Treaty was subject to two interpretations. The Catholic powers took a rigorous view: for them *Gewissensfreiheit* merely implied the right not to be forced into conversion, though individuals might be pressurised to emigrate. Protestant *Gewissensfreiheit* implied a much clearer freedom of individual choice; the Protestant Estates declared the right of all to family devotions, and understood the *jus reformandi* to include the right to extend privileges to groups outside the established Church.[28] On any interpretation, the toleration defined in 1648 was limited, and it was increasingly seen to be unsatisfactory, on grounds which ranged from the purely religious to the political, social and economic. It was this rising sense of dissatisfaction which stimulated attempts to extend the rights guaranteed in 1648, to extend laws produced by fear of strife and conflict into liberties based on confidence in harmony and human progress.

Little attention has, however, been devoted to the study of the policies which resulted from these fundamental attitudes.[29] In practice the situation of religious minorities varied enormously. Only in Prussia has official policy been studied in detail.[30] Here the Electors continued traditions laid down in the sixteenth and early seventeenth centuries by welcoming all manner of religious minorities expelled from various parts of Europe. While religious conviction was undoubtedly important, political and above all economic motives were crucial. Huguenots and Jews, for example, played

---

27 Fürstenau, *Grundrecht der Religionsfreiheit*, pp. 70–3; Conrad, 'Religionsbann', pp. 179–80.
28 Fürstenau, *Grundrecht der Religionsfreiheit*, p. 73. For a contemporary interpretation, see: Klefeker, *Verfassungen*, 8, pp. 692–704, 741–8.
29 See the comment in Kopitzsch, 'Sozialgeschichte der Aufklärung', p. 160 (note 662).
30 Fürstenau, *Grundrecht der Religionsfreiheit*, pp. 75–80.

a central role in the development of the Prussian economy after 1700 and Frederick II's tolerance was essentially a recognition of this fact.[31]

Similar policies appear to have been adopted in other territories like Hessen, Schleswig-Holstein and Braunschweig-Wolfenbüttel.[32] Religion rarely became an issue in these cases. The implementation of concessions by princely fiat seldom aroused significant opposition: the clergy were subject to princely authority in the *Landeskirchen*, while popular opposition, where it existed, often lacked an effective vehicle of expression due to the weakness of the territorial Estates.[33]

More surprisingly, even less attention has been devoted to the free cities. Often governed by mixed constitutions, the formulation of a coherent policy was far more difficult here than in the principalities. Toleration at any level aroused fears that religious constitutions might be subverted, while the clergy often played a more active and powerful role in the decision-making process.[34] At the same time, the need to accommodate minorities was generally more pressing in an independent city. The history of Cologne in the eighteenth century showed that the price paid for intolerance was economic stagnation and decline. The history of Frankfurt in the same period demonstrated the dangers inherent in pursuing the opposite course – decades of bitter constitutional conflict between Lutherans and Calvinists resolved only by decisive Imperial intervention.[35]

This book will examine the problems which ensued from the acceptance of religious minorities in the most important independent commercial centre in Germany, the Lutheran city of Hamburg. Its Jewish, Catholic and Calvinist minorities made a substantial contribution to the economy. But Hamburg avoided the constitutional conflicts which disrupted the history of Frankfurt over this issue; although at the same time the opposition of both citizenry and clergy prevented a satisfactory resolution of the issue of religious worship until 1785 in the case of the Christian groups and until 1849 in the case of the Jews.[36]

---

[31] Jersch-Wenzel, *Juden und 'Franzosen'*, pp. 25–42.

[32] Klefeker, *Verfassungen*, 8, pp. 695–7; Albrecht, *Förderung des Landesausbaues*, pp. 573–7; Kopitzsch, 'Sozialgeschichte der Aufklärung', pp. 90–1.

[33] The point is stressed by the Hamburg Syndic Johann Klefeker in Klefeker, *Verfassungen*, 8, pp. 695–7.

[34] Ibid. See also: François, 'De l'uniformité à la tolérance', *passim*.

[35] On Cologne, see Schwering, 'Entwicklung des Protestantismus'; *idem*, 'Lage des Protestantismus'; Heinen, 'Kölner Toleranzstreit'. On Frankfurt, see Soliday, *Community in conflict*, esp. pp. 208–30.

[36] On the Catholics, see Dreves, *Geschichte* and Linckemeyer, *Das katholische Hamburg*; on the Calvinists, see Hermes, *Reformierte Gemeinde* and Boué, 'Abriss'; on the Jews, see Grunwald, *Hamburgs deutsche Juden*. These works all deal primarily with the internal history of the respective communities; this book is the first general analysis which deals with all three groups and their relationship with the Lutheran authorities.

The struggle for political stability and purity of belief: Hamburg from Reformation to French Revolution

In his survey of the world of the early Enlightenment, Peter Gay wrote: 'Hamburg, one of many Free Cities in the German Empire, avoided the decay of most of the others by welcoming foreigners of all nationalities and giving them a place in civic and commercial affairs. The...Constitution of 1712, perhaps the least oligarchical urban charter of the age, reflected this liberal spirit and promoted it.'[1] Gay gives no source for his judgement, but it reflects nonetheless the views of a long line of Hamburg historians beginning around 1800 and culminating in the better-known work of Percy Schramm.[2] After the toleration mandate of 1785, and in the context of the euphoric reforming zeal of the urban elite after the 1790s, the city's historians created a myth of a free mercantile republic whose present wealth and power derived from a long tradition of freedom and toleration. 'In political and civil terms there is only one estate in Hamburg, the burgher estate', wrote Johann Daniel Curio in 1802, 'We are all citizens, no more and no less.'[3] A decade later Jonas Ludwig von Hess elaborated the myth when he declared:

The people here sometimes abused the non-Lutheran immigrants and made them fear for their lives. Yet one cannot claim that Lutheran Hamburg ever openly persecuted those whom, according to its religious principles, it would have been obliged to regard as heretics. It never deprived them of their honour, their livelihood or their lives. The appearance of intolerance which was formerly attached to the city rarely sprang from a fanatical devotion to the supposed cause of God. If such an intolerance did in fact ever rage in Hamburg, this spirit more truly possessed the minds of the clergy than those of the real citizens.[4]

Like most myths, that of Hamburg's tradition of tolerance has a certain foundation of truth. But the present study will show that the judgements of Curio and Hess, which remain influential to this day, in fact represent

---

[1] Gay, *Enlightenment*, 2, pp. 47–8.
[2] Schramm's two most important contributions are: *Sonderfall* and *Neun Generationen*, 1.
[3] Quoted by Dingedahl, 'Johann Carl Daniel Curio', p. 9.
[4] J. L. von Hess, *Hamburg* (2nd edn), 3, p. 259.

a distortion of reality. They would even have surprised eighteenth-century visitors like Jonas Hanway who noted in 1753 that Hamburg was like Amsterdam and London, except that there was no toleration.[5] For the interplay of commerce and ideology, of religion and politics, rendered the acceptance of religious minorities infinitely more complex than many later commentators would admit. What von Hess called 'the appearance of intolerance' in fact lasted for nearly two centuries. The history of its exorcism is intimately bound up with the social, political and intellectual development of Hamburg in the early modern era.

I

In the second half of the sixteenth century religious persecution and war disrupted and partially destroyed the economy first of the southern Netherlands and then of Spain itself. For many of those driven into exile in search of liberty and peace, Hamburg provided an attractive haven. It was an established port and commercial centre: it was an independent neutral city far to the north of the troubles. Above all, compared with London and Amsterdam, it was relatively underdeveloped.[6]

Italian Catholics, Sephardic Jews, Lutheran and Calvinist Dutch all began to settle there from the 1550s. They brought with them wealth and skills which rapidly transformed the city from a leading member of the declining Hanseatic League into a European commercial centre. Textiles replaced beer as the mainstay of the urban economy. The Dutch and the Sephardim particularly played a crucial role in the development of the financial market. The establishment of a Bank in 1619 underpinned the transformation of the city from a Baltic and North Sea port into one whose trading network extended down to the Iberian peninsula and westwards to London and the New World.[7]

In much the same way, the Huguenot immigrants after 1685 laid the foundations of prosperity in the eighteenth century. They too brought wealth and, perhaps more importantly, commercial contacts with France. Together with textiles and banking, the French colonial trade enabled Hamburg to survive the structural changes and crises of the era before the American War of Independence and the collapse of Dutch mercantile influence during the Anglo-Dutch War in the 1780s.[8]

[5] Hanway, *British Trade*, 2, p. 277.
[6] Wiskemann, *Welthandelspolitik*, pp. 75–9; Kellenbenz, *Unternehmerkräfte*, pp. 33–102; Vogel, 'Handelskonjunkturen', pp. 57–9; Büsch, *Handlung*, pp. 22–36.
[7] Ibid., pp. 26–39, 80–1; Kellenbenz, *Unternehmerkräfte*, pp. 179–81, 236–8, 241–3, 252–7, 258–9, 333–50; Sieveking, 'Hamburger Bank', pp. 26–47; Mauersberg, *Zentraleuropäische Städte*, pp. 278–85.
[8] Schramm, 'Zwei "Millionäre"', pp. 29–40; Büsch, *Handlung*, pp. 72–7; Jeannin, 'Hansestädte', *passim*; Huhn, 'Handelsbeziehungen', 1, pp. 20–34; Liebel, 'Laissez-faire vs. Mercantilism', pp. 211–16.

International conflicts which led to the decline of powers like Spain in the seventeenth century and Holland in the eighteenth undoubtedly enhanced Hamburg's position in the European economy. But the process of growth and consolidation was crucially determined by immigration.[9] Between 1550 and 1600 the urban population doubled from 20,000 to about 40,000, rising to 45,000–50,000 by 1620, some 60,000 by 1680, 75,000 by 1715, 90,000 by 1750 and about 100,000 by the 1780s.[10] Even allowing for natural growth, Heinrich Reincke has estimated that at any given time about 50 per cent of the population were immigrants.[11] Between 1550 and 1650 the most prominent immigrant group came from the Netherlands. Reincke estimated that around 1600 nearly a quarter of the entire population was of Dutch origin. Thereafter the pattern of immigration was characterised by migration from within Germany, especially from Lower Saxony.[12] Throughout, most immigrants were Lutherans. But the relative contribution of non-Lutherans to the economy was highly significant. For they brought to Hamburg the wealth, skills and contacts which attracted so many Germans after 1650.[13]

Trade and finance were the lifeblood of the growing metropolis on the Elbe. But the economic vitality of a predominantly immigrant society also contributed to the development of a burgeoning urban culture. After 1650 Hamburg became an attractive centre for printers and publishers producing books, and above all newspapers and journals.[14] Diplomats and noblemen in search of cosmopolitan entertainment combined with prosperous citizens in establishing and supporting the first permanent opera house in Germany in 1678.[15] Hamburg had no university, but its Gymnasium attracted respected scholars, in addition to those writers who lived in the city on private means supplemented by income from journalism and publishing.[16] By 1700 Hamburg had become an economic and cultural centre of unrivalled importance in Germany and comparable only with such great cities as London and Amsterdam.

[9] The point is stressed by Büsch, *Handlung*, pp. 52–6.

[10] For a general discussion, see Mauersberg, *Zentraleuropäische Städte*, pp. 30–48. The most reliable figures are those presented by Reincke, 'Hamburgs Bevölkerung', pp. 171–4.

[11] Ibid., p. 187.

[12] Ibid., pp. 192–3. See also the excellent analysis of seventeenth-century immigration in Reissmann, *Kaufmannschaft*, pp. 213–31.

[13] Büsch, *Handlung*, pp. 26–31, 51–7, 72–7; Reissmann, *Kaufmannschaft*, pp. 213–30.

[14] On newspapers, see Prange, *Zeitungen und Zeitschriften*; Whaley, 'Circulation of early newspapers', pp. 178–83. On publishing, see W. Kayser, *Hamburger Bücher*, pp. 11–19; idem, 'Drucker und Verleger', pp. 28–36.

[15] The opera survived until 1738: Marx, 'Hamburger Barockoper'; Wolff, 'Hamburger Oper'.

[16] Sillem, *Matrikel*, pp. ii–xiii; Klefeker, *Verfassungen*, 6, pp. 45–63. The major function of the Gymnasium was to prepare scholars for their university studies; the city also supported an ordinary grammar school, the Johanneum.

Indeed it was this extraordinary combination of economic and cultural exuberance which attracted so many travellers in the eighteenth century. The British Resident might complain in 1718 that 'that which actually happens in Hamburgh is very seldom worth printing'.[17] But the topographers and travel writers disagreed. Writers like James Vernon, Zacharias Conrad von Uffenbach, Thomas Lediard, Thomas Nugent among many others stressed the vitality of Hamburg, its prosperity, its culture, its unique blend of local tradition with a cosmopolitan culture.[18]

II

The admiration expressed by travellers for this dynamic city, combined with the immigrant character of its population, might suggest that the process of assimilating foreigners was indeed as uncomplicated as Gay implies. In so far as the newcomers were Lutherans, this was undoubtedly true. After an initial period as *Einwohner* most of them, including the Lutheran Dutch, became *Bürger*. They gained full civil and political rights, and contributed as much as the established indigenous population to the administration of urban and ecclesiastical affairs.[19]

Since by far the greatest proportion of immigrants were Lutherans, their acceptance posed no problems. The experience of the relatively smaller numbers of non-Lutherans was, however, very different. The Senate successfully resisted attempts to expel them outright in the early seventeenth century and thereafter made every effort to aid their establishment within the city. But those initiatives were severely limited, and did not extend to a recognition of the right to worship in public. The Jews were a special case: their relationship with the city remained a contractual one until the nineteenth century.[20] The Christian minorities could, however, be partially assimilated. They were encouraged to move beyond their initial contractual obligations and assume limited citizenship. If they paid taxes and obeyed the laws they might enjoy all privileges of citizenship except the right to political participation and the right to public worship.[21]

Exactly how many non-Lutheran Christians made use of this limited

[17] PRO: SP 82/99: 1 February 1717/18, Wich to Tilson.
[18] The most important accounts are: Nugent, *Grand tour*, 2, pp. 90–107; *idem*, *Travels*, 1, pp. 19–92; Vernon, *Travels*, 2, pp. 240–51; von Uffenbach, *Reisen*, 2, pp. 75–143; Hanway, *British Trade*, 2, pp. 272–82; Lediard, *German spy*, pp. 90–397. Lediard was Secretary to the British Resident 1725–7, and his account is by far the most detailed and well-informed.
[19] On the distinction between *Bürger* and *Einwohner*, see: Klefeker, *Verfassungen*, 2, pp. 272–319; Reissmann, *Kaufmannschaft*, pp. 231–42; Büsch, *Handlung*, p. 31.
[20] See Chapter 3. In Imperial law the Jews were defined as a separate 'nation', subject not to the princes but to the Emperor himself. Cf. Conrad, *Deutsche Rechtsgeschichte*, 2, pp. 223–5.
[21] Klefeker, *Verfassungen*, 2, pp. 299–303. They were also allowed to serve in the militia and in the garrison: Ehlers, *Wehrverfassung*, pp. 168–9.

freedom is unclear. Statistics relating to the minorities are rare. Little is known about the numbers who stayed permanently under the so-called *Fremdenkontrakt* as opposed to those who became citizens or indeed those who migrated away from Hamburg altogether.[22] Those who married daughters or widows of Lutheran citizens were obliged to become citizens themselves. Similarly, others who decided to settle in Hamburg permanently could apply for limited citizenship if they wished – even the minorities whose religion did not permit them to take the usual oath.[23] But in the seventeenth century at least, Martin Reissmann suggests that many preferred to remain *Fremde*: they were allowed to trade on the same terms as *Bürger*; indeed their alien status gave them exemption from militia duties and the freedom to leave Hamburg without paying a substantial tribute.[24] After 1700 the situation seems to have changed: a list of *Fremde* compiled in 1731 only gives 135 names; apparently, the official desire to have *Bürger* rather than *Einwohner* gradually prevailed.[25]

Whether as *Fremde* or as *Bürger*, non-Lutheran Christians thus enjoyed considerable freedom in economic terms. But even as *Bürger* they were excluded from political participation, so that in many ways the difference between the two conditions was minimal, and dependent largely upon the degree to which settlement in Hamburg was a permanent or a transitory move.[26]

In either case, the most important form of discrimination lay in the denial of the right to worship in public; in this sense non-Lutherans were no more privileged than the Jews. This issue was in turn intimately bound up with the lack of political rights. Lutheranism was the established religion; only Lutherans were eligible for public office or could attend the *Bürgerschaft*. In a republic where commercial success or academic standing determined social status, religion alone determined participation in the polity.[27]

This was the crux of the debate over toleration. To allow public worship for non-Lutherans ultimately implied the possibility of non-Lutherans participating in the administration of the affairs of the established Church. Quite apart from the fact that the Lutheran clergy vehemently opposed such a prospect, the Senate itself was wary of introducing a reform which might in imperceptible ways gradually undermine the urban constitution. As the Syndic Johann Klefeker pointed out as late as 1770, this was where the

[22] Reissmann, *Kaufmannschaft*, pp. 231–52.
[23] Klefeker, *Verfassungen*, 2, pp. 299–312.
[24] Reissmann, *Kaufmannschaft*, pp. 219–20, 231–42.
[25] StAH, Senat, Cl.VII Lit.Cc No.2 Vol.1 Fasc.1; Klefeker, *Verfassungen*, 2, p. 303.
[26] Ibid., pp. 296–303; Reissmann, *Kaufmannschaft*, pp. 231–5.
[27] Unlike many other German cities, Hamburg had no formal table of ranks or *Ständeordnung*. See: Reissmann, *Kaufmannschaft*, pp. 278–330; Schramm 'Adelsfrage', *passim*. The significance of discrimination in terms of religious worship is stressed by Klefeker, *Verfassungen*, 8, pp. 692–704, 741–8, 773, 776–83.

difference between principalities and independent cities lay. For princes and monarchs were more masters over their lands than magistrates whose hands were tied by constitutions, and whose authority was effective only to the extent that it was accepted by citizens and clergy. To jeopardise the pure religious base of the urban polity might throw it into turmoil, and ultimately destroy it.[28]

III

Conflict and turmoil were not merely chimeras conjured up by the Lutheran mind in order to justify mindless opposition to change. The constitutional history of Hamburg in the sixteenth and seventeenth centuries was characterised by periodic protracted conflicts between magistrates and citizens. After 1650 they erupted into a virtual civil war; a hopeless and violent deadlock ensued which was only resolved by the intervention of an Imperial commission in 1708–12. The causes of the disturbances were complex, and there is still no satisfactory account of them.[29] Even many contemporaries were baffled by the bewildering variety of issues, by the shifting alliances and uneasy compromises. After 1712 a determined effort at collective amnesia secured the future but obscured the past. Nonetheless, the history of the troubles is fundamental to an understanding of the evolution of the city in the *ancien régime*.

The power structure, which was the source of conflict, was the product of the Reformation, formally introduced in Hamburg in 1529. During the Middle Ages, the city had effectively been ruled by a city council, later known as the Senate. This body normally comprised twenty-four members (of whom four were *Bürgermeister*) drawn from the mercantile elite, although after 1465 lawyers were occasionally elected. In the fifteenth century its powers were challenged by three major rebellions of the citizenry, in 1410, 1458 and 1482–3; but the political powers of the *Bürgerschaft* never extended beyond a limited veto on taxation and on decisions relating to foreign policy. Despite the rebellions, the traditional rights of the *Bürgerschaft* to participate in the legislative process were also progressively eroded and the position of the Senate reinforced.[30]

The fundamental transition came with the gradual acceptance of the Lutheran teachings during the 1520s. This process was a peaceful one. Apart from the violent destruction of a recalcitrant monastery in Harvestehude in 1530, the reform was characterised by the acquiescence of the

[28] Ibid., p. 697. Cf. Bartels, *Einige Abhandlungen*, pp. 299–314.
[29] The best short introductions are: Bolland, *Senat und Bürgerschaft* and Loose, 'Zeitalter der Bürgerunruhen', pp. 269–87. For a more detailed account, see Rückleben, *Niederwerfung*.
[30] Postel, 'Reformation und Gegenreformation', pp. 195–6.

Senate in the demands of the citizens. Initially, the movement took the form of a demand for greater control over the clergy and over ecclesiastical affairs within the four major urban parishes. It was led by the church wardens (*Juraten* or *Kirchgeschworene*) and the custodians of the sacraments (*Leichnamsgeschworene*) who demanded the correction of clerical abuses, both in morals and teachings and in the administration of the parishes. In 1522 the wardens of all the parishes united to reassert lay control over schools. In 1526 the parishioners of St Nicholas' insisted on their right to appoint a preacher of their own choice, a Lutheran sympathiser.[31]

The next step was the most fundamental of all. In August 1527 the parishioners of St Nicholas' appointed a committee of twelve laymen (known as deacons or *Gotteskastenverwalter*) to administer the poor box. Within three months the other parishes had followed suit; and in the following year each parish appointed a further twenty-four subdeacons to assist in the new tasks which the citizenry had taken upon itself. Finally, in September 1528, the citizens agreed to nominate the three most senior deacons of each parish to serve on a body (known as the *Oberalten*) to administer the consolidated accounts of all poor boxes.[32]

Lay control over education and the poor boxes, the election of preachers, all established by 1528, thus formed the core of the Hamburg Reformation. In pursuing these aims, the citizenry had, however, also created institutions which bridged the gap between the medieval parish administration and the urban administration. The problem which had confronted the *Bürgerschaft* in the fifteenth century was the lack of representative institutions capable of pursuing its claims against the magistrates effectively. Now the deacons and subdeacons provided precisely that. Convened together, they formed the College of the 144, and were commissioned in June 1528 to promote the unity and prosperity of the city, and to negotiate with the Senate on behalf of the *Bürgerschaft*. At the same time, the deacons on their own formed the College of the Forty-Eight; while the *Oberalten*, in regular weekly session, for the first time constituted a permanent representative mouthpiece of the citizenry.[33]

The organisation of these bodies was complex; but three features are important. Firstly, the personal structure of the new Colleges was interlocking: the *Oberalten* were recruited from the Forty-Eight; the Forty-Eight were recruited from the 144; while they in turn were recruited from the *Bürgerschaft*, maintaining strict parity between all four parishes (a principle also retained in voting procedures at all levels, votes being taken by a

[31] Ibid., pp. 196–7.
[32] Ibid., pp. 197–8. See also Postel's articles: 'Reformation und Mitsprache' and 'Bedeutung der Reformation'.
[33] Postel, 'Reformation und Gegenreformation', pp. 198–200.

majority out of four rather than by a simple majority of those present). Secondly, the members of all these bodies had dual functions: in the ecclesiastical domain, they controlled the parishes; in the political domain, they represented the citizenry in negotiations with the Senate. Thirdly, the complex intertwining of secular and ecclesiastical affairs, and the crucial role played by the citizenry in creating institutions of self-government spanning the two domains, left an important historical and psychological legacy. During the next three centuries, the events of the 1520s provided both a source of justification in conflict and of inspiration in harmony.

The system which emerged during the 1520s was anchored in a new constitution drawn up with the aid of Johannes Bugenhagen, a disciple of Luther. It was promulgated in February 1529. Known as the *Langer Rezess* (or 'long treaty'), this document was the first real constitution of the city. It reinforced both the functions of the new institutions. It handed over the old medieval hospitals and the property of the various brotherhoods to the poor box administrators. Their political powers were confirmed by the establishment of the principle that power would henceforth be shared by both Senate and *Bürgerschaft*, the latter represented in most discussions by the *Oberalten*, the Forty-Four and the 144.[34]

At first the new regime operated relatively smoothly. The distribution and limited devolution of political powers ensured unusual unanimity in the completion of the Reformation reforms during the next decades. Even when financial problems began to create friction, a mutually satisfactory solution was possible when in 1563 the Senate consented to relinquish the administration of fiscal revenues to a deputation of eight citizens (the *Kämmerei*).[35] Similarly, further problems involving accusations of nepotism and corruption in the Senate did not result in significant differences. In 1603 the first major revision of the constitution was also a relatively peaceful affair. The revision essentially sought to clarify the distribution of powers set out in 1529, and, more importantly, explicitly linked political participation with adherence to the Lutheran faith.[36]

From time to time tensions did drift to the surface. In 1602 the *Bürgerschaft* strenuously rejected *Bürgermeister* vom Holte's claim that the citizenry had no right to resist the Senate, however 'godless, tyrannical and miserly' it might be. His proposition that such a state of affairs should be accepted as God's punishment for the sins of the citizens outraged them. But this blunt exchange of views had no practical consequences.[37] Again in 1618 the Senate was able to refuse to answer the question whether Hamburg was an aristocracy or a democracy: the *Bürgerschaft* seemed

---

[34] Ibid.; J. Bolland, *Senat und Bürgerschaft*, pp. 24–6.   [35] Ibid., pp. 25–6.
[36] Postel, 'Reformation und Gegenreformation', pp. 241–2.
[37] Kopitzsch, *Grundzüge*, p. 147.

content with the evasive reply that most polities embodied a mixture of both principles.[38] Initially, apathy on the part of the *Bürgerschaft* seems to have been a major buttress of stability. But during the Thirty Years War positive common interests secured the *status quo*. The desperate need to steer a neutral course, which involved the payment of substantial tributes to potential marauders, galvanised the union of Senate and *Bürgerschaft*. Equally important in this respect were the vigorous attempts by the Danes to contest Hamburg's status as an Imperial City and to reassert their own traditional claims to sovereignty. The external threat guaranteed the domestic peace for several decades.[39]

All of this rapidly changed after 1648. The following decades saw the re-emergence of fundamental issues of principle which resulted in bitter strife and chaos.

The major question at all times was that of the relationship between magistrates and citizens.[40] During the next sixty years this issue lay at the root of confrontations over administration, taxation, foreign policy and religion. At first, financial problems, resulting from the strains imposed by finding Hamburg's share of the compensation paid to Sweden by the German states, were crucial. Social factors, resulting from a rapid growth of the population, also played an important part: by the 1680s the major rebel leaders drew much of their support from the new parish of St Michael's in the Neustadt. The parish was only enfranchised at the height of the troubles in 1685, whereafter the Forty-Eight became the Sixty, and the 144 the 180.[41] At the same time, Hamburg's conflict with Denmark and her shifting position in the German balance of power repeatedly came into play. And finally, in the 1690s, religion became the issue, with the explosion of a vitriolic controversy between Orthodox Lutherans and Pietists. In many ways just as bad as the disturbances themselves were the attempts by the Imperial authorities to mediate in them by sending Imperial commissions to Hamburg. Although many of the commissioners were actually requested to come, and one of them did finally end the troubles in 1708–12, their activities were often bitterly resented – most obviously by the losing party, but more generally also by those who feared the bad publicity the city received in the world at large and who saw the commissions as a threat to the independence of the city.

At no stage, however, did any of these factors play an exclusive role. Indeed controversies often raged on long after the original grievance had been settled and ceased to be meaningful. It is this which has undermined

[38] Loose, 'Zeitalter der Bürgerunruhen', p. 270.   [39] Ibid., pp. 259, 269–70.
[40] The problems are discussed with reference to the experience of other German cities by: Brunner, 'Souveranitätsproblem'; Hildebrandt, 'Rat contra Bürgerschaft'; Schilfert, 'bürgerliche Revolutionen'.   [41] Loose, 'Zeitalter der Bürgerunruhen', pp. 277–8.

attempts by modern scholars to formulate a satisfactory general theory. As Otto Brunner convincingly demonstrated, it is impossible to employ either class conflict or democratisation as plausible explanatory concepts.[42] The fundamental issue was that of sovereignty, an issue which embraced virtually everything and which allowed virtually anything to serve as the catalyst of discord.

The first disputes were straightforward confrontations between Senate and *Bürgerschaft*. In 1650 the Senate was able to assert its primacy. In 1657 the *Bürgerschaft* temporarily succeeded in halting the erosion of its traditional rights. In 1663 the domestic peace was shattered by accusations of bribery and nepotism in the Senate elections and by the denunciation of abuses in the administration of justice. The first issue was relatively easily laid to rest by the formulation of new rules for the election and composition of the Senate (twelve seats were henceforth reserved for lawyers). The second issue was more intractable. In 1666 the *Bürgerschaft* achieved the suspension of *Bürgermeister* Lütkens. He fled the city and appealed to the *Reichskammergericht* in Speyer, with the result that an Imperial commissioner was sent to Hamburg. The compromise he engineered soon evaporated, however, and the *Bürgerschaft* continued to insist upon and exercise the right it claimed to dismiss members of the Senate.[43]

The two fronts now began to crumble into a hopeless tangle of opposing factions. Since 1650 the power of the *Oberalten* had grown considerably. They now sought to consolidate their position, and in so doing they distanced themselves from the *Bürgerschaft*, whose representatives they were meant to be. Their rise was short-lived. By 1672 the wrath of the citizens was directed against them, and the violence which ensued was again only curbed in 1674 when another Imperial commissioner intervened. Count Windischgrätz attempted to exclude the mob from politics by imposing more rigid rules concerning entitlement to attend *Bürgerschaft* meetings. Yet this was of no avail. By 1677 the tempers of the *Bürgerschaft* again boiled over, and the citizens suspended all of the *Oberalten* and one Senator. The attempts at mediation in the following years by certain members of the Senate led by *Bürgermeister* Hinrich Meurer merely produced yet another wave of unrest. In March 1684 the mob, led by Cord Jastram and Hieronymus Snitger, arrested and suspended Meurer; and the stage was now set for the most dramatic confrontation of all.[44]

Meurer fled to Celle where he attempted to enlist the support of the duke. Jastram and Snitger appealed to Denmark, whose ruler Christian V was only too eager to offer assistance, in the hope of being able to turn the

[42] Brunner, 'Souveranitätsproblem', *passim*.
[43] Loose, 'Zeitalter der Bürgerunruhen', pp. 270–2.   [44] Ibid., pp. 272–6.

situation to his own advantage. In August 1684 and again in March 1685, Celle troops tried to kidnap first Jastram and then Snitger. They failed, and the two rebels for a short time became virtual dictators in the city. Their rule was only ended in 1686 when their supposed Danish allies showed their true colours and laid siege to the city. Military assistance from Celle and diplomatic support from the Great Elector forced Christian V to withdraw his troops in September 1686. Internal order was restored; Jastram and Snitger were arrested and tried for treason, and finally executed on 4 October 1686. Their crime was to have betrayed the city to the Danes; their only achievement was to have effected the enfranchisement of the fifth parish (St Michael's) in May 1685.[45]

For four years relative peace prevailed. The shock of Christian V's treachery concentrated and harmonised the minds of all factions. Yet the underlying tensions remained. In 1690 another case of bribery and corruption once more brought them to the surface.[46] Within three years the spectre of civil war revived, this time activated by a religious controversy. The 1680s had seen a series of vituperative confrontations between Orthodox Lutheran and Pietist pastors. Fiery sermons and forthright pamphlets had brought the congregations into the disputes, which largely concerned the issue of whether theatre and opera were permissible in the eyes of God. By the end of the decade the divisions between the clergy were so acute that it was almost inevitable that they should intrude into the political life of the city.

The fuse was lit in January 1693 when the Pietist Pastor Johann Heinrich Horb of St Nicholas' distributed as a New Year's greeting a tract on education written by a Jesuit. His action was promptly denounced by his colleague Pastor Johann Friedrich Mayer of St James', an uncompromising champion of Orthodox Lutheranism. Both sides enlisted popular support – Horb among the more prosperous citizens, Mayer among the guilds and lower classes. Mayer's was the more powerful group in the *Bürgerschaft*, and by the end of the year the Senate was obliged to agree to exile Horb. The theological divisions were settled soon afterwards, but Mayer's party remained active. His followers transferred their excitable minds to other issues, to the denunciation of corruption and to opposing the Senate. Finally, in 1699 they emerged triumphant and imposed a total humiliation on the Senate. The *Bürgerschaft* abolished the property qualification for attendance at its meetings and substituted the simple criterion of Lutheran faith, thus institutionalising the power of the mob. Furthermore, it insisted that henceforth only men nominated by itself would be elected to the Senate. The old constitutional norms were thus undermined and the power

---

[45] Ibid., pp. 276–81.   [46] Ibid., pp. 281–2.

of the Senate was virtually destroyed.[47] If the Hamburg polity had hitherto been characterised by a mixture of aristocracy and democracy, the democratic principle was now exclusive.

The new *status quo* was impossible. Mayer left Hamburg in 1701 to become *Superintendent* in Griefswald, but his colleague Pastor Christian Krumbholtz of St Peter's took over his role. The struggle continued, kept flaming by a series of trivial issues, including a protracted argument over Mayer's possible reappointment to a job to which it was known he had no intention of returning. By 1708 the situation had degenerated into anarchy once more, with seven Senators suspended by the *Bürgerschaft*, the mob rampant in the Rathaus, the urban administration paralysed.[48]

Given this chaotic state of affairs, the Imperial authorities feared another attempt by Denmark to take over the city. It was thus decided to send Imperial troops to Hamburg and to despatch Count Damian Hugo von Schönborn to lead yet another Imperial commission. The city was surrounded and then occupied; the rebels' leaders were rounded up; and Schönborn began four years of investigations and consultations. The result was the restoration of law and order, and the publication in 1712 of a new constitution. It embodied the final clarification of the division of powers which had emerged in 1529; it provided the foundation for stability over the next 150 years and was not replaced until 1860.[49]

The constitution was based on two fundamental principles. Firstly, the Lutheran status of the city, as proclaimed in 1529 and 1603, was confirmed: the established religion had exclusive status and formed the basis of the urban polity. Secondly, sovereignty was vested jointly in Senate and *Bürgerschaft* (*inseperabili nexu conjunctim*).[50] The magistrates were thus essentially executives, and sovereign only in conjunction with the citizenry. The *Bürgerschaft* were both representatives of the people and *Mitregenten* or co-regents.[51]

The Senate comprised four *Bürgermeister* and twenty-four senators, of whom eleven senators and three *Bürgermeister* were lawyers, while thirteen senators and one *Bürgermeister* were merchants. Election to both posts was by co-option, provided that the candidate was Lutheran and over thirty years of age. They were assisted by four syndics (all lawyers) and four secretaries, of whom one was the archivist.[52] Although the syndics only had a consultative vote in the Senate, their position was powerful: they were responsible for the execution of foreign policy, legal matters concerning the

---

[47] Ibid., pp. 282–4.   [48] Ibid., pp. 284–7.
[49] Bartels, *Einige Abhandlungen*, pp. 1–44; *idem*, *Nachtrag*, pp. iv–v. The most reliable version of the constitution is printed in Bartels, *Neuer Abdruck*, pp. 57–102, 139–60, 197–256, 271–92.
[50] Ibid., pp. 197–207.   [51] Bartels, *Einige Abhandlungen*, pp. 95–132.
[52] Westphalen, *Verfassung und Verwaltung*, 1, pp. 33–55.

city's sovereignty, and censorship.[53] The powers of the Senate as a whole were also carefully circumscribed and ranged over foreign policy, the dispensation of justice and numerous other aspects of domestic administration.[54] In most areas this power was administered in mixed deputations consisting of senators and citizens elected by the *Bürgerschaft* from the Civic Colleges.[55]

The Senate could not, however, change or make new laws, or levy taxes, without the consent of the *Bürgerschaft*. Admission to that body was determined by two factors. The first was the ownership of freehold property in the city (*Erbgesessenheit*). Before 1712 this qualification was loosely interpreted, but the new constitution limited participation to those who held unmortgaged property worth 1,000 *taler* in the city or 2,000 *taler* in its outlying territories.[56] Before 1712 *Bürgerschaft* meetings had been attended by up to 2,000 people, but now the new limitations effectively reduced the numbers of eligible freeholders, with the result that a quorum was increasingly dependent upon the other category of participants, the *Personalisten*.[57] They comprised the 180 deacons of the parishes (with twenty adjuncts after 1720), for whom attendance was obligatory on pain of a fine, together with members of administrative bodies, the sixty officers of the militia and twenty guild masters, for whom attendance was optional. All *Personalisten* were eligible to vote regardless of whether or not they were freeholders. In practice they also dominated the *Bürgerschaft* since votes were taken according to parish and proposals were accepted when three parishes gave their consent.[58] Explicitly excluded were non-Lutherans, employees of foreign rulers, city employees, bankrupts, non-guild craftsmen, and non-freeholders.[59]

The *Bürgerschaft* generally met twice-yearly at the request of the Senate (whose prerogative this was) to decide matters relating to taxation, and at unspecified intervals to pass important legislation affecting the interpretation of the Constitution.[60] When they did so, it was only after a long process of consultation between the Senate and a series of Civic Colleges, namely the *Oberalten*, the Sixty and the 180.

The *Oberalten* sat in permanent session: they were in effect watchdogs

[53] Ewald, *Senatssyndicus*, pp. 26–30, 36–40. See also the article on Syndic Johann Klefeker in *ADB*, 16, pp. 76–7.
[54] Westphalen, *Verfassung und Verwaltung*, 1, pp. 56–74. The most detailed list of the Senate's functions is in von Hess, *Hamburg* (1st edn), 3, pp. 304–8, 311–20.
[55] The role of deputations is discussed by Joachim, *Historische Arbeiten*, pp. 134–48.
[56] Reissmann, *Kaufmannschaft*, pp. 346–9; Westphalen, *Verfassung und Verwaltung*, 1, pp. 77–82.
[57] Bolland, *Senat und Bürgerschaft*, p. 36. Of the 133 meetings called 1713–20, no less than 105 were inquorate. Cf. Wurm, *Verfassungs-Skizzen*, pp. 13, 72.
[58] Westphalen, *Verfassung und Verwaltung*, 1, pp. 89–98.   [59] Ibid., pp. 85–9.
[60] J. L. von Hess, *Hamburg* (1st edn), 3, pp. 320, 325–8.

over the constitution, the perpetual representatives of the *Bürgerschaft*, combining the controlling functions of the Athenian Areopagus and the protective functions of the Roman Tribunes of the People.[61] Their secretary (always a lawyer) played an important mediatory role in urban affairs; he was the crucial bridge between the two jointly-sovereign elements of the polity.[62]

The powers of the Sixty were less wide-ranging. They deliberated on legislative proposals passed by the *Oberalten* before sending them on to the 180. But their prime role was to act as perpetual representatives of the *Bürgerschaft* in all matters relating to education and religion. Thus, together with the Senate, the Sixty held the key to the regulation of ecclesiastical affairs. Their consent was essential in any attempt to regulate the position of the non-Lutheran minorities, although in so far as any such regulation might affect the basic principles of the Constitution, it also had to be ratified by the *Bürgerschaft*.[63]

The sole function of the 180 was to ratify formal proposals which were then submitted to the *Bürgerschaft*. In addition to this, as deacons and subdeacons, they were responsible for actually electing individuals nominated by the parishes to the *Oberalten* and the Sixty.[64]

After 1712, conflicts between Senate and *Bürgerschaft* were rare. In marked contrast to the times of trouble of the seventeenth century, political participation was distinctly unenthusiastic. Indeed in 1720 measures had to be taken to augment the number of *Personalisten* obliged to attend *Bürgerschaft* meetings in order to ensure the statutory quorum of 197.[65] But even so the extreme complexity and slow speed of the decision-making process often thwarted swift action and the formulation of coherent policies. Unpopular issues were often held up for years by the Civic Colleges, and only discussed seriously long after the need for action had passed. As the British Resident commented in 1728: 'it has allways been the misfortune of this Republick never to do anything with a good grace, which indeed one may attribute in some measure to this Form of Government, which ties up the hands of the magistrates and too often hinders them from doing things in a handsome manner...'[66] In the seventeenth century anarchy had

---

61 Westphalen, *Verfassung und Verwaltung*, 1, pp. 193–200, 202–6; Wiskemann, *Welthandelspolitik*, p. 110; Buek, *Oberalten*, pp. 1–5.

62 Bartels, *Einige Abhandlungen*, p. 140. All were born in Hamburg, and were members of the urban elite: Buek, *Oberalten*, pp. 378–93.

63 Klefeker, *Verfassungen*, 8, pp. 730–3; von Hess, *Hamburg* (1st edn), 3, pp. 342–3; Westphalen, *Verfassung und Verwaltung*, 2, pp. 158–61.

64 J. L. von Hess, *Hamburg* (1st edn), 3, pp. 343–4.

65 Reissmann, *Kaufmannschaft*, pp. 346–9; Wurm, *Verfassungs-Skizzen*, pp. 13, 72; Westphalen, *Verfassung und Verwaltung*, 1, pp. 94–8; Nirrnheim, 'Verfassungsfrage', pp. 131–2; Kopitzsch, *Grundzüge*, pp. 149–54.

66 PRO: SP 82/45: 26 November 1728, Wich to Townshend.

resulted from conflicts between magistrates and citizens in a relatively undefined constitutional framework. After 1712, stability and domestic harmony rested largely on the fact that a minutely detailed constitution enabled the Senate's opponents to frustrate almost anything beyond the day-to-day administration of urban affairs.

This new-found political harmony was also accompanied by a remarkable degree of social stability. Although periodic guild disturbances occurred in Hamburg as elsewhere, they never threatened the political order.[67] Only twice did unrest pose a potential problem. In 1728 a medical doctor, Johann Caspar Engelleder, attempted a *coup d'état*. Almost nothing is known about the event, however, and what evidence there is suggests that his conspiracy was rapidly discovered and easily destroyed.[68] In 1753 a lawyer, Dr Heinrich Kellinghusen, attempted to co-ordinate guild unrest; but he too failed.[69] Even a massive guild rebellion in 1791, involving several thousand artisans, foundered on the determination of the citizenry to put it down. Grievances continued to be voiced for several years afterwards. Yet attempts by some historians to claim that the rebellion should be seen in connection with the French Revolution, and that it represented the first 'general strike' in Germany, are far from convincing. The fact was that Hamburg's stability was only disrupted when the French occupied the city between 1806 and 1814.[70]

Just as there is no convincing account of the troubles, so it has proved difficult to explain the stability which followed them. The limitation of the franchise might account for the absence of mob violence from political negotiations; but it cannot entirely explain the apparent apathy of those who still held the vote. Equally important, and much neglected, was the psychological dimension. A century or more of strife left deep scars and haunting memories. It was in the interests of all concerned to cling to the new constitution and to forget its bloody genesis. Only this can explain the Senate's swift punitive reaction to the publication in 1781 of a text of the constitution of 1712 together with related historical documents. Its editor Ludwig von Hess (a Swedish official) touched a raw nerve when he proclaimed, rather too accurately for comfort, that 'the fundamental laws of Hamburg, while not written in dragon's blood...did still cost the blood of citizens'.[71]

---

67 See Preiss, 'Handwerkerunruhen', pp. 8–18; Gerber, *Bauzünfte*, pp. 74–5; Kopitzsch, *Grundzüge*, pp. 208–15.
68 Klefeker, *Verfassungen*, 5, pp. 398–400; Steltzner, *Versuch*, 6, pp. 178–83; Schröder, *Lexikon*, 2, pp. 193–4.
69 Preiss, 'Handwerkerunruhen', pp. 18–28.
70 The debate is summarised by Kopitzsch, *Grundzüge*, pp. 212–15.
71 L. von Hess (ed.), *Unwiederrufliches Fundamental-Gesetz*, p. iii. The scandal is dealt with by Wächter, *Historischer Nachlass*, 2, pp. 60–3 and Kopitzsch, *Grundzüge*, pp. 174–5.

IV

One theme ran consistently through the constitutional history of the city after the Reformation: the search for purity of faith. The movement of the 1520s could obviously be interpreted in this light. The constitution of 1603 firmly placed adherence to pure Lutheranism in its first article as the foundation of the polity. The constitution of 1712 reiterated this point. Indeed, in the eighteenth century, the principle of purity of belief became idiomatic to all interpretations of both past and present. Opponents of toleration prefaced their arguments with firm assertions of the principle; the advocates of toleration prefaced theirs with equally firm assurances about their own loyalty to it. Yet both the assertions and the assurances obscured a complex history: the constitutional position of the Church was ambiguous from the start, and remained so even after 1712.

The ease with which the Reformation was introduced in Hamburg was at least partly due to the lack of an effective clerical overlord. The Hamburg Cathedral, and with it the parishes, were technically governed by the Archbishop of Bremen. He was, however, an absentee, and his powers in Hamburg were administered by a relatively junior official, the Dean (technically third-in-command after the Provost or *Probst*). Episcopal authority was rapidly undermined by the movement in the parishes, which was able to push through the reforms against the opposition of the Dean and Chapter. The latter refused to accept the diminution of their powers and the confiscation of much of their property, and they appealed to the *Reichskammergericht* in Speyer in September 1528. Although they obtained a favourable judgement in 1533, and a partial restitution of their property in 1535, they were unable to regain their former position. The Cathedral itself gradually turned Protestant during the 1530s and 1540s, but still persisted in its claims to exemption from urban legislation on the grounds of external overlordship. Decades of legal wrangling were finally ended in 1561 with a treaty which confirmed the Cathedral's exterritoriality. Thereafter the Cathedral changed hands with the Duchy of Bremen, finally ending up under Hanoverian control in 1719, where it remained until it was given back to the city in 1802.[72]

The Cathedral thus became an enclave with no influence on the ecclesiastical life of the city. From the inception of the Reformation, it was the parish clergy who became decisive. Yet there was at first no legal definition of their role. Only several years after the introduction of Bugenhagen's constitution and *Kirchenordnung* of 1529 was the first spiritual leader appointed from among them.[73] In 1532 Johannes Aepinus

---

[72] See: Postel, 'Reformation und Gegenreformation', pp. 206–7, 210, 215–16, 222–5, 228–9; Otto, *Domstift*, pp. 15–32.   [73] Postel, 'Reformation und Gegenreformation', pp. 209–14.

was made *Superintendent*: he was initially commissioned to represent the city in religious matters and then, in 1539, to formulate a more precise definition of the relationship between Church and State.[74]

Aepinus' years of office until his death in 1553 were characterised by a mixture of success and failure. On the one hand he assisted in dextrously steering the city through the doctrinal and political uncertainty of the early Reformation decades. He called the first Lower Saxon synod in 1535 which denounced Anabaptism; in 1537 he represented the city at the Synod of Schmalkalden; he argued against the Imperial Interim of 1548, thus preparing the way for Hamburg's inclusion as a Lutheran city in the Peace of Augsburg in 1555. All of this helped to ensure that the city remained in line with the Lutheran forces in the *Reich*. Yet at the same time he inevitably became embroiled in theological controversies which brought him into conflict with his colleagues at home as well as theologians outside. His pronouncements on Justification and on Christ's Descent into Hell unleashed arguments which often threatened to undermine both the authority of his own office and the unity of the city.[75]

It was this threat which stimulated the Senate to intervene. Aepinus' own *Kirchenordnung* was introduced in 1556, three years after his death; but its main proposition, the formation of a consistory, was never realised.[76] The theological controversies of the 1540s and 1550s alerted the Senate to the dangers of an uncontrolled independent clergy. Not only was the idea of a consistory quietly dropped, but the Senate even hesitated for two years before appointing Paul von Eitzen as Aepinus' successor. He too was unable to bring harmony to the clergy. The Senate itself was obliged to act in 1560 with a mandate banning theological controversy in the city.[77]

The powers of the *Superintendent* were thus gradually diminished. They were further undermined by von Eitzen's departure from Hamburg in 1562 after a series of accusations concerning his alleged Crypto-Calvinism. The office remained vacant for nine years, was then occupied again between 1571 and 1574, and again from 1580 to 1593. It was then abolished. In the meantime the Senate had once more taken the initiative in accepting the Book of Concord as the basis for Lutheran teaching in the city in 1580.[78]

Two important points emerge from the above. Firstly, the experience of open disputes among the clergy, many of which also aroused the congregations, on several occasions seemed to portend the disintegration of the reforming consensus of the 1520s. It was this threat to domestic stability which obliged the Senate to take a leading and decisive role in the

---

[74] Ibid., p. 235.   [75] Ibid., pp. 235–8.
[76] Klemenz, *Religionsunterricht*, pp. 45–7.
[77] Ibid.; Postel, 'Reformation und Gegenreformation', p. 238.
[78] Ibid., pp. 252–4; Klemenz, *Religionsunterricht*, pp. 46, 59–63; Bergemann, *Staat und Kirche*, pp. 29–31.

imposition of Lutheran Orthodoxy on the city and its clergy, a process more or less complete by 1580. Secondly, it became obvious that many of these problems arose from the position accorded to the *Superintendent*, exacerbated inevitably by the personalities and opinions of the various incumbents. In 1580 the doctrinal problems were laid to rest, in a move later given constitutional force in 1603. In 1593 the institutional problems were solved by abolishing the office of *Superintendent* altogether. Both developments had far-reaching implications.

The powerful office of *Superintendent* was replaced by the relatively informal post of *Senior*. Appointed by the Senate, he was the public representative of the Ministry, its mouthpiece in negotiations with the secular authorities. The Ministry itself was composed of the *Hauptpastoren* (four until 1685, five thereafter), the junior clergy of the major parishes, together with the preachers of the seven minor chapels and churches in the city and its extramural suburbs.[79]

The constitutional position of the Ministry was not clearly defined. By abolishing the one central clerical office mentioned in the *Kirchenordnung* of 1529 the Senate had itself assumed the highest authority over the religious life of the city. Since its own powers were only exercised in conjunction with the *Bürgerschaft*, it followed that the *jus reformandi* lay in the hands of both Senate and citizenry, represented in this area by the College of the Sixty.[80] The clergy often challenged this state of affairs. In 1639, for example, the Ministry advanced the proposition that the powers of the *Superintendent* had surely passed to the Ministry as a whole, since it was obvious that the *Senior* was merely its mouthpiece. They received a brisk reply in which the Senate baldly countered that the Ministry had no competence in ecclesiastical affairs: any powers the *Superintendent* might have held derived from the Senate and reverted to it.[81]

Such exchanges recurred periodically to the end of the eighteenth century. But even the constitution of 1712 did nothing to clarify the position: the *Kirchenordnung* mentioned in its twenty-fourth article was never published because it contained prejudicial references to the role the clergy had played in the troubles.[82] In theory, then, the powers of the Ministry were limited to the organisation of the liturgy and the execution of priestly functions. According to the earliest regulations laid down by Bugenhagen, which remained valid throughout this period, the clergy had the right to be consulted about all major innovations which might be introduced by the secular authorities.[83] Ultimately the power of decision

[79] Ibid., pp. 26–31.   [80] Klefeker, *Verfassungen*, 8, pp. 733–41.
[81] Klemenz, *Religionsunterricht*, p. 63.
[82] Westphalen, *Haupt-Grundgesetze*, 1, pp. 248–50, 348–9; ibid., 3, pp. 3–27; Bartels, *Neuer Abdruck*, pp. 191–2; idem, *Einige Abhandlungen*, pp. 216–98.
[83] Klefeker, *Verfassungen*, 8, pp. 733–41.

lay clearly, if not always firmly, in the joint hands of the Senate and the Sixty.

Yet the clergy exercised formidable power. Despite the formal limitations placed upon them and despite the fact that there was no legally-recognised clerical estate, visitors to the city repeatedly commented on the prominence of the pastors. In 1740 Thomas Lediard expressed a common view, if more sharply than most, when he wrote that they were

as arrant Popes, as far as they can possibly extend their power, as his Holiness of Rome, who may, in a great measure be said to govern the whole city. For though they are in Reality, as much subject to the senate as any other Burghers, and have no direct Power over them; yet they have such an influence over the minds of the Commonalty, as makes the senate cautious of doing anything they can apprehend will disoblige their spiritual Fathers.[84]

Indeed, only after 1800 did observers like Jonas Ludwig von Hess and J. P. Fahrenkrüger note a decline in their power, which they dated from the death of Johann Melchior Goeze in 1786. Only then did the position of these 'guardians of the Hamburg Zion...these conquerors of the kingdom of God' finally succumb to the pressures of internal controversies and external opposition to them resulting from the spread of the *Aufklärung*.[85]

Several factors combined to buttress the pre-eminence of the clergy. They took seriously the spiritual duties imposed upon them by their oath of admission and interpreted them in the broadest possible way. Indeed, as *Senior* Goeze noted in 1760, the very fact that no definitive *Kirchenordnung* was ever passed gave them considerable freedom of action.[86] In his view the absence of legally-defined powers effectively implied a kind of legal immunity, which he, like many of his predecessors, exploited with impunity.

In a city without a university, the clergy stood as the sole interpreters and representatives of the Lutheran faith. The *Hauptpastoren* were all members of the *Scholarchat*, the body composed of four Senators and the *Oberalten* which governed urban education. This gave them considerable control over what was taught and how at the Johanneum and the Gymnasium.[87] They became so powerful on this body that in 1743 *Senior* Wagner attempted to assume the formal title of *ephorus scolae* (controller

---

[84] Lediard, *German Spy*, p. 189. Similar comments were made by Albrecht von Haller (1726) and Christlob Mylius (1753). Cf. Hintzsche, *Hallers Tagebücher*, p. 80 and Guthke, 'Hamburg im Jahre 1753', p. 164.

[85] J. L. von Hess, *Hamburg* (2nd edn), 3, p. 258; Fahrenkrüger, 'Sittengemälde', pp. 109–12. Cf. Nahrstedt, *Freizeit*, pp. 103–5, 159–60; Finder, *Bürgertum*, pp. 70–3; Höck, *Bilder*, pp. 187–9.

[86] StAH, Bestandsverzeichnis Ministerium 511–1, Bd. 3, p. 58.

[87] Bergemann, *Staat und Kirche*, pp. 28–9, 33; Klemenz, *Religionsunterricht, passim*.

of schools). His bid foundered on the opposition of the secular authorities.[88] Yet, even without public recognition of his status, he was able to play a decisive role in rejecting a new catechism drafted by a group of Senators which contained references to the principles of natural religion; his own text, embracing the tenets of Orthodox Lutheranism expressed in the language of rationalism, was the one finally published in 1753.[89] At parish level, the *Hauptpastoren* exercised exclusive sanction as school inspectors.[90] Thus, from the Gymnasium down to the elementary schools, clerical vigilance could ensure that purity of faith was maintained.

The influence of the clergy in this area was paralleled by the pedagogic functions of public sermons. Each pastor was obliged to preach two or three sermons a week. In all that meant up to sixty weekly sermons in churches which had a combined capacity of about 16,000 seats. Obviously it is difficult to assess the impact of these activities; but, in view of the numerous reports up to the middle of the eighteenth century of the crowds which attended the services, it cannot have been negligible.[91] Indeed, the rich Hamburg parishes endowed the position of *Hauptpastor* with a prestige and income sufficient to attract many renowned orators and scholars away from eminent academic and ecclesiastical posts in the principalities, and to induce them to refuse subsequent offers after their appointment in Hamburg. The sole qualification for the office was an established reputation for oratory and scholarship.[92]

The pastors never hesitated to voice spiritual and moral qualms from the pulpits. This public role was to a degree supported by the Senate which encouraged them to speak out against atheism, free-thinking, suicide and infanticide, though it baulked at the denunciation of sodomy on the grounds that it might merely put ideas into people's heads.[93] But since the clergy justified the exercise of their *geistliches Strafamt* or *elenchus* on exclusively theological grounds, the Senate often found itself embarrassed by sermons which intervened in delicate negotiations over such issues as the position of the non-Lutheran minorities.[94] While sermons could complement legislation to reinforce social and political order, experience proved that

[88] See the papers in StAH, Senat Cl.VII Lit.He No.1 Vol.3.
[89] Klefeker, *Verfassungen*, 8, pp. 532–5; Klemenz, *Religionsunterricht*, pp. 115–22; Mönckeberg, *Reimarus und Edelmann*, pp. 66–70; *idem*, 'hamburgischer Catechismus', *passim*.
[90] Bergemann, *Staat und Kirche*, p. 33.
[91] Loose, 'Zeitalter der Bürgerunruhen', p. 336.
[92] Bruhn, *Kandidaten*, pp. 29–33; Klefeker, *Verfassungen*, 8, pp. 816–20; *Wahl der Hauptpastoren*, pp. 3–6, 10–30.
[93] Klefeker, *Verfassungen*, 8, pp. 528–32, 746–8. On civil disobedience (1750), see StAH, Ministerium, II, 7, p. 174 and ibid., III A1t, nos. 330–3, 335–7, 339–42. On suicide (1753), see ibid., nos. 56–8. On infanticide (1711), see ibid., II 5, p. 291. On incest (1711), see ibid., p. 287. On sodomy (1749), see ibid., II 7, pp. 150–1 and ibid., III A1t, no. 59.
[94] Krabbe, 'geistliches Strafamt', *passim*.

they could just as easily undermine domestic harmony by stirring up the citizenry against the magistrates.

Because of the protracted nature of the decision-making process, this was often crucial. It was compounded by the dual functions of the deacons who belonged to the Civic Colleges, for as parish administrators they naturally came into close contact with their pastors. Political matters could rarely be kept secret, and the clergy were usually well-informed when they complained to the Senate or made denunciations on the pulpits. Similarly, the confessional was also an important source of information and influence in a relatively small and deeply religious society: the weekly confessions prescribed by the Lutheran system further ensured intimate knowledge of civic affairs.[95]

For the best part of two centuries the members of the Ministry employed their talents and influence in the service of one cause: the promotion and defence of Lutheran Orthodoxy. Of course, later theological movements did not pass Hamburg by: Pietism and rationalism found their disciples among the clergy here too. Yet such movements, which apparently threatened the pure faith, never became dominant. They caused internal rifts and divisions, often dangerous controversies, but were always in the last resort absorbed into the original tradition. They diversified its range, while never diluting its fundamental principles.

The foundations of the tradition had been laid by the Senate itself. The decision in 1580 to accept the Book of Concord as the basis for teaching and preaching in the city was intended to end the doctrinal uncertainty of the previous decades. Like the many other territories and cities which accepted the Book, the Hamburg magistrates desired clarity and security in theological matters. The dogmatic canon which they adopted offered just that. It embodied a collection of texts and pamphlets: the early Christian Creeds (the Apostolic, the Nicene and the Athanasian), Luther's two Catechisms, the Augsburg Confession and Apology, the Articles of Schmalkalden (written by Luther) and the Formula of Concord of 1577.[96] Its aim was two-fold. On the theological level it was designed to eliminate the influence of Melanchthon's disciples, and to make a clear distinction between Lutheranism and Calvinism. On the political level it was promoted in order to foster unity among the Lutheran states in the *Reich* against the incursions of both Catholics and Calvinists.[97]

In Hamburg, as in many other places, the major motive for its acceptance was the hope that it might end the doctrinal disputes which had almost

---

95 Klefeker, *Verfassungen*, 8, pp. 793–5. The importance of the confessional as a vehicle of influence was stressed by L. von Hess, *Statistische Betrachtungen*, p. 256.
96 Daur, *Von Predigern und Bürgern*, pp. 84–5; Klemenz, *Religionsunterricht*, pp. 46–7.
97 Wohlfeil, *Einführung*, pp. 37–8.

continuously threatened domestic stability. It was, however, significant that this occurred at precisely the same time as the first non-Lutheran immigrants began to arrive. As Hamburg's social and economic base became more diverse, so its confessional identity was more narrowly and rigidly defined, a development underlined by the embodiment of Orthodoxy in the constitution of 1603.

The intertwining of religious and constitutional principles endowed the clergy with a major political role. Even though their own legal position was unclear, they were always able to justify their pronouncements on purity of faith by referring to the urban constitution. This was later to cause considerable embarrassment to the Senate on many occasions, yet it was impossible to dismiss the argument out of hand.

In the first half of the seventeenth century the union of religion and politics was strengthened. The clergy made a substantial contribution to the foundation of the Gymnasium in 1613. Their own authority was then further enhanced by the fact that Hamburg survived the Thirty Years War relatively unscathed. The preachers were not slow in pointing out that this was the result of God's pleasure at the city's adherence to Orthodoxy.[98]

The first major threat to clerical solidarity came with the appointment of a Pietist in 1679, Pastor Anton Reiser. In 1684 Spener's friend, Johann Winckler, was elected Pastor of St Michael's; and a year later Spener's brother-in-law Johann Heinrich Horb was elected in St Nicholas'. Reiser's appointment was uncontentious; those of Winckler and Horb were firmly opposed by the Ministry – they were secured only as a result of the active manipulation of the church wardens by a few wealthy merchants. The election of three Pietists did not, however, lead to the triumph of their persuasion in Hamburg. When Reiser died in 1686, the church wardens of St James' vigorously resisted attempts by Winckler to effect the election of another Pietist. Instead they chose Johann Friedrich Mayer, a professor of theology at Wittenberg and a vituperative champion of Orthodoxy. With his appointment, an open clash between the two tendencies became inevitable.[99]

The counter-suggestible behaviour of the church wardens in the elections points to the way in which the conflict within the Ministry assumed wider political dimensions. The *Priesterstreit* coincided with the years of great constitutional unrest. Popular interest in ecclesiastical affairs became inextricably bound up with the confrontation between Senate and *Bürgerschaft*, with the clergy playing a bewildering variety of often contradictory, though largely divisive, roles.

At root, however, the dispute within the Ministry concerned the purity

[98] Klemenz, *Religionsunterricht*, pp. 64–5.
[99] See Rückleben, *Niederwerfung*, pp. 50, 53–9.

29

of faith. The Orthodox tradition was one which derived from a belief in the exclusive validity of Luther's witness. It regarded the Reformer as the sole fount of wisdom and truth, and elaborated a scholastic theological system on the foundation of his writings. Spener and Francke, the two leaders of the Pietist movement, rejected the historical tradition. They espoused a renewal of Lutheranism through a greater concentration on individual piety and a preoccupation with the problems of the present.[100]

In Hamburg, this fundamental difference in philosophies was manifested in two main controversies. The most intriguing was in many ways the debate over the opera during the 1680s. It began in 1682 when the Pietist Anton Reiser denounced the opera which had been founded on the Gänsemarkt in 1678. His attack had little effect. But in 1686 the issue re-emerged when Johann Winckler delivered a sermon on the same theme. This time the objections of the Pietists had a greater and more sinister resonance. Winckler's attack aroused public interest. It fell in the period of Jastram and Snitger's 'dictatorship', a time when almost any pronouncement on anything assumed a wider political significance. Above all, it stimulated Mayer to leap to the defence of the opera. The point at issue was essentially that of the morality of lavish commercial entertainment; behind it lay the thorny academic question of whether opera and theatre should be regarded as harmless activities over which the Church had no jurisdiction (*adiaphoron* or *Mitteldinge*) or whether, as Winckler argued, the preachers had a duty to point out their inherent sinfulness with a view to persuading the authorities to ban them. The debate raged inconclusively for several years and was only ended in January 1688 when the Senate issued a decree banning all further discussion of the subject.[101]

The opera controversy served to highlight publicly the divisions within the Ministry, and to arouse the passions of considerable numbers of laymen. More fundamental was the parallel controversy over the *collegia pietatis*. Each of the Pietist pastors seems to have conducted such a private group devoted to prayer and study of the Bible (as indeed did the Orthodox Mayer, a fact which was conveniently suppressed in the final stage of the conflict). The groups were largely composed of educated and relatively well-to-do citizens, and they embodied one of the most vital tenets of Pietism: the principle of personal renewal in the cause of a general spiritual revival. The Orthodox preachers regarded them with suspicion from the start. For one thing, their very existence seemed to substantiate the claims that Pietism represented an innovation, and thus a threat to the pure faith to which the constitution of 1603 bound the city. In addition, the prominent role which the *collegia* gave to the laity seemed to undermine the position of the

---

[100] A useful discussion of these two traditions may be found in *RGG*, 4, col. 1719–30 and 5, col. 370–83.
[101] Rückleben, *Niederwerfung*, pp. 50–3, 59–71.

Ministry and of the established Church.[102] These fears and suspicions were apparently justified when successive investigations into 'separatist' Pietist *collegia* also revealed the existence of groups of laymen who congregated without the guidance of any preacher. It is not clear just how close the links were between the Pietist *collegia* and the separatist conventicles. Some of the latter appear to have been quite harmless; but others undoubtedly attracted radicals and enthusiasts whose links with alternative mystical traditions were clearly stronger than their affinity with official Lutheranism. Even at the time there was considerable confusion over the issue. However, the very fact of the proven existence of some anti-clerical lay enthusiasts was sufficient to enable Mayer and the Orthodox camp to tar the Pietists with the same brush.[103]

Largely by equating religious radicalism and separatism with political sedition, the Orthodox faction managed to effect an official ban on conventicles of any kind in February 1689. In the following year the Orthodox then attempted to force the Pietist pastors into submission by issuing a Ministerial declaration, to be signed by all the clergy. It was to denounce enthusiasm, separatism, the mystical legacy of Jakob Böhme, and, more ominously for the Pietists, 'all innovations, under whatever name, even if they appear to promote the improvement of Christianity'.[104]

The Pietists refused to sign. Renewed open conflict was only averted when the Senate pronounced the document invalid – not because it supported the dissidents, but because the declaration infringed the authority of the secular powers in ecclesiastical matters.[105] Winckler and Abraham Hinckelmann (a Pietist elected in St Catherine's in 1689) made an uneasy peace with their colleagues. But it was not long before Mayer found an opportunity to attack the recalcitrant Horb in a disagreement over educational principles in 1693. This time Mayer so effectively aroused his parishioners that riots forced Horb to leave the city, a departure formally turned into exile by a Senate anxious to restore law and order. Mayer's victory was complete, underlined by a decree stating firmly that only Luther's Catechism should be used in school instruction.[106]

If there had been a Pietist threat to the integrity of Orthodoxy in Hamburg, Horb's involuntary departure marked its end. Winckler and Hinckelmann remained; and Winckler became *Senior* in 1699 until his death in 1705. Winckler in particular was influential in the educational field, responsible for the foundation of several schools on Pietist lines. In this sense, Pietism had an enduring influence in Hamburg.[107] But it was an

[102] Ibid., pp. 71–83.   [103] Ibid., pp. 83–108.   [104] Ibid., pp. 108–31, 379–80.
[105] Klemenz, *Religionsunterricht*, p. 94.
[106] Ibid., pp. 94–7; Rückleben, *Niederwerfung*, pp. 137–57.
[107] Klemenz, *Religionsunterricht*, pp. 97–8.

influence on form and not on content: the methods of Pietism were harnessed to the Orthodox cause. Ultimately, the Pietists foundered on the urban constitution. Their opponents found it all too easy to suggest a link between innovation and sedition – in the highly febrile political atmosphere of the time that proved crucial.

The reassertion of the bond between Orthodoxy and constitution in 1693 did not in the short term bring the desired peace. On the contrary, Mayer soon became more directly involved in politics, particularly in the popular opposition to the Senate which led to the latter's humiliation in 1699. Even after his departure from Hamburg in 1701, his party, still bonded by the twin causes of Orthodoxy and democracy, played a major role in the virtual civil war which ended in the occupation of the city by Imperial troops in 1708.[108] But in the long term the fundamental point was that the Ministry as a whole was from 1693 once more firmly committed to the public defence and exposition of Orthodoxy, albeit now enriched by Pietist influences. The house of the 'Hamburg Zion' had acquired another room; the building, however, was that erected with the acceptance of the Book of Concord in 1580.

Just as the promulgation of the constitution of 1712 brought peace to the city as a whole, so it ushered in a prolonged period of harmony in the Ministry. The clergy had every reason to feel relieved at the terms of the settlement. Strenuous efforts on all sides prevented the publication of clauses whose wording would have provided a public record of the clergy's role in the troubles. Orthodoxy was again made fundamental to the polity; but the way that it had triumphed over its opponents escaped comment. Among the clergy too, the memory of discord served as a powerful harmonising agent during the next decades. And again, powerful Orthodox personalities emerged to dominate the clerical stage: primarily Theodor Seelmann (*Senior*, 1715–30) and Erdmann Neumeister (*Hauptpastor* of St James', 1715–56).

Of course, not all the clergy sympathised with the uncompromising Orthodox view. In the 1720s, Johann Christoph Wolf and at least one minor preacher expressed their private disquiet at the public excesses of their colleagues.[109] Later, between 1743 and 1760, *Senior* Friedrich Wagner, who took up a neutral stance in the dispute between rationalists and Orthodox, presided over a period of relative moderation in the Hamburg Ministry.[110]

But after the struggles of the late seventeenth century, those who did

---

[108] Ibid., pp. 98–104; Rückleben, *Niederwerfung*, pp. 340–59.

[109] On Wolf's misgivings and his friendship with Neumeister's secular opponents, see Mönckeberg, *Reimarus und Edelmann*, pp. 7–12 and Röthel, *Bürgerliche Kultur*, p. 33. The minor preacher was Ernst Mushard, who refused to sign an anti-Calvinist declaration in 1722. Cf. StAH, Ministerium, III A1n, nos. 114–16, 120.

[110] Schröder, *Lexikon*, 7, pp. 552–4; *ADB*, 40, pp. 492–3.

oppose did so in private. Wolf never made public the doubts he expressed in his letters to La Croze, and was prevented from joining his friends in the Patriotic Society whose activities will be discussed below.[111] Potentially uncomfortable outsiders were excluded from the Hamburg Ministry: in 1736, for example, the clergy successfully lobbied against the election of *Propst* Reinbek of Berlin because of his rationalist Wolffian sympathies.[112] Even Wagner, who tried to remain conciliatory on the toleration issue, did so largely because he saw that the real threat to Orthodoxy came not from the recognised Christian religions but from free-thinking and atheism.[113]

Throughout, the public stage was dominated by the voice of outspoken Orthodoxy, which opposed and never hesitated to denounce anything but the most pure Lutheran faith. Johann Melchior Goeze (*Hauptpastor* of St Catherine's, 1755–86) was the last representative of this tradition. It was only during his period as *Senior* (1760–70) that the first major public divisions between the clergy emerged.[114] Until then Orthodoxy ruled all but unopposed in Hamburg, so much so that even the learned and respected Hermann Samuel Reimarus desisted from publishing his radical speculations on religion for fear of losing his teaching post at the Gymnasium.[115]

Harmony did not lead to either apathy or complacency. As later chapters will show, the proponents of Orthodoxy could never be accused of resignation. The issue which concerned them most was toleration; and, since this is dealt with in detail below, it will suffice to delineate the broader framework here.

The Hamburg clergy perceived the toleration debate in the context of what they discerned as the all-pervasive tendency of the age: the gradual spread and acceptance of heterodoxy and indifference. In a complaint of 1713 they registered their concern at the growth of 'atheism, epicurianism, indifferentism, scorning of the works of God and of the holy sacraments'.[116] The Senate consistently supported their effort to stamp out heresy and atheism throughout the eighteenth century.[117] But 'indifferentism' posed a less clearly identifiable, yet ultimately more pernicious, threat than either of the former. Individuals were easily dealt with. But the reinterpretation of the Lutheran church system in the light of the new secular legal

---

[111] See note 109 above.

[112] Müsing, 'Reimarus', pp. 59–60; Mönckeberg, *Reimarus und Edelmann*, pp. 49–56. The term Wolffian refers to its usual philosophical sense and not to the J. C. Wolf who appears in this paragraph.

[113] Müsing, 'Reimarus', pp. 60–6; Mönckeberg, *Reimarus und Edelmann*, pp. 174–83.

[114] On Goeze, see Schröder, *Lexikon*, 2, pp. 515–37; *ADB*, 9, pp. 524–30. His career is discussed in greater detail in Chapter 5.

[115] Müsing, 'Reimarus', *passim*; Grossmann, 'Edelmann und Reimarus', *passim*.

[116] StAH, Ministerium, II 5, pp. 333–4 (7 July 1713).

[117] Klefeker, *Verfassungen*, 8, pp. 526–32. See also Chapter 4, note 180.

philosophies of Thomasius, Wolff, Pfaff and Buddeus among many others, affected official attitudes to the Church rather than just the behaviour of outcasts.[118] The pressures which the dissemination of their works placed on the Orthodox are illustrated by the letters of Erdmann Neumeister in the 1720s and 1730s. Among many specific references to the impact of new ideas on the urban elite, which will be discussed more fully below, one general comment of 1738 provides a forthright statement of a view shared by many of his Orthodox colleagues. He wrote:

I have become accustomed to seeing the appearance of one excretion of the unclean spirit after the other, in which he [Thomasius] rejects many of the rights of the Church, in which he deprives our only Lord, Jesus Christ, of all his honour, and in which the Church is trampled beneath the feet of the political Antichrist. But none has aroused in me such foul odour and disgust as that which has recently been published in the form of the posthumous work of Thomasius of unblessed memory.[119]

The major manifestation of the new spirit in Hamburg was the attempt to solve the problem of religious worship for non-Lutherans. For it brought into play fundamental arguments about the role and function of the established Church. To oppose such moves successfully was to maintain the traditional exclusive supremacy of Lutheranism in the city. To fail was to open the floodgates to heterodoxy and indifference. That in itself would erode the power and prestige of the clergy. But clerical incomes were also at stake. For their regular salaries were complemented by the *jura stolae* (fees for baptisms, marriages and funerals) which all were obliged to pay regardless of whether or not they were baptised, married or buried by Lutheran pastors.[120]

Ultimately the struggle over toleration far transcended the narrow issue of freedom of conscience. On their own terms, the Orthodox were not intolerant: coercion and persecution were as alien to them as they were to the Pietists, the Thomasians or the Wolffians.[121] But they saw clearly the profound implications of the debate over the extension of individual freedom. For toleration decreed by secular magistrates threatened to undermine the very constitution of the established Church, to erode its position as the sole moral and spiritual arbiter of the polity.

[118] All of these authors are mentioned by Johann Klefeker (Syndic since 1721) in his discussion of ecclesiastical law: Klefeker, *Verfassungen*, 8, pp. 676–748. For a general discussion, see Greschat, *Tradition und neuer Anfang*, pp. 146–66, 224–33, 241–62; Schlaich, 'Kirchenrecht', *passim*; *idem*, *Kollegialtheorie*, pp. 17–22, 65–129.

[119] The letters are printed in three parts: Wotschke (ed.), 'Neumeisters Briefe' (1925), (1929), (1930). The quotation is from ibid. (1930), p. 186 (9 August 1738, to Ernst Salomo Cyprian).

[120] Klefeker, *Verfassungen*, 8, pp. 819–20. Klefeker notes that the regular salaries were eroded by inflation and that the clergy were increasingly dependent on the *jura stolae*.

[121] Heckel, *Staat und Kirche*, pp. 163–72; Schultze, 'Toleranz und Orthodoxie', pp. 200–1, 213–19; Greschat, *Tradition und neuer Anfang*, pp. 56, 146, 171, 184.

V

The Ministry was thus deeply committed to opposing even a limited recognition of the religious rights of non-Lutherans. In the case of the Jews and smaller sects such as the Mennonites, its task was easy since they were not recognised by Imperial legislation.[122] By contrast, the claims of Calvinists and Catholics were less easily denied. As members of the Churches recognised by the Treaty of Osnabrück they were guaranteed certain fundamental liberties. On the other hand, the application of the provisions of 1648 was not straightforward in Hamburg. The Treaty explicitly affirmed the supremacy of Lutheranism; and since no formal concession had been made before 1624, the clergy could rightly claim that there was no need to respect anything more than a *devotio domestica*.[123] On the basis of both local and Imperial laws an *exercitium religionis privatum* was clearly unthinkable.

The immense power of the clergy and their ability to manipulate the political system ensured that this minimalist legal attitude prevailed until 1785. But two factors beyond their control made the issue an object of continual debates and conflicts. Both were responsible for perennial efforts by the Senate to gain acceptance for a loose interpretation of the Treaty of Osnabrück.

The first was the extraordinary degree of toleration which prevailed in the small town of Altona which lay on the Elbe estuary just a few miles west of Hamburg (literally within walking distance).[124] The policies pursued by its overlords the Counts of Schaumburg (after 1640, the Kings of Denmark) provide a unique example of the use of toleration edicts for mercantilist ends. The motive behind them was clear: to try to capitalise on the intolerance of Hamburg and thereby to compensate for the natural disadvantages of Altona's harbour facilities compared with Hamburg.[125] From about 1600 all manner of religious groups were granted freedom there: Jews, Catholics, Calvinists, Mennonites, and, after 1747, even sectarians and others commonly regarded as heretics.[126]

---

[122] On the Jews, see Chapter 3. On the Mennonites, see Klefeker, *Verfassungen*, 8, pp. 367–8, 399, 411–12, 748; Roosen, 'Mennoniten-Gemeinde', *passim*; Schepansky, 'Sozialgeschichte des Fremden', *passim*. The Mennonites were officially tolerated from 1814.

[123] The legal situation is described by Klefeker, *Verfassungen*, 8, pp. 383–92.

[124] The best work is still that published in 1790–1 by Johann Adrian Bolten. Cf. Bolten, *Kirchen-Nachrichten von Altona*, 1, pp. 188–395 and 2, *passim*. See also the useful article: P. T. Hoffmann, 'Politik und Geistesleben', pp. 41–69 and the survey in Kopitzsch, *Grundzüge*, pp. 216–39.

[125] On Danish policy in Altona, see Wucher, 'gewerbliche Entwicklung', pp. 53–8 and Stoob, 'frühneuzeitliche Städtetypen', pp. 190–2. An Austrian survey of 1755 stressed the failure of these policies: Otruba (ed.), 'Bericht', pp. 272–3.

[126] On Mennonites and separatists, see Bolten, *Kirchen-Nachrichten von Altona*, 1, pp. 271–91 and 2, pp. 3–7. Jews, Catholics and Calvinists are dealt with in the relevant chapters above.

Although the town expanded from a mere fishing village with only 10–15 houses before 1567 to a flourishing town with a population of about 3,000–3,400 by 1664 (12,000 in 1710 and 30,000 by about 1750), the original aim of cutting off Hamburg's trade failed.[127] Instead, many more made use of the churches in Altona than actually lived there. Throughout, the metropolis remained economically predominant: the most successful non-Lutherans (including the Jews) preferred to live and work in Hamburg, and to suffer the inconvenience of having to travel a few miles to worship outside the city rather than settle in Altona itself.

Although ultimately unsuccessful, the very existence of a nearby competitor made a profound impact on the magistrates in Hamburg. For one thing, the Danes persisted in their attempts to assert ancient claims to sovereignty over Hamburg itself: the threat of military force waned after the unsuccessful siege of 1686, but the Danish claims were not formally dropped until 1768.[128] This uncertainty was compounded in periods of economic crisis by a twofold fear: both that the Danes might be able to attract foreigners away from Hamburg in substantial numbers, and that they might then be able to exploit Hamburg's weakness in order to further their claims to sovereignty over it. Whether they were real or not, such fears increasingly played on the mind of the Senate in the eighteenth century as piece-meal policies governed by traditional mercantile wisdom gave way to broader strategies based on more profound insights into the nature of economic growth.

The very existence of Altona was thus a constant source of anxiety in Hamburg. But it also provided an extraneous outlet, albeit unsatisfactory, for the religious needs of non-Lutheran minorities. Furthermore, after 1700, Altona's newspaper and publishing trade was subtly exploited by the protagonists of toleration in Hamburg.

Similar privileges were granted to Jews and Mennonites in the village of Wandsbek to the east of Hamburg around 1600. The village was part of the estate of the Rantzau family between 1564 and 1614, and thereafter passed through various hands. The numbers involved were, however, never very great (in 1790 the total population was still only 500); and in many ways the example of Wandsbek serves only to underline the significance of Altona.[129]

---

[127] Wucher, 'gewerbliche Entwicklung', pp. 53–60, 65. Wucher gives a figure of 23,000 for 1803 (ibid., p. 65); one contemporary source estimated 30,000 for about 1747, although this was subject to sharp short-term fluctuations. Cf. Schmid, *historische Beschreibung*, p. 134.

[128] See Reincke, 'Hamburgs Aufstieg', pp. 19–34; *idem, Betrachtungen*, pp. 9–13; Wohlwill, 'Gottorper Vergleich', *passim*. Hamburg in turn contested the Danes' right to grant Altona an urban charter in 1664, and refused to recognise it on the grounds that the concession of such charters was technically an Imperial prerogative: Specht, 'Streit zwischen Dänemark und Hamburg', *passim*.   [129] Kopitzsch, *Grundzüge*, pp. 240–2.

Inside the city itself, diplomatic chapels provided the second sanctuary for non-Lutheran Christian worship. After 1650 Hamburg became a natural diplomatic centre of the North with permanent Residents from most major European countries. Their presence was of considerable benefit to the city. The Austrian and Prussian envoys in particular played a vital role in the struggle to maintain Hamburg's neutrality and independence; while Dutch diplomats, in protecting the interests of their own state in Hamburg, also assisted in safeguarding the city's international position.[130] But there was a price to be paid. Like diplomats everywhere, they and their officials enjoyed an exterritorial immunity which was extended to their homes and above all to their chapels. Indeed, the chapel question was a crucial factor in the emergence of a generally recognised code of diplomatic conduct in the sixteenth century.[131] In Hamburg as elsewhere, diplomats continually sought to extend their own freedom of worship to others of their religion. Their legal right to do so was dubious. But its gradual acceptance in practice marked the first step towards the concession of 1785.[132]

The tireless efforts of Austrian, Dutch and Prussian diplomats in Hamburg to extend religious hospitality to Catholics and Calvinists, together with the threat posed by Altona, provides the framework within which a concession ultimately emerged. Indeed, the interplay of both factors is central to any understanding of why public intolerance did not adversely affect the economic or political development of the city.

For nearly two centuries the Senate trod a delicate path. On the one hand it saw the need to accept non-Lutherans for economic reasons. On the other hand, it sought to maintain domestic security by preserving the integrity of the constitution and by placating the powerful clergy. In this area of policy as in many others, the Senate's behaviour often baffled and infuriated outsiders. In 1723 the British Resident described some of the Senators as 'fort rustique'.[133] Thirty years later the French Resident thought they were vain, arrogant and ignorant, obsessed with secrecy; the merchants among them knew only about their own trade, while the lawyers had learnt only how to prolong and obscure the most simple issues: 'In order to gain an impression of their politics', he wrote, 'one should think of the coffee

[130] Ramcke, *Beziehungen*, pp. 23–4; Lappenberg, 'Listen der Diplomaten', pp. 416–21; Baasch, 'Hamburg und Holland', *passim*; Wohlwill, *Aus drei Jahrhunderten*, pp. 26–88; Wiskemann, *Welthandelspolitik*, pp. 75–127.

[131] For a general discussion, see Mattingly, *Renaissance diplomacy*, pp. 45–51, 279–81; Adair, *Exterritoriality of ambassadors*, pp. 177–97, 244–5; Grossmann, 'Toleration', pp. 133–4. In Cologne the Prussian Resident made a similar attempt to introduce a Calvinist chapel, 1708–10: Meister, 'Preussischer Residentenstreit', *passim*.

[132] Klefeker, *Verfassungen*, 8, pp. 613–22, 743–6.

[133] PRO: SP 101/40, 6 April 1723, Wich to Tilson.

houses, where men reason without understanding and where they become agitated without the slightest cause.'[134]

In view of the intricate system of constitutional checks and balances it was, however, hardly surprising that prevarication was elevated into an art form. And, as in many mercantile republics, secrecy and sleight of hand were essential in affairs of state. Maritime, postal and banking laws were closely guarded secrets, as indeed was the constitution of 1712. For to give outsiders too much knowledge of the laws and constitutions was to give them power to exploit them to their own advantage and to the detriment of the city.[135]

The views of eighteenth-century diplomats were, however, in many ways more applicable to the policies of the seventeenth century. Before 1700 the attitude to the minorities was indeed often inconsistent and highly volatile. To a large degree this was the result of the perpetual constitutional conflicts of the era. Faced with anarchy and revolution, the Senate was unable to prevail over either the citizenry or the clergy.[136] The minorities were bound to the city by contracts which dealt with their economic privileges, but which either avoided the religious issue or explicitly denied the right to worship. The only exception to this rule was the religious freedom granted to the Anglican members of the English Court after 1611.[137] For the rest, the availability of chapels in Altona allowed the Senate to bypass the question of worship in Hamburg. Its attitude to the diplomatic chapels was censorious in public but lax in private.

After the resolution of the constitutional conflicts in 1712, a more coherent and forceful policy emerged. Its development before the concession of 1785 went through two distinct phases: both were characterised by the influence of broader intellectual and philosophical movements on the urban elite, and marked by the formation of Patriotic Societies in 1724 and 1765. Both also coincided with profound economic crises which acted as stimuli for action on many different levels of urban government. Neither Patriotic Society was officially sanctioned or recognised: but leading members of the Senate participated in each, and both aspired to breathe new life into the traditions and institutions of the city.[138]

The foundation of the first Patriotic Society in 1724 was largely a response to the problems raised by the constitutional conflicts which had been compounded by the threats posed to the city by the Great Northern

---

[134] Quoted by Huhn, 'Handelsbeziehungen', 1, pp. 45–6.

[135] On the constitution, see Wächter, *Historischer Nachlass*, 2, pp. 60–3. On the secrecy of other aspects of the law: Ewald, 'Sammlungen hamburgischer Rechtsvorschriften', pp. 170–6.

[136] Two reports (of 1640 and 1680) give vivid pictures of the chaotic conduct of Senate affairs: StAH, Senat, Cl.VII Lit.Aa No.2 Vol.8a.

[137] Hitzigrath, *Merchants Adventurers*, pp. 1–5.

[138] Brunner, 'Patriotische Gesellschaft', pp. 333–41.

War and a severe plague in the years 1713–14.[139] It sought to make philosophical sense of the new constitution, and to remedy the poverty of urban government so clearly demonstrated by its helplessness in the face of war and plague.

The Society's concerns have often been characterised as primarily literary and linguistic, and indeed its members were drawn almost exclusively from the educated elite – men like the poet Barthold Heinrich Brockes and the scholar poets Michael Richey and Johann Albert Fabricius (the latter both professors at the Gymnasium). But Brockes was also a Senator; Johann Julius Surland and Conrad Widow were Senatorial Syndics, as was Johann Klefeker after 1725; Johann Julius Anckelmann was secretary of the *Oberalten*.[140]

The intellectual character of the Society was strongly influenced by the ideas of Locke, the English Deists, and the legal philosophies of Thomasius and Wolff.[141] Although the journal which they published between 1724 and 1726, and which was to be their sole lasting monument, contained few concrete reform proposals, it was very much concerned with the analysis of the present condition and future prosperity of the city in the light of the new philosophical and legal wisdom.[142] *Der Patriot* was more than just an imitation of the English *Spectator*. Critical and satirical, it aspired to instruct as well as to amuse. Perhaps its most radical claim was that there was a form of morality which derived from reason and which was not necessarily coterminous with traditional Christianity. The authors stressed their desire to work within the existing framework of government, and with the established Church: reason was to complement religion rather than replace it. Patriotism entailed obedience and loyalty to tradition and authority, as well as tolerance and forebearance towards others.[143] Like Candide, the Patriots ceased their public speculations after three years, declaring that it was now time to try and apply their new precepts to their daily work.[144]

The only practical result of their efforts was an ultimately unsuccessful attempt to reform the poor-relief system.[145] But the ideology of the Society

139 Wohlwill, 'Pestjahre', pp. 295–329, 401–6.
140 On its origins and membership, see Scheibe, *Der 'Patriot'*, pp. 25–43, 50–9. On the friendship of one of its members, Conrad Widow, with Leibniz, see: Braubach, 'Bartensteins Herkunft', pp. 117–28.
141 Schimanck, 'Entwicklung der Naturwissenschaften', pp. 32–7; Scheibe, *Der 'Patriot'*, pp. 155–67. For a general discussion of the religious attitudes of the 'moral weeklies', see Martens, *Botschaft der Tugend*, pp. 185–224; Martens, 'Naturlyrik der frühen Aufklärung', *passim*; Philipp, *Werden der Aufklärung*, pp. 33–47.
142 Cf. Rathje, '"Der Patriot"', *passim*.
143 Scheibe, *Der 'Patriot'*, pp. 147–67; Matthei, *Untersuchungen*, pp. 11–23.
144 *Der Patriot*, 3, pp. 418–24.
145 Von Melle, *Armenwesen*, pp. 54–61.

had a profound impact on Senate policy after the 1720s. It also characterised the attitudes of some non-members like *Bürgermeister* Sillem, said by an anonymous source to be the domineering politician whose power and influence the Society wished to undermine.[146] As the vitriolic Orthodox Pastor Neumeister recorded in his letters, the spirit of what he called 'the political Antichrist' pervaded the urban administration after 1725.[147] In two areas it affected relations with the clergy. The first was in the protracted negotiations over the publication of a new catechism which the Senate thought should contain fundamental tenets of natural religion.[148] The second was in the emergence of a new attitude to toleration.

The first Patriots were not innovators. As their role in the organisations of the festivities analysed in Chapter 6 shows, they shared many of the fundamental assumptions of the clergy. Where they differed was in the moderation which their philosophy and their position as magistrates of a mercantile republic led them to espouse. Their understanding of the legal rights of Protestant rulers discussed by Thomasius and others led them to formulate a loose interpretation of the Treaty of Osnabrück. Their political and mercantile interests convinced them that religious moderation was good for trade. They aimed to achieve an amicable solution to the problem of non-Lutheran religious worship which would both avoid the intervention of foreign powers in domestic affairs and preserve the integrity of the purely Lutheran constitution.

If genuine religious conviction demanded toleration, political and economic interests dictated that it would effectively mean connivance. In the first instance they were concerned to establish the patronage rights of diplomats. Only later, in the 1730s and 1740s, did they contemplate more radical solutions for the Jews and for the Calvinists. These later steps were based on explicitly political and economic calculations, which conformed entirely with the principle enunciated in *Der Patriot* in 1726: 'One of the foundations of the happiness of our state is the fact that until now everyone has been tolerated without any imposition on his conscience; yet at the same time we allow no one to disturb the general peace and we ensure that only one faith is predominant without prejudice.'[149]

---

[146] Scheibe, *Der 'Patriot'*, pp. 38, 239. Cf. Schröder, *Lexikon*, 7, pp. 185–7 and *ADB*, 34, pp. 324–8. Educated in Halle, Sillem emerged as a leading figure as chairman of the *Sanitätskollegium* 1710–14. Its last report stimulated the attempted poor-relief reforms. Cf. Wohlwill, 'Pestjahre', pp. 405–6.

[147] Wotschke (ed.), 'Neumeisters Briefe' (1930), p. 164. The religious views of *Der Patriot* provoked a storm of pamphlets: Martens, 'Flugschriften gegen den "Patrioten"', *passim*.

[148] Klefeker, *Verfassungen*, 8, pp. 532–5; Klemenz, *Religionsunterricht*, pp. 115–22; Mönckeberg, *Reimarus und Edelmann*, pp. 66–73; Mönckeberg, 'hamburgischer Catechismus', *passim*.

[149] *Der Patriot*, 3, p. 78. The statement was twice quoted by Johann Klefeker as a fundamental principle: Klefeker, *Verfassungen*, 2, p. 272 and 8, p. 365. The same view is echoed by two further members of the Society, Michael Richey and J. A. Hoffmann. Cf. StAH, Hss No. 273, ad pag. 258; J. A. Hoffmann, *Staats-Kunst*, pp. 34–6.

The opposition of the clergy thwarted the first serious efforts to establish a viable *Toleranz-System*. The Patriots themselves were unwilling to countenance open conflict and repeatedly acquiesced in the face of an uncompromising Orthodox clergy. Their resistance betrayed more than mere timidity. Despite the claims made for the strength of deism and natural theology amongst them, despite their belief in the rectitude of the Thomasian interpretation of the rights of magistrates in ecclesiastical affairs, they perceived clearly that political stability and sound order ultimately depended upon a harmonious relationship between State and Church.[150]

Although their efforts were fruitless, their ideas continued to be a source of inspiration. The Society continued to meet regularly until 1748.[151] But by the 1760s only Johann Klefeker remained of the original members. His monumental history of the laws and constitutions of Hamburg provided final testimony to the first struggles for religious toleration.[152]

The ideas set forth in that work were only implemented in the concession of 1785. That was the achievement of a second generation of Patriots in the context of the profound economic crisis after 1763. The foundation of the second Patriotic Society of 1765 will be discussed more fully below.[153] Its aspirations were much broader than those of its predecessor, its achievements more considerable in many areas. And it was this group which exploited the decline of clerical power to solve once and for all the problem of worship in Hamburg for those non-Lutheran Christians recognised by the Treaty of Osnabrück. Again it is important to stress the limitations of their enlightened vision. They did not resume the earlier discussion of the Jews, nor did they address themselves to the problems posed by Mennonites or sectarians. Economic crisis and *Aufklärung* combined to realise the limited aspirations of the first Patriots. But they neither rendered obsolete the Imperial religious settlement of 1648 nor questioned the fundamental principles of a polity based on the continued existence of the established Lutheran Church.

The timing of the concession, four years before the French Revolution, is significant. For all its limitations, the mandate emphasises the strength and distinct character of enlightened reform in Hamburg. Here, as indeed elsewhere in Germany, the fact that the process of reform started before the revolutionary upheavals in France had important implications. It should

---

[150] Cf. Martens, 'Naturlyrik der frühen Aufklärung', *passim*; Deckelmann, 'Glaubensbekenntnis des Brockes', *passim*. The simple fact that the clergy never publicly opposed the Patriots testifies to the tact and diplomacy with which they handled their beliefs.

[151] Klefeker, *Verfassungen*, 12, p. 373.

[152] On Klefeker, see Schröder, *Lexikon*, 3, pp. 608–12, and *ADB*, 16, pp. 76–7. His twelve-volume work was published 1765–73; it remains an indispensable reference book.

[153] See Chapter 5, pp. 149–51.

be stressed that the religious reform was but one of many associated with the generation of the second Patriotic Society. The most prominent was perhaps the foundation of the Allgemeine Armenanstalt in 1788, a poor-relief institution admired throughout Europe. But the reforming zeal embraced many other areas too, such as urban administration and education.[154] Throughout, the emphasis was on improvement rather than innovation, renewal rather than revolution.

The enthusiasm generated by the reforms of the 1780s was sustained during the next decade. In October 1789 the Patriotic Society was refounded on new statutes aiming to achieve 'more publicity, more solemnity, and more precision in the conduct of business'; and in 1790 alone the 142 members were joined by a further 154.[155] The following years also saw the proliferation of other associations – informal discussion groups, reading societies and the like – which together broadened the social base of enlightened ideas in the city. The growth of interest in public affairs is further reflected in the expansion in the circulation of existing newspapers and the appearance on the market of numerous new papers, journals and magazines.[156]

This quickening of the political pulse was undoubtedly related to the reaction to the news from France after 1789. Yet reports that Hamburg was a nest of jacobins and revolutionaries were wild exaggerations. Foreign diplomats representing monarchs who feared for their future in the revolutionary era were perhaps inevitably over-sensitive to any discussions which praised freedom and earnestly pondered the alleviation of the plight of the poor. In 1792 the Prussian envoy to the Lower Saxon Circle went so far as to claim that 'The Senate is hand in glove with the National Convention; the local Marats and Robespierres rule the roost here, the honest men [*Biedermänner*] are in a minority.'[157]

Such testimonies are, however, more a reflection of the anxieties of their authors than of the real situation. As Walter Grab has shown, there were indeed some jacobins or democratic revolutionaries in Hamburg. But they remained a relatively small and isolated group: their lack of contact with the masses is amply demonstrated by their failure to capitalise on the outbreak of the artisans' rebellion of 1791. As the years went by, the news from France was less and less encouraging, and their hopes were finally dashed by Bonaparte's assumption of power in 1799.[158]

More significant was the emergence of an influential group of 'liberals' in 1790 and 1791. Composed of merchants like Georg Heinrich Sieveking,

[154] See Whaley, 'Protestant Enlightenment', pp. 115–17; *idem*, 'Rediscovering the *Aufklärung*', pp. 193–4; Kopitzsch, *Grundzüge*, pp. 551–6, 667–711.   [155] Ibid., pp. 540–1.
[156] Ibid., pp. 539–95.   [157] Quoted by Wohlwill, *Neuere Geschichte*, p. 98.
[158] Grab, *Demokratische Strömungen*, pp. 239–55.

and associated with the poet Klopstock (then living in Hamburg), their initial enthusiasm for the Revolution was considerable.[159] Their excitement was easily misinterpreted: Goethe wrily remarked that Sieveking, for all his obvious intelligence, did not seem to realise that the *Marseilleise* was written for the 'consolation and encouragement of poor devils' and not for the prosperous.[160] Yet the important point was that Sieveking and his friends discussed the concepts of liberty and equality in the light of their own experience: in that context the new language implied a strengthening of old urban traditions, not the creation of a new world. Apart from anything else, their enthusiasm for the French experiment in liberation cooled considerably after the trial and execution of the king in 1792–3. As Franklin Kopitzsch has pointed out, Hamburg saw none of the declarations and constitutional manifestos that appeared in many South German cities in this period.[161] The debate over reform was enriched but not fundamentally redirected by the new political currents.

By the end of the decade the problems of the revolutionary era began to loom over Hamburg in earnest – not the spectre of internal unrest, but the threat of invasion. The traditional policy of neutrality became virtually impossible to sustain. In 1801 the city briefly fell victim to Danish occupation. In 1806, after the dissolution of the *Reich*, the French invaded in order to bring the Elbe into the Continental System. Four years later Hamburg became part of the *Départment des Bouches de L'Elbe*. The constitution was abolished; the Senate was replaced by a *conseil municipal* supervised by a French Prefect; and the Code Napoleon was introduced. All previous legislation became invalid, and for a brief period complete religious freedom prevailed: full civil and political equality was granted to all – in fact two Jews were appointed to the *conseil municipal*.[162]

The years of French occupation marked the first radical break in continuity in Hamburg. Yet the transformation of the Free Imperial City into a *bonne ville de L'Empire française* was short-lived. In 1814 Hamburg was liberated and the old regime was restored. The restoration was not, however, complete. The French system had aroused admiration as well as resentment; and it was this admiration which provided the stimulus for discussions and reforms which led ultimately to the promulgation of a new constitution in 1860. An integral part of that development was the concession of full political liberties to all Christians in 1819, and the more protracted debate over a similar concession to the Jews.[163]

---

[159] Kopitzsch, *Grundzüge*, pp. 610–23.
[160] Quoted ibid., p. 617. See also Wohlwill, *Neuere Geschichte*, pp. 85–104.
[161] Kopitzsch, *Grundzüge*, p. 626.
[162] Ibid., p. 177; Wohlwill, *Neuere Geschichte*, pp. 239–67, 335–489.
[163] Ibid., pp. 515–39; Kopitzsch, *Grundzüge*, pp. 171–2, 631–3; Nirrnheim, 'Verfassungsfrage', *passim*.

Those developments were, of course, crucially moulded by situations and events specific to the nineteenth century. Yet through them ran patriotic traditions and historical memories which can be traced back through the endeavours of successive generations, each inspired in its own way by the first modern reform of the city in 1529.

2

The politics of toleration: the Catholic community

In July 1773, in the month of the dissolution of their Order, the Jesuit priests in Hamburg sent a report to Maria Theresa in Vienna. They described their chapel, their organisation of the liturgical year, and gave information on the salaries of the three priests and their lay helpers. They presented the picture of a religious community living at peace with its neighbours: those problems which had once accompanied the exercise of their pastoral functions had now been smoothed over by their patron, the Imperial Resident. In a city with a total population of about 100,000, the Catholic community amounted to no more than about 1,200 to 1,500 souls: 'The number of wealthy individuals is small. The number of the middling sort is a little larger, but their numbers are not one thirtieth of those without any wealth at all.' Servants, labourers, and manual workers, rather than shopkeepers or merchants characterised the Catholic community. Poor and without apparent influence, indeed without any interests to protect where influence might be needed, the Catholics in Hamburg appeared, according to the report of 1773, to lead a peaceful existence, watched over by the Imperial Resident, protected by a pro-Austrian Senate, ministered to by the diligent and devoted Jesuit mission.[1]

And yet the tranquil vision of 1773 belied a stormy past. For despite their relative unimportance, the Catholics had aroused as much animosity as either the Calvinists or the Jews. Indeed the violent destruction of the Catholic chapel in 1719 was regarded as one of the archetypal examples of the disastrous consequences of clerical zeal when combined with popular religious fury. By the late eighteenth century enlightened men thought they could gauge the decline of the power of the Lutheran clergy by pointing out that such outrages could no longer occur. It also demonstrated to them the decline of those confessional rivalries which had periodically imposed considerable financial and political strains on the city.[2]

[1] Duhr, *Geschichte der Jesuiten*, 4, pt 1, p. 107; Linckemeyer, *Das katholische Hamburg*, pp. 353-5.
[2] J. L. von Hess, *Hamburg* (2nd edn), 3, pp. 258-61; StAH, Hss No. 304. The latter is an anonymous account written c. 1800.

The economic and social tensions which largely accounted for the struggle over the Calvinists and the Jews did not have such an important impact on relations with the Catholics. Clerical animosity and senatorial diplomacy were directed not so much against the Catholics themselves as against their preachers, the Jesuits. Until the dissolution of the Order in 1773 they symbolised all that Lutheranism most violently opposed. It is significant that many enlightened critics throughout Europe shared the views of even the most Orthodox Lutheran clergy on this score. In the eighteenth century anti-Jesuit sentiment characterised the polemics of both tolerant and intolerant Protestants. In Hamburg Michael Richey, a member of the original Patriotic Society, expressed a common view when he wrote in 1758 that suspicion of the Catholics was well founded in experience:

The principles of the papists, and particularly the Jesuits, are well known. They neglect no opportunity to broaden their influence. They are driven by the spirit of persecution to pursue, either with cunning or with boldness and violence, their campaigns against the supposed heretics.

Indeed, he claimed:

Perhaps it is a kind of divine providence that this inevitable fear of an overweening papism serves to keep those alert who do not want to believe in the possibility of an overweening Calvinism. For they might otherwise be inclined to grant the Calvinists more than is allowed by the example of our blessed forebears, and they might thus endanger the security of the Protestant [i.e. Lutheran] religion.[3]

Even in Altona, where all manner of separatist sects had been given religious freedom in 1747, the Catholics were subject to more severe restrictive measures than any other minority.[4] In 1790 the liberal Lutheran clergyman, Johann Adrian Bolten, explained why. The Catholics, he claimed, had never been satisfied with limited freedom and had always contrived to disturb the delicate confessional equilibrium in the most tolerant of communities. In 1722 they had been the first group to demand a spire for their chapel. That demand was but one further indication of what he called the *Ausbreitungssucht* of the Catholics.[5] The Jesuits exploited the proximity of Altona and Hamburg to flout the laws of both cities, to propagate their religion and to force those who entered into mixed marriages to convert their spouses and bring up their children in the Catholic Church. The reason, he believed, lay in the nature of the Roman faith:

They (or at least the bigots among them) regard their Church as the only one which can bring salvation. Because they cannot desist from converting, so they cannot

---

[3] StAH, Hss No. 273, Richey, Anmerckungen, ad pag. 259.
[4] Bolten, *Kirchen-Nachrichten von Altona*, 2, pp. 3–7.   [5] Ibid., 1, pp. 355–64.

desist from condemning: the pursuit of proselytisation is so fundamental a part of Catholicism that it would be difficult to conceive of their Church without it. To demand of the Catholics that they should not be concerned with the spread of their Church, in all places and by whatever means, would be tantamount to demanding that they should cease to be Catholics.[6]

If only they would pursue peace like members of other religions, then it might be possible to treat them more leniently; but the real problem lay in the fact that their priests were not only priests but 'apostolic missionaries sent out among the cursed heathens to convert them to the Roman see'.[7]

In Hamburg, the supposed fanaticism of the Jesuits combined with yet another all-important factor to account for their unpopularity. For what infuriated the Lutheran clergy, and periodically worried even the Senate, was the fact that they enjoyed more powerful external protection than any other religious minority. From the start, the Catholics exploited the sanctuary provided by the chapels of diplomatic residents in the city as a base for their community life. And from the 1670s they also enjoyed the uninterrupted protection of the Emperor in Vienna. The preservation of Lutheran purity thus conflicted at crucial points with the city's political, financial and diplomatic interests. As the history of the Catholic community in Hamburg was to show, the combination of confessional politics with high diplomacy was potentially explosive, for the activities of the Jesuits revived memories of Catholic aggression in the sixteenth and seventeenth centuries, memories of campaigns which had been motivated as much by politics as by religion.

I

On reading the reports of the Lutheran clergy in the eighteenth century one might be forgiven for conceiving the impression of successive waves of Jesuit fanatics hurling themselves against the walls of the Zion of the North. In fact there were never more than four priests in Hamburg and Altona combined. And while they were theoretically committed to the reconversion of the northern heathens there is little evidence that they ever converted more than a dozen people in any year.[8] Apart from the spectacular and much publicised conversion of the occasional dignitary (and most of them were not even citizens of Hamburg) their proselytising energy seems to have been devoted to exploiting the potential of mixed marriages among the relatively poor. Even so, disputes over the rights of non-Lutherans to act as godparents do not seem to have involved Catholics in the same

---

[6] Ibid., 1, pp. 370–1 (note 240).　　　[7] Ibid., 1, p. 376.
[8] Seffrin, *Katholische Bevölkerungsgruppe*, pp. 29–30; Dreves, *Annuae missionis*, pp. 45, 58, 71, 101, 121.

way as they did Calvinists in the 1740s. Indeed Johann Klefeker inaccurately, but forgivably in view of the absence of open conflicts over this issue, claimed that intermarriage between Catholics and Lutherans was relatively rare.[9]

From the start, the activities of the Jesuits were largely concerned with the problem of ministering to and securing protection for a relatively small community. During the seventeenth century they did, it is true, become increasingly involved in the plans of the Curia in Rome for a Catholic revival in the Protestant North.[10] But the history of that involvement and its negligible results in Hamburg reveals a lack of real understanding of the situation on the part of the Roman authorities. While Catholic activity periodically caused considerable disruption within Hamburg, its history illustrates the geographical limits of the Counter-Reformation Church, which increasingly concentrated on the minds of individual princes in the North rather than on cities like Hamburg, whose mixed constitution and querulous clergy proved a match for the ingenuity of even the most devious Jesuit.

The origins of the Catholic community in Hamburg were in marked contrast with its later state. In the late sixteenth century its beginnings were similar to those of the Calvinist and Sephardic communities, consisting largely of exiled merchants rather than the servants and labourers who characterised it in the eighteenth century. The first Catholics came from Italy, the Netherlands and Spain or Portugal. Like other merchants they came to Hamburg because of the trade, which grew as persecution and war made other countries unsafe.[11] The most prosperous among them was Allessandro della Rocca of Florence, and it was he who in 1592 both negotiated a religious privilege in Altona and wrote to the papal nuncio in Cologne requesting a priest for the community, which then numbered between 130 and 160 individuals.[12] In the spring of 1593 Pater Reiner Egnoius was sent up from Hildesheim. He was paid 200 *taler* per annum by della Rocca and his colleagues, and he ministered to a predominantly foreign mercantile community composed of 'Italians, Spaniards, Scotsmen, Portuguese, French, Dutch and even a few negroes'.[13]

Little is known about the early members of the community. Although most of them lived in Hamburg, they exercised their religion in Altona.

9 Klefeker, *Verfassungen*, 8, p. 802.
10 The best sources for the *Propaganda* and its activities in North Germany are: Pieper, *Propaganda-Congregation*; Metzler, *Apostolische Vikariate*, pp. 1–30; Mejer, *Propaganda*, 1, pp. 89–100; ibid., 2, pp. 177–80; Denzler, *Propagandakongregation*, pp. 53–121.
11 Klefeker, *Verfassungen*, 8, pp. 368–9; Bolten, *Kirchen-Nachrichten von Altona*, 1, pp. 355–8; Kellenbenz, *Unternehmerkräfte*, pp. 259–60.
12 Duhr, *Geschichte der Jesuiten*, 1, p. 423; Kellenbenz, *Unternehmerkräfte*, pp. 260–2.
13 Duhr, *Geschichte der Jesuiten*, 1, p. 432.

Even so, della Rocca's flamboyance and wealth attracted the attention of the Hamburg authorities. In 1603 the Senate issued a decree forbidding Hamburg residents to attend services in Altona. In 1606 the Lutheran clergy became embroiled in a polemical debate with Egnoius' successor, Henricus Neverus.[14] But on the strength of their privileges in Altona, the Jesuits survived these attacks and seem to have made six to eight converts each year up to 1611.[15] In 1607 their freedom in Altona was guaranteed for twenty years in return for an annual payment of 100 ducats, and by 1608 the community supported three priests and one lay brother.[16] The opposition of the Senate and the Lutheran clergy in Hamburg was effectively neutralised by letters of protection sent by Rudolf II in 1604 and 1608.[17]

The uneasy existence of the Jesuit mission did not last long. In June 1612 it was expelled after a dispute over property with Count Ernst of Schaumburg. Della Rocca himself had left Hamburg for Seville as a result of trading difficulties in 1610, and so for some years the community was without either missionaries or effective internal leadership. Another appeal for help drawn up by the merchant Abondio Somigliano in 1614 came to nothing, and until 1622 the community was only occasionally visited by Canon Martin Stricker of Hildesheim.[18]

The new beginning in 1622 was the result of external factors. The establishment in Rome of the *congregatio de propaganda fide* in January 1622 marked the growth of a new interest in the Protestant North, where the papal nuncios in Cologne had signally failed to make any impact.[19] The ultimate grand design was the spiritual reconquest of Scandinavia, but Hamburg and other North German cities were seen as vital stepping-stones. Two Jesuits were sent up to Altona to exploit the more liberal atmosphere which prevailed after the succession of Count Justus Hermann. But they too were expelled in the following year. In Hamburg meanwhile the Catholic cause was served by the Dominican, Dominicus Janssen, who arrived in 1622 armed with letters of protection from Ferdinand II, Philip III and the Archduke Albert, governor of the Netherlands.[20]

Aided again by Martin Stricker, Janssen worked amongst the small community of about 200 souls. But his activities were repeatedly interrupted

---

[14] Linckemeyer, *Das katholische Hamburg*, p. 214; Bolten, *Kirchen-Nachrichten von Altona*, 1, pp. 355–7.

[15] Duhr, *Geschichte der Jesuiten*, 2, pt 1, p. 135.

[16] Ibid., pp. 135–6; Denzler, *Propagandakongregation*, pp. 87–8.

[17] Advice was taken in Speyer which recommended that these letters had legal force – StAH, Senat, Cl.VII Lit.Hf No.3 Vol.2.

[18] Denzler, *Propagandakongregation*, p. 88; Duhr, *Geschichte der Jesuiten*, 2, pt 1, p. 136.

[19] Ibid., p. 137; Mejer, *Propaganda*, 1, pp. 89–100.

[20] Denzler, *Propagandakongregation*, pp. 88–9; Duhr, *Geschichte der Jesuiten*, 2, pt 1, p. 137.

by the Lutheran clergy and by the Senate, which at first omitted to publish the Imperial privilege. When it did eventually recognise the letter in 1627, it was for explicitly political reasons. The proximity to Hamburg of the Catholic armies of Tilly and Wallenstein after 1627 ensured that the Senate proceeded with due caution.[21] It was an uneasy caution for, as the Syndic Vincent Möller pointed out in a report in 1629, the Senate was obliged to pursue a dangerous course. To expel Janssen might mean military reprisals by the Imperial armies; yet to tolerate him openly might well lead to the same result, with the Catholics possibly being in a position to reclaim the Cathedral and other ecclesiastical properties lost during the Reformation.[22] In the last resort the need for Imperial support in the conflict with Denmark over the Elbe prevailed and Janssen remained in Hamburg until 1637.

Although he enjoyed the protection of an Imperial privilege, Janssen lived independently in Hamburg. After 1630, however, the Jesuits managed to establish themselves in a rather different capacity as chaplains to the Imperial Resident. It was an important development. For Heinrich Schacht's appointment as chaplain to Michael von Menzel founded a relationship which was to prevail until the dissolution of the *Reich*. The Jesuits were thereby able to exploit the diplomatic immunity of their patrons, which provided an all but impregnable buttress to their rather flimsy letters of recommendation.[23]

With Janssen, Schacht and periodically Stricker in residence after 1630, the Catholic mission managed to survive relatively peacefully for the next few years. The only setback was the failure in 1635 of an attempt to assert the rights of Catholics to worship openly in Hamburg after the Peace of Prague. The Senate was able to deny the claim that such a freedom had existed in 1627, and merely granted the right to visit the Imperial Resident's chapel.[24] The exercise of this right was made easier after 1643 by the opening of a further chapel in the house of the French Resident, Claude de Meulles, who seems to have supported a chaplain of his own, a priest who preached alternately in German and French.[25]

Thus despite occasional conflicts and the discontinuity within the mission itself, the Catholics in Hamburg survived the confessional conflicts of the Thirty Years War. The Senate also at least partially achieved its aim by averting the possibility of a re-establishment of Catholicism in Hamburg, and by restricting the community to the facilities provided by resident

[21] Denzler, *Propagandakongregation*, pp. 89–90; Klefeker, *Verfassungen*, 8, pp. 370–4; Loose, *Hamburg und Christian IV*, pp. 22–35 (esp. 23–6); Kellenbenz, *Sephardim*, p. 38.
[22] The report is printed in Ziegra, *Sammlung*, 4, pp. 5–56.
[23] Denzler, *Propagandakongregation*, pp. 37–8, 90–2.
[24] Ibid., pp. 90–1; Klefeker, *Verfassungen*, 8, pp. 374–6.
[25] Denzler, *Propagandakongregation*, pp. 92–3.

diplomats. In 1648 the Peace of Westphalia itself laid many fears to rest, for it affirmed the Lutheran status of the city and merely guaranteed the Catholic minority there against persecution. The extent to which further freedom was given was left for the consideration of the Senate from time to time.[26]

The following decades were to show that the Senate was not inclined to place a liberal construction on the clauses of 1648. But the Peace also had an important impact on Catholic policy, for it placed the final seal on the loss to Catholicism of places like Hamburg. Henceforth their religious integrity was guaranteed by the constitution of the *Reich*. Those ecclesiastical properties confiscated during the Reformation were now irrevocably lost and nothing short of a total conversion of the whole city could fundamentally alter the position of the Catholic community or the status of its Jesuit missionaries.[27]

The *Propaganda* reacted to the new situation after 1648 with a mixture of depression and uncertainty, and increasingly restricted itself to maintaining the faith of its far-flung congregations. The dream of the reconquest of the North faded; while it may have inspired individual missionaries in the field, it remained elusive. The *Propaganda* itself seemed to recognise this at times. In 1677 its secretary, Urban Cerri, reported that no real missionary activity took place in the North. The princes, he said, did not object to the Catholics, but in the towns the hostility of the populace imposed severe limitations on the work of the Jesuits. Rather optimistically, he claimed that there were about 3,000 Catholics in Hamburg, but he admitted that their numbers were not increasing.[28]

The gradual establishment of a more formal missionary hierarchy did not make a significant impact on the situation in Hamburg. The Apostolic Vicariate of the North, founded in 1667–70, proved no more effective in co-ordinating the missions than the papal nuncios in Cologne. The efforts of its first incumbents were primarily aimed at the conversion of rulers of large territories. In Hamburg the only real difference it made was when Ferdinand von Fürstenberg established a charitable bequest in 1683 which paid the stipends of the missionaries.[29]

The Jesuit mission in Hamburg, which had once been regarded as the stepping-stone to Scandinavia, had a varied history after 1648. Initially, it seems to have been supported by the French Resident de Meulles, who successfully persuaded the *Propaganda* to pay the salary of two missionaries in 1650. The community by now consisted of about 600 members, most

---

[26] The relevant passages of the Treaty are printed in Klefeker, *Verfassungen*, 8, pp. 386–90.
[27] Denzler, *Propagandakongregation*, pp. 165–72, 213–15; Mejer, *Propaganda*, 2, pp. 177–80, 182–5, 275, 294.   [28] Ibid., 1, pp. 128–48 (esp. pp. 129–31).
[29] Metzler, *Apostolische Vikariate*, pp. 12–49, 54–61.

of whom were relatively poor, the original mercantile nucleus having all but disappeared by about 1620. Although one of the Jesuits periodically lived in the home of the Imperial Resident, the community was effectively protected in Hamburg by de Meulles, since the Imperial Resident lived mainly in Lübeck and seldom came to the city.[30]

The community seems to have attracted attention to itself for a number of reasons. The French Resident's chapel was small: on high feast days many simply could not get in, and this gave the impression of crowds thronging to the Jesuit services. The Jesuits themselves always stressed these 'crowds' in their reports to Rome.[31] Occasional visits by travelling dignitaries also brought not only Catholics but Lutherans too to look and wonder. The Baroque Catholic liturgy, with its elaborate ritual involving frequent processions, also aroused both popular curiosity and Lutheran anger. The elaborate burial of Heinrich Schacht in the hereditary Schaumburg grave in the Cathedral in 1654, accompanied by coaches of state and many diplomats, again drew the attention of the Lutheran clergy to what they called 'das Faule Nest an der Faulen twiete' (the foul nest in the foul alley, a pun based on a corruption of the street's true name, Fuhlentwiete).[32]

The clergy retaliated by demanding the closure of the chapel, or at least its restriction to the Resident and his personal staff. From 1652 they protested repeatedly, requesting that the Senate insist on all services being held in French, a move which would exclude the poor German Catholics. As usual their claim that the law of God was the only relevant one in these cases cut little ice when that law conflicted with politics and diplomacy. When the Senate did finally attempt to act, de Meulles refused to comply and the dispute was only resolved by the latter's death in 1657.[33]

That event temporarily closed the Jesuit mission in Hamburg. In the following year it moved to Altona where the merchant Hugo de Terlon managed to negotiate another concession.[34] Only in 1661 did services once more begin in Hamburg when Pierre de Bidal took up the post of French Resident.[35] Another chapel was also opened in the house of ex-Queen Christina of Sweden, who was based in Hamburg while ordering her financial affairs in Sweden after her conversion to Catholicism in 1655.[36]

Bidal's chapel apparently operated relatively undisturbed. But Queen Christina soon became embroiled in conflicts with the Lutheran clergy who

[30] Denzler, *Propagandakongregation*, pp. 92–4; Duhr, *Geschichte der Jesuiten*, 3, pt 1, p. 690.

[31] Dreves, *Annuae missionis*, pp. 53, 58, 71, 101, 106, 141.

[32] Seffrin, *Katholische Bevölkerungsgruppe*, pp. 26–9; Linckemeyer, *Das katholische Hamburg*, pp. 252–6; Duhr, *Geschichte der Jesuiten*, 3, pt 1, p. 690.

[33] StAH, Ministerium, II 2, pp. 100, 105–6, 125, 130, 166, 168, 170–9, 209.

[34] Dreves, *Geschichte*, pp. 72–4.   [35] Ibid., pp. 74–7.

[36] Kellenbenz, *Sephardim*, pp. 387–92; *idem*, 'Diego und Manoel Texeira', *passim*; Arckenholtz, *Mémoires*, 2, pp. 38–88, 104–30.

knew that she had attempted to gain widespread support for religious freedom for the Catholics. They also suspected her of having converted several prominent citizens, among them Peter Lambeck who later became the Imperial Librarian in Vienna after his flight from Hamburg in 1662.[37] Matters came to a head in July 1667, when the Queen gave a splendid feast to celebrate the election of Pope Clement IX. Free wine was given to the populace, her house was illuminated with an inscription which read *Clemens IX Pont. Max. Vivat*, and *Te Deums* were sung in her chapel. Several Lutheran preachers mingled with the crowd and the result was a violent attack on the chapel which was promptly destroyed while the Queen fled the city in fear of her life.[38] Although she returned once more before leaving for Rome in November 1668, her chapel was thereafter a more modest building which eventually closed in 1674 when it became clear that she would never return. In the following year Bidal's chapel was also closed after his departure from Hamburg after the outbreak of war between France and the *Reich*.[39]

II

Bidal's departure in 1675 effectively ended the French protectorate over the Catholic community. Although he returned in 1679 and attempted to re-establish his position, the situation had by then changed radically. Even his successor, his son Étienne de Bidal, failed to establish a permanent alliance with the Jesuits, for his tenure of office was also interrupted by renewed international hostilities between 1690 and 1698 and again in 1703.[40]

After 1675 the Emperor firmly established his patronage of the community. His motives were twofold. Rivalry with France obviously played a part: protecting the Catholics in Hamburg was one way of neutralising French influence there. At the same time he sought to enhance his own influence in a city which was regarded as a crucial northern frontier-post of the *Reich*. The Catholics thus became a pawn on the elaborate board of international diplomacy, a vehicle of pressure and influence.[41]

Moves towards this end had already been made in 1671 when the Emperor commissioned Georg von Rondeck as his Resident in Hamburg with the express aim of protecting the Catholics. As a pious convert,

[37] Dreves, *Geschichte*, pp. 75–7. On Lambeck, see Schröder, *Lexikon*, 4, pp. 278–92 and Voigt, 'Bedenken der Oberalten', *passim*.
[38] Dreves, *Geschichte*, pp. 77–80; Arckenholtz, *Mémoires*, 2, pp. 127–8; ibid., 3, pp. 290–5.
[39] Linckemeyer, *Das katholische Hamburg*, p. 277; Dreves, *Geschichte*, pp. 87–90.
[40] Dreves, *Geschichte*, pp. 112–20.
[41] Lorenz, 'Eine Hamburgische Residentschaft', pp. 71–2, 74, 91–2; Rückleben, *Niederwerfung*, pp. 28–49; Wiskemann, *Welthandelspolitik*, pp. 101–8.

Rondeck was deeply committed to the cause, and when Bidal left in 1675 he immediately rented a house to serve as a chapel, adorning it with the Austrian eagle as a symbol of Imperial protection.[42] The fact that he himself did not live there, however, made the situation rather difficult since it was technically meant to be his own private chapel. After the intervention of the head of the Jesuit Order, Marcellus von Lotz, in Vienna, it was decided to buy a larger building to house both Rondeck and the chapel. The cost of 16,000 *taler* was met partly by the Emperor, who personally paid 2,000 *taler*, and partly by an allocation made from the taxes that Hamburg was due to pay the Emperor in 1678.[43] The Senate rightly suspected the role of the Jesuits in the affair, and protested strongly to the Emperor. Nonetheless, by 1678 the purchase was completed and work began to accommodate the new chapel. Meanwhile until 1680 the Jesuits held services in the house of the Spanish Resident Don Juan de Salazar.[44]

Georg von Rondeck died shortly before the purchase was concluded. But despite clerical opposition, the Ballhaus in the Fuhlentwiete had been bought by the time his son, Hans Dietrich, arrived in January 1679 to take over his post armed with a letter from the Emperor ordering the construction of a chapel and the protection of the Catholic community. The younger Rondeck did not, however, share his father's piety, while his wife apparently positively disliked the proximity of the Jesuit priests under her own roof. Thus in 1681 he resolved to sell the newly-acquired house in order to buy something more suitable for his purposes. The attempted sale dragged on for nearly two years, with the Senate unsuccessfully trying to persuade the *Oberalten* to raise enough money to buy it for the city in order to oust the Jesuits. This was essential, it was argued, since otherwise the priests would only call upon another Resident from Spain or France to protect them.[45]

The Senate's assurances to the *Oberalten*, that the Emperor himself had agreed to the sale, were, however, less than accurate and were based on information fed to them by Rondeck himself. Indeed in July 1681 Leopold I had written to his Resident expressly forbidding him to take any steps which might prejudice the position of the Jesuits. Alerted to Rondeck's anti-Catholic attitude by Marcellus von Lotz, the Emperor wrote that the whole purpose of having a Resident in Hamburg was 'that Catholic services might be held to comfort the Catholics of that area, and to promote the further growth of this religion'. Rondeck must be seen to be the public

[42] StAH, Senat, Cl.VII Lit.Hf No.3 Vol.4b, fol. 1.
[43] Dreves, *Geschichte*, pp. 88–93.
[44] Ibid., pp. 96–7; StAH, Senat, Cl.VII Lit.Hf No.3 Vol.4a, *passim*.
[45] Dreves, *Geschichte*, pp. 106–7; StAH, Senat, Cl.VII Lit.Hf No.3 Vol.4b, fols. 6–21.

patron of the Jesuits and he himself must regularly attend services.[46] Rondeck blamed the missionaries for the struggle, but although he continued his negotiations over the sale of the house, his efforts met with no success. In 1682 the matter was finally laid to rest when the new chapel was opened and regular services resumed.

Rondeck left Hamburg in 1685, but a further crisis erupted in 1687 when the new Resident, Baron von Gödens, in fact carried out Rondeck's plan to move to a larger house. He sold the Ballhaus to the city and bought instead the so-called Herren-Logiment in the Kraienkamp. After some prevarication, the Jesuits were allocated a separate house nearby, although in 1694 Gödens' successor, Count von Eck, added a new wing to the Resident's house so that Residence and chapel were once more united.[47]

Despite these domestic problems, and despite sporadic conflicts within the community occasioned by the temporary sojourns of French diplomats anxious to reassert their former influence, the community survived unscathed until the end of the century. However unwilling the younger Rondeck and Gödens may have been to carry out their religious duties, the Emperor's will prevailed. The Austrian protectorate of the Catholics was established and recognised. Even the Lutheran clergy ceased to harry the Jesuits after 1682. Their one act of defiance was to insist on the closure of the chapel for a short period after Gödens' death in 1692, pointing out that since it was a diplomatic chapel it must be formally associated with the person of an Imperial Resident. Even so their protests were muted: on 1 December they informed the Senate that services must stop, but a week later some 273 people were observed entering the chapel, which continued to operate informally until the arrival of the new Resident in September 1694.[48] Hostility to the Catholics remained latent and intense, but no single issue triggered open aggression during these years.

III

The persistent personal interest of the Emperor in the welfare of the Catholic community in Hamburg thus ultimately secured its position. The Jesuits, who had contributed so much to keeping that interest alive, exploited the situation to their best advantage. In 1696 they founded their

---

[46] Lorenz, 'Eine Hamburgische Residentschaft', pp. 93–4; the Imperial letter is printed in Dreves, *Geschichte*, pp. 107–8.

[47] Dreves, *Geschichte*, pp. 109–11; Linckemeyer, *Das katholische Hamburg*, pp. 299–301.

[48] StAH, Senat, Cl.VII Lit.Hb No.3 Vol.2b, fols. 56–9; ibid. Cl.VII Lit.Jb No.1 Vol.1b; ibid., Ministerium, II 3, pp. 64, 68 – undated anonymous notes.

first school in the city, and by 1706 five more had been established for the religious instruction of the young.[49]

The provisional *status quo* was, however, soon to be disrupted by the growing animosity of the Lutheran clergy which culminated in the violent destruction of the Catholic chapel in September 1719. The ill-feeling which led to that outburst escalated over a number of years during which the Emperor was represented in Hamburg by two envoys. For in 1708, in the midst of the most violent constitutional conflict between Senate and *Bürgerschaft*, the Imperial authorities intervened by sending Count Damian Hugo von Schönborn as a mediator. He was given the title of Ambassador, and although the new constitution was promulgated by 1712, he remained in Hamburg until 1716. Thereafter the Emperor maintained two envoys in Hamburg, one an Ambassador to the Lower Saxon Circle, the other a Resident attached to Hamburg itself.[50]

Schönborn, who was made a lay cardinal in 1715, proved no less effective a patron of the Jesuits than his predecessors or his colleague, Count von Kurtzrock.[51] The Lutheran clergy, already threatened by the Imperial Commission with the exposure of their role in the civil disturbances, were now unable to protest against the activities of the Jesuits.[52] Only on one occasion in 1709 did they attempt to assert their position, in a dispute over the children of a deceased Lutheran who were entrusted to the care of his Catholic widow and hence ultimately to the Jesuits. The conflict lasted for over a year and was exacerbated by the fact that Schönborn himself intervened and effectively arranged for the children to be kidnapped to preserve their Catholic faith. The situation was only resolved when in October 1710 the *Reichshofrat* gave custody to the Catholic mother and the Lutheran clergy accepted the decision with bad grace.[53]

Their behaviour during the affair shows how bitterly they resented the freedom which Schönborn's presence afforded the Jesuits. In July 1709 they explained to the Senate that they were obliged to preach against Schönborn in order to maintain their reputations – to show their congregations 'that they had faithful guardians and not mute dogs, an expression already used by some malcontents who out of ignorance have demanded that these things

[49] Linckemeyer, *Das katholische Hamburg*, pp. 399–400.

[50] Ramcke, *Beziehungen*, pp. 5–6. Both were effectively based in Hamburg. For a further discussion of the Emperor's influence in Hamburg, see Chapter 6, pp. 179–85.

[51] On Schönborn, see: Dreves, *Annuae missionis*, pp. 144–6, 158–61; *idem, Geschichte*, pp. 123–9.

[52] Westphalen, *Haupt-Grundgesetze*, 3, pp. 3–27. The College of the Sixty played an extremely important part in protecting the clergy against public recriminations over their role during the internal struggles.

[53] Dreves, *Geschichte*, pp. 124–7; StAH, Senat, Cl.VII Lit.Hf No.3 Vol.3, *passim*; ibid., Ministerium, II 5, pp. 187–91, 194–5, 197–213, 227–8, 236; ibid., Ministerium, III A1k, nos. 14–21, 25–63, 71, 75, 77–95, 101, 103, 256–65, 287–8.

should immediately be aired in the pulpits in order to satisfy their itching ears'.[54] Their claim appears to have been genuine for their subsequent justifications of their actions repeatedly apologised for their behaviour. They recognised that inflammatory sermons would probably harm their cause, but felt that a loss of public face, both in Hamburg and in the world at large, would be intolerable.

The dispute over the Schlebusch children demonstrated the frustration of the clergy, but it also revealed their disorganisation and lack of effective influence. It was only in 1715 that the Ministry once more gained effective leadership in the alliance between the new *Senior*, Peter Theodor Seelmann, and the newly-appointed Pastor at St James's, Erdmann Neumeister. Seelmann, Pastor of St Michael's since 1706, was consumed with a deep hatred of Catholicism which derived from his own experience of persecution in Hungary in his youth.[55] Neumeister, who became one of the leading and most uncompromising and articulate defenders of Orthodoxy in the first half of the eighteenth century, had a more mixed background. A highly neurotic and gifted man, he had suffered from severe hypochondria in his early manhood. He had once associated himself with Pietism, but he came to Hamburg in 1715 with all the fervour of a convert to the strict Orthodox Lutheran tradition, eager to show his colours by hurling himself into any religious controversy.[56]

Although willing to oppose any religious cause which differed from their own, Seelmann and Neumeister concentrated at first on Catholicism. Their minds were sharpened by a series of incidents which underlined what they saw as the rise of militant Catholicism. In 1715 the community celebrated Schönborn's appointment as a lay cardinal.[57] In June 1716 the Imperial chapel was once more the scene of an elaborate celebration, the birth of an Habsburg archduke.[58] In August 1716 Seelmann took up the cause of a blind Lutheran visiting preacher who had been banned from the pulpit because of an anti-Catholic sermon against which Count Kurtzrock had protested vigorously.[59] Seelmann argued that he should be allowed to preach again 'because the Jesuits boast inordinately, and the [Lutheran]

[54] StAH, Ministerium, II 5, p. 190.

[55] Schröder, *Lexikon*, 7, pp. 146–8.

[56] Ibid., 5, pp. 494–512. See Neumeister's assurances to his future colleagues in StAH, Ministerium, III A1l, no. 621, 31 May 1715, Neumeister to Ministry. See also ibid., nos. 648–9, where Neumeister recants his false doctrine of the soul.

[57] Dreves, *Geschichte*, pp. 128–9; idem, *Annuae missionis*, pp. 159–60; Linckemeyer, *Das katholische Hamburg*, pp. 310–11.

[58] StAH, Ministerium, III A2b, no. 41. The Lutheran clergy were especially incensed by the suggestion that the birth of the Archduke was the result of the intercession of the Virgin Mary. Ibid., no. 41, *Hamburger Relationscourier*, 16 June 1716, containing a description of the ceremony.

[59] StAH, Ministerium, II 5, pp. 394–5, 398–9; ibid., Ministerium, III A1m, nos. 95, 112, 120–2, 127–9, 154–5.

congregations criticise the Ministry and are angry, and fear the works of the Jesuits'.[60]

Only a few months later the clergy experienced their first taste of the power of the press when a rumour circulated in French and Dutch newspapers that a secret clause had been inserted in a commercial treaty with France granting religious freedom to all Catholics in Hamburg. On making their protest, the clergy learnt that the rumours were unfounded.[61] But the case was significant in that it marked the beginning of a long and frustrating struggle with the new media which henceforth avidly published any rumours concerning the religious minorities in Hamburg and the repressive attitude of the Lutheran clergy. Little is known about the operations of the press at this time, and so it is difficult to say whether such reporting was premeditated or organised. It is, however, significant that after 1712 the *Hamburger Relations Courier* was published by a Calvinist printer, a man whom Neumeister later suspected of being a particularly anti-clerical trouble-maker.[62]

The resolve of the Lutheran clergy was strengthened by what they saw as the happy coincidence of the year of the second centenary of the Reformation in 1717.[63] They decided to preach incessantly against the Catholics, and already by February 1717 Seelmann and Neumeister provoked a protest by Kurtzrock against their sermons.[64] As the year progressed, Seelmann conscientiously collected material on the pernicious activities of the Jesuits – notes on mixed marriages, poor folk bribed by the Jesuits to convert, others employed by them to sell catechisms and popular tracts.[65] The centenary itself was celebrated with such zeal and enthusiasm that the Apostolic Vicar of the North was moved to retaliate by ordering his congregations to celebrate the memory of St Ansgar, the pioneer missionary and founder of the medieval see of Hamburg.[66]

An outright confrontation was avoided despite bitter conflicts between Senate and clergy over the organisation of the centenary and especially over the extent to which it should be made into an anti-Catholic jamboree as the clergy wished. For most of 1718 the situation remained brittle but, in public at least, subdued. Matters soon came to a head, however, when it

[60] Ibid., Ministerium, III A1m, no. 112, 25 September 1716, Resol. Rev. Min.
[61] The newspaper reports are collected in: StAH, Ministerium, III A2b, nos. 298, 303; ibid., Ministerium, III A1m, nos. 184, 193. Compare: Huhn, 'Handelsbeziehungen', 1, pp. 95–6. Similar fears were voiced by the clergy in 1763; StAH, Senat, Cl.VII Lit.Hf No.3 Vol.18, *passim*.
[62] Colshorn, 'Buchhandel', p. 186. See reference to Daniel Bene (or Behn) and his son in 1724 and 1749: StAH, Ministerium, II 6, p. 27a; ibid., III A2c, no. 580. Cf. Wotschke (ed.), 'Neumeisters Briefe' (1930), pp. 193–4.   [63] See Chapter 6, pp. 189–92.
[64] StAH, Senat, Cl.VII Lit.Ja No.1 Vol.5, 19 February 1717, Kurtzrock to Senate.
[65] StAH, Ministerium, III A2b, Nos. 283–90, 292–6, 312–17.
[66] Metzler, *Apostolische Vikariate*, p. 145.

became known that Kurtzrock intended to enlarge his chapel. When building work actually started early in 1719, with the laying of a foundation stone dedicated to S. Carlo Borromeo, the clergy were set on a collision course.[67]

On 16 May they sent their first protest to the Senate. They warned against the evil intentions of the Jesuits and pointed out that the enlarged chapel would constitute a flagrant breach of both the urban constitution and the Peace of Westphalia.[68] Technically, of course, their arguments were valid, for what Count Kurtzrock intended was obviously a chapel which would effectively provide freedom of worship for the Catholics in Hamburg. The Senate did not reply to this protest and, after further futile protests on 9 and 19 June, the clergy decided to take the matter to the College of the Sixty, having first informally notified the *Oberalten* of their intentions.[69] As Seelmann put it to them: 'When the Jesuits want something, one reacts quickly: but when the Ministry protests once, twice, or even three times, there is no reply. *Ô tempora!*'[70] His most militant ally at this point was again Neumeister who recommended that their letters ought to be printed as pamphlets – 'so that our descendents may not say that the members of the Ministry were traitors and knaves at this time. Yet again, I say that Carthage, both of the popes and of the Calvinists, must be destroyed.'[71]

In the event, they were pre-empted by the Senate which itself took the matter to the Sixty on 30 June. The manoeuvre failed for they supported the clergy and, despite the warnings of the Senate, insisted that the building work must be stopped at once.[72] Neumeister himself was instrumental in effecting this decision: he was in constant contact with the *Oberalten* of his parish and gave them copies of the relevant lengthy papers so that they could consider them before their meetings.[73] His aim, he wrote to Seelmann, was to undermine the position of the Senate or, as he put it in a typically lively phrase, 'to give the whigs [*Wighs*] a soaking without even wetting their skins'.[74]

The *Wighs* were, however, not easily deterred. The Senate refused to accept the decision of the Sixty and continued to negotiate, but on 7 July the Sixty insisted that the *Bürgerschaft* be called to settle the issue once and for all.[75] On the same day the clergy took a solemn oath pledging themselves to the Lutheran cause and were rewarded by the *Bürgerschaft*'s

---

[67] Dreves, *Geschichte*, pp. 142–3.
[68] StAH, Senat, Cl.VII Lit.Hf No.1 Vol.3b, fols. 1–2.
[69] StAH, Ministerium, III A2b, no. 132.
[70] Ibid., no. 53v.   [71] Ibid., no. 51v.
[72] Ibid., nos. 58–62; Senat, Cl.VII Lit.Hf No.1 Vol.3b, fols. 5–7.
[73] StAH, Ministerium, III A2b, nos. 271–4, 276.
[74] Ibid., no. 319, undated, Neumeister to Seelmann.
[75] Ibid., nos. 61–3, 260–1, 333–44.

decision that the chapel should be demolished at once.[76] Even now the Senate refused to give in and resolved to go back to the Sixty for further talks. On 17 July it informed the clergy that it would investigate their complaints 'in so far as they are justified' and continued to prevaricate over the Sixty's renewed demand for prompt action.[77]

Owing to the relentless activity of Seelmann and Neumeister, the affair was by now widely discussed throughout the city.[78] At least two of their colleagues voiced severe doubts about the wisdom of their policies, but these objections were overruled by the militants who smelt blood.[79] On the strength of yet another massive written protest by the clergy on 13 July, the Sixty demanded the cessation of all services for both Catholics and Calvinists in the city and on 28 July forced the publication of a mandate to this effect.[80] Meanwhile accounts of the affair had again appeared in German and Dutch newspapers.[81]

On 2 August Kurtzrock himself warned the Senate against the dangers of what he called 'violent solutions' proposed by the *Bürgerschaft*. He demanded the punishment of those preachers responsible for the unrest, who threatened the 'sovereign laws of the Emperor, the public peace of the Empire, and the tranquillity of the state'.[82] The Senate was obviously impressed with this stern admonition and warned the Sixty that they should be aware 'into which labyrinth one will err as a result of the proposed violent action'.[83] The Sixty remained obdurate even in the face of a renewed warning on 21 August by Kurtzrock, who requested military protection for his chapel against an increasingly threatening rabble. In words which the Senate had cause to remember with acute embarrassment for many years, he declared that the Emperor would hold the Senate itself responsible for any disorder or damage.[84]

Further negotiations failed to resolve the deadlock. On 4 September the clergy sent the longest protest ever submitted in the history of the Hamburg Church – no less than eighty-three pages listing every single case of Jesuit malpractice Seelmann could find in his archive.[85] It ensured the solid support of the Sixty once more on 6 September.[86]

---

[76] Ibid., II 5, pp. 434–5; Kühl, *Raths- und Bürger-Schlüsse*, p. 47.

[77] StAH, Ministerium, III A2b, no. 321.

[78] *Ausführliche und recht gründliche Nachricht*, pp. 3–11. Neumeister himself regarded this as a relatively reliable account: Wotschke (ed.), 'Neumeisters Briefe' (1925), p. 112.

[79] StAH, Ministerium, II 5, p. 435; one is named as Pastor Nicolai Staphorst of St John's.

[80] StAH, Senat, Cl.VII Lit.Hf No.1 Vol.3b, fols. 18–42, 13 July 1719, Ministry to Senate; ibid., Ministerium, III A2b, nos. 391–5, 322–6; Blank, *Mandate*, 2, p. 918.

[81] StAH, Ministerium, III A2b, nos. 299, 300, 304, 305.

[82] A copy may be found in: ibid., no. 387; it was preceded by a letter from Schönborn in Vienna: ibid., ad no. 399.   [83] Ibid., no. 400, 4 August 1719, Senate to Sixty.

[84] StAH, Senat, Cl.VII Lit.Ja No.1 Vol.6, 21 August 1719, Kurtzrock to Senate.

[85] StAH, Senat, Cl.VII Lit.Hf No.1 Vol.3b, fols. 57–137.

[86] StAH, Ministerium, III A2b, nos. 377–8.

By now the whole affair had reached fever-pitch. On Sunday, 10 September, a day of fiery sermons, trouble broke out when Catholic boys began to throw stones at the Church of St Michael opposite the Catholic chapel. The Lutheran parishioners, already fuelled by Seelmann's sermon, moved to retaliate. They launched a full-scale attack on the chapel and the Residence in which it was housed.[87] An attempt by the Resident's secretary, Lempe, to subdue the crowd by brandishing a musket merely incensed it still more. By evening, both the chapel and the Resident's house had been completely demolished, its archive was destroyed, and the contents of the chapel were in the hands of a triumphant mob which paraded the monstrance and chalice round the streets in jubilant defiance. Neither Seelmann nor Neumeister took part in the riot. Both went home early and locked themselves away: but both refused to intervene.[88] The Senate itself was caught unawares and only moved in troops in the late evening after the deed had been done.

Even before the news was sent to Vienna, Count Metsch attempted to rally the support of other diplomats in the city. As he wrote to Cyril Wich, the English Resident, on 11 September: 'Je ne scais pas, Monsieur, si les quartiers et les personnes de ministres etrangers sont assez en seureté ici, dans la ville, où il semble qu'on se plait à executer des barbaries dont on a de l'horreur en Turquie.'[89] But Wich, who had followed the affair with interest since the end of August, refused to act, for as he pointed out, 'the insult has not been done to the Emperor's Envoy, but to the Popish church'.[90] He added later that 'It is certain that the accident that has happened to the Emperor's envoy's house...or rather to the Popish chappel, will create trouble and uneasiness to these magistrates.'[91]

Wich thus accurately pinpointed the problem. For although he was in a sense right in believing that the Jesuits were effectively to blame for provoking the city, the Imperial authorities took a very different view. The Senate's initial letter of apology met with little sympathy. It simply placed the blame squarely on the shoulders of the Jesuits and attempted rather unconvincingly to separate what it claimed was an essentially domestic religious problem from the Imperial reprisals it rightly suspected might ensue.[92]

---

[87] The following is based on numerous accounts of the riot: Dreves, *Geschichte*, pp. 148–51; Linckemeyer, *Das katholische Hamburg*, pp. 320–4; Steltzner, *Nachricht*, 5, pp. 505–6; Dreves, *Annuae missionis*, pp. 166–70; Höck, *Bilder*, pp. 139–41; *Ausführliche und recht gründliche Nachricht*, pp. 22–4; StAH, Handschrift No. 304; ibid., Ministerium, II 5, pp. 442–5; ibid., Senat, Cl.I Lit.Hc No.10.   [88] Ibid., Ministerium, II 5, pp. 443–5.

[89] PRO, SP 82/36, fol. 240r, 11 September 1719, Metsch to Wich.

[90] Ibid., fol. 239r, 12 September 1719, Wich to Stanhope.

[91] Ibid., fol. 259r, 26 September 1719, Wich to Stanhope.

[92] Printed in Klefeker, *Verfassungen*, 8, pp. 652–8.

Again the whole affair had been widely reported in the newspapers, which circulated the first rumours of the actual demands of the Emperor conveyed to the Senate in October 1719.[93] At first the Emperor merely demanded compensation and the arrest of the ringleaders. On 2 October, however, the *Reichshofrat* decided to demand the occupation of the city by Imperial troops and the establishment of a new Imperial Commission to investigate its affairs.[94] With the support of Hanover, Brunswick and Prussia the threat of another commission was averted, but on 27 December the Emperor sent a more precise and harsh list of demands. Full compensation was to be paid for the demolished house; a deputation consisting of two *Bürgermeister* and two *Oberalten* was to be sent to Vienna to make a public apology; in addition the city should pay a fine of 400,000 florins (200,000 *taler*) to the Imperial treasury.

Despite its success in averting military reprisals the Senate was placed in a difficult position by these demands which were both costly in financial terms and detrimental to the prestige of the city. Its policies were not made easier by the recalcitrance of the clergy and of the Civic Colleges. In the first week of October the clergy reacted promptly to rumours that Seelmann and Neumeister were to be arrested on Imperial orders, proposing to vindicate themselves publicly by publishing all the documents of the first months of that year. Although the Senate dissuaded them from taking this tactless step, the clergy continued to assert their innocence and the need to publicise it.[95] Indeed, privately, Neumeister allowed himself a certain amount of selfrighteous glee at the predicament of the Senate: 'Now the great men are sitting on ice', he wrote, '…Because we predicted these inconveniences in advance we were decried as laughable and restless men. I must say that I cannot see a single spark of political sense in the whole situation.'[96]

The complexity of the problem would have tested even the most versatile politician. With the clergy and the Civic Colleges adamant that the demolition must not be used as an excuse to grant freedom of religion to the Catholics after all, the following two years placed a severe strain on the Senate. A deputation sent to Count Metsch in Brunswick in January 1720 was turned back with the news that the Emperor insisted on the fulfilment of all his demands.[97] Although, again with Hanoverian and Prussian aid, the worst had been averted, the Hanoverians subsequently withdrew their support. Thus in May 1721 a deputation consisting of two *Bürgermeister*

---

[93] StAH, Ministerium, III A2b, nos. 310, 308, 309; CBH, S/984 (reports).
[94] Ramcke, *Beziehungen*, pp. 73–4, 85–6; StAH, Senat, Cl.I Lit.Hc No.24, report by Syndic Matsen (1790).   [95] StAH, Ministerium, III A2b, nos. 436–9, 440–2.
[96] Wotschke (ed.), 'Neumeisters Briefe' (1925), p. 112.
[97] Ramcke, *Beziehungen*, p. 75.

and two *Oberalten* accompanied by the young lawyer Johann Klefeker set off to Vienna where the apology took place in front of a small circle on 27 June. Senator Brockes read out a florid poem he had composed for the occasion and the Emperor grudgingly accepted their apology.[98] However, he still insisted on the purchase of a new house and on a reduced fine of 200,000 florins (100,000 *taler*). The fine was paid promptly in September 1721, but the question of the house proved more difficult. Metsch turned down all the houses proposed by the Senate, while the *Bürgerschaft* opposed the purchase of a house owned by the Goertz family which Metsch wanted for personal reasons.[99]

The negotiations with the Emperor over the new diplomatic residence lasted until 1727 when the Goertz house was finally purchased by the city. They were complicated by the involvement of the Colleges and the *Bürgerschaft* who strenuously resisted any attempts by Metsch to convert several rooms into one large chapel. Under the circumstances, even the renewed support of Hanover and Brunswick did not clarify the issue. From December 1722 onwards the Jesuits once more held their services in the new diplomatic chapel. Ironically, they were now able to do this at the expense of the city: until the purchase was agreed in 1727, the city treasury paid rent for the house; thereafter it became the property of the city, pledged in perpetuity to the Emperor's diplomatic representatives.[100]

The city had thus not only paid 200,000 florins in fines, but also replaced the entire contents of the former chapel and bought the new residence. As a later report put it: 'The city was burdened with a debt of a million [mark]; and just as we found a stone inscribed with the name of the holy Borromeo [in the chapel], so we laid the foundation for a perpetual drain on our treasury.'[101]

IV

Despite the devastating financial and diplomatic consequences of the riot of 1719, the following years showed few signs of a more lenient attitude to the Catholics. The clergy, who had so narrowly escaped the threat of public humiliation, remained unrepentant. Indeed in 1721 they renewed their protests about the clandestine operations of the Jesuits in the city.[102] And by the end of that year the Amsterdam newspapers once more reported

[98] Klefeker, *Verfassungen*, 8, pp. 606–9; Ramcke, *Beziehungen*, pp. 76–7.
[99] StAH, Senat, Cl.I Lit.Hc No.24, Beilage zum Gutachten (1790).
[100] Ibid., *passim*; ibid., Cl.I Lit.Hc No.6b; ibid., Cl.I Lit.Hc No.7; ibid., Cl.I Lit.Hc No. 1–5.
[101] StAH, Senat, Cl.VII Lit.Hf No.1 Vol.3g, anon. notes 1785.
[102] StAH, Ministerium, II 6, p. 8b; ibid., Senat, Cl.VII Lit.Hf No.1 Vol.3c, 2 May 1721, Resolutio Rev. Ministerii.

rumours that Neumeister and Seelmann were to be arrested on Imperial orders.[103] Neumeister maintained his usual combative stance in the face of such adversity. He blamed the prejudiced reports of the Imperial Resident and placed little faith in the support of the Senate. As he wrote to Ernst Salomo Cyprian: 'Just as I have learned from experience never to trust a politician in matters concerning religion, so I would not build straw huts, let alone castles, on the favour we are shown here [by the magistrates].' Indeed he claimed that he had a clear conscience, and that 'the many thousands of visitors to my sermons will serve as witnesses that I have never preached about the papist chapel, still less that I have aroused the people against it'.[104]

The Senate itself showed few signs of that public humility which it had displayed in Vienna. Clearly resentful of what it considered the unreasonable nature of the Imperial reaction, it made strenuous attempts to maintain a strictly legalistic stance with regard to the Imperial Resident. A complaint by Kurtzrock that a messenger sent on an errand by his chaplain had been attacked and had sustained a broken leg was dismissed as untrue and provocative.[105] And when in 1723 Kurtzrock attempted to intervene in a criminal case brought against a Catholic, he was briskly informed that he had no right to meddle in the judicial affairs of the city.[106] Similarly, in 1724 the Imperial chaplain was refused permission to visit a condemned Catholic in the city prison. Not without cause did Kurtzrock promptly complain 'that one no longer had any respect for him'.[107]

But strict interpretation of the laws did not always work to the disadvantage of the Catholics. If the laws of Hamburg restricted them, those of the *Reich* guaranteed them against persecution and public condemnation. And in view of what happened in 1719, the Senate was just as much concerned to enforce the latter as it was to follow the former. Hence in 1725 the Senate banned the sale of a pamphlet which described in graphic detail the trial and execution of ten Lutherans after an anti-Jesuit riot in Thorn in 1724. It was argued that their distribution contravened the Imperial decree of 1715 which sought to stem the tide of provocative confessional tracts.[108] That the ban was a purely formal one dictated more by diplomacy than by indifference to the fate of Lutherans in Poland is indicated by the fact that in September 1720 the Senate had agreed to a church collection

---

[103] See, for example, the *Amsterdamse Saturdaegse Courant*, 1721: Nr. 46 in StAH, Ministerium, III A1n, no. 183.
[104] Wotschke (ed.), 'Neumeisters Briefe' (1925), p. 117.
[105] StAH, Senat, Cl.VII Lit.Hf No.3 Vol.8, *passim*.
[106] Ibid., Cl.VII Lit.Ja No.1 Vol.7, 20 September 1723, Kurtzrock to Senate (10 October 1723, reply).
[107] Ibid., Cl.VII Lit.Hf No.3 Vol.11, 22 November 1724, EPS.
[108] Ibid., Cl.VII Lit.Hf No.1 Vol.1b(4), 16 May 1725, EPS; ibid., Cl.VII Lit.Lb No.16 Vol.6a2, fols. 9–16; Dreves, *Geschichte*, pp. 166–7; Weintraub, 'Tolerance and intolerance', pp. 21–2.

to aid the oppressed Churches in the kingdom, and the Senators themselves both contributed a *subsidium charitativum* of 400 mark and voted another 200 mark from the treasury to the cause.[109]

Similarly, steps were taken in 1726 to ensure that the news of the murder of a Lutheran preacher in Dresden by a Catholic did not provoke ill-feeling in Hamburg. This time even the *Oberalten* were eager to ensure that 'no cause should be given for bitterness against the Roman Catholic clergy'.[110] The muted reaction of the clergy was due at least partially to the severe illness of Seelmann, so that Neumeister was isolated. He declared firmly that 'I am bound to the magistrates with all due obedience, but they cannot and surely would not want to force my conscience.' But he agreed with the rest to preach only on the theme of the 'persecution of the Church of Christ', without specific reference to the murder.[111]

The bitterness and barely restrained animosity which followed the disastrous events of 1719 did not, however, prevent the re-establishment of Catholic life in Hamburg during the 1720s. The Jesuit schools reopened and in 1728 a seventh school was established to cope with the offspring of a community, which according to a no-doubt exaggerated estimate in 1724, included about 1,500 communicants.[112] Indeed, after 1726 there is no evidence that the Lutheran clergy paid much attention to them. As relations with the Emperor improved, so the Senate relaxed its attitude in 1733 by allowing Catholic priests to visit their charges in city prisons.[113] The Calvinists no doubt diverted attention away from the Catholics in these years, while the Jesuits themselves were involved in a series of internal disputes over the division of community funds between Hamburg and Altona where a new church had been opened in 1723.[114]

On the other hand, the reaction of the Ministry to the news of the death of Charles VI in 1740 showed that, fundamentally, little had changed. Since the Imperial chapel was technically only a diplomatic one, the clergy demanded its closure during the two-year interregnum which followed.[115] The Senate was eager to comply and published a long justification of its occupation of the Residence and the closure of the chapel.[116]

Rainer Ramcke has interpreted this event as an outright affront to the Imperial court effected by an anti-Austrian party in the Senate.[117] The

[109] StAH, Ministerium, III A2b, nos. 510–12, 13 September 1720, EPS.
[110] StAH, Senat. Cl.VII Lit.Hf No.1 Vol.1b(4), 3 July 1726, Conclusum der Oberalten; Dreves, *Geschichte*, p. 167.
[111] StAH, Ministerium, III A1c, nos. 93–4.
[112] Linckemeyer, *Das katholische Hamburg*, pp. 400–1; Duhr, *Geschichte der Jesuiten*, 4, pt 1, p. 101.
[113] StAH, Senat, Cl.VII Lit.Hf No.3 Vol.11, 17 July 1733, Kurtzrock to Senate; ibid., 17 July 1733, EPS. For later problems concerning this issue see ibid., Cl.VII Lit.Hf No.3 Vol.23.
[114] Dreves, *Geschichte*, pp. 172–87. [115] StAH, Ministerium, III A1s, no. 467.
[116] *Gründlicher Bericht, passim.* [117] Ramcke, *Beziehungen*, pp. 141–2.

evidence for this view is inadequate. The clergy were, as always, concerned to reassert the principle of non-toleration. The Senate was motivated by a desire to rid itself of the costly burden of the house, arguing somewhat tenuously that the grant had been made in perpetuity, but only in the lifetime of Charles VI.[118] Strenuous diplomatic efforts were made to solve the problem. Once more Hanoverian aid was enlisted, but this move failed since the Saxon court at Dresden regarded the closure of the chapel as an affront to all Catholics in the *Reich*. When a new diplomatic representative arrived in 1742, negotiations were continued with the new Emperor, Charles VII. A bribe of 10,000 florins was paid to the *Reichs-Vize-Kanzler*, Count Königsfeld, and a generous payment was promised to the Imperial treasury. But the Imperial authorities insisted on their right to perpetual compensation regardless of the fact that the Imperial crown was now in the hands of the Wittelsbachs. The operation was not aided by the spiteful opposition of Frederick the Great, who refused to intercede on the grounds that the Senate had proved so uncooperative over the issue of religious freedom for the Calvinists.[119]

The triumph of the pro-Austrian party in the Senate in 1742–3 analysed by Ramcke did not change official policy regarding the chapel.[120] In 1745, on the death of Charles VII, the chapel was closed again.[121] The envoy Count Bünau vacated the house in January 1745, and in April the Jesuits were ordered to cease all services in the chapel which was used as a temporary lecture hall by the professors of the Gymnasium. Again diplomatic efforts to reach a compromise on the status of the house failed, and the chapel reopened with the arrival of the new Resident, von Raab, in December 1745. The only result was a declaration by Francis I to the effect that the house was formally the property of the city of Hamburg – a minor consolation since the city was obliged to bear the costs until the occupation of the city by the French in 1806.[122]

Contrary to the views of scholars such as Dreves and Ramcke, these measures were neither particularly anti-Catholic nor anti-Austrian.[123] The real problem was simply that the very existence of the house proved a painful reminder of the city's public humiliation and a constant drain on the resources of the treasury. Before 1731 the whole affair cost the city

---

[118] StAH, Senat, Cl.I Lit.Hc No.24, Beilage zum Gutachten (1790). They were willing to concede a vague obligation to the Habsburgs, but believed that the succession of the Wittelsbach dynasty with Charles VII extinguished their legal obligations.
[119] StAH, Senat, Cl.VII Lit.Hf No.1 Vol.3d, 13 June 1742, Frederick II to Senate.
[120] Ramcke, *Beziehungen*, pp. 151–6.
[121] The move was again supported by the clergy. StAH, Senat, Cl.VII Lit.Hf No.1 Vol.3e, *passim*.
[122] StAH, Senat, Cl.I Lit.Hc No.24. Beilage zum Gutachten (1790); Dreves, *Geschichte*, pp. 265–7.
[123] Ramcke, *Beziehungen*, pp. 141–2; Dreves, *Geschichte*, pp. 188–95.

nearly a million mark, and between 1733 and 1789 the chapel cost an average of 2,052 mark per annum – sums which weighed heavily on the minds of a finance-conscious Senate.[124] Unquantifiable, though equally if not more important, was the question of sovereignty and urban pride. Though reliant on good relations with Vienna, the Senate drew the line at the kind of subservient relationship which the existence of the Imperial house implied. Well-publicised unequal agreements between sovereign bodies touched deep and sensitive nerves in early modern politicians whose world was shored up by labyrinthine legal foundations.

V

After 1745 it is possible to discern a distinct lack of interest in the Catholics. The half-hearted protests of the clergy against conversions to Catholicism in the 1750s met with little response.[125] By 1765 relations with Vienna had improved to such a degree that several Senators actually appeared at a requiem mass for Francis I held in the Imperial chapel.[126] The more relaxed behaviour of the Senate did not, however, reflect popular attitudes. Confessional animosities were still strong, as the scandal created by the prosecution of a young Catholic woman accused of incest with her father in 1766 showed. But the affair aroused interest largely because both her husband and her father were relatively wealthy men; and it was kept alive by the fact that while in prison she managed to seduce a young Lutheran preacher who had attempted to convert her.[127]

Even the Lutheran clergy appear to have devoted more attention to the Calvinist problem after 1760 than to the Catholics. *Senior* Goeze regarded the latter with greater abhorrence than he did any other minority, but his attention was increasingly directed away from the dangers of militant Papism to those of insidious Calvinism. There is little evidence to support Dreves' claim that Goeze preached incessantly against the Catholics during the 1760s.[128] He included them in his memorial of 1763, but it would have been surprising had he not done so, given the sheer range of subjects included in his list of complaints.[129] Otherwise, his own animosity during

---

[124] A list of these costs can be found in StAH, Senat, Cl.I Lit.Hc No.24.

[125] StAH, Senat, Cl.VII Lit.Hf No.3 Vol.14 and Vol.19, *passim*.

[126] Dreves, *Geschichte*, pp. 197–8; *idem*, *Annuae missionis*, p. 227. The Jesuits noted that their visit was a private gesture, but they also stressed that this was the first time when the chapel was not automatically closed on the death of an Emperor.

[127] Dreves, *Geschichte*, pp. 219–21, 225.   [128] Ibid., pp. 222–3.

[129] StAH, Senat, Cl.VII Lit.Hb No.3 Vol.13(4), 18 March 1763, clergy to Senate. Such memorials were regularly sent to the Senate. This particular document is unusual only for its sheer length, and for the attention devoted in it to the problem of the non-Lutheran minorities.

his years as *Senior* was made clear repeatedly in his persistence in reading the traditional anti-Catholic prayers before services.[130]

However, Goeze's personal rigour increasingly lost support, even among his colleagues. His resignation in 1770, after a bitter debate over the form of the annual prayer of penance, was indicative of the extent to which, even in the Ministry, the cause of Lutheran Orthodoxy was no longer as strong as it had been in the days of Seelmann and Neumeister. Goeze's resignation was not the result of either diplomatic representations from Vienna or of senatorial pressure.[131] He himself felt constrained by the confines of so prominent an office and believed that his crusade could best be carried on without the trammels imposed on him as official representative of a disunited clergy, many of whom strongly disapproved of his attitudes.[132]

After 1770, the Ministry no longer concerned itself with the Catholic community. Although many were jubilant at the dissolution of the Jesuit Order in 1773, only Goeze and one other are known to have preached on the subject. According to the Jesuit reports, most other preachers went so far as to assure them that they would refrain from mentioning the matter in public.[133]

Goeze's last skirmish with the Catholic Imperial authorities in 1779 revealed his isolation to the full. When the Imperial Resident complained about two anti-Catholic sermons he held in May of that year, his appeal for the support of his colleagues met with little response.[134] After the matter had almost got to the Imperial Courts at Regensburg in September, Goeze was forced to make a public apology. The Senate's agent in Regensburg had persuaded several theologians to write to Goeze personally. The agent thought that their advice, combined with the threat of an Imperial decree, explained why 'this great champion of Orthodoxy has decided to trim his sails to the wind'.[135] Even his most staunch supporter in Hamburg, Johann Dietrich Winckler, believed that Goeze had been misguided. Their views were similar, but the difference in their public pronouncements lay in the fact that while Winckler had always preached on the 'state of the Roman Church before the Reformation', Goeze had committed the indiscretion of directing his condemnation of the intolerance and ignorance of the Catholics to the 'state of the Roman Church as it now is'.[136]

130 Röpe, *Goeze*, pp. 7–8, 91.
131 This claim is made by Dreves, *Geschichte*, p. 223.
132 See his letter of 22 December 1770 to Johann Christian Bartholomäi quoted by Wotschke (ed.), 'Wincklers Briefe', p. 52 (note 31).
133 Dreves, *Geschichte*, pp. 225–6; *idem, Annuae missionis*, pp. 245–8.
134 StAH, Senat, Cl.VII Lit.Hf No.3 Vol.22, *passim*. Goeze's appeal to his colleagues is in StAH, Ministerium, III B (1779), 20 May 1779.
135 StAH, Senat, Cl.VII Lit.Hf No.3 Vol.22, 1 November 1779, Selpert, report from Regensburg.
136 Wotschke (ed.), 'Wincklers Briefe', p. 78.

Goeze's defeat and public apology marked the last conflict with the Catholic community and its Imperial patron in Hamburg. Its existence continued to pass all but unnoticed until in October 1782 it was mooted in the Senate that if religious freedom were to be given to the Calvinists, it must also be extended to the Catholics.[137]

The proposal came almost as an afterthought. For whatever assurances may have been given to the Imperial authorities, there is no evidence to suggest that any group other than the German Reformed community was discussed before that date.[138] The reasons are obvious, for the Catholics, as the Jesuits themselves pointed out in their report of 1772, were predominantly poor. The only economic issue they raised was the relatively minor one of whether they might be admitted to the guilds, and that was solved without difficulty by referring to the practice of other cities.[139] In any case, by the later decades of the eighteenth century, the Senate and business community of Hamburg had far greater worries than the occasional Catholic craftsman or criminal who wished to be visited in jail by a priest. The loss of a Calvinist merchant weighed heavier in their minds than the professional or spiritual welfare of a poor Catholic. The Goeze scandal of 1779 once more underlined the fact that the relationship between the city and its Catholic inhabitants was dominated by politics rather than economics. Of course, the religious issue was important throughout and should not be underestimated; but the long course of events which preceded and followed the debacle of 1719 showed that anti-Catholicism waxed and waned according to primarily political circumstances. If the passions appeared to subside as the decades passed, this was more a tribute to the diplomacy of the Senate than to the tolerance of the citizens.

[137] StAH, Senat, Cl.VII Lit.Hf No.1 Vol.3g, 23 October 1783, EPS.
[138] Ramcke, *Beziehungen*, pp. 247–8, 253.
[139] StAH, Senat, Cl.XI Generalia No.1 Vol.13, *passim*. These problems did periodically cause considerable unrest amongst the guilds, although apart from this specific economic problem there is very little evidence of genuine, spontaneous animosity to the Catholics; effectively, the clergy led the way. See: Preiss, 'Handwerkerunruhen', pp. 35–6; J. L. von Hess, *Hamburg* (2nd edn), 3, pp. 258–61.

3

The limits of toleration: Sephardim and Ashkenazim

In 1811 Jonas Ludwig von Hess looked back on the history of the Jews in Hamburg and claimed that since the seventeenth century there had been a clear forward progression from persecution and rejection to something approaching assimilation. The Senate, he wrote, had always taken pains to defend the Jews and 'through words and deeds has always brought home to their enemies...that Jews are also human beings'.[1] The way in which this was done was significant. For the Senate had simply isolated the community, encouraged it to lead a separate existence. Gradually the populace accepted the Jews and then ignored them; the clergy too desisted from their former aim of damning and persecuting the Jews and now only prayed for their conversion. The Jews, in short, had not been tolerated in the enlightened sense of that word. For, as Hess pointed out, such a toleration would have demanded close enquiry by the Christian authorities into the complex religious affairs of the Jews. Instead, successive contracts had sought to limit their religious freedom as much as was humanly possible, so that the authorities had only to concern themselves with outright abuses rather than petty transgressions of the law.[2]

Hess's views were in many ways typical of his generation.[3] Long after toleration for Christian minorities had ceased to be an issue, the question of the Jews continued to exercise the minds of his contemporaries and tax their powers of historical imagination. Writers like Johann Albert Crantz and Johann Arnold Günther recognised the contribution the Jews had made to Hamburg's economic prosperity during the last two centuries. They were concerned to stress the extent to which the Jews had always enjoyed unusual freedom within the city. But their discussions are characterised by an ambivalence which is itself testimony to the fact that the toleration mandate of 1785 was soon recognised to be not the end of a long battle with the

[1] J. L. von Hess, *Hamburg* (2nd edn), 3, p. 276.
[2] Ibid.
[3] Krohn, *Juden in Hamburg*, pp. 13–14.

Church but the beginning of an endless struggle against social prejudice and popular envy.[4]

Both Crantz and Hess stressed the economic achievement of the Jews. Indeed Crantz claimed that there was little difference between Jews and Christians when it came to trade. The Jews, he declared, had become responsible citizens: they contributed to charitable causes and public appeals, and were often remarkably generous when it came to organising financial support for enterprises which were in danger of collapsing, even those owned by Christians. The popular image of the Jews, Crantz wrote, is one invented by the prejudiced Christian mind; the negative characteristics of the race were largely the result of self-defence against persecution and rejection.[5]

Even so, the ultimate aim which emerges from these late-Enlightenment discussions is not that of the emancipation of Jews as Jews. Crantz pointed to the prejudices of Christians. Hess, by contrast, claimed that the only things which prevented the total assimilation of the Jews were their own customs, their education and their pride. The hope, in other words, was that with the gradual spread of enlightenment, Christians might become more open to the Jews; the Jews in turn might lose their pride and with it their religion in order to become rational Christians. Assimilation rather than integration dominated the debate over the Jews, which was generated not only in Hamburg but in the whole of Germany during the 1780s, and which reached a particular intensity around 1800.[6]

It is only by virtue of their discussion of this problem that late-eighteenth-century writers like Hess differed from previous generations for whom there could be no toleration for the Jews at all. Catholics and Calvinists were indeed already in a sense members of a larger Christian community, and this made them at least eligible for admission to the narrower Lutheran community of Hamburg. But with the Jews, men of the eighteenth century reached the limits of toleration. They regarded them, after all, as a race excluded from the larger Christian world by an original sin which many still resented and abhorred: the murder of Christ.

Jacob Toury has shown that a new appreciation of the Jews can be discerned at varying levels of literary sophistication from about the 1740s.[7] But in the 1770s the Syndic Johann Klefeker could still firmly reiterate the traditional view that the toleration of the Jews was exclusively a legal and not an ecclesiastical matter. Religious toleration, he stated, did not enter

---

4 Ibid., p. 13; Grunwald, *Hamburgs deutsche Juden*, pp. 55–9; Günther, *Jüdische Einwohner, passim.* Crantz and Günther were both contemporaries of von Hess.
5 Quoted by Grunwald, *Hamburgs deutsche Juden*, pp. 55–9.
6 Krohn, *Juden in Hamburg*, pp. 13–14; Kopitzsch, 'Sozialgeschichte der Aufklärung', pp. 91–4.
7 Toury, 'Jüdische Problematik', pp. 13–21.

into this problem, whose origins lay in the measures taken by the *Reich* and the cities in the later Middle Ages to provide 'civil protection' for the Jews in order to enable them to carry out their trades without persecution.[8] As so often in early modern times, it was a question of economic reality expressed and regulated by legal terminology.

However, the history of the Jews in Hamburg is marked not only by continual discussions about the legal forms which would best promote specific economic objectives, but also by a long and bitter series of conflicts between Church and State. The Senate might well insist that, in technical terms, the existence of the Jews in Hamburg had nothing to do with the clergy. But the latter took a very different view as it became abundantly clear that the Jews brought an alien religion as well as trade. Indeed the Senate itself was responsible for provoking these disputes. For political and economic rivalry with Altona and the Danish crown, complicated by important legal issues, led to a series of attempts to grant greater privileges to the Jews than even many Senators thought desirable.[9]

At the same time, the Jewish issue is important in the general context of religious toleration in that here the economic arguments were most explicit. Precisely because there was no strong religious or ecclesiastical argument for tolerating Jews, their existence could only be justified in purely economic terms.[10] Political philosemitism fluctuated in direct relation to economic prosperity. Crises in the relationship with the Jews were almost invariably stimulated either by economic crises in the city at large or by periodic conflicts with the Danish crown.

The complexity of the history of the Jews in Hamburg is intensified by the existence in the seventeenth century of two distinct Jewish communities: the so-called Portuguese community of Sephardic Jews and the German community of Ashkenazi Jews. Their histories do coincide in some aspects. But at the time they were treated as very separate communities distinguished by a differing economic status. This was reflected in the all-important legal relationship between the communities on the one hand and the city of Hamburg on the other.

[8] Klefeker, *Verfassungen*, 8, pp. 702–4.
[9] These issues are discussed by: Brilling, 'Rabbinerstreit', pp. 234–44; Graupe, *Statuten*, 1, pp. 19–28; Marwedel, *Privilegien*, pp. 48–88.
[10] Lists of rich Jews who had left the city were drawn up in 1770 and April 1775; most went to Altona. It is significant that these lists appear to have been used during the toleration debate of the 1770s, although only as evidence to back up the general economic argument advanced in favour of tolerating the Calvinists. Owing to the complex registration system, it may simply have been easier to collect material relating to the movements of the Jews rather than any other group; there is no evidence of any discussion of further privileges for the Jews at this time. StAH, Cl.VII Lit.Hf No.5 Vol.3a, Fasc.7, lists dated 1770 and April 1775.

I

Few of the older accounts of the history of the Jews in Hamburg made any distinction between the Portuguese and German Jews.[11] It is easy to see why: in the seventeenth century the Portuguese community predominated, and its decline after 1697 was matched by a rapid expansion of the Ashkenazic group without any apparent disruption of continuity. By 1800 there were some 6,300 Ashkenazim compared with only 130 Sephardim.[12] But the differences between the two communities are not confined to their relative numerical and economic importance over the centuries. The Portuguese achieved a privileged status quite unmatched by the Germans. They alone were unequivocally protected in legal terms by the Senate, in much the same way as the early communities of English and Dutch merchants. The German Jews only partially achieved this in 1710.

The first Portuguese Jews probably came to Hamburg during the 1580s. How many came, or where precisely they came from, is unclear. Indeed, the obscurity which surrounded them was at least partly of their own making. Just as in Spain and Portugal many lived as Catholics, or had actually converted, so in Hamburg they claimed to be Catholics. Their numbers increased gradually after the union of Spain with Portugal in 1580, when many Jews began to move from Portugal to Spain or further afield to escape from the persecution of the Portuguese Inquisition. The fifty or so *autos-da-fé* in Portugal between 1581 and 1600 made even the Spanish Inquisition seem lenient by comparison. Even so, many Jews or *marranos* simply moved northwards, and some ended up in Hamburg.[13]

The migration was, however, gradual, and it was only in December 1603 that the *Bürgerschaft* complained to the Senate that some of the recently arrived foreigners were Jews, and lived openly as such.[14] The *Bürgerschaft* demanded heavy taxes on the whole Iberian community and the expulsion of its Jewish members. In May 1604 the Senate replied that it had not been able to find any Jews. Two years later, it acknowledged the existence of seven Jewish families and two unmarried Jewish brokers.[15] These figures

---

[11] Cf. Reils, 'Beiträge', *passim*; Grunwald, *Hamburgs deutsche Juden*, pp. 4–12. The best general study of the differences between the Ashkenazim and the Sephardim is: Zimmels, *Ashkenazim and Sephardim*.

[12] Krohn, *Juden in Hamburg*, p. 9.

[13] Kellenbenz, *Sephardim*, pp. 25–32; Feilchenfeld, 'Anfang und Blüthezeit', pp. 199–201. See also: Yerushalmi, *From Spanish court to Italian ghetto*, pp. 8–43 and Dominguez Ortiz, *Golden Age of Spain*, pp. 216–18.

[14] The negotiations between Senate and *Bürgerschaft* are printed in Ziegra, *Sammlung*, 4, pp. 625–6. Similar confusion arose over the religious identity of the Portuguese in Antwerp, cf. Pohl, *Portugiesen in Antwerpen*, pp. 339–48.   [15] Ziegra, *Sammlung*, 4, p. 626.

were almost certainly inaccurate: by 1610 some 116 Portuguese Jews lived in the city.[16]

The revelation that a Jewish community did in fact exist led to a series of intense and heated negotiations between the Senate, the *Bürgerschaft* and the clergy. If the clergy were primarily concerned with religious issues, the citizens were also motivated by economic considerations, fearing for their own important trade with the Iberian peninsula, demanding that the Jews be obliged to pay a tax amounting to 1 per cent of the total value of all goods they brought in and out of the city.[17]

The Jews themselves were by no means inactive. They managed to exercise considerable pressure on the Senate: a petition submitted in 1605 stressed their economic power and the benefits it might bring to the city. They even threatened economic reprisals if they were expelled: their agents still had influence with the Spanish authorities, they claimed, and might easily be induced to take revenge on Hamburg merchants on the Iberian peninsula.[18]

The Senate was obviously impressed by their case, and used these arguments to dismiss the idea of a heavy tax on the Jews. Furthermore, it was pointed out that the Jews had been invited to go to Emden and Stade, to Altona and Wandsbek, so that negotiations with them must be conducted with the utmost diplomacy.[19] The Senate also armed itself against the clergy by consulting the theological faculties of Jena and Frankfurt an der Oder. The replies were on the whole favourable to the Jews. The Jena theologians were cautious: they felt that the Jews could only be allowed to stay if they effectively gave up their religion, promised not to employ Christian servants, and agreed to attend Lutheran church services. Their colleagues in Frankfurt were not as stringent and proposed only that the Jews be ordered not to slander Christianity and that some attempt be made to convert them. The Senate presented this last reply to the clergy in 1611.[20] Despite the fact that the latter accused the Senate of being more interested in the 'money and status' of the Jews than in their salvation, the first steps were taken to reach a contractual agreement with the Portuguese community which was finally sealed in February 1612 for a period of two years.[21]

The contract contained seventeen articles which clearly defined the rights

---

[16] Kellenbenz, *Sephardim*, p. 29.

[17] Ziegra, *Sammlung*, 4, pp. 626–8.

[18] Feilchenfeld, 'Anfang und Blüthezeit', p. 236.

[19] Ziegra, *Sammlung*, 4, pp. 628–36, 27 July 1609, 16 August 1610, In Propositione Senatus. See Chapter 1, pp. 35–6 above.

[20] Feilchenfeld, 'Anfang und Blüthezeit', pp. 204–6; Kellenbenz, *Sephardim*, p. 31. The use of learned opinions (*theologische Responsa*) was common in disputes between Church and State in seventeenth-century Hamburg. Cf. Geffcken, 'Theologische Responsa'.

[21] Feilchenfeld, 'Anfang und Blüthezeit', pp. 205–6, 237–9; Kellenbenz, *Sephardim*, pp. 31–2; Levy, *Rechtsstellung*, pp. 9–11.

and privileges of the Jews.[22] Like the Dutch and the English communities, they were to be accepted as *Schutzverwandte* in return for an annual payment of 1,000 mark. They were enjoined to live modestly and quietly in return for the freedom to trade and the right to conduct financial transactions in the city. They were not permitted a synagogue; in accordance with the wishes of those who hoped for their conversion, they were forbidden to circumcise their sons, and they were forced to bury their dead in Altona or 'elsewhere'.

These rigid regulations were relaxed in the following years. In 1617 the second contract allowed the Portuguese to import ritually slaughtered meat from outside the city. In 1623 the community was assured that it would not be punished collectively for the transgressions of any individual member; the Lutheran clergy were enjoined to ensure the moderation of their congregations; while, finally, the community was also allowed to slaughter its own animals inside the city on certain days. The first three contracts thus show an increasingly liberal tendency to ensure the safety and goodwill of the community.[23]

There was good reason for this leniency, which also extended to turning a blind eye to the existence of an unofficial synagogue. For the community grew rapidly after 1611: by 1617 the tax was doubled to 2,000 mark, while by 1646 the community's numbers had risen to about 500.[24]

But numbers alone did not account for their importance. While the community inevitably also attracted poor members, it was essentially a prosperous one.[25] No fewer than 28 of the 560 accounts opened at the Hamburg Bank, founded in 1619, were owned by Portuguese Jews.[26] As merchants and financiers, they had contacts throughout the whole of Europe, and many of them also enjoyed privileged status as 'court Jews' in Denmark or Sweden. The Portuguese lived like aristocrats and made no secret of their wealth and influence. Their ranks also included scholars and doctors, like the celebrated Rodrigo a Castro, whose reputation amongst the urban elite stood so high that he alone of all the Jews was allowed to own a house in the city.[27]

Educated, aristocratic, wealthy, the Sephardim lived in the most affluent quarters of the city. Indeed, it was ultimately their ostentatious existence which provoked the first significant protests against them. The sense of security which pervaded the community in the years after 1623 prompted them to practise their religion more or less openly. Indeed in 1627 the

---

[22] The contract is printed in Levy, *Rechtsstellung*, pp. 11–12.
[23] Ibid., pp. 13–14; Feilchenfeld, 'Anfang und Blüthezeit', pp. 208–10.
[24] Kellenbenz, *Sephardim*, p. 41.
[25] Gonsiorowski, 'Berufe der Juden', pp. 15–27.   [26] Kellenbenz, *Sephardim*, pp. 253–9.
[27] On a Castro, see Isler, 'Aelteste Geschichte', pp. 467–76; Feilchenfeld, 'Anfang und Blüthezeit', pp. 212–14; Kellenbenz, *Sephardim*, pp. 325–30.

Emperor was able to protest that the Senate allowed the Jews a synagogue while refusing similar privileges to the Catholics whom he protected in the city.[28] As the community became more secure, so resentment against them increased, and by the 1640s burgesses and clergy were united under the leadership of Pastor Johannes Müller of St Peter's.

Müller, who became *Senior* of the clergy in 1648, included the toleration of the Jews in his list of reasons for the decay of Lutheranism in Hamburg.[29] In 1649 he produced the first of a series of vitriolic denunciations of the 'pernicious Jews', which coincided with a marked expansion in the size of the community in 1648 and 1649.[30]

Popular agitation against the Jews had been rife for some time. At least some of the animosity was directed against the German Jews, who were expelled outright in 1649, but the Portuguese were also under great pressure. In March 1647 a decree sought to forbid the citizens to insult members of foreign nations on the streets; two years later, in April 1649, a further decree made it clear that the Jews were the prime object of attack.[31] The *Oberalten* meanwhile sought to restrict them to the letter of the contract: they demanded the abolition of the synagogue, although they did not insist on their expulsion, recognising that 'one need fear no seduction on the part of the Jews, while Calvinism always takes root'.[32] The Jews, they said, were arrogant and proud and boasted of their contacts in the Senate.

These complaints were backed up by the clergy who began to preach openly against the Jewish community. Their views, as summed up in *Senior* Müller's essay in 1649, were typical of the popular antisemitism of the age. He talked at length of their noisy and extravagant religious ceremonies, the way in which they defiled the sabbath and insulted Christian women. Even their morals spoke against them: Gabriel Gomez, it was claimed, had married his niece; Dr Rosales had divorced his wife.[33] In the following year, Müller complained that, above all, little had been done to convert the Jews.[34]

The Senate was unwilling to take immediate action. There was some concern that the Jews might leave and a deputation was set up to consider

[28] Ibid., p. 38; Feilchenfeld, 'Anfang und Blüthezeit', pp. 216–17.
[29] Johannes Müller, 'Einfältiges Bedencken von dem im Grund verderbten und erbärmlichen Zustande der Kirche Christi in Hamburg' (1648) in Ziegra, *Sammlung*, 1, pp. 1–30 (esp. pp. 10–11).
[30] Johannes Müller, 'Bedencken wegen Duldung der Juden' (1649) in Ziegra, *Sammlung*, 1, pp. 98–114. Cf. Kellenbenz, *Sephardim*, pp. 45–7.
[31] Blank, *Mandate*, 1, pp. 78–80.
[32] StAH, Senat, Cl.VII Lit.Hf No.5 Vol.4a, 7 January 1648, EPS.
[33] Ziegra, *Sammlung*, 1, pp. 98–114; StAH, Senat, Cl.VII Lit.Hf No.5 Vol.4a, 5 April 1650, EPS; StAH, Ministerium, II 2, pp. 55–7, 62–5.
[34] Feilchenfeld, 'Anfang und Blüthezeit', p. 219.

ways of 'not letting Altona grow too large'.[35] An attempt was made to restrain the clergy, while the Jews themselves were warned to keep quiet and not to gather more than sixteen or twenty families together at any one time in order to avoid arousing popular suspicions.[36] In 1649 the Senate again consulted legal and theological faculties, this time at Jena and Altdorf, once more obtaining essentially favourable replies to their questions about the toleration of the Jews.[37]

The result in 1650 was the first *Judenordnung*, a more elaborate set of regulations than ever before. Many of its clauses were simply taken over from previous regulations: the Jews were forbidden to insult the Christian faith, to engage in speculative money lending, or to own houses in the city, and were bidden to restrict themselves according to the sumptuary laws laid down for citizens. On the other hand they were given a little more religious freedom. Synagogues were still prohibited, but prayer gatherings of up to fifteen families were allowed as long as no more than four or five families entered or left a house simultaneously.[38] The regulations were presented to the clergy as a 'provisional measure', with the promise of a more detailed settlement in the future and strict supervision in the meantime.[39]

The immediate effect on the Portuguese community was twofold. It continued to grow, reaching its maximum size of about 600 members by the early 1660s.[40] And in 1652 the new freedom of action permitted the establishment of a regular religious organisation in Hamburg.[41] To some extent this move was no doubt a defensive one in the face of the bitter attacks of the 1640s, but it was only made possible by the protection of the Senate which now allowed them to employ two regular rabbis and to contemplate opening a synagogue.

Indeed after 1650 the community was more prosperous and influential than ever. Its history in these years is dominated by the fortunes of the Texeira family. The elder Diego Texeira was known in the city simply as 'the rich Jew'.[42] His son Manoel was also an international financier and merchant who became Queen Christina's diplomatic representative in Hamburg. When the latter visited the city in 1667, she stayed with Texeira rather than in the house prepared for her by the Senate.[43]

[35] StAH, Senat, Cl.VII Lit.Hf No.5 Vol.4a, 7 January 1648, EPS.
[36] Ibid., 10 April 1648, EPS.
[37] StAH, Senat, Cl.VII Lit.Hf No.5 Vol.3a Fasc.3, *passim*; Kellenbenz, *Sephardim*, p. 47.
[38] StAH, Senat, Cl.VII, Lit.Hf No.5 Vol.3a Fasc.3, fols. 119–22r.
[39] Ibid., fol. 126v, 16 September 1650, EPS.   [40] Kellenbenz, *Sephardim*, p. 41.
[41] Levy, *Rechtsstellung*, p. 20; Feilchenfeld, 'Anfang und Blüthezeit', pp. 220–2; Kellenbenz, *Sephardim*, pp. 48–9.
[42] Feilchenfeld, 'Anfang und Blüthezeit', p. 226.
[43] On the Texeira family, see Kellenbenz, *Sephardim*, pp. 385–96; and *idem*, 'Diego und Manoel Texeira', *passim*.

The Texeiras were apparently responsible for the attempts to build a synagogue in the city which led to continual friction between the Senate and the clergy. In 1652 two plots of land were bought but then promptly sold as a result of the opposition of the Lutheran clergy.[44] The latter claimed rightly that this represented a transgression of mutually agreed regulations. They complained that many of the clauses of 1650, which had sought to limit the freedom of the Jews and to prevent popular disturbances, in fact hindered the clergy's efforts to convert them. They did not, they claimed, wish to 'force anyone with fire or the sword', but to convince them with the word of God. Thus once more they demanded the appointment of a Christian teacher with knowledge of both Hebrew and Portuguese as the first step towards the conversion of the Jews.[45]

Apart from a warning to the Jewish elders about the possibility of popular disturbances if the synagogue were built, no official action was taken. Indeed, once more the Senate placed much of the blame on the clergy, especially *Magister* Wiese of St Nicholas', whose claim that the Jews had circumcised Christian boys nearly provoked a riot.[46]

The synagogue plan re-emerged on three further occasions, in 1660, 1668, and in 1672 when it was decided to extend the prayer house in the Wallstrasse with money donated by Diego Texeira.[47] On all three occasions the Senate initially ignored the plans, deferring action until the clergy submitted a formal objection. They reacted with characteristic alacrity. Couched in sharp and direct terms, their letters essentially reiterated what were by now well-known arguments. The protest of 1669 was perhaps the most elaborate of all. It sought to contradict the view, held even by the *Bürgerschaft* in 1650, that the Portuguese community was in any way important to the urban economy: Hamburg was a prosperous city before their arrival, so that their departure would hardly reduce the city to 'the size of a village'. Once more the clergy stressed that they did not want to behave 'like the Spanish Inquisition', but they argued that because the Sephardim were so persistent in their religion, strong measures would be needed to convince them of the superiority of Christianity. This was an important point, they felt, for if no attempt were made to convert the Jews, then they might well have cause to complain at the Last Judgement that the Lutherans in Hamburg had done nothing to help them find salvation.[48]

---

[44] Kellenbenz, *Sephardim*, p. 49; StAH, Senat, Cl.VII Lit.Hf No.5 Vol.3a Fasc.3, fols. 128r–130r, 22 June 1652, EPS; StAH Ministerium, II 2, pp. 86–92, 101, 126–8.

[45] StAH, Senat, Cl.VII Lit.Hf No.5 Vol.3a Fasc.3, fols. 129v–130r.

[46] Ibid., fols. 130v–132r, 1 October 1652, EPS.

[47] See the anon. notes in StAH, Senat, Cl.VII Lit.Hf No.5 Vol.1b Fasc.1, fol. 1r–v; and StAH, Ministerium, II 2, pp. 232–6, 321–7.

[48] StAH, Senat, Cl.VII Lit.Hf. No.5 Vol.3a Fasc.5, April 1669, Pro Memoria.

The direct impact of such protests was minimal, although continual sermons on the subject inevitably whipped up popular support for the clerical cause. By 1672 the captains of the militia declared that they could no longer guarantee that their men would be able or indeed willing to defend the Jews in the event of a riot.[49] This obvious sign of unrest led directly to the closure of the synagogue in the following year. The Portuguese community was once more forced to accept the old system of small unofficial prayer houses, and further attempts to enlarge these failed in 1682 and 1684.[50]

The 1660s probably marked the peak of the community's prosperity and size. Constant clerical harassment and internal problems arising from the upheaval over the false Jewish prophet Sabbatai Zwi after 1665–6 led to a gradual decline in numbers from about 600 in 1663 to only 300 in 1692. It was predominantly the poorer Jews and the scholarly community who left first. The Texeiras, the richer merchants, financiers and diplomats stayed until the 1690s, when the community was confronted by its last major crisis.[51]

The constitutional conflict between the Senate and the *Bürgerschaft*, in which the clergy played so central a role in the 1680s and 1690s, at first diverted attention away from the Jewish question.[52] Despite declining numbers, the community had not become much less prosperous, and in 1690 it agreed quietly to raise its annual tax contribution to 4,000 mark.

It was the obvious prosperity and wealth of the Portuguese community, combined with a rise in the number of Ashkenazim, which again brought the Jewish question to the fore in the context of a debate over new ways of raising taxes.[53] The burgesses opposed the idea of a wealth tax for themselves but, encouraged by the clergy, eagerly seized on the idea of an extra tax on the Jews. To help the city out of its financial difficulties the Portuguese were to pay a special levy of 20,000 mark, the German Jews 30,000 mark. In addition, a new contract was to be drawn up which effectively proposed to treat the Portuguese in the same way as the German Jews.[54]

The imposition of the tax and the new contract effectively destroyed the Portuguese community. They protested both about the amount of money they had been asked to pay and about the terms of the contract. For

---

[49] StAH, Senat, Cl.VII Lit.Hf No.5 Vol.1b Fasc.1, fol. 2r.
[50] Kellenbenz, *Sephardim*, p. 50.
[51] Ibid., pp. 50–2. On Zwi's significance in general, see Graupe, *Entstehung*, pp. 55–9; Brilling, 'Rabbinerstreit', pp. 219–24; Scholem, *Sabbatai Sevi*, pp. 566–91.
[52] Rückleben, *Niederwerfung*, passim.
[53] Kellenbenz, *Sephardim*, pp. 52–3; Feilchenfeld, 'Anfang und Blüthezeit', pp. 230–2.
[54] StAH, Senat, Cl.VII Lit.Hf No.5 Vol.1b Fasc.1, fols. 4r–11r, Extractus Nuclei Recessum.

although it was similar to previous agreements, it did not mention what they regarded as their special legal status. To be treated in the same way as the Ashkenazim, who were not technically *Schutzjuden* at all, was an insult.[55] Their arguments were futile. For they put a case for religious freedom, for special treatment, which had long been recognised unofficially by the Senate, but which the clergy and the *Bürgerschaft* had always opposed vehemently.

Under the circumstances, the Senate was powerless to resist overwhelming popular pressure. Faced with heavy taxes, collective insecurity and personal degradation, the wealthiest Portuguese Jews left the city in 1698. Many followed Manoel Texeira to Amsterdam; others went first to Altona and Glückstadt, and then to the growing Sephardic communities in the Netherlands.[56]

The contract of 1697 and the subsequent emigration marked the end of the Portuguese community as a major economic force in Hamburg. Although the Sephardim were also included in the new *Judenreglement* of 1710, their significance in the eighteenth century was minimal.[57] A list of 1730 showed that they had been reduced to some forty-nine families; in 1732 there were only twenty-seven taxpayers within the community, and few were merchants of the type which had dominated the community before 1697.[58] They lived a quiet and enclosed existence, regarded now by most people as old-established inhabitants worthy of paying their taxes individually rather than collectively.[59]

II

For nearly a century the Sephardic Jews thus enjoyed a privileged position. Wealth, noble birth and education brought them into close contact with the urban elite, a relationship cemented by regular gifts and bribes to individual Senators.[60] The obvious reason for their acceptance was their economic power, displayed primarily in their share of the important Iberian trade and in their participation in the formation of the early money market in Hamburg. Indeed their sumptuous life-styles gave rise to periodic complaints that they were too much admired by the populace.[61]

---

[55] StAH, Senat, Cl.VII Lit.Hf No.5 Vol.3a Fasc.5, Hochnöthige, Anmerckungen...von Seiten der Portugiesischen Nation, 1697.

[56] Kellenbenz, *Sephardim*, pp. 53–4; Feilchenfeld, 'Anfang und Blüthezeit', pp. 232–3.

[57] Klefeker, *Verfassungen*, 2, 313–14.

[58] StAH, Senat, Cl.VII Lit.Hf No.5 Vol.3a Fasc.7, a list dated 1730; Kellenbenz, *Sephardim*, pp. 54–7.

[59] Klefeker, *Verfassungen*, 2, pp. 389–90; Feilchenfeld, 'Anfang und Blüthezeit', p. 233.

[60] Kellenbenz, *Sephardim*, p. 48.

[61] StAH, Senat, Cl.VII Lit.Hf No.5 Vol.3a Fasc.3, fol. 126v, 1 December 1650, EPS. See also Zimmels, *Ashkenazim and Sephardim*, esp. pp. 39–67.

In a sense the Sephardim were already half-assimilated and they could be regarded as a kind of aristocratic caste. Only in the eighteenth century did their concentration on certain areas of economic activity lead to a weakening of their position.[62]

The more limited nature and smaller scale of the economic activities of the Ashkenazim made their establishment a more difficult and complex process. In 1583, for example, the Senate had rejected a petition by a pearl dealer, Isaak of Salzuffeln, requesting the right to settle in Hamburg for himself and twelve other families. He offered to pay regular and generous taxes, and intimated that he had started similar negotiations with Count Adolf von Schaumburg and Heinrich von Rantzau about settlement in Altona and Wandsbek respectively.[63]

The reasons for the Senate's attitude in this case are not entirely clear, since no justification has survived. But there were differences between the two communities. Isaak of Salzuffeln was obviously not poor, but the Ashkenazim, who came from Germany and Poland, driven north-west by persecution and attracted to Hamburg for its trade, were on the whole not as wealthy as the average Portuguese family. The richest among them were jewellers or small money lenders, the poorest were craftsmen and labourers: in 1652 eighteen German Jews were listed as 'servants of the Portuguese nation'.[64] In the early 1660s, when the Sephardic community in Hamburg was one of the largest in Europe, there were only forty or fifty Ashkenazic families in the city. Their numbers only began to grow after 1670, and while some made their fortunes, the majority remained at the middling or poorer levels. Certainly, until the 1690s there were relatively few Ashkenazim compared with the community which existed in the 1720s.[65]

Whatever the precise reasons (and clerical opposition seems certain to have played a part) the Senate's rejection of Isaak of Salzuffeln's plea had important long-term consequences. By 1612 the Ashkenazim had negotiated their first general privilege in Altona with the Counts of Schaumburg. Just as the Sephardim became *Hamburgische Schutzjuden*, so the Ashkenazim became *Schaumburgische* (and after 1640, *Dänische*) *Schutzjuden*. Although officially protected by the rulers of Altona, many were still drawn to live in Hamburg, where they paid taxes to the city on an informal basis.[66] But in religious terms they remained a separate group from those who were

---

[62] This relative weakening of the position of the Jewish communities was the result of the expansion and diversification of the economies in which they had established themselves, and also of increased competition from Christians in areas previously dominated almost exclusively by Jews. Cf. Kellenbenz, *Sephardim*, pp. 452–62.

[63] Reils, 'Aelteste Niederlassung', pp. 157–66; Graupe, *Statuten*, 1, pp. 13–14.

[64] Levy, *Rechtsstellung*, p. 18; Grunwald, *Hamburgs deutsche Juden*, p. 10.

[65] Ibid., pp. 10–11; Kellenbenz, *Sephardim*, p. 458.

[66] Graupe, *Statuten*, 1, pp. 13–15, 19–28.

registered as servants of the Portuguese community. By about 1680, as a result of complex legal and internal Jewish ecclesiastical struggles, a federation of the three communities of Altona, Hamburg and Wandsbek was established under the jurisdiction of a Chief Rabbi in Altona and officially protected by the Danish crown. Members of all three communities lived in Hamburg. In effect, therefore, even those who called themselves Hamburg Jews were part of what amounted to a Danish enclave in the city. The legal situation was obscure even to contemporaries and was further complicated by the Danish claims to sovereignty over Hamburg which were not dropped until 1768.[67]

The fact that the Ashkenazim were technically subject to Denmark prevented the conclusion of any formal agreement on the terms of their residence in Hamburg. Although the Senate closed an eye to their presence, objections from the *Bürgerschaft* or from the clergy were inevitable. During the 1620s a small number of them seem to have paid taxes informally in return for unofficial trading and residence rights.[68] Their numbers soon increased thereafter. But in 1648–9, at a time when renewed negotiations began over the Portuguese contract, it seemed that the Ashkenazim would have to be expelled. Henceforth Altona Jews would only be allowed into the city for two or three days at a time on payment of an escort tax (*Geleitsgülden*).[69] The new regulation was not effective. By May 1651 the *Oberalten* complained that Altona Jews had been seen regularly at the Exchange.[70] And after the Swedish invasion of Altona in 1657, the whole community moved back to Hamburg where the Senate again opposed the wishes of the *Bürgerschaft* by allowing them to stay.[71]

The Senate seems to have had at least some support for this policy from the inhabitants of the new quarter of the city, in the western area nearest to the border with Altona. In April 1649, for example, a group of citizens submitted a petition asking that not all be expelled since many houses would be left empty. Altona, they claimed 'would only become bigger, and then we would be still less able to compete with it'.[72] The Jews were nonetheless expelled in the following year, but a similar plea of 1672 prevented a second expulsion in 1674.[73] The Senate was not alone in its awareness of the positive economic potential of toleration: just as many citizens opposed the Jews because of the competition they threatened, so others were equally

[67] Ibid., pp. 16–19; Levy, *Rechtsstellung*, pp. 20–5.
[68] Graupe, *Statuten*, 1, p. 19.
[69] StAH, Senat, Cl.VII Lit.Hf No.5 Vol.1b Fasc.1, fol. 17r, 10 July 1650, 17 July 1650, EPS.
[70] Ibid., fol. 21r, 2 May 1651, EPS.
[71] StAH, Senat, Cl.VII Lit.Hf No.5 Vol.1a, fol. 27r, notes by Syndic Klefeker.
[72] Ibid., Cl.VII Lit.Hf No.5 Vol.4a, fols. 12r–v, 29 January 1649, 4 April 1649, EPS.
[73] Ibid., Cl.VII Lit.Hf No.5 Vol.1a, fol. 27r, notes by Syndic Klefeker; ibid., Cl.VII Lit.Hf No.5 Vol.1b Fasc.1, fol.2r; Levy, *Rechtsstellung*, pp. 17–18.

afraid of the disastrous effect that their departure might have on the accommodation business.

The interests of certain sections of the population thus reinforced the philosemitic policies of the Senate. Although no precise figures are available, contemporary accounts leave no doubts about the growing size and prosperity of the community. By the 1670s they had achieved considerable success as money lenders and gold and jewellery dealers with contacts throughout northern Germany. Glückel of Hameln, a Jewess married to a pearl merchant in Hamburg, stressed this in her memoirs: around 1650, fortunes of about 30,000 mark were rare; the majority worked with capital sums much nearer 6,000 mark. But as the community expanded, it suffered from increasing internal social tensions.[74] Glückel herself belonged to one of the wealthier families, whose lifestyle gradually lost many of the characteristics of the ghetto mentality. She spoke French fluently, she read German books and played music with her companions.[75] Indeed by the 1680s the rabbinicial authorities themselves seem to have been concerned at the partial assimilation of members of their community into urban life: the statutes of the Wandsbek community in 1687 forbade attendance at bowling alleys, theatres or fencing schools, while women were forbidden to attend the opera.[76]

Of course, incidents like the murder of a Jewish money lender in 1687 graphically demonstrated the impotence of the Jews against popular agitation.[77] But the extent to which the community had grown is illustrated by the fact that when in 1697 renewed demands were made to expel the Ashkenazim, even the *Bürgerschaft* was prepared to make a concession in return for a substantial payment of 30,000 mark together with an undertaking that they henceforth pay an annual tax of 4,500 mark. More significant than the efforts of the Senate to reduce the sums involved was the fact that the Ashkenazim agreed to pay, while the Sephardim declared that they could not afford the lesser sum of 20,000 mark demanded of them.[78]

Clearly, even the Ashkenazim were not entirely happy about the arrangement. They pleaded for greater economic privileges similar to those given to the Jews in 'Venice, Amsterdam, London and Frankfurt', and they requested the formulation of a legal contract which would secure their position in the city. Without such security they would neither be able to carry out their trades nor borrow the money they needed to pay the 30,000

---

[74] *Denkwürdigkeiten der Glückel von Hameln*, p. 16.   [75] Ibid., p. 21.
[76] Graupe, *Statuten*, 1, pp. 43, 86–7, 283.
[77] Grunwald, *Hamburgs deutsche Juden*, pp. 14–17.
[78] StAH, Senat, Cl.VII Lit.Hf No.5 Vol.1b Fasc.1, fols. 4r–11r, Extractus Nuclei Recessum; ibid., Cl.VII Lit.Hf No.5 Vol.1b Fasc.2, fols. 4r–5v, 1697, EPS.

mark tribute. Despite their misgivings, however, they were willing to make the financial sacrifice demanded of them, and seemed confident that the next Leipzig Fair would enable them to settle most of their debts.[79]

In return, they were offered a contract identical to that drawn up with the Sephardic community: they were not permitted to own houses in the city or to construct a synagogue, although they were allowed to hold their religious services in the privacy of their own homes. The significance of this contract was, however, more symbolic than real, for the *Bürgerschaft* in fact refused to ratify it; so the legal position of the community remained ambiguous until 1710.[80] No further discussions were initiated about the relationship between Jewish traders and Christian guilds after 1697, while the Senate persisted in its policy of playing down clerical complaints about the existence of synagogues in the city.

At the end of the seventeenth century the Ashkenazim were thus already well-established in the city and to a large degree protected by the Senate despite their formal adherence to the Danish crown. Like the Sephardim who had originally sheltered them, they were able to live as a Jewish community under the guidance of the Chief Rabbi in Altona. And by the 1690s at the latest, they had developed a consciousness of their economic and fiscal value to the city which was their most important defence against intolerance and expulsion.

III

It is relatively easy to account for popular attitudes to the Jews. Antisemitism was the result of a general hostility to non-Christian foreigners but more importantly of fear of competition, and of resentment at the high rates of interest the Jews allegedly charged.[81]

The attitude of the clergy, while obviously influenced by such considerations, was more complex. They repeatedly demanded expulsion, but their complaints about Jewish religious practices in the city had at least as much to do with the aspiration to convert the Jews as with the desire to be rid of them. As they pointed out on several occasions, the universities of Jena and Frankfurt an der Oder had advised the Senate in 1611 that the Jews could only be permitted to live in a Christian city as long as they were restricted in their religion and as long as attempts were made to show them

---

[79] Ibid., fols. 15r–22v, 4 June 1697, German Jews to Senate.
[80] Graupe, *Statuten*, 1, p. 25; StAH, Senat, Cl.VII Lit.Hf No.5 Vol.4a, fol. 20r, 10 June, 17 June 1697, Extractus Nuclei Recessum. The Senate later admitted that the contract was invalid: ibid, Cl.VII Lit.Hf No.5 Vol.4c, no. 15, 29 June 1746, EPS.
[81] In August 1648 the *Oberalten* had complained that Jewish money lenders charged interest rates of 24–30 per cent: ibid., Cl.VII Lit.Hf No.5 Vol.4a, fol. 8r, 11 August 1648, EPS.

the error of their ways.[82] The Senate paid little attention to these stipulations, but the clergy regarded the conversion of the Jews in Hamburg as the ultimate challenge. If they succeeded, then their claims to represent the best and most Orthodox Lutheran traditions would be vindicated.

Two developments coincided to produce a new concentration on the problems of Judaism not only in Hamburg but in most Protestant areas in the seventeenth century. In general terms, the Reformation, with its stress on a return to the fundamental roots of Christianity, inevitably drew attention to its Jewish roots. The growth of Hebraic studies at the universities did not, of course, directly affect the treatment of the Jews. Protestants everywhere still firmly rejected the Jewish interpretation of the Bible. But the discovery that there was such an interpretation created some common ground, and gave rise to hopes that by reasonable argument the Jews might be persuaded to convert to a Christianity cleansed of papal corruption. Such considerations played an important part in the gradual erosion of the traditional scapegoat image of the Jew in Protestant areas at a time when the Jewish population of north-western Europe was rising rapidly as a result of renewed persecution in Poland and the East.[83]

The migrations also had profound effects on the Jews. Just as the 'court Jews' were gradually assimilated at the top of society, so the so-called *Betteljuden* (or 'begging Jews') became more and more like Christian vagrants at the bottom.[84] The impact of these changes was minimal at first. It became important in the wake of the confusion and, ultimately, the severe rifts created in the Jewish diaspora by the appearance of the false Messiah Sabbatai Zwi of Smyrna, who in 1648 proclaimed that the messianic era would begin in 1666. The significance of Zwi's kabbalistic prophecies lay in the central idea that a divided and atomised world would be reunited by the returning Messiah, and that the Jews might well have to abandon their religion and unite with others in order to create a new and vital synthesis. Zwi himself turned to Islam, but others turned to various forms of mystical religion close to the Christian sects. Indeed some, like one of the Sephardic rabbis in Hamburg, were even prepared to take serious steps to convert to orthodox Christianity, convinced that the common biblical heritage was the most promising common denominator among a large mass of the world's population.[85]

The numbers of those who converted, either to Islam in Adrianople or

---

[82] Feilchenfeld, 'Anfang und Blüthezeit', p. 205; Levy, *Rechtsstellung*, p. 11.

[83] Healey, 'The Jew in Protestant thought', *passim*; Graupe, *Entstehung*, pp. 47–8, 72–6. This problem has recently been analysed in depth for England: Katz, *Philo-semitism*.

[84] Graupe, *Entstehung*, pp. 43–5.

[85] Ibid., pp. 55–9; Brilling, 'Rabbinerstreit', pp. 219–24; Scholem, *Sabbatai Sevi*, pp. 461–602, 687–93, 749–64.

Saloniki, or to Christianity in Europe, was probably relatively small. But, as the messianic year of 1666 approached, most Jewish communities throughout Europe were apprehensive about the future, and many were uncertain about the extent to which there was still any point in adhering to their own rigid legal and liturgical system.

The theological justification for conversion to another religion and the vision of the dissolution of Jewish law thus coincided with a period in which the Protestant Churches were themselves more interested in Judaism than ever before. Both general tendencies are evident in Hamburg. In 1649, for example, *Senior* Johannes Müller pleaded for the introduction of Hebraic studies at the Gymnasium. Without Hebrew, he argued, no Christian could really know anything about his own religion. Since the arrival of the Jews, he continued, 'the need of this Church and congregation demands that the Hebrew language be studied among us, because of the Jews, who live here in great numbers. The Jews...boast that we cannot judge their religion because their language is unknown to us.' Universities all over Germany and the Netherlands were beginning to study Hebrew intensively, he claimed, so that the Gymnasium would do potential students a great service by giving them elementary instruction.[86]

More specifically, several demands were made that the Senate should employ someone who spoke Hebrew and Portuguese, or a 'Christian rabbi', who might teach the Jews the error of their ways. In 1650 the Senate declared that it could not find such an individual.[87] Even when the clergy announced in 1660 that they had found someone who would be willing to learn both languages within three months, the Senate did not respond.[88]

Despite the emphasis placed on this issue since the earliest discussions about the Jews, there is little evidence that practical steps were taken before the 1660s. Indeed the first serious attempts at conversion were the work of one man, Esdras Edzardi, who in 1667 founded what later became known as the Edzardische Proselyten-Anstalt. Edzardi was not a clergyman; he lived in Hamburg after 1656 on private means, having studied theology and oriental languages at several universities. He repeatedly refused university appointments and declined the offer of the chair of oriental languages at the Gymnasium in 1675. Instead, he worked as a private scholar and

---

[86] StAH, Akademisches Gymnasium, C1, no. 66, Rationes und Ursachen warum man für nöthig erachtet, die Professionem der Hebräischen Sprache im Gymnasium zu bestellen (1649). The first Professor of Oriental Languages at the Gymnasium (Heinrich Rump) died in 1626. His successor, Ägidius Gutbier, was not appointed until 1652: see Schröder, *Lexikon*, 3, pp. 33–5 and ibid., 6, pp. 407–10.

[87] StAH, Senat, Cl.VII Lit.Hf No.5 Vol.4a, fol. 15v; ibid., Cl.VII Lit.Hf No.5 Vol.1b Fasc.1, fol. 14r. They presumably meant a rabbi who had converted to Christianity.

[88] Ibid., fol. 1r.

attracted large numbers of students from all over Germany, whom he instructed in biblical and rabbinical studies.[89]

In 1667 he established a fund for the conversion of the Jews, appealing for contributions from the urban elite and from his many former students and well-wishers. The response was favourable: some Senators contributed sums of several hundred mark; while distinguished outsiders like the Princess Antonia, Duchess of Württemberg, presented a legacy of 100 *taler*.[90] By 1675 the fund had an annual income of 1,064 mark, which rose to a peak of some 3,000 mark shortly before Edzardi's death in 1703.[91] The money was used to buy books for the instruction of Jews and to give the converts small presents at Easter and Christmas; it also supported those poorer Jews and their families unable to earn a living since they had been rejected by their own community and not yet fully accepted by the Christian citizens.[92]

It is not known how many Jews were converted. Bishop Kidder noted in 1698 that 'in the last seven years several hundred Jews have been converted to the Christian faith in Hamburg'.[93] This is almost certainly an exaggeration. However, other accounts confirm that Edzardi himself instructed more than 200 converts. Most were German Jews, although a few Sephardim were converted with the help of Eberhard Anckelmann, Professor of Oriental Languages at the Gymnasium, who spent two years on the Iberian peninsula learning their language for this purpose. Most seem to have remained faithful to their mentor and only about one in forty reverted to Judaism.[94]

The later history of the Proselyten-Anstalt, however, showed that its early success was almost entirely dependent upon the prestige and talent of its founder. After Edzardi's death in 1703, the fund was administered by his heirs, but the interest he had generated in it gradually declined. By 1705 the administrators were no longer able to support the thirty or forty individuals awaiting instruction and the eighty-five families of unemployed converts. Even a church collection in that year, which brought in 1,393 mark, did not ease the situation.[95] The converts complained that too much attention was devoted to the work of conversion, and that, immediately after baptism, they were thrown back on their own resources. Sebastian Edzardi

[89] Gleiss, *Edzardi*, pp. 10, 30–1; Schröder, *Lexikon*, 2, pp. 126–8.
[90] Gleiss, *Edzardi*, pp. 26–9; StAH, Edzardische Proselyten-Anstalt, B1, p. 169.
[91] Gleiss, *Edzardi*, p. 29; StAH, Edzardische Proselyten-Anstalt, B3, Kurze historische Nachricht (no pagination).
[92] Gleiss, *Edzardi*, p. 47; StAH, Senat, Cl.VII Lit.Hf No.5 Vol.5a Fasc.2, no. 1a, Nachricht von der Hamb. Juden Cassa, 11 March 1761.   [93] Gleiss, *Edzardi*, p. 22.
[94] Ibid., p. 21; Schröder, *Lexikon*, 1, pp. 63–4.
[95] Gleiss, *Edzardi*, p. 22; StAH, Hss No. 305, Erträge der Hamb. Kirchen Collection, entry for 1705.

could only direct them to other Christian charities.[96] He himself was less interested in the Anstalt than his father. For Sebastian Edzardi believed that his life-work lay in the fight against Catholics and Calvinists, and it is significant that in 1717 he set aside a sum of 1,700 mark for their conversion. By 1710 weekly expenditure on the Jewish converts had declined to 5 mark, from about 55 mark in the 1690s.[97]

Although interest in the Anstalt revived periodically, Esdras Edzardi's original success was never emulated. There were two main reasons for this. Firstly, the work of conversion of Jews increasingly became associated with Pietism, particularly with Callenberg's Institutum Judaicum, founded in Halle in 1728. For the Orthodox clergy in Hamburg, such contacts between religions as were espoused by the Pietists in Halle were anathema and they aroused nothing but contempt fuelled by fear. Secondly, as the number of Jews in Hamburg increased, it became clear that accommodation rather than conversion must be the first priority. The search for satisfactory laws and regulations was more immediately important than the ultimate subversion of Judaism.[98]

IV

Whether or not Esdras Edzardi's successors shared his aspirations, they certainly lacked the money and influence to carry on his work effectively after 1703. Indeed, by that time any thought of the wholesale conversion of the Jews in Hamburg had become all but futile. What had been a minute Ashkenazi community even up to the 1670s was now an established sub-group, sufficiently large and wealthy to build up defences against sporadic antisemitism and to gain the support of the Senate against the clergy.

In 1697 the position of the Ashkenazim was still ambiguous, dependent upon the goodwill of the Senate. But the *Judenreglement* of 1710 finally gave them almost as much security as the Sephardim. The *Reglement* was drawn up by the Imperial Commission led by Count Damian Hugo von Schönborn at the same time as the new constitution which ended the long and bitter struggle between Senate and *Bürgerschaft*. The Commission aimed to bring the legal status of the Jews in Hamburg into line with that which they enjoyed in other areas under the general jurisdiction of the Emperor. At all events, it was important that the terms of the Windischgrätz

---

[96] See undated complaints and replies by Sebastian Edzardi *c.* 1709 in StAH, Ministerium, III A1k, nos. 184–6, 203–5, 207–8.

[97] Gleiss, *Edzardi*, pp. 30, 48.

[98] The best survey of Callenberg's work, and of eighteenth-century Protestant attitudes to the conversion of the Jews, is still Le Roi, *Die evangelische Christenheit und die Juden*, pp. 200–407.

Treaty of 1674, which banned the Jews from Hamburg outright, be amended.[99]

The twenty-three articles of the *Reglement* dealt with everything from religion to trade and taxation.[100] The Jews were enjoined to lead a 'quiet and pious life', to hold their services in private and to avoid provoking the Christian community. They were no longer encouraged to attend Lutheran church services, but they were still forbidden to attempt to prevent children over fourteen or fifteen years from converting to Christianity. In return, they were promised protection and assured that they would only be asked to pay ordinary taxes. In economic terms, they were allowed virtually everything in so far as it did not either conflict with the privileges of the guilds or involve handling stolen goods, or charging extortionate rates of interest. An attempt by the College of the Sixty to insert a clause stating that the *Reglement* was not a *lex perpetua*, and that it was subject to revision by agreement between Senate and *Bürgerschaft*, was foiled by the Senate, which argued that this might encourage renewed attempts to expel the Jews.[101]

Although the *Reglement* dealt with a wide range of subjects, it was a vague document compared with previous contracts. As J. F. Voigt put it in 1881: it was more a Habeas Corpus Act than a precise definition of liberties and limitations. It remained valid until 1849, for its content was so minimal that it could survive virtually any change in policy.[102]

Indeed the *Reglement* was perhaps most notable for its omissions. It gave privileges and protection to the Jews in Hamburg, but did not define their status: the delicate issue of Danish overlordship was left on one side. Similarly, it gave the Jews limited legal autonomy in things like marriages and inheritance, but left open the extent to which the Senate would permit the Chief Rabbi in Altona to exercise his authority in Hamburg. The Jews were not told where to live: they were thus freed once and for all from the compulsion of a ghetto; but the potentially contentious issue of whether they had the right to buy property, and whether they had the right to live wherever they wished, was left open.[103]

---

99 Voigt, *Rückblick*, p. 3. The Windischgrätz Treaty was one of the many attempts to conclude a truce between the Senate and the *Bürgerschaft* in the seventeenth century: Bartels, *Nachtrag*, pp. 178–238. The position of the Jews in the numerous German states differed considerably since the *Judenschutzrecht* had passed from the Emperor to the princes in the Golden Bull. They were, however, in general governed by similar laws and allowed a similar degree of communal autonomy in domestic and personal legal affairs. Cf. Conrad, *Rechtsgeschichte*, 2, pp. 223–4.

100 The *Reglement* is printed in Klefeker, *Verfassungen*, 2, pp. 386–93.

101 StAH, Senat, Cl.VII Lit.Hf. No.5 Vol.1b Fasc.3, fols. 53–7, 16 June 1710, Extractus Protocolli Caesarae Commissionis.   102 Voigt, *Rückblick*, p. 4.

103 Levy, *Rechtsstellung*, pp. 25–7; Krohn, *Juden in Hamburg*, p. 10; StAH, Senat, Cl.VII Lit.Hf No.5 Vol.1a, fol. 35v, notes by Syndic Klefeker; ibid., Cl.VII Lit.Lb No.18 Vol.2a2, *passim*.

The real significance of the *Reglement* was that it provided a foundation upon which a complex administrative practice was later built. The clause which dealt with taxation was a typical example of this. The Ashkenazim were to pay taxes collectively in view of their migratory habits and confusing family relationships. Two problems were thus solved: firstly that of administering the collection of taxes, and secondly that of the poor Jews or *Betteljuden*, since it was obviously in the interests of the Jewish elders to keep them out if the tax load was to be distributed equitably.[104]

Equally important from a mercantile point of view was the fact that few restrictions were placed on the economic activities of the Jews. They were forbidden to trespass on the privileges of the guilds, but since these privileges were in any case vaguely defined, the *Reglement* again created an open-ended framework within which all manner of substantive issues were subject to negotiation. As events were to show, the shopkeepers' guild increasingly felt that its privileges had not been adequately protected.[105]

Later observers, like Senator Johann Arnold Günther, held that the strength of the *Reglement* lay in the freedom it gave to both Jews and Senate. It marked, he thought, the triumph of the commercial spirit and of humanity, the triumph of a spirit once found only in a small minority but now universal. The *Reglement*, he wrote, was and is: 'not only an impressive monument of healthy mercantile politics, but also [a monument] of the purest and most honourable humanity, a monument once placed before the world by the dawning eighteenth century, and now gratefully transmitted undiminished by the dying century to the next'.[106]

If the *Reglement* was designed to attract more Jews to Hamburg, it succeeded. Although no reliable figures are available for the period after 1663, when only forty or fifty houses were occupied by Jewish families, it seems clear that there was a substantial increase in numbers after 1710. By about 1730 estimates indicate that about 600 Jewish taxpayers lived in the city.[107] Gilbert Leiding, a church warden used by the Senate as an expert on Jewish affairs, quoted a figure of about 10,000 by 1733, an estimate based on Jewish tax assessments and an average family size of five.[108] Whatever the exact figure, contemporaries were certainly struck by the size of the community and its rate of growth. Leiding himself was concerned to scotch

---

104 Ibid., Cl.VII Lit.Hf No.5 Vol.1d3, 21 January 1763, Nachricht von denen Juden...insebesondere deren Contributions-Wesen betreffend. Poor Jews were the subject of repeated negotiations between the Senate and the Jewish elders: ibid., Cl.VII Lit.Lb No.18 Vol.1l. Cf. Grunwald, *Hamburgs deutsche Juden*, pp. 19–26; Levy, *Rechtsstellung*, pp. 22–3.
105 StAH, Senat, Cl.VII Lit.Hf No.5 Vol.1a, fols. 33r–v, notes by Syndic Klefeker; Gonsiorowski, 'Berufe der Juden', pp. 34–63; Krohn, *Juden in Hamburg*, pp. 11–13.
106 Günther, *Jüdische Einwohner*, p. 13.
107 Grunwald, *Hamburgs deutsche Juden*, p. 20.
108 StAH, Senat, Cl. VII Lit.Hf No.5 Vol.2a1, no. 8, 20 October 1733, Leiding to Senate.

rumours that there were 70,000 Jews in Hamburg, but even informed observers stressed immigration and above all a phenomenal reproductive rate to account for the growth of the Jewish communities; although their perspective was probably distorted by the fact that many Jews who plied their trade in Hamburg actually lived in Wandsbek or Altona.[109]

Since poor Jews or *Betteljuden* were generally not admitted to the communities, the average level of prosperity seems to have been relatively high. Although the communities sometimes protested against the level of taxation, they paid 7,000 mark annually between 1723 and 1741, when it was reduced to 5,000 mark.[110] The problem seems to have been one of liquidity rather than lack of wealth: in 1733, for example, it was estimated that the total wealth of the communities was about 6,000,000 mark, while their annual wealth tax of 7,000 mark (one quarter per cent of total wealth) only assessed them at 2,800,000 mark.[111]

The difficulties they claimed to find in raising this annual sum derived largely from the nature of their economic activities. Details on this aspect of Jewish life in Hamburg are sparse. The material collected by Gonsiorowski, based mainly on lists drawn up in 1720 and 1764, reveals that, while the number of merchants increased from 250 to 350, the number of small shopkeepers declined from 330 to 130.[112] Apart from activity in the traditional Jewish professions of money lending and changing, the Jews seem to have been particularly involved in the textile trade, both in the import and export of textiles, and in their manufacture, which was not subject to guild regulations. Other products handled by Jews included colonial goods such as chocolate, coffee, tea and tobacco.[113] They were, in short, active in all those areas not clearly circumscribed by guild privileges. For the most part, in the mercantile sectors, they had little to fear from such restrictions, but problems frequently arose over the retail sale of goods by Jews in the city. Owing to the privileges of the *Krameramt* (shopkeepers' guild), they were not permitted to open shops with trade signs: Jewish retail activity thus took the form of either underselling goods from unadvertised shops or street selling, which both infuriated the guild and ultimately laid the Jews open to charges of unfair and dishonest trading.[114]

As the size and prosperity of the Jewish communities increased during the 1720s, their desire to establish synagogues and schools grew once more.

---

[109] In 1734 it was known that 152 Jews commuted daily from Altona: ibid., Cl.VII Lit.Lb No.18 Vol.1g, fols. 37–9.
[110] Grunwald, *Hamburgs deutsche Juden*, pp. 19–25; StAH, Senat, Cl.VII Lit.Hf No.5 Vol.1d3, 21 January 1763, Nachricht (as in note 104 above).
[111] Ibid., Cl.VII Lit.Hf No.5 Vol.1a, fols. 73–86, Ammerckungen über die ad Supplicam der hochdeutschen Juden d. 22 April 1733 anliegende gravamina und desideria.
[112] Gonsiorowski, 'Berufe der Juden', pp. 40–63.
[113] Ibid., pp. 40–56; Krohn, *Juden in Hamburg*, pp. 10–13.   [114] Ibid., pp. 11–12.

In this they seem to have been supported by the Senate. The legal situation was ambiguous: the *Reglement* forbade them to have what it called 'public buildings', but permitted them to worship in private as long as they refrained from ostentatiously provoking their neighbours by using ceremonial horns and trumpets or by publicly displaying liturgical lanterns.[115] The distinction between a private prayer house and a synagogue was, however, largely formal, and one which the Senate had little desire to clarify. With characteristic watchfulness, the clergy protested on several occasions that synagogues were being built, but in 1719, 1722, 1723, 1727 and again in 1728, the Senate claimed that, on investigation, it had found nothing.[116] Only in 1732 was it privately admitted that no less than fourteen unofficial synagogues existed together with forty-one schools which taught Hebrew and the Talmud.[117]

The benevolent attitude of the Senate in those investigations provides the clue to official attitudes towards the Jews after 1710. For what Günther later saw as humanitarianism was in fact a desire to avoid all public controversy, and above all to avoid antisemitic violence. This feeling was particularly strong owing to the fear that popular disturbances of any kind might once more draw the attention of the Imperial authorities to the city: the anti-Catholic riot of 1719 had already raised the spectre of another Imperial Commission, a spectre which loomed large over official policy during the 1720s.[118]

There is no evidence of a more enlightened or more tolerant attitude to the Jews in this period, at least not in the sense that those words later assumed. The moral weekly, *Der Patriot*, widely regarded by contemporaries, and scholars today, as the most enlightened of the genre, still spoke scathingly of the Jews as the 'blood leeches of the Christians' and the 'seducers of our youth'.[119] One of its authors, Michael Richey, elsewhere wrote of 'this lecherous and lascivious race which multiplies like vermin' and of their 'swinish nature'; while official documents of the period are at best neutral in their phraseology.[120]

The official mind was guided by *Policey* rather than *Humanität*; so that many of the freedoms enjoyed by the Jews in Hamburg were primarily the result of a desire to preserve law and order. In 1711 burial rights were given

---

[115] Klefeker, *Verfassungen*, 2, p. 387.
[116] The material for these cases is unfortunately scattered throughout three files: StAH, Senat, Cl.VII Lit.Hf No.5 Vol.1b Fasc.5, fols. 56–7, 13 November 1719, EPS; ibid., Cl.VII Lit.Hf No.5 Vol.4a, fols. 46, 62, 66, 16 April 1722, 14 September 1725, 30 April 1727, EPS; ibid., Cl.VII Lit.Hf No.5 Vol.1b Fasc.6, fol. 30, 30 April 1728, EPS.
[117] Ibid., Cl.VII Lit.Hf No.5 Vol.1d1, fols. 52–6, 28 February 1731, EPS and Nachricht von den jüdischen Schulen.
[118] Cf. StAH, Hss No. 273, Richey, Anmerckungen, ad pag. 180.
[119] *Der Patriot*, 1, pp. 261, 337–44.
[120] StAH, Hss No. 273, Richey, Anmerckungen, ad pag. 260.

to the Jews in order to prevent them from carrying infection from Altona (currently stricken by plague) into the city.[121] Poor Jews were excluded with firm regularity in order to lessen the danger of disorder on the streets.[122] The Jewish elders themselves collaborated with the city authorities on many of these issues by enjoining their communities to lead quiet and modest lives, and by drawing up their own sumptuary laws.[123] And while the Senate did not officially recognise the jurisdiction of the rabbinical court in Altona, few attempts seem to have been made to enquire more closely into its operations as long as disputes within the communities did not become public.[124] It is in a sense a tribute to the success of this policy that the topographer, Christian Ludwig von Griesheim, was obliged to admit in 1759 that 'a great obscurity shrouds the history of the Jews in Hamburg'.[125]

V

Many of the difficulties inherent in the tenuous relationship between the city and its Jewish communities were never resolved. The Danes continued to protect not only the Wandsbek and Altona communities but also the Hamburg group.[126] Members of all three groups lived in Hamburg; but the Hamburg group too seems to have preferred to obey the Altona rabbis as this gave them greater freedom from interference by the Senate. Even in cases where the Senate was moved to act, the situation was always complicated by the fact that it did not always understand the religious problems involved: it might demand the lifting of a ban of excommunication, but to little effect.[127] The problems experienced in finding an oath which would be binding on the Jews were typical of the difficulties encountered by the Senate in dealing with these aliens who adhered to a religion which was all but impenetrable to an outsider.[128] Similarly, the fact that so much

---

[121] StAH, Senat, Cl.VII Lit.Hf No.5 Vol.7, *passim*; ibid., Cl.VII Lit.Lb No.18 Vol.1k, *passim*; ibid., Cl.VII Lit.Hf No.5 Vol.1b, Fasc.4 *passim*.

[122] Klefeker, *Verfassungen*, 2, pp. 314–19.

[123] Graupe, *Statuten*, 1, p. 44; Grunwald, 'Hochzeits- und Kleiderordnung der Hamburger Juden', pp. 32–44. The elders were once reminded of their traditional co-operation in this respect: StAH, Senat, Cl.VII Lit.Lb No.18 Vol.1n, 2 November 1763, EPS.

[124] Grunwald, *Aus dem Hamburger Staatsarchiv*, pp. 16–21; Levy, *Rechtsstellung*, pp. 23–5.

[125] Von Griesheim, *Anmerckungen und Zugaben*, p. 89.

[126] Graupe, *Statuten*, 1, pp. 27–8; Grunwald, *Aus dem Hamburger Staatsarchiv*, pp. 16–25; Brilling, 'Rabbinerstreit', pp. 234–6, 241–4; Marwedel, *Privilegien*, pp. 50, 55, 84–5.

[127] See the account of the case of Jacob Isaak *c*. 1730 in Grunwald, *Aus dem Hamburger Staatsarchiv*, pp. 16–21. Cf. Marwedel, *Privilegien*, p. 82.

[128] StAH, Senat, Cl.VII Lit.Lb No.18 Vol.4, Von der Juden Eide, *passim*. This file contains various essays on the question of whether Christian oaths were binding on Jews, and negotiations over the formulation of an appropriate oath for Jews in 1734. Cf. Klefeker, *Verfassungen*, 3, p. 649. The Danish authorities in Altona encountered similar difficulties over this issue. Cf. Marwedel, *Privilegien*, pp. 99–100.

was left in the hands of the Jewish elders often led to confusion and misunderstanding. Since the Jews were taxed collectively, and allowed to raise their annual payments according to their own internal assessments, it was never quite clear either how many Jews there were in the city or what they were worth; while many suspected that the criteria by which the elders accepted new members from other parts were not entirely in the best commercial interests of the city.[129]

The relatively untroubled growth and consolidation of the Jewish communities after 1710 was not, however, entirely due to the successful implementation of the *Reglement*. It was also undoubtedly aided by the fact that other, more pressing, problems preoccupied both the Senate and the clergy. The city's recovery from the plague in 1715 was followed by the fiasco over the Catholic chapel riot, the aftermath of which kept the secular and ecclesiastical authorities busy, and in mutual conflict, until 1722. No sooner had that crisis been resolved, than the clergy launched themselves into an hysterical attack on the Calvinists, which embroiled the Senate in years of domestic and diplomatic strife. Throughout, the pace was set by the clergy and, despite ritual antisemitic protests, they clearly felt that the major threat to the Lutheran community lay elsewhere.

In 1730, however, the only serious antisemitic riot of the eighteenth century gave rise to a new preoccupation with the Jews. It resulted in conflict between Church and State and in a new appraisal by the Senate of the economic and social position of the Jews.

The riot, which raged from 24 to 27 August, seems to have had various causes.[130] It broke out in the Neustadt, in the area where most of the Jews lived in close contact with Christians, close to the harbour district south of St Michael's Church. That was undoubtedly important, for 1730 was a year of crisis in the mercantile trades in Hamburg.[131] Hence the most detailed contemporary account of the riot stressed the involvement of sailors in the crowd of several thousands who thronged the streets. The other group mentioned repeatedly was the *Krameramt* (shopkeepers' guild), whose members complained of unfair competition and underselling by Jewish traders. The clergy in the parish of St Michael also apparently contributed to the disorder by preaching against the excesses of the Jews.[132] The Jews themselves were embroiled in internal disputes which it was

[129] StAH, Senat, Cl.VII Lit.Hf No.5 Vol.1a, fols. 73–86, Anmerckungen über die ad Supplicam der hochdeutschen Juden d. 22 April 1733 anliegende gravamina und desideria.
[130] The most detailed account of the riot is printed in Grunwald, *Hamburgs deutsche Juden*, pp. 29–31; other details have been taken from Grunwald, 'Judentumult', and a Jewish account in StAH, Senat, Cl.VII Lit.Hf No.5 Vol.4a, fols. 40–4.
[131] Vogel, 'Handelskonjunkturen', p. 64.
[132] Grunwald, *Hamburgs deutsche Juden*, p. 29.

difficult to conceal from the public eye. These controversies arose out of the expulsion from the community by the rabbinical court of the son of one of the rabbis, Jacob Isaak. His crime was to have made false accusations against several Jewish traders to the Hamburg authorities. He vigorously denied the charges and tried to enlist the support of the Senate. His campaign to clear his name, which ultimately failed in October 1730, led him to send repeated denunciations of Jewish malpractices to the Senate and to the Lutheran clergy in 1730, and this undoubtedly contributed to the generally unsettled atmosphere.[133]

Tension between Jews and Christians in the Neustadt obviously built up over a number of weeks. Witnesses later questioned by the judicial authorities told stories of impudent behaviour by Jewish youths, one of whom apparently threw plum pips into the wig of a choir master, and of Christian aggression towards Jewish women on the streets.[134] At the same time rumours were circulated by sailors that Jewish merchants were responsible for the recent loss of Hamburg sailors to pirates in Algiers.[135]

On the afternoon of 24 August a crowd gathered on the Grossneumarkt, threatening the Jews with violence. It was easily dispersed by the militia, but it reassembled on the following day in the predominantly Jewish Elbstrasse nearby. Stones were thrown at Jewish houses and several Jews were chased through the streets. That evening, the Senate met in special session and resolved to pass an emergency mandate condemning the violence, and to move in troops to quell the unrest. The mandate was communicated both to the *Oberalten* and the clergy on the following day (26 August), and then published.[136] More troops were moved in, while members of the Senate, foremost among them *Bürgermeister* Garlieb Sillem, rode around the streets and apparently thus managed to prevent any further trouble. By 27 August, the violence was over and official enquiries into the disturbances began, although, predictably, little helpful evidence was found, and only six men, including one Jew, received minor punishments on 13 September.[137]

By any standard the riot was a relatively mild affair. It passed without bloodshed, without even destruction of property. The militia had never lost

---

[133] Ibid., p. 27; Grunwald, *Aus dem Hamburger Staatsarchiv*, pp. 16–21. See also: StAH, Senat, Cl.VII Lit.Hf No.5 Vol.1b Fasc.5, fols. 25–35.

[134] Ibid., Cl.VII Lit.Lb No.18 Vol.1f, statements taken by the judiciary 26 August–6 September 1730. There is no pagination.

[135] Ibid., 5 September 1730, statement by Jacob Metzdorff. Hamburg sailors captured by pirates in the Mediterranean were often freed with the aid of Jewish merchants whose contacts and linguistic skills usually succeeded where diplomacy failed. Cf. Baasch, *Convoy-Schiffahrt*, pp. 49, 52, 61, 67, 193.

[136] Blank, *Mandate*, 2, pp. 1107–8; Grunwald, 'Judentumult', pp. 587–9.

[137] StAH, Senat, Cl.VII Lit.Lb No.18 Vol.1f, 13 September 1730, EPS.

control of the situation and, at a crucial point on 26 August, the appearance of Sillem on the streets probably saved the day. The Jews too behaved discreetly by keeping off the streets for a few days.

More important in many ways was the spectre of violence which the events of these days raised, and the discussion of its causes. On 26 August the *Oberalten* had approved the mandate condemning the violence, but had been moved to point out that popular hatred of the Jews was surely caused by their extreme provocation of the Christian community. It was not only their synagogues and their schools, their general insolence, but above all the economic threat they posed to the *Krameramt*, which they had all but driven to ruin in recent years.[138]

The *Oberalten* were content with the Senate's promise to investigate the problem of Jewish street traders; but communications with the clergy were less straightforward. The Senate had sent them the mandate to be read out again in the churches on the following Sunday, but had also enclosed a letter which effectively accused them of instigating the violence through irresponsible preaching.[139] On 30 August, the clergy reacted with an outraged reply in which they denied all accusations made against them. On the contrary, they blamed the Senate for the riot: its 'overly great connivance with the Jews up to now' was surely the cause of their excesses, and that which justified the complaints of the *Krameramt*. So few were the restraints imposed upon the Jews, they claimed, that many of them boasted that the clergy were 'patrons of the Jews'. Hence the preachers declared that they could not promise to refrain from preaching against the Jews.[140]

Although not entirely inaccurate, the charge that the Senate had connived with the Jews, and thus alienated the populace, gave rise to understandable anger. The Senate accused the clergy of exploiting the dubious grievances of others to create trouble, and of interfering in areas in which they had no authority. Its reply bleakly pointed out that the clergy were after all subjects just like anyone else, and thus bound by both law and professional conscience to promote truth and peace. The Senate recommended the clergy to use what it called 'theological wisdom and moderation' in future, and use its position to promote 'harmony and love between rulers and ruled, teachers and taught' in the city.[141]

The dispute continued until May 1731 and even then only ceased when the Senate firmly declared that it had no wish to continue discussions on this matter. In December 1730 the clergy had produced a massive

---

[138] Ibid., 26 August 1730, Conclusum der Oberalten.
[139] Ibid., 26 August 1730, EPS. Neumeister scornfully reported the charges to his correspondent, Ernst Salomo Cyprian; cf. Wotschke (ed.), 'Neumeisters Briefe' (1929), p. 1456, letter of 2 September 1730.
[140] StAH, Senat, Cl.VII Lit.Lb No.18 Vol.1f, 30 August 1730, Resolutio Rev. Ministerii.
[141] Ibid., 27 September 1730, EPS.

justification of their position, prefaced by a firm statement that in matters of conscience they did not consider themselves bound in the same way as other subjects. Although they modified their previous accusations, the preachers resorted to their traditional face-saving tactic of producing long lists of extracts from previous laws concerning the Jews. They wanted no innovations, they said, but merely pointed out how the Jews had exceeded the limitations imposed upon them by seventeenth-century laws which were still valid.[142]

There was no simple answer to this argument. For the Senate was forced to admit that the *Reglement* of 1710 had not superseded all previous arrangements. But they could in turn point out that the growth of the Jewish communities inevitably necessitated greater concessions in the interests of public order; to allow the Jews schools and synagogues would surely be a more effective way of isolating them from the Christian community. Again it was stressed that law and order rather than Lutheran Orthodoxy were at stake, thus reinforcing the claim that Jewish affairs were an entirely secular, rather than ecclesiastical, concern.

For the moment it seemed that the Senate had indeed achieved its aim. The clergy did not reply to the last communication of 16 May 1731 and indeed no longer seem to have paid particular attention to the Jews during the 1730s.[143] However, having established its public patronage of the Jews against both popular and clerical attacks, the Senate soon found that it was perhaps more difficult than at first envisioned to ensure the Jews a viable existence in the city.

The problems which emerged after the riot of 1730 were twofold. The dispute over the excommunication of the Jewish renegade, Jacob Isaak, in October 1730 once more raised the thorny issue of the Danish protectorate of the Jews in Hamburg. His appeal to the Senate, and its subsequent attempts to persuade the rabbis and elders to lift their ban on him, once more clearly demonstrated the impotence of the Senate with regard to the affairs of communities which owed their allegiance to a rabbi over whom it had no power. But in the last resort it was concluded that even if the Danes were to acquiesce in the provision of rabbis in Hamburg, the Jews themselves would probably never agree, since this might lead to a restriction of their internal communal jurisdiction.[144]

That was, however, strictly speaking a technical problem, and one whose importance was perhaps largely symbolic. More concrete were the issues

---

[142] Ibid., 16 December 1730, Resolutio Rev. Ministerii; 16 May 1731, EPS.

[143] Only one minor public protest was made against the public burial of a rabbi in June 1738. Cf. StAH, Ministerium, III A1r, No. 149, 12 June 1738, Pro Memoria; Blank, *Mandate*, 3, p. 1314.

[144] Grunwald, *Aus dem Hamburger Staatsarchiv*, pp. 16–21; see also notes 127 and 133 above. A report dated February 1732 on the problems arising out of this case is in StAH, Senat, Cl.VII Lit.Hf No.5 Vol.1a, fols. 56–9.

raised in 1733 by the Jews themselves, when they petitioned the Senate for a reduction in their annual tax assessment and for greater economic freedom, especially for their shopkeepers and street traders.[145] Their pleas for lower taxes were greeted with a certain amount of scepticism since it was well known that their real wealth was well over 6,000,000 mark, more than double the sum on which they were actually assessed. The Senate's report thus dismissed most of the specific requests made by the Jews, but it dealt at length with the problem of their economic and social position. It claimed: 'There is virtually no area of high commerce, of manufacture and of daily work where they do not have a strong connection, and where indeed in many cases they take the bread out of the mouths of our own citizens. They have in fact become a necessary evil for us.' The report went on to outline the need for stricter controls, and to criticise the liberal policies of the past, which had contributed to the growth of so potentially disruptive a force. The riot of 1730 had shown how explosive the situation could become, and that, the report claimed, was surely due to the rapacity, cunning and immorality of the Jews. There could be no simple answer, and the report stressed that neither suppression nor expulsion would be appropriate since they would simply move on to Altona and ruin Hamburg's trade. But some form of limitation should be imposed upon them, otherwise they would soon ruin the city anyway.[146]

Just what these limitations should be was never quite clear. The Jewish elders were subsequently requested to draw up lists of all their members and to keep a closer check on those who came into the city.[147] But as Senator Lucas Corthum declared: 'The question of whether the Jews should be allowed more freedom than heretofore in trade and in their way of life gives rise to many doubts and great difficulties.' Further concessions would surely attract still more Jews, and thus merely magnify the problem. Nor would the Civic Colleges readily agree to such concessions, for too many of their members had material interests to defend. Yet Corthum argued that the question should be considered seriously, for to deny them such freedom would be to restrict them to trade, and that would lead to the impoverishment of the vast majority of those Jews who were not merchants. The important point, he claimed, was that 'He who has gained the right to live in any place is given a silent assurance that he has the freedom to pursue his livelihood there.'[148]

---

[145] Ibid., fols. 71–2, 22 April 1733, Jews to Senate.

[146] Ibid., fols. 73–86, Anmerckungen über die ad Supplicam der hochdeutschen Juden d. 22 April 1733 anliegende gravamina und desideria.

[147] Ibid., fols. 99–102, 21 January 1734, Senate to Jews; Blank, *Mandate*, 3, pp. 1229, 1253.

[148] StAH, Senat, Cl.VII Lit.Hf Vol.1a, fols. 87–92, undated report by Lucas Corthum. On Corthum, see Schröder, *Lexikon*, 2, pp. 584–5. He was a lawyer who had studied in Leipzig and Leiden; he was elected Senator in 1729.

The limits of toleration: Sephardim and Ashkenazim

The significance of Corthum's report lay in the fact that, for the first time, it considered the position of the Jews in the same way as that of other citizens. The Jews had expectations just like the *Krameramt*, and the function of government was to mediate between them impartially where they conflicted. He thus recommended that, when the economic climate improved, the Jews should be permitted to sell a whole range of goods and to take up several crafts like wig-making, clock-making and shoe-making, which the guilds had previously objected to. Since the *Bürgerschaft* would not agree to complete freedom, he proposed that individual Jews should apply for licences in return for an annual fee.

A subsequent decision of 21 January 1734 postponed the issue of trade freedom for the moment; but it seems that a commission was set up to consider the matter which did eventually implement Corthum's proposal, in that individual Jews were granted trading licences in the following decades.[149] Although no immediate practical results ensued, the whole discussion since 1731 had at least broached many of the fundamental issues and forced the Senate to clarify its ideas. What emerged, under pressure from both clergy and guilds, was a more explicitly tolerant attitude to the Jews which was in part based on opposition to both of the former. The intervention of the clergy in 1730 stimulated the Senate to take its stand firmly behind the Jews, while the opposition of the monopolistic guilds led to the theoretical recognition of the Jews as legally established inhabitants with concomitant economic rights.

VI

In 1734 the Senate justified, at least in theory, the concession of greater economic freedom to the Jews. Their religious rights had, however, not been mentioned during that debate, although it was taken for granted that the *Reglement* of 1710 allowed them to exercise their faith in private. Twelve years later those rights were themselves discussed at length in the context of a bitter dispute over the proposed construction of a synagogue in the Doctorgang on the western periphery of the city.

The plan was initiated by the largest of the three communities, the Altona group, whose elders in Hamburg signed a contract in April 1746 for the rental of a building site for thirty years. Essentially, the proposed building was unusual only in that it was larger than most previous prayer houses, and in that the contract specifically stated that it was to be used as a synagogue.[150] The Senate apparently gave its tacit assent to the project,

---

[149] StAH, Senat, Cl.VII Lit.Hf No.5 Vol.1a, fols. 99–102, 21 January 1734, Senate to Jews; Gonsiorowski, 'Berufe der Juden', pp. 36–7.

[150] StAH, Senat, Cl.VII Lit.Hf No.5 Vol.4c, no. 8, 4 April 1746, contract between Johann Joachim Stieteleben and David Isaac Wallach. Although numbered, the documents in this file are not ordered chronologically.

partly because it was seen as a further step towards the ultimate goal of prising the community away from its Danish patron.[151] It was, however, virtually impossible to keep the plan secret. Although the Doctorgang was one of the smallest and narrowest alley-ways in the city, the inhabitants of the area were of mixed religions: both Jews and Christians lived in close proximity, often renting different floors of the same houses.[152] The news soon leaked out, and the first protest of the clergy on 13 May 1746 inaugurated the last great conflict over the right of the Jews to worship in Hamburg.[153]

The dispute was notable not only for the arguments which the Senate put in favour of the building but also for the uncharacteristically tactful behaviour of the clergy who, under the guidance of *Senior* Friedrich Wagner, ultimately achieved their ends without ever expressing their views in public.[154] Wagner's behaviour in the affair was ambiguous. While participating in the official debate, he made strenuous attempts to defuse the situation by holding secret talks both with members of the Senate and with the Jewish elders.[155] Although he was officially committed to the demolition of the building, he was reluctant to resort to the traditional clerical tactic of preaching against it. In his letters to the Syndic Johann Klefeker, he expressed what virtually amounted to personal indifference to the building, and he stressed that only the high feelings of his colleagues and the belligerence of the Civic Colleges were to blame for the failure of the plan.[156] His private humility and tolerance seems, however, to have been more strategic than Christian in nature. For Wagner's own notes on the case clearly show how strong his private opposition was. The difference between him and his less restrained colleagues was one of tactics rather than philosophy. It was important, he stressed, to show that the clergy had been wronged, that unjust aspersions had been cast on their reputation. While his predecessors relied on the power of the public sermon, Wagner exploited the intricacies of the urban constitution in order to rally the support of the all-important College of the Sixty. His aim throughout was to show that non-toleration was not necessarily synonymous with repression.[157]

His patience and guile were appreciated by some members of the Senate,

[151] Ibid., no. 11, 23 May 1746, EPS.   [152] Ibid., nos. 1–3, plans of the Doctorgang area.

[153] Ibid., no. 10, 13 May 1746, EPS.

[154] See Wagner's notes in StAH, Ministerium, II, 7, p. 37.

[155] StAH, Senat, Cl.VII Lit.Hf No.5 Vol.4c, no. 16, 27 June 1746, Wagner to Klefeker; StAH, Ministerium, II 7, pp. 24–5.

[156] StAH, Senat, Cl.VII Lit.Hf No.5 Vol.4c, nos. 16, 32, 27 June and 17 September 1746, Wagner to Klefeker.

[157] StAH, Ministerium, II 7, pp. 24–5, 28–9, 31–7; ibid., III A2c, nos. 134–5, 19 December 1746, Wagner to Greve.

which seems to have been divided on the issue. Although it is not clear exactly who was involved, the debate moved through two distinct phases. In the first, the Senate boldly upheld the rights of the Jews. In the second, it seemed to modify its original position. Faced with the possibility of extensive riots and the outright opposition of the Sixty, the synagogue was demolished at the end of September. In the case of Johann Klefeker, his ultimate loss of enthusiasm for the synagogue plan was entirely due to the threat made by the Sixty that, if the Senate persisted, they would insist on the matter being brought before the *Bürgerschaft*, which would mean further unwelcome publicity and almost certain ignominious defeat. In the last resort, his support for the Jews dissolved when it became clear that the 'honour and authority' of the Senate were at stake. On the other hand, the Senate did persist in the search for a compromise, even in the face of popular unrest, until the final uncompromising rejection of the synagogue by the Sixty on 26 September.[158]

The crisis did not become acute until the end of August. Until then, Senate and clergy had been involved in an acrimonious correspondence, which revolved around the usual issue of whether the Jews were a secular or an ecclesiastical problem. While the clergy produced three predictably Orthodox papers, all festooned with the appropriate legal references, the Senate was concerned not to enter into detailed arguments.[159] It was thus able to concentrate on matters of principle. On 1 June, the clergy were informed that the Senate had absolute confidence in the integrity of the Jewish elders, whose co-operation in recent years had contributed significantly to a more satisfactory relationship with the Jews. While insisting that the issue was a purely political one, the Senate did not refrain from scoring points on the theological plane. It recommended that the clergy adopt an attitude of 'compassionate inclination and sincere pity towards the Jewish people, whose situation is in any case already pitiful', and referred the pastors to the recent works of prominent Protestant theologians which defended toleration. One principle was stressed above all: 'that as long as Christian magistrates tolerate the Jews in their lands, there can be no just hindrance to them in the exercise of their religion'.[160]

---

[158] StAH, Senat, Cl.VII Lit.Hf No.5 Vol.4c, nos. 67–8, 25 September 1746, Klefeker to Senate. Klefeker was confined to his bed with severe diarrhoea and was thus obliged to communicate his feelings in writing.

[159] Ibid., nos. 12, 14, 17, 42: 25 May, 15 June, 29 July, 26 August 1746, clergy to Senate.

[160] Ibid., no. 13, 1 June 1746, EPS. The works by Protestant theologians are not specified in this letter; two books of particular importance had, however, appeared in 1741: Justus Henning Böhmer, *De Causa Judaeorum Tolerantia* (Halle-Magdeburg, 1741), and Johann Jacodus Beck, *Tractatus de juribus Judaeorum* (Nuremberg, 1741). Cf. Toury, 'Jüdische Problematik', pp. 16–17. Böhmer's work was first published in Halle in 1708; it appears to have been used by the Hamburg Senate and is cited with approval by Johann Klefeker. Cf. Klefeker, *Verfassungen*, 8, pp. 703–4.

Just as in 1734 the Senate had formulated the right of inhabitants to economic freedom, so now it firmly stated their right to expect certain fundamental, if limited, religious liberties.

The clergy were, needless to say, hardly reassured by the distinction made between a public synagogue and a private one. By the end of June, Wagner was convinced that his colleagues would accept nothing less than a total demolition of the half-finished building. He himself had spoken to the Jews and they seemed willing to amend their plans and even withdraw them, if necessary, in order to preserve peace.[161] His claim that he himself maintained a neutral attitude in the affair was not entirely accurate. Only two weeks later, he reported to his colleagues that he had informed the Jews that the clergy would not be satisfied with anything short of demolition, and on 19 August he assured them that his views had received the tacit support of 'some honest men of the highest rank in the Senate'.[162]

However, all attempts to find a peaceful solution failed and, by the end of August, the Senate resolved to end the dispute with the clergy by taking the matter to the College of the Sixty. The latter were presented with a statement of the facts of the case so far, and in particular with an aggrieved account of the unruly behaviour of the clergy.[163] After some prevarication, however, the Sixty sided with the clergy and, on 12 September, they too demanded the demolition of the synagogue.[164] All attempts to reverse this decision met with no response; indeed the Senate's initial refusal to accept defeat led to the growth of considerable popular ill-feeling. As soon as it became known that the Senate intended to go against the decision of the Sixty, crowds began to gather in the Doctorgang area and threatened to demolish the building by force. The atmosphere was intensified by the expectation that the clergy would speak out in their sermons on the annual day of penance of 15 September.[165] That they did not do so probably decided their victory. On Sunday, 18 September Wagner himself did not mention the synagogue at all, and preached instead on the virtues of peace and toleration, thus reinforcing the image he had been concerned to project of a peace-loving clergy whose patience had been provoked beyond all reasonable limits by the impetuous, illegal and unconsidered actions of the Senate.[166]

By thus posing as innocent bystanders, the clergy were able to encourage the Sixty in the belief that the Senate was responsible for the threat to public

---

[161] StAH, Senat, Cl.VII Lit.Hf No.5 Vol.4c, no. 16, 27 June 1746, Wagner to Klefeker.
[162] StAH, Ministerium, II 7, pp. 24–5.
[163] StAH, Senat, Cl.VII Lit.Hf No.5 Vol.4c, nos. 21–4, 9 September 1746, EPS.
[164] Ibid., no. 25, 12 September 1746, Conclusum der Lxger.
[165] Ibid., nos. 21, 33, 7 September, 14 September 1746, orders to the militia.
[166] Ibid., no. 35, a printed summary of Wagner's sermon.

order. Thus, despite last-minute efforts to save the situation, the Sixty remained firm, and on 26 September the Senate declared that, out of 'love of peace', it would order the demolition of the disputed building and the dissolution of the contract between its owner and the Jews.[167]

As Wagner noted in the ministerial minutes, the whole affair had been a remarkable victory. For, without once speaking out in public, the clergy had won their case, and the Senate had been outwitted. All that the clergy had done was to write four long letters. In the end that had proved crucial: for their legal arguments, based on the Jewish legislation of 1650, 1697 and 1710, had proved of great value to the Sixty, who might otherwise not have known where to find the relevant information.[168] Thus the synagogue was pulled down and the owner of the building was paid compensation by the Jews, while a similar, though smaller, project on the Dreckwall was stopped without any discussion at all in November.[169]

Although the battle had been won without resort to violence, the clergy did not, however, emerge as unqualified victors. Their campaign had been fought in private, but news of their uncompromising stand was soon broadcast far beyond the confines of the city. On 18 November, Wagner notified his colleagues that no less a journal than the *Mercure historique* of The Hague had published a notice of the affair in October.[170] The article was obviously based on an accurate insight into what had happened, even if its understanding of the constitutional mechanism was far from penetrating. The synagogue, it wrote, had been approved by the Senate – 'mais sur les representations faites par les ecclesiastiques, dont la haine et la passion de se mêler de tout ne dort jamais, jointes à l'apprehension d'un soulèvement de la part de la populace, animée par les prédicateurs, les juifs ont été obligés de cesser le bâtiment...'[171] It is not clear who wrote the piece or how it got into the *Mercure*. But Wagner suspected it was probably written by someone who knew the situation intimately, and may well have been the work of someone like the Calvinist newspaper editor, Behn, whom Pastor Neumeister suspected of conducting a campaign against the clergy.[172]

The discussions which ensued demonstrated the helplessness of the clergy in the face of such adverse publicity. Wagner himself drafted a reply which stressed that the Jews had synagogues in Altona, and that the constitution of Hamburg did not permit them to worship publicly there.

---

[167] Ibid., no. 71, 26 September 1746, EPS. On 21 September it had been necessary to issue a mandate in order to avoid violence, and this ultimately persuaded the Sixty to remain firm: Blank, *Mandate*, 3, pp. 1585–7.   [168] StAH, Ministerium, II 7, p. 37.

[169] StAH, Senat, Cl.VII Lit.Hf No.5 Vol.4c, nos. 72–4. On the second synagogue see: ibid., Cl. VII Lit.Hf No.5 Vol.4b, *passim*.

[170] StAH, Ministerium, II 7, p. 46.   [171] Ibid.   [172] See Chapter 2, note 62 above.

He pointed out too that the anger of the populace had been spontaneous, and not provoked by the clergy, who had been concerned to keep the peace: 'Everyone knows here,' he wrote, 'that this article lays the blame for such things at the feet of the preachers without any justification and with the greatest injustice.'[173] The formulation of a reply was the least of his problems. The question of how to get it published was far more difficult. Extensive enquiries ultimately found an anonymous messenger willing to hand in the essay.[174] But by June 1747, nothing had appeared, and it was mooted that it might be better to insert it in the Orthodox Lutheran journal at Wittenberg, the *Acta historico-ecclesiastica*, although by then the whole affair was no longer relevant and the article never in fact appeared.[175]

VII

The debates of 1730–4 and 1746 were the last important milestones in the history of the acceptance of the Jews in Hamburg in the eighteenth century. If they demonstrated, as Jonas Ludwig von Hess later claimed, that the Senate was always concerned to show that Jews were human beings, they also demonstrated the limits of toleration. The recognition of the right of the Jews to an economic existence, and the attempt to extend their limited religious liberties, marked the furthest extent of Christian efforts to come to terms with the existence of the Jews. In the seventeenth century their safety was entirely dependent upon the goodwill of the authorities; now their position was theoretically guaranteed in what amounted to a contractual relationship between Christian rulers and Jewish inhabitants.

It was an important advance. But just how little it meant in real terms is illustrated by the fact that, as late as 1744, the Jews in Hamburg were still concerned to reaffirm an agreement with the community in Altona, which allowed them to flee there from Hamburg in the face of persecution.[176] Indeed the Jews themselves seemed to realise how much the Senate's policy was effectively based on the desire to solve the problem of the Danish protectorate. In 1754 and 1768 the Senate failed to persuade first the Jews and then the Danes to dissolve the legal nightmare of the three communities. The Danes were unwilling to see either their sovereignty or the economic position of Altona prejudiced in any way. The Jews clearly appreciated their Danish legal privileges, while, on the other hand, the majority continued

---

[173] StAH, Ministerium, III A2c, nos. 134–5, 137–9, 19 December 1746, Wagner to Greve, with a draft of the official reply.
[174] Ibid., II 7, pp. 49–50, 52–3; ibid., III A2c, nos. 142–3, 19 December, 22 December 1746, Wagner to Greve.
[175] Ibid., II 7, pp. 56, 59, 62, 64, 71, 76–7, 82–3, 90, 92–3.
[176] Grunwald, *Hamburgs deutsche Juden*, p. 52.

to live in Hamburg because of its greater economic opportunities. The Danes thus failed to attract them away from Hamburg; while the Senate equally failed to detach them from Altona.[177]

However, even if this legal and political problem had been solved, it is doubtful whether any further steps would have been taken towards emancipation. There is no evidence that the relatively enlightened attitude of the Senate became any more advanced during the eighteenth century; and there is certainly no indication that popular attitudes to the Jews underwent any change. What at first sight appears to be a more relaxed atmosphere was in fact merely an interlude in which the Jews were placed in a kind of limbo.

Indeed, this is hardly surprising in view of the general ambivalence of enlightened thought in Germany, and indeed elsewhere, towards Judaism. It was, after all, as late as 1754 that Lessing's play *Die Juden* (1749) provoked heated discussion about whether there was such a thing as a good Jew. The first demand for the social and political emancipation of the Jews was only published in 1753. By the later 1770s, such demands appeared more often in journals and pamphlets; while Joseph II's toleration edict of 1781 intensified the discussions already stimulated by C. W. Dohm's *Über die bürgerliche Verbesserung der Juden* (1781).[178] Demands for the complete emancipation of the Jews only became frequent during the 1780s and 1790s, and even then they were often ambivalent. Enlightened observers condemned the intolerance of the Orthodox clergy, but they themselves were unwilling to accept the Jews as Jews. Most, like Wieland, believed that the best way to convert the Jews was to bind them to Christian society by the rule of law. 'Give them freedom,' he wrote, '...and bind them by your laws. Do to them as you would have others do to you!...And see, you too will succeed in bringing them to recognise Him, through Whom we were once assured of the greatest happiness.'[179] For many *Aufklärer*, to tolerate the Jews would have been to give way to religious indifference.

The significance of these debates lies not in their practical impact, but in the fact that they were held at all. For it was a period in which Christian society increasingly became aware of the Jews as a permanent feature of the environment and gradually became concerned to learn more about them. It is also important to remember that very few Jews themselves participated in this debate. Those Jews who, like Moses Mendelssohn, were accepted by polite and educated society, were accepted as individuals rather

---

177 Grunwald, *Aus dem Hamburger Staatsarchiv*, pp. 21–5; Graupe, *Statuten*, 1, pp. 27–8; Brilling, 'Rabbinerstreit', pp. 234–44.

178 Toury, 'Jüdische Problematik', *passim*; Rengstorf, 'Judentum', *passim*; Schoeps, 'Aufklärung', *passim*. See also Kopitzsch, 'Lessing und seine Zeitgenossen', and *Grundzüge*, pp. 505–16.

179 Quoted by Kopitzsch, 'Sozialgeschichte der Aufklärung', p. 92.

than as Jews. Contacts between Jews and Christians were almost exclusively commercial and professional. In only a few places were Jews admitted to Christian schools or universities. Altona, again, was exceptional in this respect, since Jews were regularly admitted to the Gymnasium there after 1778, while in Hamburg Jews were only admitted to the Johanneum after 1802.[180]

While not as advanced as Altona, Hamburg too undoubtedly saw the social emancipation of a few individual Jews during the later eighteenth century. Perhaps the most prominent was the merchant and writer, Moses Wessely, a friend of Lessing, Mendelssohn and Johann Christoph Unzer. But Wessely, like Mendelssohn, represented the enlightened tradition of Judaism whose progressive ideas inspired them to reject the authority of the rabbis and demand a total separation between Church and State.[181]

The extent to which the position of the Jews in general was improved by such theoretical debates and specific personal contacts was, however, limited. Perhaps the most marked feature of the existence of the Jews in Hamburg after 1741 was the absence of open clerical opposition. During the last decade of *Senior* Wagner's period of office no further protests were made, and there is no evidence that the Church concerned itself with the Jews in any way.[182]

Even Johann Melchior Goeze failed to revive the Jewish question in 1763. Goeze had complained about the excesses of the Jews ever since he assumed the office of *Senior* in 1760. In March 1763 he produced one of the longest memorials ever submitted to the Senate by the clergy, complaining that his representations had simply been ignored. The complaints were the traditional ones, but Goeze's arguments showed a significant shift of emphasis. Previous papers by the Church had argued in legal or theological

---

[180] Kopitzsch, 'Jüdische Schüler des Christianeums', *passim*; Freimark, 'Juden und Christen', p. 254.
[181] Graupe, *Entstehung*, pp. 131–4; Kopitzsch, *Grundzüge*, pp. 757–76.
[182] There were two series of events which drew the attention of the public to the Jewish communities. The first, in 1750, concerned the heresy of a recent Jewish convert to Christianity named Eberhard Carl Friedrich Oppenheimer. He not only proclaimed a bewildering variety of millenarian and chiliastic heresies, but also declared that all atheists would be saved; he compounded his misdoings by leading astray his former confessor, Gottfried Bennewitz of Halle. Bennewitz was imprisoned on grounds of insanity; Oppenheimer seems to have sunk into obscurity after being banished from Hamburg. Cf. StAH, Senat, Cl.VII Lit.Hf No.4 Vol.5; ibid., Ministerium, II 7, pp. 184–7; ibid., III A2g, nos. 265–319, 335–52, *Acta historico-ecclesiastica*, 14, pp. 777–89. The second series of events was a dramatic and lengthy conflict between two rabbis in the community which began in 1750 and was only resolved in 1756. The issues involved were extremely complex and have not been studied in detail; but it seems clear that it was, in part at least, a bitter debate about the Sabbatarian legacy, about the extent to which the Jews should gradually adapt their religion and their laws to the environment in which they lived. Cf. Brilling, 'Rabbinerstreit'; Graupe, *Entstehung*, pp. 81–9. Among other things, the dispute was significant for the fact that it provoked the publication of the first poem about a rabbi in German: Brilling, 'Gedicht'. Neither the Oppenheimer affair nor the rabbinical dispute caused a public scandal in Hamburg.

terms: Goeze's letter dwelt at length on the economic situation and attempted to reconcile his own views with those of the Protestant theologians, whose views were so readily quoted by the Senate in 1746.

The argument that the Jews were an economic necessity was, he claimed, a sign of the decay of the polity:

How greatly is Hamburg to be pitied if its condition is such that it must regard the Jews as foundations of its prosperity, and if it must expect its prosperity, abundance and growth to come from this unholy race...Did Hamburg become Hamburg, and up to now remain Hamburg, through the Jews and their usury, or was it not through God's mercy, protection and blessing?

He argued that Jewish money was 'blood money'; their ostentation and arrogance was an affront to Christian society. At the same time, Goeze was careful to stress that he did not disagree with those theologians who now accepted the toleration of the Jews. They themselves, he claimed, had stressed that a tolerant attitude was permissible in so far as it did not extend to a recognition of religious freedom. If the existence of Jewish communities in Christian society was a fact of life, then they should at least be severely limited in the exercise of their religion. Despite his vitriolic condemnations, Goeze did not demand the expulsion of the Jews, but merely insisted that the *Reglement* of 1710 be rigidly enforced. In the last resort his argument rested on weak foundations, for he thus implicitly admitted that the Jews were effectively not a religious problem.[183]

For this reason his complaints met with an indifferent response. The Senate merely pointed out that most Jews did in fact live according to the law, and it did not even bother to discuss Goeze's memorandum in detail.[184] Its only action was to warn the Jews once more, and to point out that it was in their own best interests to live modest and quiet lives.[185] By ignoring the details of Goeze's argument, the Senate thus restricted itself to the role of a mediator, neutralising the claims of the clergy, while attempting to ensure that the Jews themselves did not provoke undue adverse attention. In a sense the issue of the Jews had indeed been secularised at last, reduced to a simple problem of government.

The fate of Goeze's attempt to revive the Edzardische Proselyten-Anstalt after 1760 reflects a similarly indifferent attitude. The Senate participated in the formulation of new statutes in 1761, and donated 100 *taler*, but the Anstalt's efforts were not particularly successful. By 1767 it had once more nearly exhausted its resources, and the Senate refused to permit a general church collection to be made on the occasion of its first centenary.[186]

---

[183] StAH, Senat, Cl.VII Lit.Hb No.3 Vol.13, 18 March 1763, clergy to Senate.
[184] Ibid., 31 October 1763, EPS.
[185] StAH, Senat, Cl.VII Lit.Lb No.18 Vol.1n, 2 November 1763, EPS.
[186] Ibid., Cl.VII Lit.Hf No.5 Vol.5a Fasc.2, *passim*.

Between 1762 and 1783, only forty-nine persons were converted (only twenty-two in the period 1784–1803), and many if not most of them seem to have been either poor or criminal, more in search of alms than salvation. City dignitaries continued to donate small sums periodically but nothing comparable to the amounts that Edzardi had collected in the late seventeenth century.[187] The reasons were probably twofold. Once the Jews were accepted as commercial partners, the desire to convert them declined; while the sheer size of the community (approximately 4,500 by 1764)[188] inevitably placed the role of such an institution in a different light. Its small scale and limited resources now made the Anstalt more a tribute to civic piety than a significant vehicle for the solution of the Jewish problem.

Goeze's failure to make any headway, either with his complaints against the Jews or with their conversion, effectively marked the end of the Church's struggle to preserve the purity of Lutheran society by limiting or expelling at least this non-Christian element. His failure illuminated yet another area of public life where the concerns of Church and State were diametrically opposed. The claim of the Church to act as moral arbiter was replaced by the provisions of a secular authority concerned with the material welfare of the community.

However, while in the case of the Catholics and Calvinists the Senate was later able to draw the logical conclusion by granting freedom of worship, it did not do this with the Jews. Indeed there is in fact no evidence to suggest that any further freedom for the Jews was even discussed before the 1790s. Groups like that in Altona, which discussed and attempted to act upon C. W. Dohm's famous tract of 1781, do not seem to have existed in Hamburg.[189]

The obstacles to any further progress were still great. For if the clerical opposition had been silenced, many of the views expressed by Goeze were still vehemently represented by the Civic Colleges during the last decades of the eighteenth century. The College of the Sixty took up the cause where Goeze had failed. In 1764 the Sixty took the unusual step of initiating negotiations with the Senate itself, instead of waiting to be approached as the constitution demanded.[190] If the Senate was unwilling to investigate the claims of the clergy, then the College felt itself to be 'obliged by our

---

[187] Gleiss, *Edzardi*, p. 50; StAH, Edzardische Proselyten-Anstalt, B 2 and B 3. The *Anstalt* continued to function until it was dissolved by the National Socialists in 1942. Cf. Graupe, *Entstehung*, p. 75. A foundation of that name still exists today.

[188] Grunwald, *Hamburgs deutsche Juden*, p. 60.

[189] Kopitzsch, 'Jüdische Schüler des Christianeums', *passim*. By 1783 the synagogue in Altona was even recommended to tourists in a guide to Hamburg written by Johann Peter Willebrandt, *Polizeidirektor* in Altona until 1771: Willebrandt, *Vermehrte Nachrichten*, pp. 124–5. On Willebrandt, see Schröder, *Lexikon*, 8, pp. 48–50; *ADB*, 43, pp. 261–2.

[190] StAH, Senat, Cl.VII Lit.Lb No.18 Vol.2c3, 20 January 1764, Conclusum der Lxger.

office to make this representation to the Senate about the excesses of the Jews, which are known throughout the whole city'. In particular, the Sixty protested against the fact that the Jews were buying houses in expensive streets in the west of the city, a fact which had been the subject of petitions by groups of citizens since 1758. The obviously prosperous inhabitants (one group included a cousin of the Syndic Johann Klefeker) who sent these petitions were above all concerned with the impact which the proximity of Jews would have on house prices. As one group put it: 'Without wishing to succumb to vituperation, it is possible to assert without dispute that cleanliness is not exactly the characteristic of the Jewish nation.'[191]

At the root of the problem lay the usual legal ambiguities. For although there had never been a clearly-defined ghetto in Hamburg, it had always been understood that the Jews would live close together in narrow streets in order to avoid public disturbances. Similarly, like other foreigners, the Jews had not been permitted to own houses, merely to enter into contracts whereby a citizen might buy a house on their behalf (*ad manus fideles*). Although not mentioned in the *Reglement* of 1710, these provisions had been renewed by the *Bürgerschaft* in 1723 and 1733.[192] The Sixty now insisted that, since these decisions were still valid, the Jews should be deprived of those properties whose freehold they had acquired, and that they should be restricted to those streets in which they had traditionally lived. The result in 1768 was the institution of what amounted to an informal ghetto when a list of nineteen streets (fourteen in the Neustadt and five in the Altstadt) in which the Jews should live was drawn up.[193] Like all such provisions previously, this one was soon ignored. Even so, in 1770, the Sixty once more insisted that it would not contemplate any change in official policy. They did not do so until the *Reichskammergericht* declared their restrictions illegal in June 1801.[194]

Where the power of the clergy faltered after 1760, the intricacies of the constitution thus intervened to prevent any substantial change in the position of the Jews in Hamburg. To the last, the Civic Colleges remained alert to any obvious infringements of the labyrinthine statutes concerning the Jews: their freedom to trade was contested by the guilds; their freedom to live where they wanted was contested by the Sixty; and in 1789 their freedom to worship in public was once more contested by the *Oberalten*.[195] The opposition of the citizens bore little fruit since the regulations were

---

[191] Ibid., Cl.VII Lit.Lb No.18 Vol.2a2, 2 October 1758, August Wilhelm Schwalbe et Consorten to Senate. Further petitions may be found in ibid., Cl.VII Lit.Lb No.18 Vol.2c3.

[192] Kühl, *Raths- und Bürger-Schlüsse*, pp. 52, 63.

[193] Levy, *Rechtsstellung*, pp. 26–7. Levy only gives sixteen streets, but the lists drawn up in 1771 and 1773 give nineteen: StAH, Senat, Cl.VII Lit.Lb No.18 Vol.2a2 and ibid., Vol. 2c3.

[194] Levy, *Rechtsstellung*, p. 27. See also: Kopitzsch, *Grundzüge*, pp. 502–4.

[195] StAH, Senat, Cl.VII Lit.Hf No.5 Vol.4f, *passim*.

capable of such varied interpretations. But all the same it is significant that it was still worthwhile to enter into debates about whether Jews had or had not once been permitted to live in certain streets, or whether a synagogue was private or public. If in some senses these were symbolic disputes about mere words, they only barely disguised a deep fount of prejudice, envy and hatred which neither legislation nor the liberal policies of the Senate could diminish.

For in the last resort, the toleration of the Jews in the eighteenth century simply meant that one ceased to persecute them. And Goeze was right when he had claimed in 1763 that the main motive in this was not Christian charity and moderation but mercantile cupidity. As the long and bitter struggle over Jewish emancipation in the nineteenth century was to show, the translation of economic functions into human values was both difficult and ultimately unsuccessful.[196]

---

[196] Cf. Voigt, *Rückblick*, pp. 6–8; Krohn, *Juden in Hamburg*, pp. 55–78; Zimmermann, *Hamburgischer Patriotismus, passim*. The legal emancipation of the Jews in Hamburg was effected in February 1849; the Jewish community as a whole was only formally recognised as a *Religionsverband* in November 1864. Cf. Krohn, *Juden in Hamburg*, pp. 73–4, and Kopitzsch, *Grundzüge*, pp. 515–16.

4

The growth of toleration: the Calvinist communities

The history of the gradual acceptance of the Catholics and Jews demonstrates two extremes of the experience of religious minorities in Hamburg. The Catholics were tolerated almost exclusively because of the city's perennial dependence on their patron, the Holy Roman Emperor. Political and diplomatic factors predominated, while the economic considerations, which had led to the initial acceptance of Catholic merchants in the period around 1600, diminished in importance as the community lost its mercantile character. Social isolation and poverty, rather than wealth and status, characterised the Catholic community after about 1630. In the case of the Jews, who lacked an official Imperial or princely patron, economic factors were of crucial importance; they continuously played an important economic role, even though the character of the community changed considerably with the decline of the original Sephardic element and the increasing predominance of the Ashkenazim. For the Jews supplied skills and trades which did not on the whole compete with those of the citizens of Hamburg, and which made a valuable contribution to the urban economy. It was the recognition of this fact which stimulated the efforts of the 1730s and 1740s to find a more satisfactory solution to the synagogue issue.

Attitudes to neither group, however, ever went substantially beyond the desire for a more clearly defined legal relationship. Despite the periodic accusations and recriminations of the clergy, it cannot be said that the Senate ever contemplated anything other than a *modus vivendi* which would in the one case placate the Emperor and in the other prevent the Jews deserting the city in favour of its nearby Danish competitor, Altona. Enlightened and progressive though it may have been in some respects, the official mind shared many of the religious prejudices of its subjects and the clergy. The Catholic presence conjured up disturbing images of the dark papal past of the Middle Ages, to which the very constitution of the city was an explicit antithesis. The religion of the Jews was so alien that any open concession to it might be construed as a manifestation of religious indifference. The conflict between the progressive ideology of the Senate and the tradition-bound Orthodoxy of the clergy was often glaring. But both in their different ways were fundamentally agreed that Protestant Christianity, in a more or less clearly defined reformed Lutheran tradition, provided the best framework for the felicitous development of human society in general and Hamburg in particular.

Such limitations, the result of both prejudice and practical calculation, did not apply to the third significant minority group, the Calvinist community. As Klefeker remarked in 1770: 'No people who have come here have been so favoured...as those who fled the Netherlands on grounds of religion.'[1] The Dutch Calvinists who came to Hamburg in the last two decades of the sixteenth century, and their co-religionists, the Huguenots, who arrived after the revocation of the Edict of Nantes in October 1685, enjoyed greater status and were more privileged than any other group.

Wealth and commercial expertise accounted for much of this. While both the Catholic and Jewish communities changed in character soon after the initial immigration, the Calvinists maintained their original mercantile activities. And, in a city where high status was defined either in terms of legal learning or, more usually, in terms of commercial success, the Calvinists became more obviously indispensable in the eyes of those concerned with the condition of the urban economy; and they were assimilated to its society by marriage to an unusual degree.[2] To some extent this process was facilitated by the fact that the Dutch community originally consisted of both Lutherans and Calvinists. Both groups were included in the first contract of 1605, but the Lutherans rapidly entered the Hamburg elite, and by the late seventeenth century already held prestigious civic offices. Indeed, as Heinrich Reincke has noted, to be able to prove Dutch ancestry was for many the republican equivalent of noble status.[3] And although the religious issue was divisive, common ethnic origins undoubtedly served to reinforce the acceptability of the Calvinists, who shared so many of the cultural and political values of the urban elite.

These affinities were compounded by more obvious economic factors. The Iberian and colonial trade of the Dutch transformed the Hamburg economy. Their expertise in commercial matters had a profound effect on the organisation of economic affairs and was instrumental in the establishment of the Hamburg Bank in 1619.[4] The Huguenots made a similar

---

[1] Klefeker, *Verfassungen*, 8, p. 367.
[2] Ibid., p. 802: Hauschild-Thiessen, *Armen-Casse*, pp. 14–40; *idem*, 'Johann Berenberg', *passim*.
[3] Quoted by Schellenberg, *Hamburg und Holland*, p. 14. Cf. Klefeker, *Verfassungen*, 2, p. 301; Kellenbenz, *Unternehmerkräfte*, p. 180; Schilling, *Exulanten*, p. 158.
[4] Kellenbenz, *Unternehmerkräfte*, pp. 179–81, 236–8; Büsch, *Handlung*, pp. 28–9; Sieveking, 'Hamburger Bank', pp. 26, 30.

impact. Though less numerous than their Dutch counterparts, they too brought with them both trading contacts and skills. The flourishing French trade proved one of the mainstays of the Hamburg economy after about 1730.[5] Individuals like Pierre His and Pierre Boué ranked among the most prosperous merchants of the eighteenth century, endowed with fabulous wealth, international contacts and the sumptuous lifestyle of merchant princes, which aroused the studious admiration of indigenous merchants even if it incensed the clergy, who claimed that men like them were depriving ordinary citizens of prosperity and opportunities.[6]

It would, however, be misleading to give the impression that all Calvinists were both wealthy and successful. While this is largely true of the smaller Huguenot community, which by 1777 consisted of just over 200 souls,[7] the Dutch community was far more differentiated, and it is more difficult to make accurate statements about it.[8] Estimates of the size of the community range between 1,000 and 2,000 in about 1600.[9] By 1700, the number of communicants in the Church had reached about 3,500, while after the 1720s this figure declined to about 1,100 by 1770.[10] Several problems arise regarding these figures: before 1716, when the consistory was based in Altona, they include residents of both places, and, although it is often said that the wealthiest lived in Hamburg, precise information does not

---

[5] Huhn, 'Handelsbeziehungen', 1, pp. 13–26, 157–94, 205–7, 213–14; Büsch, *Handlung*, pp. 72–7, 98–102; Jeannin, 'Hansestädte', *passim*.

[6] Schramm, 'Zwei "Millionäre"', pp. 29–40; Huhn, 'Handelsbeziehungen', 1, pp. 167–9.

[7] Boué, 'Abriss', p. 17; Schramm, 'Zwei "Millionäre"', pp. 29–32.

[8] For the sake of clarity, I have used the term 'Dutch community' throughout. Contemporary sources refer to both a 'Dutch' and a 'German' community, but the distinction was in fact largely artificial; it arose out of the heterogeneous ethnic and linguistic nature of what only later became the Deutsch-evangelisch-reformierte Gemeinde. Although divisions did undoubtedly exist, and in the 1790s a Dutch group still travelled from Hamburg to worship in Altona (J. L. von Hess, *Hamburg*, 2nd edn, 3, p. 263), there was in fact only one 'Dutch'/'German' community until the split into Altona and Hamburg groups in 1716 (Bolten, *Kirchen-Nachrichten von Altona*, 1, p. 204). Each community thus descended from the original sixteenth-century Dutch exile Church, but also included subsequent immigrants both from the Netherlands and from the German territories. The language spoken by all elements was a mixture of Low German and Dutch dialects, the difference in the spoken language being minimal, but in the written language increasingly pronounced during the seventeenth century (Schilling, 'Calvinistische Presbyterien', p. 411, note 100b). Only much later did ethnic differences lead to the partition of 1716, and ultimately to conflicts within the Hamburg community itself: the more culturally and linguistically assimilated groups wished to dispense with the services of a native Dutch preacher in favour of one who spoke High German; until then the community had employed two preachers, one Dutch and one German (Hermes, *Reformierte Gemeinde*, pp. 94–105, 156–9). Similarly complex divisions are found in Dutch cities of the same period: in Leyden after 1644 there were no less than four distinct Calvinist communities – the Low German (*Nederduits*), the Walloon (*Waals*), the High German and the English Reformed Churches. Cf. Schilling, 'Calvinistische Presbyterien', pp. 409, 411.

[9] Schilling, *Exulanten*, p. 178.

[10] StAH, Senat, Cl.VII Lit.Hf No.2a Vol.13 – an undated list enclosed in the supplementary papers probably compiled in 1777.

exist. Secondly, the community was in an almost continual state of flux: the available lists of foreign merchants for the seventeenth century show that new families continually replaced others who left either for other places or to return to the Netherlands.[11] In the eighteenth century too, many merchants left for a variety of reasons – some undoubtedly for fear of persecution in Hamburg, and others in search of better opportunities in London and Amsterdam.[12] Thirdly, the lists of merchants who remained in the *Fremdenkontrakt* do not take account of those who chose to take up citizenship without political rights, for whom no reliable figures exist.[13] In addition, many families, like that of the late-eighteenth-century merchant Peter Keetmann, seemed to live a permanently peripatetic existence, dividing their time between periods of residence in Hamburg and in various parts of the Netherlands.[14] Those who, like the Keetmanns, were included in the *Fremdenkontrakt* formed the core of the community – ranging in size from 131 in 1605, to 160 in 1639, to 195 in 1731 (though this list also includes Huguenots). With an average family size of five or six they thus account for a group of up to about 2,000.[15] We also know that many of the original immigrants were poor artisans, while in the eighteenth century some were involved in printing and publishing and other trades.[16]

Even this rather unsatisfactory and obscure statistical situation allows certain conclusions. Unlike the Catholics, the Calvinists maintained a substantial mercantile presence in Hamburg after the 1630s and 1640s. Wealth, literacy and an appropriate lifestyle distinguished Calvinists from both the majority of the Catholics and the Ashkenazic Jews. The relative and qualitative importance of their contribution to the economy became obvious enough to justify efforts to secure their position in the city and, after 1770, to stimulate efforts to undertake a radical change in religious policy.

That transformation, however, lay in the future. It was very much the product of a new situation after about 1760, characterised primarily by a profound economic crisis. Until then attitudes to the Calvinists were ambivalent. Despite their cultural and economic respectability, in the eyes

---

[11] Reissmann, *Kaufmannschaft*, pp. 215, 243–4.

[12] Ibid., pp. 243–4; fear of persecution is mentioned in an undated report in the hand of Syndic Matsen in the supplementary papers to StAH, Senat Cl.VII Lit.Hf No.2a Vol.13.

[13] The *Fremdenkontrakt* defined the status of those foreign residents in the city who neither enjoyed diplomatic immunity nor wished to commit themselves to full citizenship. It was largely concerned with merchants and tradesmen. Poor people simply became *Schutzverwandte*, like the Jews, a low status which precluded them from exercising any regular craft or trade. Cf. Klefeker, *Verfassungen*, 2, p. 312; Reissmann, *Kaufmannschaft*, pp. 130, 231–6.

[14] Keetmann, 'Lebenserinnerungen', pp. 135–6.

[15] Reissmann, *Kaufmannschaft*, p. 215; the 1731 list is in StAH, Senat, Cl.VII Lit.Cc No.2 Vol.1 Fasc.1.

[16] Beneke, 'Eingewanderte Reformierte', *passim*; Hauschild-Thiessen, *Armen-Casse*, pp. 14–40; Barrelet, 'Liebeswesen', *passim*.

of many they posed a more pernicious, if less obvious, threat to the purity of Lutheranism than the Catholics. Indeed, as late as 1758, Michael Richey felt obliged to warn that the 'inevitable fear of an overweening papism serves to keep those alert who do not want to believe in the possibility of an overweening Calvinism. For they might otherwise be inclined to grant the Calvinists more than is allowed by the example of our blessed forebears, and they might thus endanger the security of the Protestant [i.e. Lutheran] religion.'[17] He argued forcefully against the view that limited toleration of the Calvinists had brought overwhelming economic advantages:

As if Hamburg would never have become Hamburg if it had only contained and accepted Protestant [i.e. Lutheran] inhabitants. A man will be able to make a fair judgement of this if he has an accurate insight into the history of our state and its trade, and if he does not confuse the occasional windfalls from adventurers with the best and most constant fund of wealth in the possession of the citizenry.[18]

The argument was somewhat dubious, since Richey was forced to admit that the Lutheran Dutch had indeed made a significant contribution to both trade and urban administration. But whatever its inaccuracies, his statement is remarkable for the affinities it revealed with the arguments of the clergy. Richey, one of the members of the first Patriotic Society, was here as concerned as clergymen like Erdmann Neumeister or later Johann Melchior Goeze to maintain strict legal limitations on religious freedom for non-Lutherans. He wished to prevent his contemporaries from being blinded by what he saw as materialist and indifferentist arguments which would inevitably undermine the religious constitution of the city.

It was precisely this sense of ambivalence and unease which the clergy were able to exploit to great effect for over a century. They regarded the Calvinists with even greater suspicion than any other group. The fact that a substantial section of the community was affluent, cultured and literate, the fact that they were eloquent and articulate victims of persecution, gave them a privileged place in a city where commercial success was the prime yardstick of status, and which had made freedom and tolerance into a republican ideology. But, as the clergy were quick to point out, they were rarely passive recipients of Christian charity. The history of other German cities amply demonstrated the corrosive effects of Calvinist political radicalism. In the late sixteenth century their arrival had transformed the political life of Emden, Wesel and Aachen.[19] In 1561, Bremen had been taken over by a Calvinist elite, the Lutherans being expelled from the city council and from the major city churches. Lübeck, it was continually pointed out, had avoided such a fate by resolutely refusing to grant more than minimal privileges.[20] In the eighteenth century, Frankfurt was thrown

---

[17] StAH, Hss No. 273, Richey, Anmerckungen, ad pag. 259.   [18] Ibid., ad pag. 258.
[19] Schilling, *Exulanten, passim.*
[20] On Bremen see *RGG*, 1, cols. 1395–6; on Lübeck see *RGG*, 4, cols. 467–70.

into turmoil by the desire of powerful Calvinist mercantile groups to obtain constitutional rights and political parity with the original Lutheran population.[21] The moral was drawn succinctly by the Senate in its reply to the *Oberalten* over the synagogue issue in 1648: 'One need fear no seduction on the part of the Jews, while Calvinism always takes root.'[22]

Fears that special concessions to the Calvinists might ultimately undermine the Lutheran constitution were compounded by efforts, made in the late seventeenth and early eighteenth centuries, to effect a union between Lutheranism and Calvinism in Germany. Hamburg was not directly involved in these negotiations, which were motivated both by theological universalism and by the practical political aim of preserving the constitutional position of Protestantism in an Empire ruled by a Catholic Emperor. But Lutheran apologists such as Sebastian Edzardi and Erdmann Neumeister were quick to take up the offensive, and to claim that Prussian and Hanoverian ecumenicalism was but the thin end of the wedge: to condone such a movement would logically lead to a concession to the Calvinists in Hamburg.

Political adroitness, a greater theological compatibility (especially accentuated in the period 1700–30), wealth and culture – all account for the fact that the Lutheran clergy met their match in the Calvinist community. For most of the seventeenth century, however, the battlelines were far from clearly drawn. Unlike the Catholics, backed by the Emperor, the Calvinists had no obvious patron. It was only after 1716 that the efforts of the Dutch and Prussian Residents succeeded in providing official diplomatic protection for the Dutch and Huguenot communities. Even then they achieved no more in legal terms than the Imperial Residents. Despite the effective use of newspaper propaganda after 1720, facilitated both by the fact that one of their community was himself a publisher and by their close contacts with printing entrepreneurs in Holland and Berlin, the Calvinists gained no more formal concessions before 1760 than any other group. If Klefeker was right in asserting that they were more favourably accepted and accommodated than any others, this lenience was manifested in spirit rather than in fact. Cogent arguments for radical change were only found by an enlightened elite in the last decades of the eighteenth century. That group first questioned fundamental assumptions which liberal politicians before 1700 – and even the progressive first Patriotic Society – had accepted as the *sine qua non* of the civic and ecclesiastical polity.

[21] Cf. Soliday, *Community in conflict*, esp. pp. 208–30. The histories of Bremen, Lübeck and Frankfurt provided later clergymen with their main arguments against the Calvinists. Cf. Goeze, *Zeugniss*, *passim*.
[22] Quoted by Grunwald, *Hamburgs deutsche Juden*, p. 9.

I

Unlike the Huguenots of the seventeenth century, the Flemish and Walloon merchants and artisans who began to leave the Netherlands in the 1520s and 1530s entered a perilously uncertain and strife-ridden confessional world.[23] Shortly after the inception of Luther's Reformation, but long before the emergence of clearly-defined dogmatic canons, it was by no means clear where they would choose to go – whether to London, or to one of the many German cities or states. The exiles themselves reflected this fluidity. Some were Catholics, driven out by economic depression and harsh Spanish taxation; others were Lutherans, Anabaptists and, later, Calvinists, fleeing from religious persecution and in search of security.[24]

The choice of the place of exile was made more difficult by the deeply ambivalent reactions of many of the receiving authorities. These governments were themselves often caught up in bitter religious and political conflicts which resulted from the introduction of new gospels. The advent of yet more problems in the shape of exiles about whose religion little was known often engendered caution and suspicion, which conflicted with the desire to attract artisans and merchants with valuable skills and contacts.

This dilemma was particularly evident in Hamburg after 1566.[25] The Reformation was introduced peacefully in 1529 and the reform of urban institutions proceeded smoothly thereafter. But the content of the new faith was not worked out until, in 1560 and 1563, the Senate itself intervened to impose a religious solution upon the divided clergy.[26] For some decades afterwards it was concerned to maintain that equilibrium, and this concern inevitably influenced its attitudes to foreigners whose beliefs might inflame the strident preachers and their excitable congregations. Two further factors inhibited a straightforward liberal policy: until the 1590s the clergy were able to rely on the resistance of the guilds, particularly the weavers and shopkeepers, to outside competition (although some new branches like the textile trade and sugar refining posed no problems); external pressures were also applied by the Hanseatic League, which like the guilds still held to traditional monopolistic policies.[27]

Caution with regard to religious stability and economic policy are clearly revealed in the reactions to the first attempts by foreigners to settle in Hamburg. When the Calvinist community headed by Johannes a Lasco was

---

23 Schilling, *Exulanten*, p. 21.   24 Ibid.
25 Ibid., pp. 22–3, 36, 122–3; Roosbroeck, 'Niederlassung'.
26 Cf. Klefeker, *Verfassungen*, 8, pp. 32–76; Klemenz, *Religionsunterricht*, pp. 43–6; Postel, 'Bedeutung der Reformation', *passim*.
27 Schilling, *Exulanten*, pp. 36–7, 77–9, 157–8. The Hanseatic League ceased to be effective after the 1590s, however, and was all but destroyed by the Thirty Years War. Cf. Dollinger, *German Hansa*, pp. 362–9.

expelled from London in September 1553 after the death of Edward VI, it migrated first to Copenhagen, from where representatives were sent to Hamburg to request permission for residence. Lasco had already been embroiled in a theological controversy over the communion with the Hamburg Pastor, Joachim Westphal, who in March 1554 induced the Senate to pass a decree expelling the foreigners. Lasco and his followers were obliged to leave, and they ultimately found sanctuary in Frankfurt am Main and Hanau.[28]

The Anglican Merchants Adventurers, who left Antwerp in 1566, met with a more favourable reception. Largely unopposed by the clergy, the merchants were able to conclude a ten-year contract with the Senate, which allowed them to transfer their cloth staple to Hamburg.[29] This move, however, met with opposition from the other Hanseatic cities at their conference in 1572.[30] Five years later the contract was not renewed, and the Adventurers dispersed to Emden, Elbing, and Stade (after 1587). Only in 1611 did they return to Hamburg with a new contract which gave them both economic privileges and religious freedom – the latter recognised by the clergy in 1617 when they decided that the Anglicans were not to be equated with the Calvinists.[31]

Both the London community and the Merchants Adventurers were relatively closed groups. They could be dealt with *en bloc*; this fact accounts for the straightforward rejection of the first, and the short-lived attempt to make concessions to the second. The Dutch immigrants, who began to arrive in the late 1560s, and in greater numbers after 1585, were however a different matter.[32] Some were Lutheran, others Calvinist, or possibly Anabaptist. They spoke different languages and were masters of different crafts and trades. Above all, the fact that they came as individuals or in small scattered groups at successive intervals gradually enabled the Senate to find a way through the opposition of guilds and clergy.

In 1569 Herman Rodenbroch, an Amsterdam cloth manufacturer, was granted an individual contract. It allowed him the freedom to set up a factory in Hamburg and freed him from restrictive guild regulations.[33] But clerical opposition soon halted this liberal policy. In 1569 a decree against Calvinist heretics was renewed, and in 1572 a further decree ruled that Dutch exiles who refused to convert to Lutheranism must leave the city

[28] Hermes, *Reformierte Gemeinde*, pp. 5–7; Schilling, *Exulanten*, pp. 22–3, 36, 122; Mönckeberg, 'Ausweisung der Englischen Exulanten', *passim*; R. Kayser, 'Johannes a Lasco', *passim*.
[29] Hitzigrath, *Merchants Adventurers*, p. 1; Schilling, *Exulanten*, pp. 39, 77.
[30] Sillem, 'Niederländer', pp. 557–8; Klefeker, *Verfassungen*, 2, pp. 296–7.
[31] Sillem, 'Niederländer', pp. 557–8; Hitzigrath, *Merchants Adventurers*, pp. 1–4; Hermes, *Reformierte Gemeinde*, pp. 8–9; Klefeker, *Verfassungen*, 2, pp. 297–9; ibid., 8, pp. 366–7.
[32] Sillem, 'Niederländer', pp. 501–3.
[33] Lappenberg, 'Ansiedlung der Niederländer', pp. 243–7; Schilling, *Exulanten*, p. 36.

by the following year.[34] On the intercession of William of Orange, the ultimatum was never carried out.[35] But the position of the Dutch was not improved. During the 1570s and 1580s the clergy instituted a series of inquisitions against the newcomers, during which even the Lutheran Dutch were often accused of Crypto-Calvinism. It is, however, a testimony to the persistence of the Senate that no action was taken; a decree issued in 1586 merely encouraged the Dutch to take an oath of loyalty to the city, and warned that any attempt to proselytise their religion would be punished severely.[36]

The Dutch themselves found the interim solution which secured their position. The establishment of a consistory in nearby Stade in 1588 allowed them to live in Hamburg while worshipping outside the city. Services held in French, Dutch and German satisfied the wishes of the Hamburg contingent, while in 1590 the consistory appointed a *consolateur des malades* to minister to them in their homes.[37] The physical removal of the religious issue from the city gave the Senate the opportunity to mollify the clergy while beginning to drive a wedge between them and the guilds. Although a petition of 1590, requesting greater freedom for the Dutch, had little effect, the authorities seem to have continued their efforts to persuade them to enter into a more formal contractual relationship with the city.[38] But the immigrants refused to take up any form of citizenship, since this would have prejudiced their religious integrity. The result in 1605 was a ten-year contract whereby 130 merchants promised loyalty to the city authorities and the payment of all ordinary taxes in return for the Senate's protection of their right to pursue their livelihoods.[39]

The contract did not mention religion. But here too changes had taken place. By 1599 the Senate felt secure enough to step out openly in favour of the Calvinists. In order to avert the passions of the clergy and the anger of the populace, Senators attended two Calvinist burials.[40] This unofficial protection was the prelude to another major change which was to determine the situation of the Calvinist community for the next century. Ultimately dissatisfied with the inconvenience of having to travel to Stade in order to

[34] Sillem, 'Niederländer', p. 560.
[35] Beneke, 'Nichtlutherische Christen', pp. 319–20. William of Orange's letter is printed in Klefeker, *Verfassungen*, 8, pp. 445–7.
[36] The reports on the inquisitions are printed in Beneke, 'Nichtlutherische Christen', pp. 325–44; the mandate of 1586 is printed ibid., p. 321.
[37] Sillem, 'Niederländer', pp. 562–4; Hermes, *Reformierte Gemeinde*, pp. 18–20.
[38] Sillem, 'Niederländer', p. 560; Klefeker, *Verfassungen*, 2, pp. 299–300; Schilling, *Exulanten*, pp. 41–2.
[39] Reissmann, *Kaufmannschaft*, pp. 215, 231–2; Schilling, *Exulanten*, pp. 41–2, 78–9.
[40] Ziegra, *Sammlung*, 4, pp. 469–70; Schilling, *Exulanten*, p. 39; Roosbroeck, 'Niederlassung', pp. 69–70. The general significance of burials is analysed more fully in Whaley, 'Symbolism for the survivors', pp. 85–6.

worship, the Hamburg community applied to the Count of Schaumburg in 1601 for the right to build a church in Altona. The request was granted in 1602 after the intercession of *Landgraf* Maurice of Hesse-Cassel and the Estates General of Holland.[41] Again, both clergy and guilds protested vigorously: they obliged the Senate to remonstrate with the Count, and to embody in the constitution of 1603 a clause forbidding Hamburg residents to attend church services in Altona. Their protest was motivated by primarily political and economic concerns since it was apparent that Altona was already a potential commercial rival of its larger neighbour. But the Count rightly pointed out that, since Catholics and Jews had already been granted similar privileges, there was really no case to answer.[42] Indeed, the Senate itself showed little interest in pursuing the matter. No further action was taken; the religious issue was not mentioned in the contract of 1605; and a renewed publication of the mandate against heretics of 1535 was a private initiative of the clergy, and thus had no official validity.[43]

As far as the Senate was concerned, a major battle had been won by 1605. Despite clerical opposition, it had successfully reversed both traditional guild and Hanse policies. While the Dutch were not full citizens, they had been brought into a satisfactory legal relationship with the city, which now profited from their wealth, expertise and international commercial networks. The Dutch too were satisfied. They were not obliged to compromise their religion; and while they paid taxes like any others, they were free from the obligations of military service, and also free to leave the city without paying any of the customary tributes imposed on full citizens who wished to emigrate.[44] The contract was renewed in 1615, and again in 1639 (with effect from Easter 1638), when a permanent commission was established to register and tax all new arrivals.[45]

Faced with a *fait accompli*, the Lutheran clergy could do little. Their only bone of contention after 1605 was the issue of Calvinist burials in Lutheran churches. In 1614 they protested vigorously that heretics should not be allowed this privilege; but a further protest in 1617 merely had the effect of producing another compromise. The Calvinists were permitted to bury their dead in the Cathedral, which did not come under the jurisdiction of the city clergy.[46]

[41] Sillem, 'Niederländer', pp. 573–8; Schilling, *Exulanten*, pp. 39, 123–5; Roosbroeck, 'Niederlassung', pp. 72–5.

[42] Sillem, 'Niederländer', pp. 578–82; Hermes, *Reformierte Gemeinde*, pp. 25–8. The Stade community survived until 1619, when its remaining members migrated to Hamburg: Bolten, *Kirchen-Nachrichten von Altona*, 1, p. 199.   [43] Sillem, 'Niederländer', pp. 582–3.

[44] Reissmann, *Kaufmannschaft*, pp. 231–2; Klefeker, *Verfassungen*, 2, pp. 299–300.

[45] Ibid., p. 301; Hauschild-Thiessen, *Armen-Casse*, pp. 41–3.

[46] Ziegra, *Sammlung*, 4, pp. 470–3. The Cathedral belonged to the Duchy of Bremen and Verden and, together with the Duchy, was ceded to Hanover in 1719. Cf. Otto, *Domstift*, pp. 16–32. See also note 40 above.

Continued sporadic protests during the 1620s and 1630s, during which the clergy sought support from prestigious theological faculties outside Hamburg, brought no change. The Senate continued to support the Dutch and ignored the complaints of the clergy. Indeed in 1633 it refused to print an opinion given by the theologians of Leipzig, on the grounds that the issue was fundamentally a political one and thus nothing to do with religion at all.[47]

Yet at the same time official policy was strictly legalistic. This was clearly demonstrated in the reaction to the attempts made in 1635 and 1644–5 to establish a Calvinist church in Hamburg itself. On both occasions the move was initiated by the Calvinists themselves who felt increasingly threatened by the marauding troops involved in the Thirty Years War. In 1633 the matter was hardly discussed at all, since the Lutheran clergy in Hamburg launched a bitter campaign against the proposal from the start. Their opposition was reinforced by the *Oberalten*, who in April and June 1634 demanded harsh measures against Calvinist services in the city.[48] In 1644–5 negotiations were more protracted. For, in addition to the difficulties which the Calvinists claimed to have in reaching their chapel in Altona, the existence of a permanent Dutch Resident in Hamburg since 1640 gave the matter a greater complexity.[49] Attendance at the services held in his house in 1641 provoked bitter protests and denunciations by the clergy and by *Senior* Müller. This does not seem to have deterred the Calvinists, who appealed to Holland for support. The magistrates in Amsterdam summoned the Lutheran pastors of their own city to discuss the situation, while the magistrates in Zwolle apparently applied pressure amounting to blackmail on the Lutherans there. The resulting flurry of mutual recriminations brought no solution.[50] The clergy stood by their solemn oath of January 1644 to resist unequivocally the establishment of a Calvinist church in Hamburg, and in September the Senate issued a mandate warning the Dutch Resident that public services in his house would not be tolerated.[51] The services did, however, continue, especially well-attended after May 1645, when the Altona church was destroyed by fire and not rebuilt until the end of the year.[52]

Although the attempt to establish a public place of worship failed, the Calvinists had by 1645 achieved a position similar to that of the Catholics. Their consistory was still based in Altona, but services were possible in Hamburg in the Dutch Resident's house. The difference was that the latter were not fully recognised either by the clergy or by the Senate; and this

[47] Ziegra, *Sammlung*, 4, pp. 473–4.
[48] Hermes, *Reformierte Gemeinde*, pp. 42–3.   [49] Ibid., pp. 57–61.
[50] The correspondence is printed in Ziegra, *Sammlung*, 4, pp. 521–90.
[51] Hermes, *Reformierte Gemeinde*, pp. 58–60.   [52] Ibid., pp. 50–1, 60–1.

resulted from the fact that Calvinism was still, even in terms of Imperial law, regarded as a sect, in contrast to the Catholic and Lutheran faiths recognised by the Peace of Augsburg in 1555.[53]

II

The Peace of Westphalia finally recognised the formal existence of the Calvinist faith in the *Reich*. It guaranteed the Calvinists protection against persecution, and gave them rights similar to those enjoyed by Catholics and Lutherans. However, although the implications of this change were pointed out forcefully in a letter written to the Senate by the Great Elector in April 1649, the position of the Calvinists in Hamburg did not improve immediately.[54] Officially, they were free to exercise their religion publicly in Altona; but in Hamburg itself they were merely allowed to worship in the privacy of their own homes.[55]

Just how much use they made of these privileges, and the extent to which they attempted to exploit them by using diplomatic protection is unclear. Until 1685 services seem to have been held periodically under the aegis of the Dutch Resident, while other small groups congregated in houses belonging either to the community collectively or to individual members.[56] Their right to assemble in this way was, however, never legally established. All efforts by the Dutch Resident, and in 1674 by the English Resident, Sir William Swan, to extend formal protection over the community failed.[57]

It seems that clerical opposition was largely responsible. In 1667 the pastors renewed their solemn oath never to permit the establishment of a Calvinist church in Hamburg, and in 1671 they republished various documents relating to the controversy of 1644 over the building of a church and the issue of public burials for Calvinists.[58] The attempt in 1674 by the Imperial Commissioner, Count Windischgrätz, to reconcile the clergy to the idea of limited civic and religious rights also foundered. The Jesuit reports claimed that he had been bribed by the Calvinists to negotiate with the Lutheran clergy; but the situation remained unresolved. Despite their

[53] Conrad, 'Religionsbann', pp. 169–75; Fürstenau, *Grundrecht der Religionsfreiheit*, pp. 9–49.
[54] StAH, Senat, Cl.VII Lit.Hf No.2a Vol.1a, 20 April 1649, Great Elector to Senate.
[55] Klefeker, *Verfassungen*, 8, p. 411.
[56] Hermes, *Reformierte Gemeinde*, pp. 61–3, 98, 129; see also notes collected by the archivist Otto Beneke, 13 August 1873, in StAH, Senat, Cl.VII Lit.Hf No.2a Vol.1c.
[57] Hermes, *Reformierte Gemeinde*, p. 86.
[58] StAH, Senat, Cl.VII Lit.Hf No.1 Vol.3a, 22 February 1667, clerical oath. The pamphlet is entitled: *Erörterung der Frage: Ob denen Calvinisten eine Kirchen-Versammlung in der Stadt Hamburg zu vergönnen?* – the date 1671 is given by Otto Beneke in his notes in StAH, Senat, Cl.VII Lit.Hf No.2a Vol.1c.

reputation for political radicalism and stealth, the Calvinists achieved no greater freedom than the Jews.[59]

The decades after 1648 were marked by piecemeal and hesitant policies rather than by great crises or public issues. The Calvinists themselves were embroiled in internal theological and financial controversies in Altona, which ultimately led to a formal split between the Dutch- and French-speaking groups in March 1686.[60] The Senate for its part had no desire to intervene in what were regarded as internal Danish affairs; as long as the Altona authorities continued to tolerate the consistory, its own policy could remain constant. The most wealthy Calvinists still lived in Hamburg and showed no desire to forsake the city: the minor physical hardship involved in travelling a few miles to worship in Altona was still more than outweighed by the economic advantages of residence in Hamburg.

The first serious disruption of this equilibrium occurred as a result of the arrival of Huguenot exiles from France after the revocation of the Edict of Nantes in October 1685.[61] During the months after the revocation hundreds of thousands of Huguenots poured out of France: most went to England and the Netherlands, some to Ireland; a substantial group of about 30,000 went to Germany, where many princes competed eagerly for their wealth and skills.[62] Indeed, in the same month as the revocation, the Great Elector issued the Edict of Potsdam offering Brandenburg as a refuge and promising religious and economic privileges in return for their help in promoting the economy; his agents in Amsterdam and Hamburg were instructed to give every encouragement to potential immigrants, including money to cover their travel expenses.[63] Relatively few came to Hamburg, some 900 in all, many of whom merely travelled through: the majority, who ended up in Prussia, Hesse-Cassel, Lüneburg and Bavaria, entered Germany by Switzerland and the Rhine route rather than via Amsterdam.[64]

However, even the arrival of such limited numbers was sufficient to increase the size of the Calvinist community in Hamburg considerably. And although the Senate made no effort to encourage this immigration, it was inevitably soon embroiled in the problems which ensued as a result. They

[59] Dreves, *Geschichte*, p. 89; Steltzner, *Nachricht*, 3, pp. 1028–9.
[60] Hermes, *Reformierte Gemeinde*, pp. 68–77; Barrelet, 'Geschichte', pp. 11–14. The split was the prelude to a lengthy legal argument over the division of community finances and property which was only resolved in 1734. Cf. Bolten, *Kirchen-Nachrichten von Altona*, 1, pp. 249–55; Klefeker, *Verfassungen*, 8, pp. 617–18.
[61] Erbe, *Hugenotten*, pp. 19–21; Scoville, *Persecution of Huguenots*, pp. 2–7. Small groups had already left due to mounting persecution after the accession of Louis XIV; in exile, they joined the French Walloon communities established in the late sixteenth century.
[62] Preetz, 'Privilegien', *passim*; Scoville, *Persecution of Huguenots*, pp. 121–5; Erbe, *Hugenotten*, pp. 29–34.
[63] Scoville, *Persecution of Huguenots*, pp. 349–50.
[64] Ibid., p. 125; Beuleke, 'Landsmannschaftliche Gliederung', pp. 22–3.

were various in nature, but all largely concerned with the Great Elector, the major patron of the Huguenots, who since 1682 had also been instrumental in protecting Hamburg from attack and annexation by Denmark.[65]

Already in 1685 the Calvinist preacher Jean de la Fontaine had been sent to Potsdam. He requested the Great Elector's help in establishing a consistory in Hamburg, since the hostilities with Denmark (culminating in the siege of Hamburg in August 1686) made it all but impossible for the community to worship in Altona. The Calvinists also claimed that the Senate was now more favourably inclined to contemplate 'the right to worship publicly within the gates of this laudable city, which has hitherto been prevented by untimely zealots'.[66] The arrival of the Huguenots in 1685–6 made the matter more urgent, and on 14 September 1686 the elders of the community again wrote to Potsdam pressing for action.[67] The Great Elector not only wrote to the Senate, pointing out the debt which the city owed him for his action against Denmark, for which a concession to the Calvinists would be a modest return, but also wrote to the Dukes of Celle, Hanover and Wolfenbüttel to rally support.[68] The Dukes of Wolfenbüttel showed great sympathy for the Senate in a city 'where the magistrates do not have absolute control',[69] but in November nonetheless signed a joint plea for toleration.[70] In the meantime the Lutheran clergy had in fact already voiced their opposition in sermons, culminating in a concerted effort on the day of thanksgiving for the recent peace with Denmark on 31 October. Having been warned by the Senate on 30 October, they did admittedly restrict their comments to a rather general level; but by then the damage had already been done.[71] On 30 November the Great Elector once more protested vigorously against anti-Calvinist sermons, protests which were reinforced in January 1687.[72]

The Senate was now placed in a delicate position. Concerned with diplomatic reprisals and unrest in the city itself, it attempted to persuade the clergy to ignore the dogmatic and theological issues, and to consider the possibility of a purely legal concession. The advantages, both diplomatic

[65] Rückleben, *Niederwerfung*, pp. 38–49; Wohlwill, *Aus drei Jahrhunderten*, pp. 39–62.

[66] StAH, DRG, I A 13, nos. 1–2, 27 April 1685, petition to Great Elector and letter of recommendation for Jean de la Fontaine.

[67] Ibid., no. 4, 14 September 1686, Calvinists to Great Elector.

[68] Ibid., no. 5, 16 October 1686, Great Elector to rulers of Celle, Hanover and Wolfenbüttel; StAH, Senat, Cl.VII Lit.Hf No.2a Vol.2, 25 September 1686, Great Elector to Senate.

[69] StAH, DRG, I A 13, no. 6, 22 October 1686, Dukes of Wolfenbüttel to Great Elector.

[70] StAH, Senat, Cl.VII Lit.Hf No.2a Vol.2, 13 November 1686, Dukes of Wolfenbüttel and Georg Wilhelm of Osnabrück to Senate.

[71] StAH, Ministerium, II 3, pp. 38–9, 41–2.

[72] StAH, Senat, Cl.VII Lit.Hf No.2a Vol.2, 30 November 1686, Great Elector to Senate; StAH, DRG, I A 13, 18 January 1687, Great Elector instructions to Resident von Guericke.

and economic, would be obvious.[73] The clergy, however, remained unmoved, and insisted on their duty to oppose outright any deviation from the obligations which the constitution and their holy office imposed on them.[74] Thus they continued to preach against Calvinism, and their implacable opposition put paid to the Great Elector's second plea of March 1687.[75]

The intervention of a prince upon whose favour the city depended thus failed to tame the Lutheran clergy, and the Calvinists had failed to acquire a formally-recognised patron in Hamburg. The independent church they desired was out of the question; they had not even established the right to worship under diplomatic protection. By pressing for the former, the Great Elector had failed to gain the latter. In the process, he had so incensed the clergy that their opposition continued undiminished in 1688 and 1689; and in 1691 they thwarted the attempts by the English Resident, Sir Paul Rycaut, to gain permission for the construction of a chapel.[76]

The Calvinists thus had little to show for their agitation. As before, services were held informally in the house of the Dutch, Prussian and, for a brief period, English Residents.

The vulnerability of their position was demonstrated during the early 1690s when the Calvinists became embroiled in the Pietist disputes as the more Orthodox clergy led by Johann Friedrich Mayer accused their opponents of leniency towards all manner of separatists. The details of those controversies are not entirely relevant to the issue of toleration. Calvinism was a term bandied around in a very loose way together with Pietism, Syncretism and Separatism, something accounted for by the fact that Spener himself preached a more moderate and tolerant gospel than that of the Orthodox.[77] In 1694 the Prussian Elector once more protested against Hamburg sermons, but both the German and the French Calvinists denied that they felt themselves personally attacked or even threatened by these utterances.[78] Even so, the Senate took the Elector's threat of reprisals

73 StAH, Senat, Cl.VII Lit.Hf No.2a Vol.2, 29 November 1686, Senate to clergy. The point was reinforced in an undated petition by the Huguenots which appears to have been submitted at about this time: ibid., Cl.VII Lit.Hf No.2a Vol.1a, no. 35.

74 Ibid., Cl.VII Lit.Hf No.2a Vol.2, n.d., clergy reply to Senate communication of 29 November 1686.

75 StAH, DRG, I A 13, no. 10, 17 March 1787, Great Elector to Senate.

76 StAH, Ministerium, III A1e, no. 1427, 6 December 1688, clergy to *Oberalten*. The diary of Pastor Schultz records most of this campaign: StAH, Senat, Cl.VII Lit.Hb No.3 Vol.2b, esp. pp. 15, 57, 59. The English initiative was dropped after the death of William III: Hermes, *Reformierte Gemeinde*, pp. 86–7.

77 See Rückleben, *Niederwerfung*, pp. 50–178; Geffcken, *Johann Winckler*, pp. 266–320, 373–84. Cf. too Müsing, 'Speners *Pia Desideria*', *passim*.

78 StAH, Senat, Cl.VII Lit.Hf No.2a Vol.1a, no. 11, 20 June 1694, Great Elector to Senate; ibid., nos. 13–17, 21, undated responses by various Calvinist groups to enquiries about their security. Cf. too Pastor Schultz's comments in ibid., Cl.VII Lit.Hb No.3 Vol.2b, pp. 278–9.

against Hamburg citizens in Brandenburg seriously enough to hesitate to carry out a decree banning French Calvinist services in the Wandrahm in 1696.[79]

The initiatives of the Prussian Electors thus secured the informal position of the Huguenots. Meanwhile, the Dutch Resident, de Kuystens, continued to do the same for the Dutch; but again, his plan to build a large chapel behind his house in 1697 was thwarted by the vigilance of the Lutheran clergy. They once more obliged the Senate to protest and restate the official policy: foreign diplomats undoubtedly had the right to maintain chapels for themselves and their households, which might be used informally by other members of their faith; but the construction of a public chapel, with the avowed aim of providing a place of worship for non-Lutherans, ran against both the *jus gentium* and the constitution of Hamburg.[80]

III

The period 1700 to 1730 was marked by the gradual establishment of recognised diplomatic patronage for the Dutch Calvinists. Despite the opposition of the clergy, services continued in the Dutch Resident's house, and in 1709 the community found a solution which proved to be the key to its future. They decided to buy the house in which the Resident lived, and let it to either the Dutch or Prussian Resident, so that diplomatic immunity might be extended to their preacher.[81] The offer to the Prussian Resident was made largely because of his efforts to persuade the Imperial Commission to grant civil and religious freedom to the Calvinists. Once he failed to achieve this, he stepped down, and the house on the Valentinskamp was let to the Dutch Resident, van den Bosch, for 600 mark per annum.[82]

This in itself did not bring official recognition by the Senate. The community was still based in Altona where its institutions and finances were protected by Danish privilege; but the new diplomatic chapel encouraged the Hamburg group to think in terms of a secession from the Altona consistory. When in 1713 communications between the two places were severed by the plague, the Senate was persuaded to give them a burial place just outside the Steintor, and to permit the enlargement of the Resident's chapel to accommodate more than 500 people.[83] Although the plague

[79] Ibid., Cl.VII Lit.Hf No.2a Vol.1a, no. 26, 11 November 1696, Senate to clergy.
[80] Hermes, *Reformierte Gemeinde*, pp. 130–1; cf. correspondence in StAH, Senat, Cl.VII Lit.Hf No.2a Vol.3a.
[81] Hermes, *Reformierte Gemeinde*, pp. 131–2; StAH, DRG, I C 34, 3 November 1709, proposals by Calvinist Elders.
[82] Bartels, *Einige Abhandlungen*, pp. 299–300; Hermes, *Reformierte Gemeinde*, p. 132.
[83] Ibid.; Klefeker, *Verfassungen*, 8, pp. 599–600, 781–3; StAH, Senat, Cl.VII Lit.Hf No.1 Vol.2b(b), 15 April 1739, clergy to Senate (report on the history of the Calvinist graveyard).

measures were rescinded in 1715, these concessions strengthened the secessionist group. In 1716 they broke away from the Altona consistory and, apparently with Senatorial permission, became based in Hamburg under the aegis of the Dutch Resident. The only proviso was that the *actus parochiales* (baptisms, weddings, burials) were to be performed in Altona as before.[84]

It is unclear just how official this solution was in the first instance. The frequent use of the word *connivenz* is indicative of the dubious legal status of the arrangement.[85] In July 1719 the Senate was obliged to issue a mandate condemning the exploitation of diplomatic chapels.[86] But this occurred in the context of the anti-Catholic agitation, and it was pointed out that there was a clear distinction between the new Jesuit church and the Dutch Resident's chapel. The former represented an illegal innovation, while the latter conformed with both the *jus gentium* and the urban constitution.[87] Thus during the 1720s the Dutch Calvinists were merely warned that they should avoid conspicuous gatherings and ostentatious display.[88] By 1728 the use of the chapel had become so established that the new Resident, Mauricius, was able to sign a formal contract with the community, promising to protect the preachers they chose, while the community undertook to consult the Resident about any changes in the organisation of the chapel. Above all, it was stressed that in legal terms the religious community was not independent: it depended explicitly upon the goodwill of both the Dutch Resident and the Senate.[89]

Their French counterparts were not as successful. They too had purchased a house in 1701 where services were conducted with short interruptions until July 1719, when the Senate imposed a ban.[90] In 1724 services were resumed, although in the following year they ceased again when the Senate dismissed the community's claim to have been granted unofficial permission.[91] Only then did the Prussian Resident, Jean Destinon, attempt to intervene by proposing to build a chapel of his own which would

---

[84] Hermes, *Reformierte Gemeinde*, pp. 105–27; Klefeker, *Verfassungen*, 8, pp. 600–1. For the Hamburg community this step involved the loss of most of its funds. Cf. Bolten, *Kirchen-Nachrichten von Altona*, 1, pp. 203–5.

[85] The word is used throughout the files which deal with this subject.

[86] Blank, *Mandate*, 2, p. 918.

[87] See for example: StAH, Senat, Cl.VII Lit.Hf No.1 Vol.3c, fols. 172–3, 13 September 1720, EPS.   [88] Klefeker, *Verfassungen*, 8, pp. 600–1.

[89] Hermes, *Reformierte Gemeinde*, pp. 132–3; Klefeker, *Verfassungen*, 8, pp. 600–1 (note S); StAH, DRG, II Aa Bd. 12, 5 December 1740, a report on the legal position regarding services in Hamburg.

[90] Klefeker, *Verfassungen*, 8, pp. 601–4; StAH, Senat, Cl.VII Lit.Hf No.2a Vol.1c, 15 August 1873, notes collected by Otto Beneke; ibid., Cl.VII Lit.Hf No.1 Vol.3a, Kurtzer Auszug, 1719.

[91] Ibid., Cl.VII Lit.Hf No.2a Vol.1c, transcript of a note submitted to Senator Widow (1725); ibid., Cl.VII Lit.Hf No.2a Vol.3b, fol. 24, 3 March 1725, report by Senator Widow; ibid., fol. 26, 7 March 1725, EPS.

operate on the lines of the Dutch arrangement.[92] This initiative was, however, quickly thwarted by the Senate; in 1728 Destinon cancelled his contract with the French, and agreed with Mauricius to share equal privileges in the Dutch chapel.[93] The different treatment of the Dutch and French resulted from their relative positions in Altona: while the Dutch broke away from the Altona consistory in 1717, the French continued to enjoy the full protection afforded by Denmark until 1744.[94]

The account of these events written by Johann Klefeker in 1770 gives the impression of an almost peaceful gradual evolution: the major complications are ascribed to the controversy over the Catholic chapel which began in 1719.[95] This is, however, misleading. For the Lutheran clergy did not accept the limited concessions to the Dutch without a bitter struggle which brought the city of Hamburg into international disrepute. Their implacable opposition was the result of two unrelated factors: firstly, the more strident policies of the Senate, and secondly, the incensed reaction of Orthodox Lutherans to plans for a union of the Protestant Churches.

The development of a more forceful Senatorial policy was influenced by a variety of factors. At the most obvious level, the problems which ensued from the anti-Catholic agitation of these years led to the formulation of a clearer conception of how religious minorities could and must be accommodated without actually infringing on the laws and constitution of the city. The publication in 1715 of an Imperial decree reminding all German rulers of their duty to uphold the religious peace of 1648 had reinforced this need.[96] The Calvinists also profited from the disaster of the anti-Catholic riot in 1719, and from the close involvement of Holland and Prussia in their cause. After 1725 the cause of the Dutch was considerably strengthened by the close contacts which their patron, Mauricius, had with the governing elite.[97] Concern for diplomatic goodwill and internal harmony underpinned the process of establishment and informal recognition.

Economic factors and the emergence of the Patriot group in the 1720s

[92] Ibid., Cl.VII Lit.Hf No.2a Vol.5a, no. 4, 14 March 1726, contract between Destinon and the Elders of the French Reformed Community; ibid., Cl.VII Lit.Hb No.3 Vol.6, extract from *Suite des Nouvelles d'Amsterdam*, 8 November 1726 and clergy to Senate, 12 November 1726.

[93] Klefeker, *Verfassungen*, 8, p. 617; StAH, Senat, Cl.VII Lit.Hf No.2a Vol.5b, Receuil de Stukken behorende tot de Hamburgshe Kapel-Quastie (1726–8), pp. I–XVIII; ibid., Cl.VII Lit.Hf No. 2a Vol.5a, no. 22: 5 and 19 January 1728, EPS.

[94] Boué, 'Abriss', p. 15; Barrelet, 'Geschichte', pp. 15–16; Bolten, *Kirchen-Nachrichten von Altona*, 1, pp. 249–55.

[95] Klefeker, *Verfassungen*, 8, pp. 599–604, 613–22.

[96] Ibid., p. 742. The Edict (18 July 1715) is preserved in StAH, Senat, Cl.VII Lit.Hf No.2a Vol. 3b, no. 14. It marked the only, and unsuccessful, attempt by the Imperial authorities to legislate against inflammatory religious tracts. Cf. Eisenhardt, *Kaiserliche Aufsicht*, pp. 55, 58.

[97] Winckler, *Nachrichten*, 2, pp. 1–8; Schröder, *Lexikon*, 5, pp. 85–6. Mauricius was Dutch Resident in Hamburg 1725–42 and again 1756–68.

also played a vital part. One of the reasons why the Senate was so eager to reach a compromise with the Calvinists was its increasing concern over the profound economic depression of the period, and in particular over the threat posed by the commercial expansion of Altona.[98] Although fear of persecution drove many Calvinists away after 1726, migration had started much earlier. The dangers posed by internal instability before 1709 and external insecurity due to the Great Northern War induced many merchants to turn to the expanding markets of London and Amsterdam after 1700.[99]

Domestic strife, plague, the threat of involvement in a major European conflict, prolonged economic crisis — all of these factors dominated the policies of the Senate. In 1716 Syndic Sillem had presented a long and detailed report on the dire state of the economy to the *Bürgerschaft*, a theme to which he returned in his annual addresses to that body as presiding *Bürgermeister* during the 1720s.[100] Similar preoccupations characterised the emergence of the Patriotic Society in 1724, whose aims were to revive the flagging spirits of the Lutheran community and to make philosophical sense of the legal heritage and the new constitution of 1712.[101] Unlike their predecessors in the seventeenth century, the Senators of the period after 1715 advanced more cogent arguments for limited toleration which combined traditional mercantile wisdom with new philosophical insights into the relationship between government and society. Lutheran purity, they concluded, was compatible with the acceptance of minorities.[102]

To some extent the indomitable opposition of the clergy was a reaction against this philosophy. As Orthodox Lutherans, they were bound to reject arguments which drew on the philosophies of Thomasius, Wolff, Pfaff and others. During the 1720s Pastor Neumeister's letters show how he reviled the Patriots as Thomasians, arrogant despots, indifferentists, the embodiment of the 'political Antichrist'.[103]

However, over the whole period, their collective reactions to the Calvinists can only be explained by reference to the protracted negotiations

98 Ehrenberg, 'Hamburgs Handel', pp. 261–97; Vogel, 'Handelskonjunkturen', pp. 61–4; Wiskemann, *Welthandelspolitik*, pp. 112–14, 120–1; Jeannin, 'Hansestädte', *passim*; Wucher, 'Gewerbliche Entwicklung', pp. 57–66; StAH, Senat, Cl.VII Lit.Ka No.4 Vol.5, Unvorgreifliche Gedanken, a report on the decline of Hamburg's trade *c.* 1726.

99 Reissmann, *Kaufmannschaft*, pp. 243–52, esp. p. 250. StAH, Senat, Cl.VII Lit.Hf No.2a Vol.13 (supplementary papers), n.d., report in the hand of Syndic Matsen.

100 StAH, EB, No. 1 Bd. 12, pp. 442–53; ibid., Bd. 13, pp. 266–70, 329–32, 354–6, 513–16; ibid., Bd. 14, pp. 801–5; ibid., Bd. 15, pp. 5–8, 81–6, 99–103, 480–6.

101 Rathje, '"Der Patriot"', *passim*.

102 Cf. Matthei, *Untersuchungen*, pp. 13–15. The new attitude is clearly demonstrated in the work of a leading member of the Society: J. A. Hoffmann, *Staats-Kunst*, pp. 35–45. Klefeker, himself a member of the Society, drew explicitly on the arguments of *Der Patriot* (Klefeker, *Verfassungen*, 2, pp. 270–2 and ibid., 8, pp. 365–6). The crucial statement appears in *Der Patriot*, 3, p. 78.

103 Wotschke (ed.), 'Neumeisters Briefe' (1925), pp. 108–42; ibid. (1929), pp. 136–42. Cf. Greschat, *Tradition und neuer Anfang*, pp. 144–57, 281–307.

over the plans for the union of the Lutheran and Calvinist Churches. The Senate of Hamburg was never involved in them, but Neumeister clearly saw them as a manifestation of the same spirit which inspired the Patriots.

Plans for the restoration of religious concord and unity were as old as the Reformation itself. Such aspirations gained a greater sense of urgency after the Peace of Westphalia which set an end to a century of bitter confessional conflict. Scholars like Leibniz and clerics like Bossuet participated in serious discussions of a reconciliation of Catholicism and Protestantism. These universalist dreams were, however, shattered by mutual distrust, and by the outbreak of major European wars after the 1670s which once more drove a political wedge between the Christian faiths. By about 1700, the idea of union had become restricted to the Protestant Churches alone and had assumed a political as well as a theological dimension, particularly in Germany.[104]

While men like Leibniz and the ubiquitous Prussian Court preacher Daniel Ernst Jablonski pursued their irenical vision, the cause of union was also promoted by the political ambitions of princes in Prussia and Hanover.[105] Both the Great Elector and his successors were – quite genuinely – interested in the theological issues; but they also had other motives. Firstly, a reconciliation of Lutheranism and Calvinism would solve the domestic problems of a state with two official religions. Secondly, such a union would strengthen Protestantism in the *Reich* as a whole, and underpin Prussian leadership of its non-Catholic members. It was this idea which lay behind the negotiations with the Anglican Church in the years 1710–14.[106] Both the internal Prussian projects and the Anglican initiative failed, but efforts to keep the cause alive were untiring. Leibniz in particular was well aware of the worldly aspect of the whole affair, and constantly sought to bring his ideas to the fore at points where diplomatic and political crises might induce sympathetic rulers to take action, when otherwise they might have acquiesced in the intransigence of the clergy. The last and most serious crisis of this kind was the conflict between Calvinists, Lutherans and Catholics in the Palatinate which came to a head in 1719–20 and nearly started another major European war.[107] Even then, however, it proved possible only to unite the *corpus evangelicorum* for the limited purpose of

---

[104] The best general survey is still Hering, *Kirchliche Unionsversuche*. See also Schieder, 'Kirchen-unionspläne'; Hiltebrandt, *Reunionsverhandlungen*; Kiefl, *Friedensplan*; Evans, *Habsburg monarchy*, pp. 305–6.

[105] Hering, *Kirchliche Unionsversuche*, 2, pp. 313–76; Gericke, *Glaubenszeugnisse*, pp. 48–58; Brandes, *Kirchliche Politik*, 1, pp. 383–463; von Thadden, *Hofprediger*, pp. 199–204.

[106] Levis, 'Anglo-Prussian ecumenical effort', *passim*; von Thadden, *Hofprediger*, pp. 130–9.

[107] Borgmann, *Deutscher Religionsstreit*, *passim*; Hering, *Kirchliche Unionsversuche*, 2, pp. 367–72, 376–82. The conflict arose out of a complex dispute between the Catholic Elector Karl Philipp and his Lutheran and Calvinist subjects.

effective constitutional action against the Catholic Elector Carl Philipp. The ensuing discussions of a theological reconciliation of the Protestant faiths foundered once more, and thereafter interest in the subject flagged as the ideal of toleration gradually supplanted that of union.[108]

Several factors thwarted the ambitions of the unionists. It has rightly been pointed out that political and diplomatic incompatibilities played an important part.[109] But the opposition of substantial sections of the clergy on both sides was also crucial. Especially on the Lutheran side, the plans were seen as a Calvinist conspiracy to destroy Lutheran Orthodoxy, still regarded as the one Protestant confession destined to replace Catholicism as the true faith. On both sides, however, the fact that the initiatives were ultimately stimulated by politicians and princes aroused intense suspicion. The unionists seemed to elevate politics above theology, and thus, in the same way as contemporary legal theorists such as Thomasius, Wolff, and Pfaff, they appeared to derogate the position of religion in society. To impassioned partisans, union represented indifference.[110]

There is no evidence that the magistrates of Hamburg ever participated in any of these protracted negotiations. While in the 1720s some Senators may have had considerable sympathy for the general spirit of the movement because it aspired to eliminate confessional conflict, the Senate itself was careful to stress that it did not wish to pass judgement on the theological issues involved.[111] But the reasons for stressing this point were diplomatic. For, since 1703, Hamburg had become notorious for the number of vitriolic pamphlets published there which condemned the unionists and their supporters in terms which led to protests by Prussia, Holland and England, and ultimately to the intervention of the Imperial Courts.

The first Hamburg citizen to take up the sword of Orthodoxy was not a clergyman, but Professor Sebastian Edzardi. A friend and admirer of the querulous Pastor Mayer, Edzardi was the son of the founder of the Proselyten-Anstalt. He had studied theology in Wittenberg, and in 1699 became Professor of Logic and Metaphysics at the Hamburg Gymnasium. Even as a student, he had written tracts condemning such intellectual giants as Grotius; but those invectives were a mere youthful prelude to his later activities.[112]

He first aroused the ire of the Prussian King in 1703 when, in a polemic against Pietism and Calvinism, he denounced the University of Halle as

[108] Schieder, 'Kirchenunionspläne', p. 605.
[109] Levis, 'Anglo-Prussian ecumenical effort', p. 399.
[110] Greschat, *Tradition und neuer Anfang*, pp. 144–57, 281–307.
[111] StAH, Senat, Cl.VII Lit.Hf No.1 Vol.3c, 13 October 1719, Senate to clergy and 16 January, ditto.
[112] Schröder, *Lexikon*, 2, p. 135; Mutzenbecher, 'Sebastian Edzardi', pp. 210–12.

the *universitatem infernalem – höllisch* (hellish) rather than *hallisch*.[113] Two years later the King once more protested at a flood of short tracts which denounced the union as a Calvinist conspiracy, its perpetrators as godless and indifferentist politicians.[114] Despite the fact that his works were publicly burned in Prussia in February 1705, and despite a severe warning from the Senate, Edzardi continued to publish.[115] In 1707 the Prussians took the matter up with the *corpus evangelicorum* in Regensburg which issued an edict condemning Edzardi's works.[116] The indomitable professor was not, however, to be deterred by the commands of mere politicians, nor even restrained by the dictates of the Emperor, whose edict against defamatory theological writings in 1715 seems to have left Edzardi unimpressed. Using a variety of pseudonyms (a particular favourite was Joannis Jeveris Wiburgensis), he continued to produce anti-Calvinist pamphlets at the rate of several a year, pausing only in 1717 to join his clerical friends in celebrating the second centenary of the Reformation by writing an invective against Catholicism.[117]

Edzardi's activities had, at the very least, kept the Orthodox pulse beating strongly in Hamburg. The clergy defended him from the start, and after 1715 he enjoyed the friendship and support of Pastor Neumeister and *Senior* Seelmann.[118] By 1719 their polemics had roused the passions of the mob to fever pitch; and in the wake of the anti-Catholic riot it became apparent that the Calvinists too might be in danger. Hence in September 1719 both Prussia and Holland wrote protesting against Edzardi's latest offering, which denied that Calvinists believed in the true Augsburg Confession.[119] In fact, Edzardi had this time taken the precaution of publishing under the name of his son, who, despite the father's attempt to justify him, was banned from preaching until 1726.[120]

[113] StAH, Ministerium, III A1h, no. 90, 2 May 1703, Edzardi to clergy; ibid., no. 91, 15 April 1703, Frederick I to Senate; ibid., no. 92, 16 March 1703, Professors of Halle to Frederick I (copy).

[114] StAH, Ministerium, III A1i, no. 51, 14 May 1705, Frederick I to Senate; the work concerned was his *Pelagianismus Calvinianorum*.

[115] StAH, Senat, Cl.VII Lit.Hf No.2a Vol.3b, no. 10a, 23 February 1705, Royal Edict; Mutzenbecher, 'Sebastian Edzardi', p. 213.

[116] Ibid.; cf. StAH, Senat, Cl.VII Lit.Ja No.3 Vol.2, 24 July 1706, Burchard to Senate, contains a threat that this course of action will be taken.

[117] Mutzenbecher, 'Sebastian Edzardi', p. 213; Klefeker, *Verfassungen*, 8, p. 742; Schröder, *Lexikon*, 2, pp. 138–44, contains a complete list of the pamphlets of these years.

[118] StAH, Ministerium, II 4, pp. 74–5, 77, 93, 111; ibid., II 5, pp. 4, 9–10, 12, 15–16, 33, 39, 41–3, 70–2, 83.

[119] StAH, Senat, Cl.VII Lit.Hf No.1 Vol.3c, 16 September 1719, Frederick William I to Senate; ibid., 25 September 1719, van den Bosch to Senate.

[120] Bruhn, *Kandidaten*, pp. 194–5; StAH, Senat, Cl.VII Lit.Hf No.2a Vol.4a, 23 April and 14 July 1720, interrogation of Esdras Hinricus Edzardi; StAH, Ministerium, III A10, no. 78, 8 February 1726, decree permitting E. H. Edzardi to resume sermons. The father's defence was published as Edzardi, *Kurtze Anzeige*.

While his son bore the punishment with filial forbearance, the elder Edzardi escaped unpunished; but the warnings of the Senate and the threat of action by the Imperial Courts effectively restrained him for some years. The cause did not, however, die. In 1720 Erdmann Neumeister stepped into the breach with a series of sermons culminating in the publication of a notorious pamphlet in 1721, in which he condemned both unionists and Calvinists with equal venom.[121]

The pamphlets appeared at a difficult time. The Protestant princes were involved in intricate manoeuvres at Regensburg over the Palatinate conflict, which could only be prejudiced by the inopportune polemics of the Orthodox clergy.[122] Neumeister's own position was also delicate: together with *Senior* Seelmann, he was already under the threat of Imperial punishment for his role in the destruction of the Catholic chapel. Newspapers in Berlin and Amsterdam now reported that the Dutch Resident might be the next object of the mob's passion.[123] For although Neumeister had been careful not to mention Hamburg specifically, his general arguments were clearly designed to reinforce the repeated protests of his colleagues against the Senate's lenient attitude to Calvinist services in the Dutch Resident's house.[124]

Neumeister's pamphlet, published with the full approval of his colleagues, provoked predictable objections from Holland, Prussia and Britain; the Prussian authorities also pressed the *corpus evangelicorum* in Regensburg to take drastic legal action against the recalcitrant pastor.[125] The Dutch and Prussian protests were actually printed in Hamburg.[126] On 16 January 1722 the Senate remonstrated with the clergy, and shortly afterwards banned the offending tract. As it explained then, it was concerned both to assuage the anger of the Protestant princes and to protect Neumeister.[127] The clergy

---

[121] Neumeister, *Kurtzer Beweis*. Cf. Hering, *Kirchliche Unionsversuche*, 2, pp. 350–6.

[122] Borgmann, *Deutscher Religionsstreit*, pp. 44–55.

[123] See Chapter 2, pp. 61–4 above. StAH, Ministerium, III A1n, 101, 23 December 1721, *Berlinische Privilegirte Zeitung*; ibid., no. 183, 6 December 1721, *Amsterdamse Saturdaegse Courant*.

[124] StAH, Senat, Cl.VII Lit.Hf No.2a Vol.4b, fols. 121–3, Neumeisterische Special Antwort, n.d.; ibid., Ministerium, II 6, pp. 2a, 8b; ibid., Senat, Cl.VII Lit.Hf No.1 Vol.3b, fols. 157, 161: 8 March and 28 August 1720, clergy to Senate. Further complaints of a similar nature may be found in ibid., Cl.VII Lit.Hf No.1 Vol.3c.

[125] Klefeker, *Verfassungen*, 8, pp. 613–14; Hering, *Kirchliche Unionsversuche*, 2, pp. 376–82; the Dutch, English and Prussian protests are in StAH, Senat, Cl.VII Lit.Hf No.2a Vol.4b.

[126] *Copia des Schreibens Welches....Die Hn. Staaten General...an den Magistrat abgehen lassen*, and *Copia des Schreibens Welches Ihro Königl. Majestät in Preussen...An dasigen Magistrat abgehen lassen*. They seem to have been extracted from Dutch newspapers and were not printed with the authority of the respective authors or of the Senate. See StAH, Senat, Cl.VII Lit.Hf No.2a Vol. 4b, no. 11, 14 January 1722, Evens to Senate, conveys Prussian displeasure at the publication. Neumeister claimed that the Calvinists were responsible: Wotschke (ed.), 'Neumeisters Briefe' (1925), p. 120.

[127] StAH, Ministerium, III A1n, nos. 43–4, 16 January 1722, Senate to clergy; ibid., no. 94, 28 January 1722, EPS.

remained adamant.[128] Indeed, in the first days of February, they printed a justification both of Neumeister's work and of their own sermons over the past years. If the connection between anti-unionism and opposition to Calvinism inside Hamburg was hitherto implicit, the clerical *Vorläuffige Erklärung* left no doubts.[129] It reiterated all the traditional legal and constitutional arguments against limited toleration; it particularly emphasised that the Calvinists were deliberately exploiting the international press in order to print provocative and inaccurate accounts of the situation in Hamburg.[130]

In the event, although the Protestant princes wrote a strongly-worded letter to the Senate in March, no formal action was taken.[131] Neumeister continued to write polemical tracts, but he was now more careful to restrict his public comments to theology. In addition, two things soon became clear. Firstly, the union plans were doomed to failure and little more was heard of them.[132] Secondly, in Hamburg itself, the clergy failed to reverse the Senate's lenient policy towards the Dutch Calvinists.

Indeed, when in 1729 Edzardi once more emerged to condemn Pietism and Calvinism, the Senate now undertook more forceful measures.[133] After long disputes he was suspended from office in 1733 for three years, forbidden to publish anything without official permission, and immediately fined 3,000 mark together with legal costs.[134] The triumph of Senatorial moderation was underlined when, on the occasion of the second centenary of the Augsburg Confession in 1730, outbursts of clerical zeal against Calvinism similar to those against Catholicism during the second centenary of the Reformation in 1717 were averted.[135]

While the clergy had left no one in any doubt about the purity of their faith, their policy of militant opposition failed to upset the *status quo*. The Calvinists themselves had contributed significantly to this outcome. They skilfully exploited their diplomatic patrons. Their contacts with printers and newspapers, both at home and abroad, ensured that diplomatic pressure was publicised to a degree that Senators became profoundly

---

[128] Ibid., nos. 47–9, 3 February 1722, clergy to Senate.
[129] Ministerium, *Vorläuffige Erklärung*. The main point made was that the Peace of Westphalia did not apply to the Calvinists in Hamburg since they had not enjoyed any privileges in the *annus decretorius* 1624. [130] Ibid., pp. 7–8.
[131] StAH, Senat, Cl.VII Lit.Hf No.2a Vol.4b, fols. 187–9, 31 March 1721, Protestant Princes to Senate.
[132] Hering, *Kirchliche Unionsversuche*, 2, pp. 376–81. Schröder, *Lexikon*, 5, pp. 501–3, contains a complete bibliography of Neumeister's pamphlets 1721–30.
[133] Edzardi, *Verzeichniss Allerhand Pietistischer Intrigen*, *passim*.
[134] Mutzenbecher, 'Sebastian Edzardi', pp. 214–17; StAH, Senat, Cl.VII Lit.Hf No.4 Vol.1c, Acta Extractus Prot. A.S. betr...dem Professor Seb. Edzardi 1729–34; Klefeker, *Verfassungen*, 5, pp. 373–6. The clergy again stood by him: StAH, Ministerium, III A1p, no. 195, 4 Nov. 1729, Resol. Rev. Min.; ibid., no. 197, 25 November 1729, Senate to clergy.
[135] See Chapter 6, pp. 192–4 below.

worried about their reputations as wise and just magistrates of a freedom-loving city. Thus the Thomasian Patriots, whom Neumeister denounced in his letters to Ernst Salomo Cyprian, persevered.[136] Christian prudence, based on a consideration of diplomatic and economic factors, and on the desire to maintain domestic order, prevailed over the dictates of Orthodoxy.

IV

The major obstacle to the formulation of a coherent policy during the early 1720s was the fact that the clergy continually drove a wedge between the Senate and the civic bodies. Clerical vigilance and the instant use of the pulpits meant that the Senate rarely had time to set the cumbersome machinery of consultation in motion. The result was that the Civic Colleges generally first heard of crises and disputes from the clergy. Once alerted to signs of danger and illegality, the *Oberalten* and the Sixty were in no mood to take a lenient view. They repeatedly accused the Senate of arrogating to itself authority in ecclesiastical affairs which the constitution clearly vested in the combination of executive and representative powers.[137] The clerical *Vorläuffige Erklärung* provided them with powerful arguments: most significant was its firm view of the implications of the Peace of Westphalia, and the irrefutable argument that, since neither Calvinists nor Catholics had enjoyed any formal privileges before 1624, the city was not obliged to give them any now. The fact that the Peace allowed rulers to go further at their own discretion was deemed irrelevant in Hamburg: for, unlike princes and monarchs with more or less absolute powers, the hands of the Senate were firmly bound by local laws and constitutions.[138]

Once clerical passions had subsided, however, the way was open for a fresh initiative. Already in 1726 the Senate had praised the Ministry's moderation.[139] By 1731 the death of *Senior* Seelmann and the fate of Professor Edzardi seemed to encourage a more moderate attitude amongst the clergy. Their protests were now confined to the denunciation of 'excesses' in the use of diplomatic chapels, and to complaints that the performance of baptisms, marriages and funerals by preachers from Altona and the diplomatic chapels were making substantial inroads on clerical incomes.[140] The Senate was sympathetic to this latter argument. The

---

136 Wotschke (ed.), 'Neumeisters Briefe' (1925), pp. 116–27; ibid. (1929), p. 149 (note 1); ibid. (1930), pp. 181–3.
137 See for example: StAH, Senat, Cl.VII Lit.Hf No.1 Vol.3c, 31 July 1722, Conclusum der Lxger.
138 Ministerium, *Vorläuffige Erklärung*, pp. 8–12. Cf. Klefeker, *Verfassungen*, 8, pp. 695–7.
139 StAH, Ministerium, III A10, no. 101, 20 November 1726, Extractus Protocolli.
140 Ibid., II 6, p. 61; StAH, Senat, Cl.VII Lit.Hb No.3 Vol.8, 17 December 1731, clergy to Senate. These practices had already been the subject of a Senatorial ban: ibid., Cl.VII Lit.Hf No.2a Vol.6a, 8 May 1731, Extract Wedde Protocoll; ibid., 9 February and 10 March 1731, Conclusum A.S.

Lutheran monopoly on the fees paid on these occasions (*jura stolae*) was never in doubt; but the attempt to persuade the clergy to allow religious freedom to the Calvinists, in return for a promise that they would pay the Lutheran pastors all the relevant fees, met with a cool reception. In March 1732 the new *Senior*, Johann Friedrich Winckler, declared that his colleagues would never accept such a compromise. Further talks in August produced a more forthcoming, but nonetheless ambivalent and noncommittal, response.[141]

At the very least, however, the clergy were pacified. They had been consulted and assured that no steps would be taken without their knowledge. The matter was then shelved. But the unresolved question of the Huguenots (whose desire to worship in the Prussian Resident's chapel had been denied in 1728) once more inaugurated an attempt to reopen the issue. In December 1733 they petitioned the Senate for permission to hold discreet and silent services in a house belonging to Jacques Le Gras.[142] Having gained their assurances that they would be willing to pay the *jura stolae*, the Senate decided to approach the *Oberalten* in April 1734.

The proposals it now made and the arguments used to justify them mark a significant new departure. For while the Dutch Calvinists were restricted to the chapel of their diplomatic patrons, it was now envisaged that the *Refugiés* should be allowed an independent place of worship. Their motives for desiring this were largely the result of conflicts with their Altona relatives, and a rising sense of resentment against the fact that the wealthy Hamburg group was obliged to carry most of the costs of the Altona chapel.[143]

The Senate exploited this state of affairs to elaborate an altogether more compelling argument.[144] It pointed to the toleration exercised by the Prussians: if Hamburg did not follow suit, then they would undoubtedly try to reopen the diplomatic chapel initiative. And this could only cause trouble with the clergy – particularly undesirable at present because the city was once more dependent upon Prussian aid in a currency dispute with Denmark.[145] Economic arguments were also stressed: the Huguenots were victims of religious persecution; but their emigration had brought prosperity to the lands where they settled. If Hamburg were to treat them generously then more might be induced to come. All that was needed was permission for an informal concession which might easily be revoked if trouble ensued. They were not to be allowed public worship, nor admitted to the civic

141 Ibid., 10 March and 27 August 1732, reports by Syndic Klefeker.
142 Ibid., 11 December 1733, Huguenots to Senate.
143 Barrelet, 'Geschichte', pp. 15–16.
144 StAH, Senat, Cl.VII Lit.Hf No.2a Vol.6a, 14 April 1734, Extractus Protocolli.
145 Cf. Oellrich, 'Währungsstreit', *passim*; Wohlwill, *Aus drei Jahrhunderten*, pp. 63–8.

polity; they would be tolerated as Christians but not assimilated as citizens. Hence the economy would be improved, foreign powers placated, the Lutheran constitution preserved; and the clergy would be assuaged by the guarantee of the *jura stolae*.

The document was the first clear statement of the ideas proclaimed in *Der Patriot* in 1726.[146] It is remarkably similar both in tone and in argument to the statement made later in the same year with regard to the Jews.[147] Political expediency, theology and economics were combined in a mixture which later characterised the ultimately successful arguments for a concession after 1774.

The *Oberalten* requested time to discuss the matter, but promised to maintain silence and discretion.[148] In fact they did not bother to reply at all. In 1739, when it became clear that the Prussian Resident, Destinon, intended to build a chapel after all, the Senate found itself confronted with precisely the dilemma it had hoped to avoid. As a new proposition to the *Oberalten* pointed out, if Destinon were allowed to go ahead and place the Huguenots 'under the protection of a powerful monarch', then any hope of a satisfactory resolution, of a successful limitation of the minorities, would be lost forever.[149]

This consideration was indeed crucial; for the continued exploitation of diplomatic chapels effectively meant that the magistrates were never masters of the situation. All they could do was to strive to restrain excessive abuse. A resolution of the problem was impossible in view of the indisputable rights of diplomatic agents. By virtue of these, the Christian minorities had become virtual foreign enclaves in legal terms – protected by powerful foreign potentates under the dubious mantle of the principle of exterritoriality.[150]

Placed under pressure by Destinon's purchase of a new and bigger residence, the *Oberalten* took a more favourable view of the proposal and agreed to allow it to be put to the Sixty, who alone could make a final decision. They, however, rejected the matter outright 'for highly convincing reasons'.[151]

Although the issue went as far as the Sixty, the clergy once more proved instrumental in defeating the Senate. The pastors had not intervened in public and had shown an uncharacteristic restraint on the pulpits, but their private intervention rapidly turned the Sixty against the Senate. As Neumeister reported gleefully in a letter to Cyprian, he had been informed

---

[146] See note 102 above. [147] See Chapter 3, pp. 98–9 above.
[148] StAH, Senat, Cl.VII Lit.Hf No.2a Vol.6a, 14 April 1734, Conclusum der Oberalten.
[149] Ibid., 20 January 1740, Extractus Protocolli.
[150] See Chapter 1, note 131 above.
[151] StAH, Senat, Cl.VII Lit.Hf No.2a Vol.6a, 12 and 19 August 1740, Extractus Protocolli.

of the new negotiations by a 'Nicodemus'. He had agreed with the *Senior* not to preach on the subject: 'For if we had preached directly on this matter, then great unrest might have ensued in the city.' Instead they lobbied several of the Sixty 'and gave them the most important documents'. Thus the 'Bubenstück' (knavish trick) was rejected, and the Senators, 'who have been possessed by the Thomasian spirit and infected by the indifferentist plague', were thwarted.[152]

Such devious politics could not prevail over the polemical enthusiasm of the clergy for long. On the *Busstag* (day of penance) of 15 September, a traditional day for invectives against heathens of all kinds (especially the non-Lutheran Christian variety), Neumeister and others delivered bitter denunciations from the pulpits, which were eagerly reported in the Altona newspapers.[153] The Senate protested vigorously; the Prussians and Dutch remonstrated and demanded the punishment of Neumeister; the clergy once more rallied behind their fiery champion.[154] The printed text of the offending sermon was banned.[155] Neumeister felt victimised: he had merely taken particular pains to point out the errors of Calvinist dogmas, and to explain the stance which every Lutheran should adopt if a Calvinist church were ever established in Hamburg. But, he wrote to Cyprian, 'Because I must always be the one who sets the Elbe on fire, both Lutherans and Calvinists have made vigorous complaints about me to the Senate.'[156]

Anxious to defuse the situation, the Senate parried the Prussian demands for retribution, and assured the clergy that it had no intention either of proceeding with the concession or of allowing Destinon to open a chapel.[157] A Calvinist pamphlet about the affair to be published in Altona was suppressed with the collaboration of the Danish authorities; and the Dutch Resident was assured that his own chapel would be allowed to function as usual.[158]

Although the concession was rejected, it had also been possible to thwart the ambitions of the Prussian Resident. The Prussians soon moderated their demands for the punishment of Neumeister, merely insisting that he be

---

[152] Wotschke (ed.), 'Neumeisters Briefe' (1930), pp. 193–4, letter dated 24 September 1740.

[153] StAH, Senat, Cl.VII Lit.Hf No.2a Vol.6a, 19 September 1740, Extractus Protocolli.

[154] Ibid., 5 October 1740, Extractus Protocolli; ibid., 14 December 1740, Estates General of Holland to Mauricius.

[155] StAH, Ministerium, III A1s, no. 9, 19 September 1740, Extractus Protocolli.

[156] Wotschke (ed.), 'Neumeisters Briefe' (1930), p. 194, letter dated 24 September 1740; StAH, Ministerium, III A1s, no. 11, 23 September 1740, Neumeister to clergy.

[157] Ibid., nos. 15–23, 16 December 1740, Senate to clergy. The Prussian complaints were not answered immediately: see note 159 below.

[158] StAH, Senat, Cl.VII Lit.Hf No.2a Vol.6a, 19 October 1740, Extractus Protocolli; ibid., 30 December 1740, instructions to Syndic Klefeker; StAH, DRG, II Aa Bd. 12, December 1740, Consistory deliberations (n.p.).

warned against such outbursts in future.[159] In strategic terms, all options were still open.

Another diplomatic scandal had thus been averted. The affair ended in failure, but it was at least significant that before the clergy intervened the *Oberalten* had agreed with the Senate's arguments. That partial success provided hopes for a more felicitous outcome when, in August 1742, Destinon notified the Senate of his intention to build a summer house on the outskirts of the city, where he proposed to hold services in more commodious surroundings than those provided by his residence in the centre.[160] His proposal was preceded by a characteristically forthright letter from his master, Frederick the Great, which pointed out the economic advantages to be gained from such a concession to the Huguenots. He urged them to emulate his own disregard for the labyrinthine obscurities of the Peace of Westphalia, and to seek refuge in the less contentious waters of diplomatic exterritoriality.[161]

The negotiations of the next two years were complicated by two factors, quite apart from the predictable opposition of the clergy. The first was that Destinon's initial plan stretched the principle of diplomatic patronage far beyond its nebulous limits. In effect, he proposed to extend his immunity and patronage to a house in which he did not in fact live.[162] Only in May 1743 did he himself recognise the implications of this problem by moving into a larger house, where he proceeded to adapt several rooms into a domestic chapel which was formally opened in October 1744.[163]

The second problem was that the Huguenots were themselves divided.[164] Although the Hamburg contingent was still dissatisfied with financial arrangements in Altona, a small section, led by Jean Pierre Chaunel and Pierre His, opposed the patronage of Prussia, in which they saw no advantages: they wanted either limited informal independence in Hamburg, or to stay in Altona.[165] Financial considerations combined with a reluctance to place their fate in Prussian hands: the Dutch had lost all their capital to the Altona consistory after 1716. The Altona communities were reluctant to lose their wealthiest members to diplomatic chapels in Hamburg, and

[159] StAH, Senat, Cl.VII Lit.Hf No.2a Vol.6a, 14 November, 2 December and 28 December 1740, 17 February 1741, Destinon to Senate; ibid., 30 December 1740, Senate to Destinon.
[160] StAH, Senat, Cl.VII Lit.Hf No.2a Vol.6b, 3 August 1742, Destinon to Senate.
[161] Ibid., Cl.VII Lit.Hf No.1 Vol.3d, 13 June 1742, Frederick II to Senate.
[162] Ibid., Cl.VII Lit.Hf No.2a Vol.6b, 10 August 1742, Extractus Protocolli.
[163] Ibid., 3 May 1743, Destinon to Senate; ibid., 28 February 1744, Extractus Protocolli. The formal opening was proclaimed in the *Supplement à la Gazette de Cologne* (27 October 1744) and in the *Reichs Postreuter* in Altona (20 October 1744) – both in the same file.
[164] Barrelet, 'Geschichte', pp. 16–19; Klefeker, *Verfassungen*, 8, pp. 617–18.
[165] This emerges from the later correspondence between Chaunel and Syndic Lipstorp in StAH, Senat, Cl.VII Lit.Hf No.2a Vol.6b: especially Chaunel's letters of 17 April, 15 July, 26 August, 9 October 1744.

were successful in persuading the Danish authorities to forbid the distribution of shares of community capital to those who no longer wished to worship in Altona. Chaunel and His thus vigorously opposed the inopportune enthusiasm of their colleagues, the preacher Chauffepié and the church elder Jean Trugeaud, for Destinon's patronage.

This internal division among the Huguenots encouraged the Senate to resurrect its original proposal for a solution which would grant freedom while bypassing the diplomatic question.[166] But the events of 1740 had alerted the clergy, who not only submitted further petitions to the Senate, but also appealed directly to the *Oberalten* and the Sixty.[167] By September 1743 the Senate had been thwarted again.[168] At the same time, Destinon's purchase of a new and larger house in May 1743 laid open the way to his patronage of the Huguenots in the chapel opened in October 1744. As *Senior* Wagner reported to his colleagues in that month: Destinon had outwitted both Senate and *Oberalten*; all parties were now obliged to accept a situation which gave the Prussian Resident the same privileges and functions as the Dutch and Imperial Residents.[169]

Chaunel and His were also obliged to accept the success of Destinon and their opponents within the community. Their prediction that complex disputes over money would ensue proved correct. The formal separation of the Altona and Hamburg contingents only took place in 1761, when the Danish authorities finally decided that the resources of the community should be divided equally.[170]

Ultimately their dream of complete freedom in Hamburg was impossible, even though it was inspired by the good intentions of the Senate. Chaunel's friend and adviser, the Prussian diplomat von Bielfeld, made this quite clear in a letter of advice written in April 1744. He wrote that 'l'etablisment d'une Eglise Francoise à Hambourg sous la protection du Magistrat est une chose entierement incompatible avec les constitutions de la ville, contraire aux intentions du Senat, dangereuse pour les suites, et dont le succés est aussi long que douteux'. The Senate was obliged by law to allow diplomatic chapels, he argued, but constrained both by its constitution and by the clergy from granting more. Indeed, if the Senate gave way to the Huguenots, it would logically be obliged to grant as much to the Catholics, the Dutch Calvinists, even the Greek Orthodox. The Senate itself would then realise how complex the matter was, and even the direct intervention of the Prussian King would not prevent the whole affair dragging on for

---

[166] Ibid., 10 August 1742, Senate to Oberalten.
[167] StAH, Ministerium, III nos. 30–40, 1 November 1742, clergy to Senate; ibid., II 6, pp. 153–4, 158. [168] Ibid., pp. 207–9. [169] Ibid., pp. 307–9.
[170] Klefeker, *Verfassungen*, 8, pp. 617–18; Barrelet, 'Geschichte', pp. 16–19; Bolten, *Kirchen-Nachrichten von Altona*, 1, pp. 253–5. The correspondence relating to these disputes is in StAH, Senat, Cl.VII Lit.Hf No.2a Vol.6c–d.

several decades. Acceptance of Prussian patronage was the only solution: the community could then worship in Hamburg, while careful negotiations would avoid a rift with Altona. Above all, the Senate would be spared embarrassment and domestic strife. It could both accept and defend the compromise with equanimity, for, as Bielfeld wrote, 'En tolerant on est charmé de pouvoir sauver les apparences.'[171]

Until 1761 the Huguenots thus enjoyed the protection of the Prussian Resident in Hamburg, while they did not secede from the Altona community. This arrangement had considerable advantages, for the contentious issue of the *actus parochiales* and the *jura stolae* did not arise: baptisms, weddings and funerals were performed in Altona. The Lutheran clergy in Hamburg had no cause for complaint.

V

The Prussian Resident opened his chapel in October 1744. It marked the last step in the gradual establishment of the Calvinists in Hamburg. Both the Huguenots and the Dutch community now enjoyed the same informal privileges as the Catholics, and their situation remained unchanged until 1785. They were integrated into the economy, yet excluded from political life.[172] They were allowed to worship and were free from active persecution, yet only with the connivance of a city which was obliged to tolerate them more or less gracefully because of their diplomatic patrons.[173]

The magistrates strictly maintained the legal distinction between the public freedom of Lutheranism as the religion of the state and the *exercitium religionis privatum* of the minorities. The Lutherans worshipped in churches with spires and bells; the minorities were restricted to chapels without either.[174] The Lutheran preachers alone enjoyed the full exercise of the *Parochial-Rechte*, with all the revenues that they brought with them. The minorities were still dependent upon their preachers in Altona for the performance of the sacramental rites of passage, while obliged as residents in Hamburg to pay the *jura stolae* to the Lutheran clergy.[175]

Despite strenuous efforts, the Senate had failed to persuade the civic bodies to grant greater freedom. The economic arguments first advanced in 1734 made little impact; the claim that the Huguenots did after all worship the same God was similarly ineffective.

The technical reason for the failure to gain recognition for these views was the opposition of the *Oberalten* and the Sixty. For they alone had the

[171] Ibid., Cl.VII Lit.Hf No.2a Vol.6b, 10 April 1744, Bielfeld to Chaunel.
[172] Cf. Büsch, *Handlung*, pp. 76–7, 103; Schramm, 'Zwei "Millionäre"', pp. 31–40.
[173] Klefeker, *Verfassungen*, 8, pp. 618–19, 741–6.
[174] Ibid., p. 773.   [175] Ibid., pp. 618–22, 820.

constitutional right to make changes in the ecclesiastical polity in conjunction with the Senate. But their opposition was both reinforced, and in a sense created, by the intransigence of the clergy. They alerted the *Oberalten* to signs of danger, and, at crucial points, provided them with arguments and documentation. The dual functions of the members of these bodies as political representatives and parish administrators made them uniquely susceptible to such clerical intervention.

Yet even amongst the clergy, the 1730s and 1740s brought a slight moderation of the zeal of earlier times. For they now appeared to accept the existence of the diplomatic chapels, and their use by the minorities, as long as that use was neither excessive nor ostentatious. This new attitude, which clung to the strictures of local laws and constitutions, while recognising the dictates of the *jus gentium* as applied to diplomats, was especially marked in the period 1743–60. *Senior* Seelmann died in 1730, Edzardi in 1736, and, as Pastor Neumeister became less combative with age (he died in 1756), the most strident Orthodox champions ceased to dominate the stage.

The appointment of Friedrich Wagner as *Senior* in March 1743 inaugurated nearly two decades of relative peace and harmony. Wagner was close to the Wolffian and Thomasian Patriotic group in the Senate, and his policies in his first year of office had averted another public confrontation over the Prussian chapel.[176] He corresponded with Syndic Lipstorp, and applied indirect pressure on Destinon to persuade him to desist from his plan to build a chapel outside his formal residence.[177] Above all, he dissuaded his colleagues from publishing a pamphlet about the matter in Altona, a move which, as he rightly pointed out, might have turned the *Oberalten* against the clergy.[178]

His diplomacy ensured that peace prevailed after 1744 too. He led his colleagues in a formal protest against the public consecration of the Prussian chapel, but did not press the matter when, by February 1745, no reply had been received.[179]

In view of his behaviour, it is tempting to conclude that Wagner was not interested in the toleration issue. As a respected theologian educated

---

[176] On Wagner, see Winckler, *Nachrichten*, 1, pp. 8–12; *ADB*, 40, pp. 492–3; Höck, *Bilder*, pp. 193–4. His appointment was supported by the Wolffians, Syndic Lipstorp and Senators Widow and Brockes, who had wanted to appoint him as *Senior* as early as 1737. See: StAH, Ministerium, III A1т, no.1, an undated account of the appointment by Erdmann Neumeister.

[177] StAH, Senat, Cl.VII Lit.Hf No.2a Vol.6b, 1 May 1743, Wagner to Lipstorp; StAH, Ministerium, III A1s, no. 77, 5 September 1743, Lipstorp to Wagner; ibid., no. 78, 12 August 1743, note by Wagner on talks between Destinon and the Prussian preacher Kleinschmidt.

[178] Ibid., II 6, pp. 198–203.

[179] Ibid., III A1s, nos. 83–9, 13 November 1744, clergy to Senate; ibid., no. 510, 26 February 1745, clergy to Senate.

in Halle, it is certainly true that he was more obviously concerned with the spread of free-thinking. He conducted a thorough campaign against Johann Christian Edelmann and other 'fanatics'; and his tenure of office was characterised by the attention paid to the disturbing prominence of free-thinking journalism in the newspapers and journals which burgeoned in Hamburg and elsewhere in the 1740s and 1750s.[180]

But the emergence of a greater, less tangible, and ultimately more pernicious enemy did not cause him to lose sight of the traditional bugbears of the Lutheran Church in Hamburg. The fact was that Wagner saw the sense of the legal arguments put forward by the Senate in previous decades. He was the first to take serious stock of the debates of the past, and to concede that which had already been lost. It is significant that his first step on taking office as *Senior* was to gather together the archives of the Ministry, which had become scattered and disorganised through neglect: he made the first attempt to organise the material which survived, and to take a balanced view of the struggles of the last one and a half centuries.[181] The result was a moderation which characterised all his dealings with the Senate – over the Calvinist chapel, the Jewish synagogue in 1744, the publication of a new catechism, and the reform of the *Busstag* service in 1747, when biblical readings cursing the people of Israel were omitted in favour of others which stressed their promise of obedience and loyalty.[182]

Indeed after 1744 few problems arose. The only minor bone of contention was the thorny question of whether Calvinists could stand as godparents at Lutheran baptisms. The legal position was far from clear: even distinguished ecclesiastical lawyers, like Justus Henning Böhmer, had been uncertain on this point.[183] Since not even acknowledged authorities knew the answer, it was unlikely from the start that it could become a significant issue of debate in Hamburg where such disputes generally only arose where treaties, laws, constitutions and the writings of learned men could be bandied around. The discussion of this issue is interesting largely for the light it sheds on the degree of intermarriage between Calvinists and

---

[180] Cf. Winckler, *Nachrichten*, 1, p. 11; Mönckeberg, *Reimarus und Edelmann*, pp. 174–83. References to Wagner's concern with heretics and newspapers can be found in Goeze's index to the Church archive: StAH, Bestandsverzeichnis Ministerium (511–1) Bd. 3 and Bd. 4 under the headings *Zeitung, Edelmann, Fanatici*.

[181] StAH, Ministerium, II 6, pp. 169–80: the record of Wagner's first meeting with his colleagues as *Senior*, during which he made proposals for reorganisation and reform.

[182] Klefeker, *Verfassungen*, 8, pp. 532–5, 538–40. The synagogue affair is analysed above in Chapter 3, pp. 99–104. On the catechism see: Mönckeberg, 'Catechismus' and *idem, Reimarus und Edelmann*, pp. 66–9. Wagner's attitude to Calvinism is demonstrated by his relieved report in 1750 that the Calvinists had given up all hope of complete freedom in both Hamburg and Frankfurt: StAH, Ministerium, II 7, pp. 170, 180, 182–3.

[183] This uncertainty was underlined by his colleagues in Frankfurt: StAH, Ministerium, III A2c, no. 576, 19 September 1749, Fresenius to Wagner. Cf. Klefeker, *Verfassungen*, 8, pp. 799–800.

Lutherans.[184] It only became a matter of public concern briefly in 1749 when Neumeister was accused of being the author of a provocative anti-Calvinist pamphlet on the subject.[185] Inevitably, he pointed out, 'The Elbe is immediately set on fire.'[186] For once, the ageing pastor had been wrongly accused.[187] After much desultory discussion a compromise emerged: in cases where Calvinists were asked as godparents, the minor clergy and *Landprediger* should be allowed to officiate in order to save the *Hauptpastoren* the embarrassment of having to bless a non-Lutheran.[188] The Orthodox face was saved by a fiction as transparent as that which held that Hamburg had no religious worship other than that performed in the five main Lutheran churches.

The *Pathen-Sache* was the last minor dispute relating to the Calvinists. Both communities lived undisturbed for the next decade. For the Huguenots particularly, the peace coincided with the years of their greatest prosperity, when men like Pierre His and Pierre Boué entered the ranks of Hamburg's most wealthy and successful entrepreneurs. Their manufacture of and trade in products like textiles enabled Hamburg to rival France in this area. They also played a crucial role in the trade with French goods, an area of activity which became of central importance to Hamburg's economy after 1730 – one of the few sectors not seriously affected by the crisis of 1763 and the depression which followed it.[189]

But this prosperity alone did nothing to change their position. It was only with the appointment of Johann Melchior Goeze as *Senior* in 1760 that the issue of toleration was revived. But then novel factors transformed the relative position and attitudes of both Senate and clergy, factors which were to lead at last to the official recognition of the *exercitium religionis privatum* under the protection of the Senate as originally envisaged in 1734.

[184] Ibid., p. 802.
[185] StAH, Ministerium, III A2c, nos. 533–8, 14 April 1749, Senate to clergy.
[186] Ibid., no. 580, 4 December 1749, Neumeister, Pro Memoria. He blamed the Calvinist printer Behn.
[187] Ibid., no. 582, 24 November 1749, Pastor Christoph Buck of Rahlstedt to Neumeister. Buck admitted having written the pamphlet.
[188] The issue is fully documented in StAH, Senat, Cl.VII Lit.Hf No.2a Vol.7a–c and StAH, Ministerium, III A2c, nos. 490–598. See also Klefeker, *Verfassungen*, 8, pp. 802–3. *Landprediger* were those who held benefices in the city's extramural territories.
[189] Büsch, *Handlung*, pp. 76–7, 98–102; Schramm, Zwei "Millionäre"', pp. 31–40; Huhn, 'Handelsbeziehungen', 1, pp. 157–94; Liebel, 'Laissez-faire vs. Mercantilism', pp. 215–16.

5

Patriotism versus Orthodoxy: the struggle for limited religious freedom, 1760–85

On 19 September 1785 the *Bürgerschaft* assented to a law giving religious freedom to Catholics and Calvinists. The proposal aroused no opposition.[1] The Lutheran clergy were not consulted. Indeed, they only heard of the initiative three days previously. Their hands were bound: they could but wait for official notification of the inevitable.[2] The city abounded with rumours of 'die Toleranz Bürgerschaft', and the news of the decision was greeted as a triumph of *Aufklärung*.[3] At last the intransigence of the citizenry had been overcome; politics prevailed over the pulpit.

Pastor Goeze's comment on hearing the news, that 'the public has been sufficiently prepared [for this step] by the newspapers', provides the clue to the general context in which the reform took place.[4] In the first decades of the century the literature on toleration was relatively small. It consisted largely of translations from English, and the works of men such as Thomasius, Buddeus, Wolff, Pfaff. After 1740, the literature began to grow significantly. The emergence of writers like Johann Michael von Loen marked the prelude to a broad stream of writings on the subject of religious toleration in the 1760s. This flood of books and pamphlets was reported and reviewed in self-consciously enlightened journals (Nicolai's *Allgemeine Deutsche Bibliothek* is the most prominent example) and also in newspapers all over Germany.[5]

Indeed the issue of religious toleration lay at the heart of the debate about *Aufklärung*. As Klaus Scholder and others have pointed out, this was a phenomenon peculiar to the Enlightenment in Germany.[6] For here the

---

[1] StAH, Senat, Cl.VII Lit.Hf No.1 Vol.3g (no. 30), 19 September 1785, Resolutio Civium.
[2] StAH, Ministerium, III B, Fasc. 6, 16 September 1785, *Senior* Gerling to clergy.
[3] Ibid., 16 September 1785, note by Pastor Heidritter on the reverse of Gerling's letter.
[4] Ibid., 16 September 1785, note on the reverse of Gerling's letter.
[5] A chronological bibliography of the most important works is printed in Schultze, *Lessings Toleranzbegriff*, pp. 128–72. Cf. Kiesel, 'Toleranz', *passim*; Kopitzsch, 'Sozialgeschichte der Aufklärung', pp. 89–91; Kantzenbach, *Protestantisches Christentum*, pp. 184–90.
[6] Scholder, 'Grundzüge der theologischen Aufklärung', *passim*; Pütz, *Aufklärung*, pp. 10–50, 53–73; Kopitzsch, 'Sozialgeschichte der Aufklärung', pp. 63–5.

scepticism of a Voltaire was conspicuously lacking. Indifference bred of genuine uncertainty about the fundamental truth of Christianity or any of its permutations was rare amongst the *Aufklärer*.[7] They seldom questioned the inherited dogmatic framework, but concentrated rather on developing those aspects of Christianity most conducive to serving God by improving man's lot in society.[8] Rather than ask what a man believed, they would ask how conscientiously he believed, how much effort he had expended in the search for truth.[9]

Such a philosophy carried within it an implicit condemnation of the old Orthodoxy. The traditionalists were capable of asking only one question about human beings, namely that which asked them to define their attitude to a given set of dogmatic principles. The new theology, propounded by preachers and laymen alike, looked further and ranged more widely. It enabled the *Aufklärer* to ask questions about social ethics and the contribution of individuals to society. Ultimately, it enabled them to conceive of progress through education, to place faith in the pedagogic functions of law and government.[10]

Of course, the discussion was highly theoretical. Many of the propositions regarding toleration which emerged from it were so radical that even two centuries later they remain mere aspirations. But the important thing was that the problem itself became a matter of general interest and concern amongst the educated groups who constituted what Rudolf Vierhaus has called 'die Aufklärungsgesellschaft'.[11] As tireless propagandists for *Aufklärung*, journalists like Nicolai were also eager to point out examples of actual reforms. Joseph II's toleration edict of 1781 received immense publicity in newspapers and pamphlets all over Germany.[12] Even the Ottoman Emperor's edict of toleration for Catholics and Protestants of 1784 was hailed by one Altona newspaper as 'a glorious monument to toleration and enlightenment worthy of our age'.[13]

There is no satisfactory survey of the toleration edicts in Germany.[14] Prussia had always been more advanced than other German states, while Altona was unique in the degree of toleration which prevailed there since the seventeenth century. But in the context of the enlightened reform

---

[7] Schultze, *Lessings Toleranzbegriff*, p. 19; Scholder, 'Grundzüge der theologischen Aufklärung', p. 295; Kantzenbach, *Protestantisches Christentum*, pp. 81–5; Wild, 'Freidenker', *passim*.

[8] Scholder, 'Grundzüge der theologischen Aufklärung', pp. 295–303.

[9] Schultze, *Lessings Toleranzbegriff*, p. 19.

[10] These themes are discussed more fully in Whaley, 'Protestant Enlightenment'.

[11] Vierhaus, *Deutschland*, p. 108.

[12] See the bibliography in Schultze, *Lessings Toleranzbegriff*, pp. 161–2; Kopitzsch, 'Sozialgeschichte der Aufklärung', p. 90; Conrad, 'Religionsbann', pp. 168, 180–9.

[13] StAH, Senat, Cl.VII Lit.Hf No.1 Vol.3g (no. 17), 11 December 1784, *Reichs Post-Reuter*.

[14] Kopitzsch, 'Sozialgeschichte der Aufklärung', pp. 90–1; Conrad, 'Religionsbann', *passim*; Fürstenau, *Grundrecht der Religionsfreiheit*, pp. 78–83.

movement, many other states followed suit to a greater or lesser degree. Although the press hailed these edicts as simple victories for *Aufklärung*, the motives behind them were complex. As in the case of the union projects after 1690, there was a genuine religious conviction. But princes and magistrates were also moved by more mundane truths: the history of the Huguenots showed that toleration could bring prosperity; and the principle of legal equality for all Christians provided the prospect of the easier regulation of both economy and society. Once men were treated exclusively as citizens, rather than as Lutherans, Calvinists or Catholics, their role in society and their contribution to the economy could be more easily assessed and enhanced.[15] Contemporaries were fully aware of these factors: in Hamburg the works of Johann Peter Willebrandt and Ludwig von Hess were explicit on the political and economic advantages of toleration. Willebrandt wrote in 1776: 'Happy is a city where one need only worry about how much the peaceful inhabitants and foreigners contribute to the common good, and not about what they believe' – an idea which he had already elaborated in 1765.[16] Von Hess advanced a similar argument in 1780, in a work specifically concerned with the controversy in Hamburg.[17]

It is difficult to assess the popular impact of either the theological or the political and economic arguments. But it would be dubious to explain the success of the concession in 1785, as Rudolf Hermes did in 1934, in terms of 'the spirit of the age'.[18] For this begs an important issue. It may be true that a certain literate section of the population was conditioned by what it read. But that reading in a sense only provided them with a justification for action. It is still essential to examine the specific context in which such ideas were able to provide a motive for reform. In the case of the principalities, this involves primarily the study of the motives of the rulers. In cities like Hamburg it is essential to examine the behaviour of the Senate and the reasons why it was able in 1785 to prevail over the clergy – something it had failed to do for a century. The growth of even a limited Enlightenment in Germany after 1760 cannot provide a satisfactory answer: in Cologne, for example, a move to grant freedom to Protestants in 1787 ended not only in failure but in the loss of privileges which they already held.[19] There the opposition of clergy and citizenry was crucial, despite the persistence of the magistrates and the application of external pressure.

---

[15] The early literature on this theme is discussed by Hassinger, 'Wirtschaftliche Motive', *passim*. Cf. Kiesel, 'Toleranz', pp. 379–82; O'Brien, *Ideas of toleration*, pp. 5, 13–17, 22–31, 70–1; Karniel, 'Toleranzpolitik', *passim*. Economic and political considerations in the Duchy of Brunswick-Wolfenbüttel are discussed by Albrecht, *Förderung des Landesausbaues*, pp. 570–7.

[16] Willebrandt, *Grundriss einer schönen Stadt*, 2, p. 15. Cf. *idem*, *Abrégé*, pp. 56–9.

[17] L. von Hess, *Statistische Betrachtungen*, *passim*. The author was the uncle of Jonas Ludwig von Hess, the topographer.   [18] Hermes, *Reformierte Gemeinde*, p. 160.

[19] Heinen, 'Kölner Toleranzstreit', *passim*.

A similar constellation of powers ultimately operated more favourably in Hamburg. In the general context of wide-ranging national and local debate over toleration after 1760, important changes took place in both Senate and Church. The relative power of the clergy and their ability to intervene in the constitutional process declined. The Senate not only changed its arguments, making them more explicit and urgent, but was also able to exploit the decline of the informal constitutional authority of the clergy in order to persuade the *Bürgerschaft*.

Finally, it is important not to lose sight of the extreme utilitarianism of the enterprise. An examination of the terms of the concession itself should warn against taking too ecstatic a view of the impact of *Aufklärung* on the religious issue.[20] It gave only limited religious freedom. The constitution was to remain fundamentally Lutheran; the minorities were still excluded from the *Bürgerschaft*. Their chapels were denied both spires and bells; indeed, they were to avoid any appearance of being places of public worship. Their preachers could perform *actus parochiales*, but the *jura stolae* were to be paid to the Lutheran pastors as before. It was, in short, a classic statement of the limits of the *exercitium religionis privatum*. All that had really changed was that the patronage of the communities had been transferred from the diplomats to the Senate, which explicitly reserved the right to abolish the concession if its terms were contravened. In fact, nothing much had changed since the proposal of 1734.

Furthermore, these limited privileges were granted only to those religions recognised by the Peace of Westphalia. The Jews were excluded, as were such Christian sects as the Mennonites. The decree was in every sense a concession rather than a declaration of freedom.

I

Despite its obvious limitations, the concession did, however, mark a portentous breakthrough. It was a prelude to further reforms which extended political rights to the minorities in 1814 and 1819, steps which ultimately led to the separation of Church and State in 1860. But these developments were the product of a very different world which struggled to come to terms with the legacy of the French occupation of 1806–14, and with the political problems thrown up by rapid social and economic change thereafter.[21] Some, like Pastor Goeze, saw clearly that the separation of

[20] The concessions are printed in: Hermes, *Reformierte Gemeinde*, pp. 202–4; Bartels, *Einige Abhandlungen*, pp. 301–4; Dreves, *Geschichte*, pp. 236–41. They were identical for all three communities, except in the case of the Catholics, where monastic orders were expressly forbidden to settle in the city (ibid., p. 238).

[21] Bartels, *Einige Abhandlungen*, pp. 307–14; Bergemann, *Staat und Kirche*, pp. 38–40, 61–74. See also below, pp. 210–16.

Church and State must inevitably ensue from the relaxation of traditional religious policies.[22] But the struggle between Senate and clergy which preceded it can only be understood in the context of fundamental changes in their attitude and relative position after 1760. In both cases the development is characterised by the theme of resurgence and renewal. In the case of the Senate, that renewal led to victory in 1785; in the case of the clergy, it led to the defeat of Orthodoxy.

As in most German states, the end of the Seven Years War marked the inception of a profound and protracted economic crisis in Hamburg. The city suffered particularly acutely due to the harsh Prussian mercantilist and monetary policies.[23] As Helen Liebel and Franco Venturi have pointed out, the significance of this general crisis in generating enlightened reforms has been neglected. In most states such reforms were a direct response to dire economic and social problems: a new sense of urgency enhanced the need to know more about the structures of social and economic life.[24] Both princes and their administrators became more convinced of the necessity to collect information about their environment as a prelude to its reform. Topographies, learned treatises on political economy, popular pamphlets on subjects as diverse as population growth and the promotion of industry and agriculture, were both produced and discussed by enlightened elites everywhere.[25]

In Hamburg this kind of response to the general crisis was evident in the formation of the second Patriotic Society in 1765. It was inspired by English models (especially by the work of William Shipley and the Society of Arts in London), and aspired to promote the general welfare of the city by encouraging individual rather than merely state initiative.[26] At the same time it drew upon local traditions, particularly on those of the first Patriotic Society founded in 1724. That Society had ceased to meet regularly after about 1750, for, as its original members died, they were not replaced (Johann Klefeker was its last surviving member in the 1760s).[27] The new group of 1765 emerged from very much the same constellation of families. The Society was formally proclaimed by Johann Ulrich Pauli in 1765, but the project grew out of discussions held in 1763 in the house of Hermann Samuel Reimarus. The author of the *Wolffenbütteler Fragmente* later

---

[22] Schultze, 'Toleranz und Orthodoxie', pp. 218–19; Röpe, *Goeze*, p. 90.

[23] Liebel, 'Laissez-faire vs. Mercantilism', pp. 229–38; Büsch, *Handlung*, pp. 114–41. See also note 34 below.

[24] Liebel, 'Aufgeklärter Absolutismus', *passim*; Venturi, 'Crise de l'ancien régime', *passim*.

[25] For a more general discussion, see Whaley, 'Protestant Enlightenment', and *idem*, 'Rediscovering the *Aufklärung*'.

[26] For the following, see: Liebel, 'Laissez-faire vs. Mercantilism', pp. 224–9; Brunner, 'Patriotische Gesellschaft', *passim*; Hubrig, *Patriotische Gesellschaften*, pp. 46–54; Braun, *Technologische Beziehungen*, pp. 127–33; Kopitzsch, 'Hamburgische Gesellschaft', *passim*.

[27] Klefeker, *Verfassungen*, 12, pp. 372–4.

published by Lessing, Reimarus was a pupil and son-in-law of Fabricius, a friend of Brockes, and, as Professor at the Gymnasium, a colleague of Richey – all three members of the original Patriotic Society. He gathered around him a small group of relatives and friends, all of them wealthy and educated, who formed the core of the fifty-three original members of the new Society.[28]

As was the case in 1724, the Society was a private initiative and had no official standing. Like its precursor, its members were largely drawn from a small group – often kinsmen. They were scholars, lawyers, doctors, politicians and successful merchants. Their aim was to provide a forum for practical discussion, and they hoped that individuals would subsequently seek to apply the insights and principles discussed in the Society to their respective fields of activity. Significantly, the initial membership included Senator Dorner, who was to play a crucial role in the toleration debate.[29] For it was Dorner, together with Senate Secretary (later Syndic) Matsen and Syndic Sillem, who formed the core of the most powerful group in the Senate in the 1770s and 1780s.[30] A further member of the same circle was the Secretary of the *Oberalten*, Johann Gottfried Misler, whose collaboration was ultimately crucial in gaining the support of the representative bodies.[31]

It is not easy to measure the indirect impact of the Society on government in general. But most scholars have agreed with Helen Liebel's conclusion: 'The Patriotic Society represented the informed opinion of almost all of the Hamburg elite.'[32] The Society's public schemes are well known. Its promotion of useful projects for poor-relief and education conformed with its ambition to provide the kind of initiative of which governments were not capable. But the whole ideology of the Society went further than that: in Helen Liebel's words, it 'provided the city's governors with the active aid of the intelligentsia who were otherwise absent from the halls of government...'[33] It was an enlightened pressure group, at once more established and more closely concerned with the specific problems of the city than the contemporaneous friendship circles of Lessing and Klopstock.[34]

[28] Matthei, *Untersuchungen*, pp. 12, 40; Liebel, 'Laissez-faire vs. Mercantilism', pp. 224–5; Kopitzsch, 'Hamburgische Gesellschaft', pp. 72–8.

[29] Ramcke, *Beziehungen*, pp. 244–9; Büsch, *Dorner und Sieveking*, pp. 9–34; Buek, *Bürgermeister*, pp. 260–2.

[30] On Matsen, see Schröder, *Lexikon*, 5, pp. 61–2 and Ramcke, *Beziehungen*, p. 252. On Sillem, see Schröder, *Lexikon*, 7, pp. 187–8 and Buek, *Bürgermeister*, p. 294.

[31] Schröder, *Lexikon*, 5, pp. 297–300; Schramm, *Neun Generationen*, 1, pp. 159, 202–16; Günther, 'Bildergallerie', p. 150; Buek, *Oberalten*, p. 386. The important function of the *Oberalten* Secretaries is noted by Bartels, *Einige Abhandlungen*, p. 140.

[32] Liebel, 'Laissez-faire vs. Mercantilism', p. 227. Cf. Kopitzsch, 'Hamburgische Gesellschaft', pp. 78–82.   [33] Liebel, 'Laissez-faire vs. Mercantilism', p. 228.

[34] Kopitzsch, 'Lessing und Hamburgs Gelehrte', pp. 19–55.

Its commitment to those problems was clearly demonstrated in Pauli's pamphlet of 1765, a work which also significantly stressed the author's commitment to Christianity and his opposition to 'praktische Freygeisterei' (practical free-thinking).[35]

The ideals of the Society, its new awareness of the need for private initiative and public reform, its fundamental commitment to the commercial principles on which Hamburg society was based, provide the wider context of the debate over a religious concession after 1774. Similarly, the Society's links with the past, especially with its precursor of the 1720s, accounted for the limitations of the concession. For the new Patriots were just as Lutheran as the old. Like them, they had no desire to establish a truly heterodox society. They merely wished to moderate the prohibitive legislation of the past in order to conform with the economic and political needs of the present. In the context of what many contemporaries saw as a prolonged economic depression after 1763, that led inevitably to a preoccupation with one of the city's major assets – its Calvinist communities.[36]

These changes amongst the enlightened elite coincided with equally significant developments within the Lutheran Church. Its history after 1760 is dominated by the character of one man: Johann Melchior Goeze, Pastor of St Catherine's since 1755, who succeeded Wagner as *Senior* in 1760. Although he resigned the *Seniorat* ten years later, he did not die until 1786; and whether as *Senior* or as Pastor, the controversies in which he engaged shook both Hamburg itself and indeed the whole of Protestant Germany. With good reason Waldemar Oehlke wrote of the years of the *Goezekriege* (the Goeze wars).[37] Reviled as 'Der Papst Hammoniens', 'Der Inquisitor',

---

35 Pauli, *An alle wahren Patrioten*, p. 38.

36 There is no good modern study of Hamburg's economy in this period, on which there are conflicting views. Writing in 1806, J. E. F. Westphalen spoke of continued growth after 1763, particularly rapid after 1783 (StAH, Hss No. 381, *passim*.). Other manuscript sources, however, especially those cited in this chapter, continually contradict this view, as does J. G. Büsch who claimed that the period 1763–88 was one of continuous depression (Büsch, *Handlung*, pp. 141, 109–40). This view is also confirmed by other later writers: Sieveking, 'J. G. Büsch', pp. 79, 592–3; Matthei, *Untersuchungen*, pp. 37–9; Vogel, 'Handelskonjunkturen', pp. 60, 64. There was undoubtedly a recovery from the severe crisis of 1763, but it seems equally clear that levels of prosperity remained relatively low until *c*. 1778–80, when slow growth began once more. In a city used to almost constant, and often dramatic, growth since the sixteenth century, such periods of low-level stability inevitably looked very much like the crises into which they were magnified on the level of political and polemical discourse. The one area which seems to have been immune from short-term fluctuations, and subject to continuous growth throughout this period, was trade with France (see Huhn, 'Handelsbeziehungen', 1, pp. 20–34, 42; Jeannin, 'Hansestädte', pp. 61–2; Liebel, 'Laissez-faire vs. Mercantilism', p. 216). This overall pattern is not altogether dissimilar from that found in many other areas of Germany, where economic expansion only became marked after about 1775 (see Dreyfus, 'Die deutsche Wirtschaft um 1815', pp. 353, 369–70, 378).

37 Oehlke, *Lessing*, 2, p. 311. For a concise survey of Goeze's life, works and controversies, see Schröder, *Lexikon*, 2, pp. 515–37. See also note 40 below.

'Götze des Pöbels' ('the idol of the rabble', a neat pun on his name), even as 'Melchior Cromwell', Goeze was the last of the great Orthodox giants.[38] He was the self-conscious heir to the tradition of J. F. Mayer and Erdmann Neumeister in Hamburg, of Ernst Salomo Cyprian and Valentin Ernst Löscher in the wider Lutheran world.[39] A respected scholar and a brilliant orator, he was the most outspoken opponent of any form of *Aufklärung*. During the course of a lifetime he published over a hundred books (many of them weighty tomes). He denounced Lessing's publication of the *Wolffenbütteler Fragmente*, and disputed with Semler and Teller, Alberti and Friderici.[40] He even found time to write a work condemning Goethe's *Werther* as 'an apology for suicide'.[41] Indeed, during these decades, to have been attacked by Goeze was almost in itself to be enlightened.

Goeze's disputes with theologians and laymen throughout Germany were by no means his sole concern. He found inevitably that new and more moderate ideas appeared in Hamburg too. His attempt to hold back the floodwaters of the *Aufklärung* in his own city was made difficult, and ultimately impossible, by the opposition he encountered in his own Ministry. His bitter denunciation of a whole series of colleagues, two of whom were said to have died as a result, inevitably aroused indignation and opposition.

The most significant of these local campaigns was conducted in 1769 against Julius Gustav Alberti, a deacon of his own parish. Alberti, friend of Senator Dorner and Klopstock, had refused to read out the old *Busstag* prayer with its appeal to 'Pour out thy wrath upon the heathen that have not known thee, and upon the kingdoms that have not called upon thy name' (Psalm 79:6).[42] His refusal encouraged other clergymen to demand the amendment of the prayer. Goeze's official complaints to the Senate were ignored on the intercession of seventeen preachers who, with official approval, effected the amendment of the prayer to read:

Pour out thy anger upon the people that do not recognise thee, and upon the kingdoms that do not venerate thy name, but treat it with hostility and slander it, if through thy bounty they do not allow themselves to be led to repentance, so that they too recognise that you, O Lord, are the ruler over the whole world…

[38] Höck, *Bilder*, pp. 203, 223–5. Goeze is compared with Cromwell in *Kleine Charakteristik von Hamburg*, p. 53.

[39] Röpe, *Goeze*, pp. 41–59; Schultze, 'Toleranz und Orthodoxie', pp. 197–9.

[40] The best accounts of these disputes are still: Röpe, *Goeze*, pp. 103–210; Oehlke, *Lessing*, 2, pp. 304–68; Schmidt, *Lessing*, 2, pp. 248–321. The most recent discussion is by Kopitzsch, *Grundzüge*, pp. 452–82.

[41] Quoted by Höck, *Bilder*, p. 220. This particular dispute, involving both Goeze and Lessing, is discussed by Röpe, *Goeze*, pp. 232–54.

[42] *ADB*, 1, pp. 213–14; Schröder, *Lexikon*, 1, pp. 32–4; Büsch, *Dorner und Sieveking*, p. 15.

The new prayer thus implicitly did not include a curse on all non-Lutherans, merely on those who rejected or maligned God.[43]

Rather than preside over the introduction of this reform, Goeze resigned as *Senior*. He refused to participate in the meetings of the clergy and continued to denounce the members of what became known as the 'Alberti party'.[44] He supported his colleagues in their opposition to toleration, but otherwise remained distant, if not openly hostile. Alberti's death in 1772 (supposedly of a broken heart) merely reinforced the sense of division amongst the clergy – the 'Alberti party' having considerable support in the Senate.[45] Even Goeze's supporters, like Pastor Johann Dietrich Winckler, disapproved of his vitriolic and savage manner, which became more accentuated once his hands were no longer bound by the constraints of the *Seniorat*. As Winckler wrote to a colleague in Weimar: 'It is unfortunate that Pastor Goeze pursues his learned disputes with such fire. In my view a more modest quill is always more successful.'[46]

The *Goezekriege* have little direct bearing on the toleration debate in Hamburg. But they did attract the attention of educated men all over Germany to the city. They provided the specific controversy about toleration with a wider geographical dimension than ever before.

Controversies over the most diverse aspects of the new theology, and Goeze's tireless advocacy of what he called 'the just cause of the Lutheran Church', also produced the first serious open divisions amongst the clergy.[47] In the 1720s the more moderate clergy were a small minority: they expressed their disapproval of Neumeister's Orthodox zeal in private, if at all. But many had become uneasy about the dogmatic stance of old. The Ministry still maintained a united front in its representations to the Senate over the toleration issue. However, that unity was now largely the product of fears about the future of Lutheranism as the foundation of the urban constitution; for that affected not only the constitutional position of the Church but also the income of its ministers. Religious freedom implied both heterodoxy, a theologically indifferent polity, and the loss of personal revenue if the *jura stolae* (upon which the clergy increasingly depended due to the erosion of their regular income through inflation) were to be shared by Catholics and Calvinists too.[48] But the fact that the clergy were divided over the new theology meant that opposition to toleration was no longer wholeheartedly based on the belief in the exclusive dogmatic superiority

---

[43] Röpe, *Goeze*, pp. 103–23; Oehlke, *Lessing*, 2, 314–17; Klefeker, *Verfassungen*, 12, pp. 738–48. Klefeker's original draft of this section was withdrawn when Goeze objected to explicit and derogatory references to himself: StAH, Senat, Cl.VII Lit.La No.3 Vol.9d.

[44] Wotschke (ed.), 'Wincklers Briefe', pp. 55, 80.

[45] Ibid., pp. 57, 61.   [46] Ibid., pp. 91–2.

[47] The title of a work published in 1771.   [48] Klefeker, *Verfassungen*, 8, p. 820.

of Orthodox Lutheranism. Ultimately, the Ministry came to oppose not the spirit of the concession but its long-term constitutional and ecclesiastical implications.

II

The arguments of the clergy opposing limited toleration in 1774 and after were essentially no different from those which Goeze elaborated after 1766. His polemics of that period are important for the way in which they appealed to both the Orthodox and their critics. The former could persuade themselves that their integrity remained intact; the latter could console themselves with the argument that at least no one was actually being persecuted.

Two points are important. Firstly, although decades of internecine strife ultimately reduced the public standing of the clergy, individuals like Alberti who openly opposed the ecclesiastical regime from within were rare. Goeze later attacked Pastor Moldenhauer for his excessively charitable view of the chances of salvation for good heathens and Turks; but Moldenhauer himself never saw any contradiction between his theological convictions and the intolerant demands of his public office as pastor in the city of Hamburg.[49]

Secondly, it is easy to take a cynical view of the continual clerical references to the *jura stolae*. Contemporaries like J. B. Basedow and Johann Olearius were quick to deride clerical cupidity and greed.[50] But the *jura stolae* also had immense symbolic importance. They were more visible to the world at large, especially to the congregations, than old laws and constitutions.

Indeed, Goeze's own views on toleration shared more common ground with those of his opponents than was generally recognised.[51] In a sense, he held a view similar to that of the first Patriots, similar indeed to that of the new Patriots, except that he dismissed as irrelevant and pernicious the economic considerations which were to become so central. His first major public pronouncement on toleration in 1766 was provoked by a series of newspaper articles published since 1760 in Hamburg and Altona. One reported the opulent public funeral of Pierre His in 1761. Others concerned the fiftieth anniversary of the ordination of the Dutch Calvinist preacher, Mäsius, in 1761, and his death in 1765.[52] All of them referred to the

[49] Oehlke, *Lessing*, 2, pp. 320–1; Schröder, *Lexikon*, 2, pp. 536–7. On Moldenhauer, see ibid., 5, pp. 333–41 and Jensen, *Hamburgische Kirche*, 1, pp. 39–40. He was *Lector secundarius* and *Pastor* at the Cathedral; as such he ranked as the most junior *Hauptpastor*: ibid., p. 27.
[50] [Basedow], *Exemplarischer Gebrauch...des Zeugnisses*, pp. 48–9; Olearius, *Gute Sache der...Reformirten*, pp. 6–7. [51] Schultze, 'Toleranz und Orthodoxie', pp. 199–201.
[52] StAH, Senat, Cl.VII Lit.Hb No.3 Vol.13(1); StAH, Ministerium, II 8, pp. 60–2; Goeze, *Zeugniss*, pp. 6–8.

Preacher, congregation, Elders and Consistory of the Calvinist Church in Hamburg. Although superficially harmless, they did distort the actual legal situation. For, officially, there was no such thing as a Calvinist Church in Hamburg – merely a diplomatic chaplain with a diplomatic chapel which was used unofficially by Calvinists who lived in the city.

Goeze's repeated complaints to the Senate met with no response: merely a statement that the Senate was powerless to prevent private individuals from using a certain form of words in that section of the newspapers not subject to censorship.[53] His memorial of March 1763 protested vigorously against this view, but again the Senate insisted that no action could be taken.[54]

Thus Goeze decided to confront the Calvinists in public. In February 1766 he published his *Zeugniss der Wahrheit*, which aimed to clarify the situation once and for all. The pamphlet itself represented the fruit of his systematic reorganisation and study of the ministerial archive during his first two years as *Senior*.[55] It quoted all previous ministerial protests, and in many ways added nothing new. His argument that the Calvinist community had no right to call itself by the name of a 'Gemeinde zu Hamburg' (congregation in Hamburg) rested on a strict interpretation of the Peace of Westphalia, and on local laws and constitutions. It was, however, necessary to reiterate these points, he declared, for otherwise the Calvinists would in the future refer back to these newspapers to claim rights which they never in fact had; for 'a hundred years of wrong do not make an hour of right'.[56] He appealed to 'upright patriots who are so solemnly bound to take conscientious care of the well-being of their descendants and to faithfully transmit to them the rights which they themselves received from their own blessed forebears'. They must look forward not merely to the next ten or twenty years, but to the long term.[57]

At the same time he was concerned to stress that the Calvinists were not in fact persecuted or oppressed in Hamburg. They had no political rights, but they were often more prosperous than the citizens themselves; they lived in the best houses, and, in many cases, paid lower taxes than most citizens. They also had their *exercitium religionis publicum* in Altona. To grant greater religious freedom in Hamburg itself would be to undermine the constitution; the history of Bremen, Frankfurt and Worms provided a salutary warning.[58] Such lenience would ultimately give the prosperous

---

53 StAH, Ministerium, II 8, p. 62.
54 StAH, Senat, Cl.VII Lit.Hb No.3 Vol.13(1), 18 March 1763, clergy to Senate, and 31 October 1763, Senate to clergy.
55 The work of indexing and cataloguing was started in September 1760 and completed in November 1762. See the title pages to StAH, Bestandsverzeichnis Ministerium 511–1, Bd. 2–4.
56 Goeze, *Zeugniss*, pp. 5–6, 27.   57 Ibid., p. 19.   58 Ibid., pp. 2–3, 11–12.

Calvinists the upper hand. 'What will remain for our descendants?', he asked. 'At first the smallest houses, apartments and basements, and finally only the yoke or the wanderer's staff.'[59]

Only in this sense did Goeze differ from the Patriots. They came to believe that Lutheran purity was compatible with religious concessions motivated by economic considerations. Goeze appealed to the Civic Colleges, both to their traditional vigilance over their inherited rights and to their fears of increased competition from wealthy and industrious outsiders. His view of the economy was essentially a static one: a given pool of wealth divided amongst a greater or lesser number of individuals. The Patriots believed that, by enlarging the whole pool of wealth, all would prosper; by contrast, Goeze insisted that, if the community only nurtured 'the priceless treasure of the true religion given to it by God', divine providence would take care of trade and commerce.[60]

However blinkered his argument appears in the light of modern economics, Goeze's view struck a raw nerve in the world of the *Aufklärung*. For where indeed was the line to be drawn between the principle of liberty of conscience on the one hand and indifference leading to anarchy on the other? The Senate itself had demonstrated its opposition to Pelagianism and indifference in mandates against heretics in 1761 and 1764.[61] Only later was it able to make a convincing distinction between indifference and limited toleration.

More important than the fact that both Frederick II and the magistrates of Bremen sent official protests against Goeze's *Zeugniss* were the pamphlets which appeared in the following years.[62] They obliged Goeze to explain his position more fully and to make clear that he bore no grudge against the Calvinists themselves. J. B. Basedow mocked the *Senior*'s elaboration of the *jura stolae* issue; Andreas Rediger, a Calvinist preacher in Worms, defended his Church against Goeze's accusations in two pamphlets of 1767 and 1768.[63] Most influential of all was the work of August Friedrich Wilhelm Sack, *Hofprediger* in Berlin, who pleaded for religious peace, and pointed to the fact that decisions in these matters properly belonged to the magistrates and not to the clergy.[64] Doctrinal controversies, Sack argued, could only impede the cause of Christianity: the *Aufklärung*, and the theological debates it provoked, provided the greatest threat of a return to the scholasticism of old. The only hope lay in the observance of 'a reverent

[59] Ibid., p. 47.   [60] Ibid.
[61] Klefeker, *Verfassungen*, 8, pp. 530–2; Schultze, 'Toleranz und Orthodoxie', pp. 211–12.
[62] StAH, Senat, Cl.VII Lit.Hf No.2a Vol.9a.
[63] [Basedow], *Exemplarischer Gebrauch...des Zeugnisses*, pp. 48–9; Rediger, *Rettung*; idem, *Bestättigte Unschuld*.
[64] [Sack], *Ein Wort zu seiner Zeit*, p. 5. The work appeared anonymously; Sack is identified as the author in *ADB*, 37, p. 299.

silence' on all issues 'over which God himself has cast a sacred shroud of darkness'.[65]

Despite the imposing moderation of Sack's argument, neither his nor any other of these pamphlets effectively answered Goeze's claims. On the contrary, they provoked him to strengthen them and to remove all doubts about his motives. In a sermon of 1768 he preached *Von der Liebe gegen fremde Religionsverwandte* (concerning the love to be shown to non-Lutheran Christians).[66] In 1770 he published his *Die gerechte Sache der Lutherischen Kirche* (the just cause of the Lutheran Church). Both works explicitly stated that he had no wish to enter into doctrinal controversies.[67] For him it was clear that Lutheranism was right; but at the same time he did not desire to persecute those who believed otherwise. The real point was whether or not a Lutheran community like Hamburg could afford to be indifferent to the truth and the political traditions which rested upon it.

Toleration threatened to erode the very fabric of the Hamburg polity. For Goeze's Church was not the enlightened Church of Christian human-kind, but the *ecclesia militans* defined by a specific faith. Like the Jews, Calvinists and Catholics might enjoy 'full liberty of conscience and all civil rights'.[68] But the visible Church remained the State Church, without which the social and political order would collapse. As Goeze's nineteenth-century apologist, Pastor G. R. Röpe, pointed out, his vision extended far beyond the exigencies of the present to the real dilemma of Röpe's own day, to the ultimate separation of Church and State in 1860.[69]

III

The debates of the 1760s provided the wider context in which the concession was first proposed in 1774. It was the work of a relatively small group in the Senate led by Senator Dorner, Syndic Sillem and Secretary Matsen, supported by *Bürgermeister* Scheele; as Sillem later noted, many of their other colleagues were far from convinced. Secondly, the concession plan concerned only the Dutch Calvinists: the Huguenots and Catholics were only included in the discussion in 1782.[70] That the matter was raised at all was due to the determination of a small group of enlightened Patriots. That it went as far as the *Bürgerschaft* was a tribute to their perseverance, and to the active sympathetic collaboration of Johann Gottfried Misler,

---

[65] [Sack], *Ein Wort zu seiner Zeit*, p. 20.
[66] The sermon is summarised by Röpe, *Goeze*, pp. 93–102.
[67] Goeze, *Gerechte Sache*, preface n.p. and pp. 248–9.
[68] Quoted by Schultze, 'Toleranz und Orthodoxie', p. 217.
[69] Röpe, *Goeze*, p. 90.
[70] StAH, Senat, Cl.VII Lit.Hf No.1 Vol.3g (no. 5), 23 October 1782, EPS.

Secretary of the *Oberalten*. His support cleared many a misunderstanding; his tenacity and diplomacy persuaded his colleagues in the Civic Colleges to go further than ever before. Only the intervention of the clergy doomed the enterprise to failure.

The immediate stimulus to action was a minor crisis in the life of the Dutch community. In 1773 Resident van Hop returned to Holland and his successor, Baron Hogguer, announced that, on his arrival, he was determined to rent a larger house than that owned by the community on the Valentinskamp. The community's offer to build a new house was disregarded. Hogguer rented a larger residence on the Speersort, thus leaving the community with the prospect of losing the diplomatic protection which it had enjoyed since 1709.[71]

From the speed with which negotiations were started, it seems likely that such an eventuality had already been discussed. In January 1774 Syndic Sillem wrote in confidence to the Hamburg Resident in The Hague, asking him to enquire discreetly whether the Estates General would object to relinquishing their right of patronage.[72] Having gained a favourable impression, the next step was to approach the Calvinists themselves, who were still awaiting Hogguer's arrival in May. A meeting with Sillem, Dorner and Matsen again produced a favourable result. Matsen himself agreed to draft a petition which would then be submitted to the Senate in the name of the Calvinist community.[73]

These secret negotiations were accompanied by attempts to convince a majority in the Senate that action should be taken. Matsen apparently played a crucial role. In a moving speech he deployed both theological and economic arguments. He announced: 'I find it harsh and cruel that one should prevent fellow Christians, who only deviate from our own present system in a few dogmatic trivialities, from freely exercising their religion.' He dismissed the legal objections based on the Peace of Westphalia and concentrated on the economic advantages that toleration might bring. Cologne had, after all, declined as a result of intolerance. Holland, Prussia and 'even Altona' had gained immeasurably from benevolent policies. In view of the vicissitudes of the economy since 1763, Hamburg had no choice but to follow suit. The clergy must be obliged to acquiesce: their solemn oath against Catholics and Calvinists had no legal standing. Senate and *Bürgerschaft* alone had the right to make decisions regarding the ecclesiastical polity.[74]

[71] Hermes, *Reformierte Gemeinde*, pp. 148–9.
[72] StAH, Senat, Cl.VII Lit.Hf No.2a Vol.11, 11 January 1777, Sillem to M. M. Klefeker, and 25 January 1777, M. M. Klefeker to Sillem.
[73] StAH, DRG, II Aa Bd. 13, entries for March–April 1774.
[74] StAH, Senat, Cl.VII Lit.Hf No.2a Vol.11 (Collectanea), n.d., Matsen.

This argument, subdued compared with his later speeches, was effective: in March 1774 the *Oberalten* had agreed to the proposal, and on 11 April the matter went to the Sixty.[75] Throughout, it was stressed that there was no intention of granting anything more than an *exercitium religionis privatum*. The Sixty too assented, subject to the condition that the Calvinists agreed to give up all rights of appeal to the Imperial Courts.[76] The Ministry appeared nonplussed when it was informed, and refused to submit a detailed case for nearly three weeks. Indeed, its memorial was only submitted on 3 May, two days before the *Bürgerschaft* meeting. The letter added nothing new to the traditional legal arguments. It did, however, contain a powerful appeal to the economic interests of the citizenry, claiming that even limited freedom would attract more outsiders to the city who would deprive good Lutherans of their livelihood. Goeze had made a similar claim in 1766. Its novelty now lay in the fact that it was employed to disguise the *jura stolae* argument: the decline of clerical revenue was put forward as but one of many dire economic consequences of a concession.[77]

This late submission proved to be crucial.[78] The Senate itself had prepared a moderate proposal. It sought simply to allay fears rather than present lengthy arguments: the proposal contained assurances that the Calvinists alone would be given these privileges, and that even they would never be given full political rights. Above all, the Senate pointed out, nothing would really change in practice, apart from the fact that the rights of patronage would now be held by the Senate rather than the Estates General of Holland.[79]

The *Bürgerschaft* was, however, persuaded by the apparently more urgent arguments of the clergy. At a meeting attended by 219 citizens, the concession was rejected outright by a majority of thirteen votes.[80] The Senate reserved the right to reintroduce the proposal. But for the moment nothing could be done. Baron Hogguer arrived on 8 May, and the community was forced to reach a compromise with him by rebuilding and enlarging the house on the Valentinskamp.[81]

Further talks over the summer brought no progress. Syndic Sillem reported that the fears of the *Bürgerschaft*, that the Calvinists might seek

75 StAH, Senat, Cl.VII Lit.Hf No.2a Vol.11, 23 March 1774, Conclusum der Oberalten and 11 April 1774, Senate to Sixty.
76 Ibid., 11 April 1774, Conclusum der 6oger.
77 Ibid., 3 May 1774, clergy to Senate. Cf. Goeze, *Zeugniss*, p. 47.
78 Wotschke (ed.), 'Wincklers Briefe', p. 63.
79 StAH, Senat, Cl.VII Lit.Hf No.2a Vol.11, 5 May 1774, Propositio in forma.
80 StAH, EB, No. 1 Bd. 24, pp. 762, 767–8; ibid., Senat, Cl.VII Lit.Hf No.2a Vol.13, June 1776, report by Senator Dorner.
81 StAH, Senat, Cl.VII Lit.Hf. No.2a Vol.11, 10 May 1774, Sillem to M. M. Klefeker. Hermes, *Reformierte Gemeinde*, pp. 151–2.

to undermine the constitution, were too great. The opposition of the clergy was so violent that any further initiatives might provoke a riot. The diplomats too were now doubtful, and another failure might well place the city in a delicate position abroad and prejudice hopes for a solution in the future.[82] By August it was quite clear that neither the Colleges nor Baron Hogguer would contemplate any change in the existing arrangements.

Even so, the refusal of the *Bürgerschaft* aroused a storm of controversy. For over a year pamphlets appeared on behalf of both sides.[83] The clergy themselves printed a letter they had sent to the Senate justifying their opposition in June 1774.[84] Their memorial of 3 May was also printed by one of their opponents, with annotations which dismissed the Ministry's claims point by point.[85] In many ways the pamphlets were more important for the publicity they gave the issue than for what they said. But two in particular, published in 1775, voiced the economic arguments.[86] One made the telling point that the income of the Lutheran Church would best be preserved by a prosperous economy for: 'If trade flourishes, there will be prosperous Lutherans, and their Church will suffer no privation.'[87]

But pamphlets alone could achieve little. For the clergy had the insuperable advantage of the pulpits. Once more Goeze excelled himself. Indeed his vehemence both in the pulpit and in print provoked the Calvinists themselves to a rare public response. In a newspaper statement, they denied that they wanted anything more than an *exercitium religionis privatum*, and declared that they had no ambitions to attain political rights.[88]

Although the initiative failed, it had become clearer than ever that the clergy were the real backbone of the reaction. Their legal arguments had won the day. The invocation of their private oath of 1719 (to which all new preachers were obliged to subscribe on taking office), and of their official *formula committendi* (oath of admission), pointed to the crux of the issue; but also to a major inconsistency. For, while taking refuge in laws and constitutions, they also claimed to be answerable not to politicians but to God alone. That claim inevitably placed the urban constitution in a dubious light. For the constitution clearly placed the *jus circa sacra* (laws concerning religion) in the hands of Senate and *Bürgerschaft* in terms which were difficult to reconcile with the divine laws invoked by the clergy.

[82] StAH, Senat, Cl.VII Lit.Hf No.2a Vol.11, n.d., Sillem, 'Gründe...die Sache...liegen zu lassen'.
[83] Two important collections have survived in StAH, DRG, I A 21, 23, 25 and StAH, Sammelband A670/9.   [84] *Ein wichtiges Document...oder letzte Vorstellung.*
[85] *Beytrag zur Geschichte der Toleranz.*
[86] *Patriotische Vorstellung: Erwägung der Gründe.*
[87] *Erwägung der Gründe*, p. 16.
[88] The declaration, published in Hamburg and Altona, is enclosed in a letter of protest to the Senate in StAH, Senat, Cl.VII Lit.Hf No.2a Vol.11 (Collectanea), 14 December 1774. Goeze had defended his sermons in two pamphlets: *Beweis* and *Vertheidigung.*

This inconsistency was ultimately the Ministry's undoing. For over a century the Civic Colleges had been prompted by the clergy to defend their own constitutional rights against an overbearing Senate. Now some believed that those same rights must be defended against an overbearing clergy. The Secretary of the *Oberalten*, Johann Gottfried Misler, was instrumental in effecting this shift in attitude. A pious and devout Lutheran, Misler held strong views on the subordinate constitutional position of the Church, over which he was to exchange a series of pamphlets with Goeze in 1780 and 1781.[89] More than any other individual, Misler was responsible for persuading his colleagues that the clergy had no right to meddle in the political aspects of ecclesiastical government. He worked tirelessly to prepare the ground for a favourable reception of the arguments of the Senate, to enable Christian political prudence to prevail over tradition-bound Orthodoxy.

The dispute of 1774 clarified the issues and placed the clerical opposition in a more rigorous constitutional perspective. But a second attempt to grant a concession to the Calvinists in 1777–9 showed just how strong the power of the clergy still remained.

In the Senate itself the arguments became more complex and more forceful. Matsen's assiduity seems to have won over those in its ranks who were doubtful in 1774. He compiled a detailed critique of the Ministry's objections of 1774, together with reports on religious toleration in Sweden, and an account of a recent debate over the issue of toleration for Catholics in the Irish House of Lords.[90] He also collected a mass of material on the contribution of the Calvinists to the urban economy. Some 75 per cent of those Calvinists living in Hamburg in 1700 had left the city during the last five decades. This, he claimed, was at least partly the cause of the present depression, and certainly the reason why some 1,300 houses in the city currently stood empty. The lack of precise statistics inevitably prevented anything more than very general statements. But the fact that the population of Altona had grown from 6,000 to 20,000 in the last forty years, he claimed, substantiated his argument about the direct relationship between toleration and economic growth – for 'there is nothing more natural than that a man should prefer to live in a place where he enjoys just freedom in matters concerning religion, rather than in a place where because of his religion he is, if not hated, then at least regarded with mistrust'. Those still in search of a fortune might not be prevented from coming to Hamburg by this fact, but 'the wealthy man who, through great

---

[89] Schröder, *Lexikon*, 5, pp. 299–300. He had also been involved in the defence of Pastor Frederici against Goeze's accusations of Socinianism in 1776: StAH, Senat, Cl.VII Lit.Hb No.5 Vol.4. His religious views are discussed by Schramm, *Neun Generationen*, i, pp. 202–16. Cf. note 30 above.
[90] Undated reports in StAH, Senat, Cl.VII Lit.Hf No.2a Vol.13 (Collectanea).

fortune and manufactures, can help others on their way will not lightly come to a place where he is bothered on account of his faith; and still less will he choose Hamburg when everywhere, and even in Catholic territories, toleration is now being introduced'.[91]

Matsen's report, which relied largely on deduction and assertion, demonstrated one of the major problems of those who advanced economic arguments for toleration. Detailed information was scarce. Attempts were made to form an accurate estimate of the city's population as early as 1750.[92] A rudimentary survey of the economy was made by a financial official, Franz Nicolaus Lütjens, in 1768. But no systematic evaluation was possible since the urban administration was simply not equipped to collate it in a useful way. As Lütjens himself remarked: 'It cannot be denied that some important things have been thoroughly and nicely worked out from time to time; yet they are but pieces of paper which get lost; they are bound away and finally get into the archive, into an eternal captivity, without anyone being able to make use of them.'[93]

Ten years later the situation had not improved, despite the new interests of the Patriotic Society. This deficiency made it difficult to produce an effective answer to the claims of the clergy, that more Calvinists would mean less money and trade for the Lutherans. Recognising this, Matsen produced a case study of the economic potential of one merchant, Berend Roosen (ironically, a Mennonite who would not have profited from a concession). Roosen owned fifty ships and had in recent years invested 200,000 mark in housing. He thus employed, fed, and housed literally hundreds of Lutherans; since they paid the preachers their *jura stolae*, did not this one heathen contribute substantially to the prosperity of both State and Church?[94]

This material was collected in 1775 and 1776, while Senator Dorner continued talks with the Calvinists, who were constantly at odds with their patron, Baron Hogguer.[95] In June 1776 Dorner proposed a secret conference with members of the Sixty to avert an untimely intervention by the clergy. But they refused to act in such an unconstitutional manner, and in April 1777 Syndic Sillem was deputed to make a new formal proposal to them.[96]

---

[91] Ibid., undated report.   [92] Reincke, 'Hamburgs Bevölkerung', p. 173.

[93] StAH, Senat, Cl.VII Lit.Dd No.4 Vol.3, Cammer-Meditationes, preface n.p. The report is erroneously dated 1764 by Reincke, 'Hamburgs Bevölkerung', pp. 173–4.

[94] StAH, Senat, Cl.VII Lit.Hf No.2a Vol.13 (Collectanea), undated report. The case was also mentioned in 1782: ibid., Cl.VII Lit.Hf No.1 Vol.3g (no. 3), n.d. On Roosen, see Roosen, *Geschichte unseres Hauses*, pp. 75–88. This account of his life did not use the above material which seems to have been widely discussed in the 1770s and 1780s. See also: Schepansky, 'Sozialgeschichte des Fremden', pp. 220–1.

[95] StAH, Senat, Cl.VII Lit.Hf No.2a Vol.13, 16 May 1776, report by Senator Dorner.

[96] Ibid., June 1776, report by Senator Dorner and 27 January 1777, Sixty to Senate. Hermes, *Reformierte Gemeinde*, pp. 154–7. The disputes concerned the election of a new preacher.

He drew substantially on the material collected by Matsen. Altona, he declared, 'has largely become great because of the intolerance which prevails here'. In times of prosperity, the old restrictive laws could be justified; one could afford to maintain strict orthodoxy; but now things had changed, and it was clear that 'coercion in matters concerning religion and intolerance' were maxims 'which obviously inhibit the growth of a state. This is demonstrated by Spain, Portugal and France, and the opposite is shown by England and Holland.'[97]

Once more the Sixty agreed, demanding only minor amendments to the concession.[98] But it did not prove possible to keep the lengthy correspondence between the two bodies secret for long. Already in March the clergy had protested against renewed rumours of a concession.[99] They reiterated their protests in June: incensed by the non-commital reply they received, they resolved to print their letter in Altona in order to pre-empt scurrilous writers who might seize the opportunity to annotate it with criticisms as had happened in 1774.[100]

The pamphlet itself said nothing new. But its publication did two things. Firstly it shattered any hope of a concession for the present. For, as Sillem pointed out in November 1778, the present situation was worse than that of 1774: a second public defeat for the Senate would undoubtedly close the matter once and for all.[101] It was thus with obvious relief that in May 1779 the Senate heard that the Calvinists had settled their differences with their patron, and felt obliged to withdraw.[102] Open defeat had thus been averted. Above all there was no repetition of the pamphlet and newspaper controversy of 1774–5. As far as the public at large was concerned, the matter was still under discussion.

Secondly, however, the success of the pastors in the short term led to their undoing in the longer term. By printing their protests the clergy prevented the new concession plan from ever being submitted to the *Bürgerschaft*. Their intervention in 1777 and their refusal to submit a more reasonable argument in the following year prevented the Senate and the Sixty from proceeding further. The Calvinists lost faith, and their withdrawal rendered further discussion meaningless. But equally the politics of the clergy had the important negative effect of finally arousing the indignation of the Sixty against them. In December 1777 they had complained to the Senate that the clergy were seeking to usurp rights which

97 StAH, Senat, Cl.VII Lit.Hf No.2a Vol.13, 28 April 1777, Senate to Sixty.
98 Ibid., 7 May 1777, Conclusum der 60ger.
99 Ibid., 7 March 1777, clergy to Senate.
100 StAH, Ministerium, III B (1778), 10 June 1778, Goeze to Herrenschmidt. The memorial of 7 June was printed as Ministerium, *Vorstellung*.
101 StAH, Senat, Cl.VII Lit.Hf No.2a Vol.13, 16 November 1778, Sillem, 'Lage der Sache'.
102 Ibid., 21 May 1779, report by Sillem and Dorner.

did not properly belong to them. They protested vehemently that the Ministry's letter of 7 June had been printed and sold before it even reached them – this was, they claimed, a 'Staats-Verbrechen' (political crime) of the most outrageous kind.[103] Indeed it was as a direct result of this outrage that the Sixty for the first time applauded the Senate's claim that the clerical oath of 1719 was illegal. They thus formally recognised that it posed no constitutional obstacle to a concession mutually agreed between Senate and *Bürgerschaft*.[104]

IV

Even apart from the difficulty of steering so contentious an innovation through the Civic Colleges to the *Bürgerschaft* without the intervention of the hostile clergy, the initiatives of 1774 and 1777–9 also illuminated the delicate nature of the proposal itself. It was all very well to claim that the concession was limited in nature and that it would apply only to one group of Calvinists. But in practice it was difficult to answer the charge that this was merely the prelude to a wider reform involving Catholics and Huguenots (and possibly others too), and more difficult still to reassure the public that such a reform would not ultimately prejudice the exclusive position of the Lutheran Church.

The clergy appealed to established traditions. They could point to their own unblemished record of pure Lutheranism, to Imperial laws and local constitutions: all of them reinforced the claim that toleration meant indifference, both to the true faith and to the past. Similarly, they could point to the fact that Orthodoxy had never meant persecution: the *Fremde* were after all established in the city and enjoyed both civic freedom and prosperity. They could exercise their religion undisturbed in the diplomatic chapels. What need was there to change a system so successfully and peacefully established?

The arguments in favour of change were more complex. Ultimately, even Dorner and Matsen admitted that the sole immediate advantage would be to reduce the city's dependence on foreign powers and thus enhance its sovereignty in public. It was essentially a symbolic gesture, but one they thought was essential, since it might persuade the rich Calvinists already in Hamburg to stay and others to come in the future. They too appealed to traditions, but to traditions which were less easily comprehensible than those invoked by the clergy. It was easier to defend the strict letter of the law (whether the Peace of Westphalia or the urban constitution) than its loose interpretation by either the Patriots of the 1720s or those of the 1760s.

---

[103] Ibid., 10 December 1777, Conclusum der 6oger.
[104] Ibid., 22 May 1778, Conclusum der 6oger.

The vision of heterodoxy placed within limits, of equality in all things but public worship and political rights, was grasped only by a few. Their deep Lutheran convictions, their concern for social and political order, led the reformers to hedge their proposals with qualifications which were all but incomprehensible to citizens whose view of life was moulded by the pulpit rather than by the Wolffian legal tradition or the *Allgemeine Deutsche Bibliothek.*

Ultimately, a variety of reasons motivated the Senate to persist. Economic considerations were paramount, as were the examples provided by other German rulers, notably Joseph II in 1781. The desire to demonstrate to the world that Hamburg could afford true protection to religious minorities also played a part. This feeling was in turn intimately bound up with the view that the imperiousness of the clergy must be put down at all costs. The Senate was determined to advertise both its sovereignty and its tolerance without compromising either its faith or the constitution it upheld.

All of these considerations became apparent when, in October 1782, Secretary Matsen was again asked to report on the history of the affair and to propose a new course of action.[105] This time he declared that the concession should be extended to all those groups recognised in the Peace of Westphalia: to both Catholics and Calvinists, for 'In all of the Christian religions the major and fundamental teachings are the same. The differences lie only in peripheral matters, which have been misunderstood, and which have partly also already been modified; and, in any case, they belong more to the spheres of academic theology than to the realms of practical Christianity.' Even Catholic rulers, he claimed, had begun to recognise this fundamental truth, and the Emperor himself had recently set an excellent example. At the same time, he stressed that recent changes in the balance of commercial power due to the Anglo-Dutch War made it all the more imperative that Hamburg should now at last attempt to prise the *Fremde* away from the diplomatic chapels. If this were done, the city might easily profit from a renewed influx of foreign merchants who had contacts with the new trading societies which were emerging in Western Europe.

He did not underestimate the potential political difficulties. But just as he himself was now more explicit in his statements regarding the minimal differences which existed between the Christian religions, so he thought that the last few years had changed popular attitudes. Firstly: 'Even the common people now think more correctly and in a more enlightened manner about the essentials of religion than they did a few years ago.' Secondly, the Emperor's toleration edict had made a great popular

[105] StAH, Senat, Cl.VII Lit.Hf No.1 Vol.3g (no. 5), 23 October 1782, EPS.

impression. Thirdly, the Anglo-Dutch War had revived the economy and given many Lutheran merchants more hope for the future. Finally, he believed that 'the influence of the clergy has been considerably diminished by the squabbles which have continued among them for a few years now'. If the matter were kept secret and the clergy not informed until after the event, he was now optimistic that the Senate might succeed.[106]

The Senate agreed. The same arguments and proposals were immediately sent on to the *Oberalten*. They were again treated to a discourse on toleration and political economy, and the Senate appealed to them to make use of their constitutional rights without first consulting the clergy.[107] The *Oberalten* did not reply for over two years. They were reminded several times but remained silent without explaining why. In earlier decades their stance might have reflected hostility. But this was not now the case, for in July 1784 the Sixty (whose core the *Oberalten* formed) responded eagerly to a suggestion that the clergy might be forbidden to oblige newly appointed preachers to take the customary solemn anti-Catholic and anti-Calvinist oath.[108] Sworn since 1644 (and reformulated in 1667 and 1719) the oath was a purely private one, but over the years the Ministry had endowed it with quasi-legal status. Surprisingly, the clergy now acquiesced in its abolition with a docility which must have confirmed Goeze's worst fears about his colleagues. Desiring to show their 'modesty and love of peace', the clergy declared that they would ignore the harsh language of the Senate's letter. More tellingly, they admitted that 'the present attitudes of the majority of our citizens' would no longer tolerate so forthright a statement of the true aims of the Lutheran clergy.[109]

This minor victory was achieved almost effortlessly and without any public discussion in September 1784. It seems to have given renewed impetus to the idea of a concession; and in February 1785 the *Oberalten* at last replied to the proposal of October 1782. They did not oppose the idea of a more all-embracing concession. Their dilatory response, they said, was due to the fact that they saw no need for it. The Calvinists had, after all, resolved their differences with Baron Hogguer, and had nothing to gain from accepting a concession from the magistrates. Would not the diplomats themselves resent a change in what was, after all, a most satisfactory *status quo*? In addition, they wondered whether the Senate was in fact right in assuming that the *Bürgerschaft* would now accept what it had previously rejected.[110]

---

[106] Ibid. (no. 12), 23 October 1782, Matsen, 'Lage der Sache'. On the impact of the Anglo-Dutch War on diplomatic relations with Hamburg, see Baasch, 'Hamburg und Holland', pp. 96–102.
[107] StAH, Senat, Cl.VII Lit.Hf No.1 Vol.3g (no. 14), 23 October 1782, Senate to Oberalten.
[108] StAH, Senat, Cl.VII Lit.Hb No.3 Vol.18a, 21 July 1784, Conculusum der 6oger.
[109] Ibid., 27 August 1784, clergy to Senate.
[110] StAH, Senat, Cl.VII Lit.Hf No.1 Vol.3g (no. 18), 21 February 1785. Oberalten to Senate.

The Senate's reply was revealing. Firstly, it was again stressed that 'the enlightenment which has become much more general during the last few years', and the previous support of the *Oberalten* and the Sixty, had undoubtedly made a great impression on the citizenry. That alone augured well for the present initiative. More important was the Senate's response to the objection that the *Fremde* might not actually want to accept the patronage of the city. If they did, then all was well; if they did not, then at least two beneficial ends would be achieved:

that by this means our way of thinking about one of the most important duties of humanity and religion will be made public, and the widespread accusation of intolerance will be removed from us. [Secondly] We may also be able to justify before the eyes of the whole world the sharper measures we will take against all eventual future transgressions by non-Lutheran clergymen.[111]

In the last report, the offer of a concession would be as much an exercise in public relations as a demonstration of tolerance and Christian charity.

The *Oberalten* concurred in this view and agreed to proceed. They also accepted the terms of the concession; they insisted only that the first clause should contain an explicit statement that the constitution would remain firmly Lutheran, and that it should be stressed that the concession could be revoked at any point if its limits were exceeded. Once the *Oberalten* were satisfied, the papers were sent on to the Sixty.[112] They too gave their consent, but raised the question of prior notification of the Ministry. To proceed without doing so would be an intolerable insult. Indeed, the constitution itself provided for prior consultation of the clergy, even if it excluded them from the legislative process.[113] Again, the Senate insisted on secrecy, and persuaded the Sixty that the concession should be communicated to the Ministry only after it had been approved by the *Bürgerschaft*, although before it was formally published.[114]

Once agreement had been reached with the Sixty, the process of consultation ended. On 19 September 1785 the concession was placed before the *Bürgerschaft*. At a meeting attended by 217 citizens it was accepted without bitterness and controversy.[115]

It is unclear how aware the clergy were of these lengthy negotiations. They did, it is true, have other things on their minds. For since 1780 the ageing Goeze had again diverted his polemical gaze from the heresies of the *Aufklärer* in Berlin to the threat of heterodoxy nearer home. He attacked his colleagues in a series of pamphlets on such vexed issues as the validity

[111] Ibid. (no. 20), 27 May 1785, Senate to Oberalten.
[112] Ibid. (no. 21), 1 June 1785.
[113] Ibid. (no. 24), 31 August 1785, Sixty to Senate.
[114] Ibid. (no. 26), 2 September 1785, Senate to Sixty; (no. 27), 7 September 1785, Sixty to Senate.
[115] Ibid. (no. 30), 19 September 1785, Resolutio Civium. StAH, EB, No. 1 Bd. 27, p. 78.

of marriages between blood relatives, the historical origins of the office of *Hauptpastor*, and whether even heathens might aspire to salvation through good works and virtuous lives alone.[116] These controversies, as Syndic Matsen noted, did much to undermine the morale and prestige of the Ministry and probably account for their acquiescence in the abolition of the intolerant oath in 1784.[117] When they heard the news of the concession on 16 September, it came apparently as a surprise, and all agreed that nothing could be done in the three days before the *Bürgerschaft* meeting.[118]

When they were informed of the concession, the clergy decided to take legal advice.[119] On 24 October they protested to the Senate that according to the constitution they should have been consulted before the matter went to the *Bürgerschaft*. They made no comment on the concession itself.[120] The Senate dismissed their legal objections to the way in which the law had been passed, and the concession was published in November.

Faced with a *fait accompli*, the Lutheran clergy could do nothing. Indeed they had every reason to accept what had happened. Their position as representatives of the established Church remained unchanged; their income too was undiminished since the concession obliged the *Fremde* to continue to pay them the *jura stolae*. The *Fremde* also accepted these limitations without demur. Only the Huguenots rightly pointed out that the '*jura stolae*, about the imposition of which we have known nothing until now, seem to contrast with the principle of toleration'.[121] But they too relented.

Their foreign patrons also agreed to the concession with alacrity. Frederick the Great professed himself to be 'charmé de ces progrès de l'esprit de tolerance'.[122] But in fact, as the Senate had insisted throughout, nothing much had changed. The full implications of the concession were only realised after 1814, when freedom of conscience was gradually translated into full political liberty. Only then were other groups, like the Mennonites and the Jews, considered. Those debates were more wide-ranging: for they were no longer constrained by the concept of Christianity enshrined in the Peace of Westphalia, but rather extended by the concept of humanity proclaimed in the French Revolution.

[116] Schröder, *Lexikon*, 2, pp. 534–7; Wotschke (ed.), 'Wincklers Briefe', pp. 80–2, 91–2.
[117] StAH, Senat, Cl.VII Lit.Hf No.1 Vol.3g (no. 12), 23 October 1782, Matsen, 'Lage der Sache'. Cf. notes 108–9 above for material relating to the oath and its abolition.
[118] *Senior* Gerling heard the news from Pastor Zornickel on 16 September: StAH, Ministerium, III B Fasc.6 (1785), Zornickel to Gerling; ibid., II 8, p. 521.
[120] StAH, Senat, Cl.VII Lit.Hf No.1 Vol.3g (no. 37), 24 October 1785, clergy to Senate.
[121] StAH, Senat, Cl.VII Lit.Hf No.2a Vol.17a II (no. 1), 16 November 1785, Huguenots to Senate.
[122] Ibid. (no. 7), 20 December 1785, Frederick II to Senate.

6

The image of the city: the search for a tolerant society in early modern Hamburg

The implementation of the toleration mandate in 1785–6 marked a true watershed in the history of Hamburg. The struggle for the liberties it granted had dominated the city since before 1600. The gradual realisation of the mandate's constitutional implications was to preoccupy the city's elite for much of the following century. Of course, both before and after 1785, other issues also stand out, and certainly other European developments had a crucial bearing on Hamburg's evolution. But from the point of view of the local dignitary, whether in the secular or in the ecclesiastical domain, the present was interpreted and articulated in primarily religious terms. The city's relationship with its non-Lutheran minorities thus provided a touchstone on which attitudes were tested and broader issues defined. For this reason the debate over religious toleration can only be fully understood in the context of the broad social and cultural development of early modern Hamburg. This chapter will thus amplify many of the problems raised in the first five chapters, and, by looking at the self-image of the city, explore some of the political, social and cultural dimensions of the debate.

One major question arises from much of the analysis above: why did it take so long to concede so little? Throughout, it might seem that the battle lines were relatively clearly drawn. On the one hand, one might sympathise with a tradition-bound, reactionary Church, desperately clinging to a crumbling supremacy, ruthlessly exploiting its hold over the minds of the untutored populace in order to preserve a simple and honest world. On the other hand, one might be tempted to applaud the valiant efforts of a progressive and enlightened secular elite: sensitive to the demands of humanity, and perceiving with wisdom and foresight the inevitable heterodoxy of a truly free and flourishing economy, its members struggling to force their reluctant fellow-citizens to follow the path of just moderation. Such a juxtaposition, of blinkered faith against the higher wisdom of secular philosophy, would, however, be both crude and misleading.

Apart from anything else, the resulting picture would endow the clerical position with a spurious antiquity. The apparent strength of the clergy's arguments lay in their claim to represent not only God, who was timeless and therefore above history, but also an historical tradition which literally reached back to biblical times. This combination of divine trusteeship and ancient historical right lent their arguments an air of impeccable rectitude; against them, the political and economic considerations of the Senate, although couched in quite genuine heart-felt humanitarian terms, could only appear trivial and ephemeral. In fact, however, the traditions represented by the clergy were no more ancient than those upheld by the Senate: both originated in 1529, the year when Johannes Bugenhagen introduced the Reformation in Hamburg.

The date was not the only thing the two traditions shared. Both were in fact substantially identical in content, only interpreted in different ways and with differing emphasis on their various implications. The relatively recent origin of their history had an important bearing on the struggle over the position of the religious minorities. For in every sense, early modern Hamburg was a city struggling to define itself. The sense of insecurity which accompanied this struggle inevitably prejudiced the assimilation, or even plain acceptance, of aliens who, in the eyes of many, threatened the integrity of Lutheran Hamburg by their very existence. This was a problem which the German Protestant princes did not confront. Their legitimacy was strengthened by the Reformation; but the lines of continuity from the Middle Ages still ran strong and visible. The same was true of many Dutch towns where the Reformation did not have a dramatic or revolutionary impact on the urban constitution. In both cases, more tolerant policies could emerge at a relatively early stage: for nothing was threatened by the concession of limited or even total freedom to those who worshipped God under a slightly different name.[1]

In Hamburg, by contrast, the Reformation effectively created a new city. Of course, the constitution of 1529 had its fifteenth-century antecedents; but Bugenhagen's document of 1529 provided the foundation and framework for the next 330 years.[2] Furthermore, for the next 200 years, until 1712, much of the history of the city was dominated by discussions, disputes, often armed conflicts, over its interpretation. These two centuries were also marked by dramatic economic and social change, the transformation of Hamburg from a Hanseatic port into a European entrepôt, and, by 1700, the emergence of a highly complex differentiated social structure. As a result, the stability of the city was often delicate. Only the virtual civil war and profound economic crises of the later seventeenth century stimulated attempts to find a lasting equilibrium, which, aided by the

---

[1] See, for example, Klefeker, *Verfassungen*, 8, pp. 695–7. The difference between Dutch and German towns is stressed by Schilling, 'Religion und Gesellschaft', pp. 207–18, 250.

[2] On the earlier constitutions, see Bolland, *Senat und Bürgerschaft*, pp. 7–23.

intervention of Imperial troops, produced the constitution of 1712. Only then was it possible to construct something like an official historical profile of the city, a series of myths about its past, its social realities, its cultural and economic aspirations, and about the beliefs which endowed the former with meaning and cohesion; the myths from which all societies derive a sense of present balance and future direction.[3]

This chapter will examine the construction of these myths. It will relate them to the struggle for toleration by showing the problems inherent in the acceptance of outsiders in a society which had only recently acquired a sense of itself; a society, moreover, only too well aware of the necessary social fluidity of a commercial metropolis.

This awareness and the ambivalence which it generated is but one of the many themes illustrated by an analysis of the extraordinary state festivals which were staged in Hamburg primarily in the first half of the eighteenth century. Three main types of festivity will be considered: the celebration in Hamburg of Imperial births, marriages, coronations and deaths, the celebration of the great Lutheran centenaries, and the centenaries of civic institutions. All of them have two features in common. Firstly, they all contributed to the general process of defining the community, to the construction after 1700 of an historical myth of Hamburg's past and present. And secondly, all more or less directly touched on the issue of toleration. By raising questions about how stridently and in what precise form the Lutheran community should be presented to the world, many of these festivities raised important issues that were often a source of bitter controversy between the secular and ecclesiastical authorities who collaborated in their organisation.

This fact once more emphasises an extremely important point which emerges from the chronological analysis presented above. The fact was that the common ground between Senate and clergy was in reality far greater than it often appeared to be in the heat of controversy. The Orthodox clergy in Hamburg, from the seventeenth century to Goeze himself, regarded themselves as tolerant on their own terms, in contrast to the oppressive, intolerant medieval Papacy. Similarly, the Senate was nothing less than utterly Lutheran. Even the impact of two waves of potent enlightened ideals, in the 1720s and in the 1760s, only served to reinforce this. Like the clergy, the secular elite saw Hamburg as a specifically Lutheran society; and at no time was there anything less than an explicit insistence that the concessions made to other Christians within the limits set by the Peace of

---

[3] A parallel process in a more broadly cultural sphere was analysed in 1930 by Hans Röthel. He based his observations on the group of artists and intellectuals associated with J. A. Fabricius, Barthold Heinrich Brockes and Michael Richey. See Röthel, *Bürgerliche Kultur*. He did not, however, discuss the festivities investigated in this chapter.

Westphalia could only be contemplated if they expressly denied to their recipients the political and constitutional rights enjoyed by the Lutherans. Here, after all, lay the significance of the fact that 1785 brought only 'private', not 'public', freedom of worship for certain minorities.

The extremely vague nature of the two positions accounts largely for the fact that the struggle lasted so long and ultimately brought so little. As it was, the struggle ended only after the identity of the Lutheran community had been firmly established. Nowhere is this nebulous common ground more accessible, because more publicly proclaimed, than in the state celebrations of the late seventeenth and eighteenth centuries. To study them is to grasp more comprehensively the problem which religious toleration posed to a society like early modern Hamburg. For they shed light on what it was that both clergy and Senate, in their various ways and for their differing ends, were trying to conserve and promote.

I

Although these festivities must be considered in their respective categories, two salient general problems arise regarding them all. Firstly, why it was that what appears to be a unique 'festive renascence' occurred in Hamburg at this particular time. And secondly, the more practical question of the kinds of resources and skills required to execute elaborate festivals of State and Church.

The most remarkable thing about the state festivities in Hamburg was not the fact of their occurrence, but that they happened when they did. Before 1700 the occasions which were celebrated or commemorated so magnificently during the following decades were hardly noticed at all, or at least celebrated relatively modestly. It might seem paradoxical that the urban elite became obsessed with such extravagant occasions in the century of the *Aufklärung*. But the paradox is superficial. While the *Aufklärer*, like the French *philosophes*, rejected the waste and disorder endemic to the traditional popular festivals and bacchanalia of Church and community, they applauded, and indeed proposed the elaboration of, festivals which drew on the public traditions of the Italian Renaissance.[4] These had provided a source of creative inspiration for many European states: for the Habsburg monarchy in the first half of the sixteenth century; for Louis XIV, who established traditions which remained potent and splendidly ostentatious to the end of the *ancien régime*.[5] The small states in Germany

---

[4] For a general discussion of Enlightenment views of festivities, see Ehrard, 'Les Lumières et la fête', and Narr, 'Fest und Feier'.
[5] On Austria, see Vocelka, 'Manier – Groteske – Fest – Triumph'. On France, see Gruber, *Les grandes fêtes et leurs décors*, pp. 1–5.

survived as the festive heirs of the Italian princes and towns in this as in so many other ways. Indeed, some, like Goethe, believed that splendid ceremonial and communal public feasts were the only things which held together an Empire normally submerged in a sea of parchment.[6]

The world of civic pageants, of triumphal processions, fired both the imagination and the intellect of the early modern era. For there was no artistic genre which gave more adequate expression to the ideals and the reality of the early modern state than the occasional official celebration. Architecture, pyrotechnics, music, choreography, opera and a whole series of minor arts and skills were employed in the creation of theatrical ceremonials which truly reflected the character of a civilisation. In a world obsessed with symbols, emblems and artifice, the public festival of state represented the ultimate theatre of life.[7]

They were more than just enjoyable public occasions. For they played a uniquely cohesive role in a society deeply divided by ranks and estates. This was most obvious in the monarchies, where the very person and movements of the monarch were surrounded with political and religious rituals which constantly displayed terrestrial majesty surrounded by all the symbols of its power. And while the Italian republics and other free cities throughout Europe may have lacked a Versailles, they too developed civic rituals which expressed the social and political order just as well. The differences lay in their smaller scale, rather than in their intentions, or in the complexity of their symbols.

In all areas, the development of such festivities can be related to the gradual consolidation of state power and to the aspiration to stability, both political and social. State festivities both reflected this process and were themselves an important part of it. They were a highly ornate mode of political discourse concerned with issues which words alone had a habit of turning into armed conflicts and civil wars.[8]

In Hamburg, the new state festivals can be quite clearly related to a self-conscious desire on the part of certain sections of the city's governing elite to revive what they saw as a declining city. They were designed to proclaim and to anchor the newly stable polity after the end of the great crisis of the first two decades of the eighteenth century. To a degree it seems that they were also intended to replace the traditional festivities of the community or of the guilds, which either declined through neglect or were suppressed. The old *Stadttanz* (city dance, a kind of carnival), for example, was no longer held after 1559: it became meaningless as the urban

[6] Berbig, 'Krönungsritus im alten Reich', p. 640.
[7] The best general survey is still Fähler, *Feuerwerke des Barock*.
[8] See, for example, the remarks made about Venice by Muir, 'Images of power'.

population began to grow rapidly.[9] The brewery workers' biennial meeting became more modest after 1700, and was last celebrated in the traditional manner in 1736.[10] The carpenters' processions were banned repeatedly in the late seventeenth century, for fear that they might exacerbate an already precarious political situation: the last regular *Höge* was held in 1727, and the guild was only twice again permitted to indulge in its traditional festive ritual, in 1775 and 1829.[11]

The process partly reflected a desire for greater control over rituals which were often unruly and dangerous. But the desire for more social distance between rulers and ruled also played a part: the *Kollegium des Klingelbeutels* at the Cathedral, an association of alms collectors, continued to hold its annual *convivium* until 1760, but after 1720 the *Domherren*, members of the Chapter, ceased to attend.[12] The behaviour of the Senate reinforces this impression: the elite both withdrew from traditional communal festivities and ceased to take any active interest in continuing such internal private celebrations where social exclusivity had always prevailed. For in 1725 it was decided not to continue the traditional *Petri- und Matthiä-Mahlzeiten* on 21 and 24 February – elaborate feasts which accompanied the declamation of the city's laws, the presentation of the accounts, the redistribution of offices among the Senators, and new elections to the Senate. From time to time it was hinted that financial considerations weighed heavily in the decision. But this is implausible in view of the massive sums of money being paid out for the state festivities of the same period. One can only conclude that such occasions had lost their meaning and function.[13]

The rise of the new state festivity was thus accompanied by a decline in the traditional communal festive rituals. In one sense the coincidence of so many new centenaries and special occasions in the period before 1765 was fortuitous. That they were celebrated at all, however, and with such grandeur, was a matter of collective choice. In the early seventeenth century, for example, Imperial events were hardly mentioned at all. The religious centenaries of that time were commemorated simply and modestly. But increasingly, from the later decades of the century, it seemed that Hamburg had become a city intoxicated with the desire to celebrate and commemorate.

There can be no simple explanation of this 'festive renascence'. Many

---

[9] Finder, *Hamburgisches Bürgertum*, pp. 328–9, 375–7. Even its successors, the communal *Reigentänze*, ceased about 1650.

[10] Ibid., p. 308; Beneke, *Geschichten und Sagen*, 2, pp. 276–82; Schlüter, *Tractat von denen Erben in Hamburg*, 2, pp. 304–15, 354–76.

[11] Jaacks, *Festzüge in Hamburg*, pp. 3–4; Fehring, *Sitte und Brauch der Tischler*, pp. 143–4; Gerber, *Bauzünfte*, pp. 62–5.

[12] Koppmann, 'Kollegium des Klingelbeutels', p. 330.

[13] Beneke, *Geschichten und Sagen*, 2, pp. 309–50.

different groups were involved, as organisers, actors and spectators; many different themes were broached; many different audiences were addressed, ranging from the populace at home to the Emperor in Vienna. One might relate the zeal of the clergy in the celebration of the Lutheran centenaries to their desire to act as public arbiters of the collective conscience. In the political sphere, Hamburg's position as a neutral entrepôt and as the diplomatic forum of Northern Europe was of paramount importance: for many shows were put on primarily for the benefit of resident diplomats and their masters.

Perhaps most important of all is the general context within which the most splendid festivities occurred, and the generation of Hamburg citizens which organised them. The context is that of the emergence of the city from the troubles of the seventeenth century. The promulgation of a new constitution in 1712 ended these disputes; but the further coincidence of the plague of 1713–14 and the uncertainty created by the Great Northern War induced something approaching a terminal crisis which clearly revealed the bankruptcy of urban government in Hamburg. The crisis had threatened more than just poverty and decline: the very independence of the city was at stake.[14]

The traumatic experience of that period proved crucial for the next generation or so. Those who emerged to lead the city in the next decades, whether in the Senate, in education, or in the Church, were deeply conscious of the need to establish stability, and to provide a sure foundation for prosperity and growth. The Patriotic Society of 1724 was typical of such a group; its journal can be read as an attempt to take stock of the past and to project the outlines of a new civic morality which would both respect tradition and promote salutary change. The Patriots' interpretation of the world conflicted with that of the clergy at many points: the latter insisted on strict adherence to the most Orthodox Lutheran traditions, while the former were willing to contemplate a more liberal approach to the resolution of the moral dilemmas of government. But the clergy too were well aware of the need for stability, of the need to cultivate traditions in order to give perspective to the present and to guarantee the future.[15]

This desire for stability, variously interpreted though it was, provided the ultimate rationale for the festivities of the eighteenth century. They were designed to project an image of the city, not only to the world at large but also to the urban community itself. Senators, pastors, professors at the Gymnasium, all manner of private individuals, participated in these celebrations of consensus. Indeed, to the educated contemporary, the study

---

[14] The best analysis of the crisis is still Wohlwill, 'Pestjahre'.
[15] Cf. Whaley, 'Protestant Enlightenment', pp. 114–15.

of such events, the collection of memorabilia and souvenirs in the form of broadsheets and coins and medals, was an immensely important educative activity. Michael Richey, Professor at the Gymnasium, author of many an oratorio and festive ode, and one of the most assiduous local numismatists of his day, stressed that the collection of these materials should be a prime duty for any true patriot concerned with the history and contemporary welfare of his fatherland.[16] With much the same idea in mind, J. A. Fabricius, J. F. Blank and Johann Klefeker all included collections of such material in their works on the history of Hamburg, while Blank and Klefeker also complemented the work of J. P. Langermann in cataloguing the coins and medals minted on such occasions.[17]

The educated elite in general became obsessed by these celebrations; but they were largely organised by its most active section, the members of the Patriotic Society of the 1720s. Many of them were Senators and Syndics, and thus instrumental in commissioning the festivities in the first place. Senator Brockes was also a renowned poet and a scholar, and he not only co-ordinated many festivities but also wrote numerous texts for oratorios himself.[18] Other texts, orations and arias were written by his fellow Patriots, J. A. Fabricius and Michael Richey, both Professors at the Gymnasium. Richey also designed commemorative medals, while Fabricius published vast amounts of material relating to the history of public festivities in Hamburg.[19] Johann Hübner, another name prominent on these occasions, was not a Patriot himself, but he was closely associated with the Society and had been a member of its precursor, the *Teutsch-übende Gesellschaft*.[20]

The work of this group of creative and forceful men was complemented by the music of the most innovatory German composer of the age. In 1721 Georg Philipp Telemann was appointed *Cantor* of the Johanneum school and, on assuming control of all official music in the city, transformed subsequent events with more elaborate and more powerful musical accompaniments than ever before.[21] Until his death in 1767, no occasion, whether secular or ecclesiastical, was complete without a new composition by this staggeringly prolific man. Both in conception and in form, his music proved to be ideal. For while Bach persisted in the cultivation of traditional forms of 'regular old music' to be performed in churches before an audience engrossed in prayer, Telemann wrote music for entertainment and for

---

[16] [Richey], 'Anleitung zum studio historiae hamburgenses', pp. I–XXXVI.
[17] The collections are: Fabricius, *Memoriae hamburgenses*; Blank, *Mandate*; Klefeker, *Verfassungen*; Langermann, *Medaillen-Vergnügen*. The latter was completed 1850–76 by Gaedechens, *Münzen und Medaillen*.   [18] Schröder, *Lexikon*, 1, pp. 394–403.
[19] On Fabricius, see ibid., 2, pp. 238–59. On Richey, see ibid., 6, pp. 262–72.
[20] Ibid., 3, pp. 413–19; Petersen, 'Teutsch-übende Gesellschaft', p. 539; Röthel, *Bürgerliche Kultur*, pp. 28–9.   [21] Petzoldt, *Telemann*, pp. 37–65.

instruction.[22] Even his church oratorios were performed repeatedly in a more secular setting in the Drillhaus – the first regular public concerts in North Germany.[23]

Once the desire to celebrate and commemorate was conceived, the educated masters of ceremonies found that the very physical environment of the city and its buildings was ideally suited to the expression of their creative muse. Hamburg had none of the premeditated grandeur of Versailles or Whitehall; it was relatively small and cramped.[24] But it was well-endowed with locations in which public life could unfold in the most theatrical manner. The five major churches were spacious and richly decorated; the auditoriums of the Johanneum and Gymnasium and the old monastery Church of St John proved ideal for oratorios and orations. The Drillhaus and the Baumhaus near the harbour gates provided elegant surroundings for many a solemn feast, and both were often illuminated with complex emblematic displays which both entertained and drew the attention of the citizens to the festivity proceeding within. Even the city walls and the twenty-three bastions set within them served a festive purpose. On public feast days interminable gun salutes sounded from them, while on religious occasions the closure of the six city gates physically reinforced the notion of a community in prayer and contemplation.[25]

The stretches of water which surrounded the city were equally important. The convoy ships which lay in the harbour were often illuminated and used to fire gun salutes. The most magnificent of all such ships, the *Wapen von Hamburg*, launched in 1722, was a veritable 'floating baroque palace', ideally suited to represent the most powerful mercantile city of the North.[26] The most unusual of all festive locations lay on the north-western side of the city by the Alster, a vast land-bound expanse of water. Its inner basin within the city walls provided a show ground for firework displays and gigantic floating illuminations which few European cities could match.[27] The lake's natural potential was further enhanced in 1710 by the construction of the Jungfernstieg, an elegant raised promenade flanked with trees, which ran along the waterfront.[28] It was this road which led from the heart of the city in the east, past the Alster, to the opera house on the Gänsemarkt. The house itself was one of the largest in Germany, and its unusually deep

[22] Valentin, *Telemann in seiner Zeit*, p. 8. [23] Petzoldt, *Telemann*, pp. 49, 52–5.

[24] The most accessible historical topographical account of the city is still G. Bolland, *Hamburg wie es einmal war*.

[25] Nahrstedt, *Entstehung der Freizeit*, pp. 103–4; Finder, *Hamburgisches Bürgertum*, pp. 396–9.

[26] Bracker, *Die 'Wapen von Hamburg'*, n.p. Convoy ships were warships first introduced in 1668 to protect native ships from foreign, especially Barbary, aggression.

[27] Melhop, *Alster*, pp. 631–42; Finder, *Hamburgisches Bürgertum*, pp. 394–6, 405–7; J. L. von Hess, *Hamburg* (1st edn), 1, pp. 74–8.

[28] Finder, *Hamburgisches Bürgertum*, pp. 378, 393–4; Lediard, *German Spy*, p. 335; Neddermeyer, *Topographie*, p. 65.

stage was again ideal for indoor illuminations and other festive celebrations.[29]

Nature and artifice had thus combined to provide what contemporaries referred to as an ideal *Schau-Platz*, where all manner of state festivities could be presented with appropriate splendour and style. Manpower was also important. At the most basic level of labourers and small craftsmen, who built elaborate scaffolds for firework displays and illuminations, Hamburg was able to draw on the services of a large floating force of under-employed labourers. At the more elevated level of orators and musicians, the city was also well-endowed. The city supported large numbers of clergy, many of whom were renowned for their gifts as orators and hymn-writers. The existence of endowed church choirs and orchestras attracted musicians from all over North Germany; and, until 1738, the opera attracted large numbers of musicians and minor composers hoping to make their fortunes in this great musical centre.[30] Indeed, the crafts and talents needed to organise splendid festive occasions were so plentiful that even the foreign diplomats used the city's facilities during the 1720s. During that decade, Thomas Lediard, Secretary to the British Resident, emerged as a kind of impresario to the diplomatic corps, and organised firework displays, illuminations and operas to celebrate and commemorate the births, marriages, coronations or deaths of various royal houses in Europe.[31]

The 'festive renascence' in Hamburg was thus generated by the coincidence of the aftermath of a profound political, social and economic crisis with the emergence of a highly-talented and artistically-inclined generation of magistrates and intellectuals. This generation seized on certain kinds of occasion (which in the past had been marked relatively modestly, if at all) and elevated their celebration to the very highest level. If the first Patriots had a monument apart from their journal, it consisted of the printed records of the festivals which they organised.

The celebrations themselves reveal more than just the spirit of an age. They reveal an image which Hamburg had of itself and the controversies which certain aspects of that image aroused. It was inevitable that in the process of defining insiders, the outsiders should pose thorny problems. They did so particularly with regard to the Lutheran centenaries. But the reasons for this only become clear when this type of celebration is considered in comparison with others where such controversies did not arise, but where the projection of an exclusive image was no less explicit.

[29] Imme, 'Bilddarstellungen des Opernhauses'; Wolff, 'Hamburger Oper', pp. 72–91.
[30] See Krüger, *Musikorganisation*; Jaacks, '"Engelgleiche Musik"', "Elbschwäne" und "Salomos Tempel"'; Marx, 'Hamburger Barockoper'.
[31] On Lediard, see Wolff, 'Engländer'. Little is known about the displays Lediard organised in the 1720s apart from the material he himself printed. See Lediard, *Collection curieuser Vorstellungen*.

II

No type of festivity demonstrated the relationship between ritual and politics better than the elaborate commemoration in Hamburg of the lives of the Holy Roman Emperors. The celebration of Imperial births, marriages, coronations and deaths was common throughout the *Reich*, especially after 1648. Although they have been largely neglected by historians, these celebrations were regarded as extremely important occasions in the eighteenth century, and they bore eloquent testimony to the importance which the *Reich*'s members attached to its well-being and survival.[32] This demonstrative patriotism, a sense of belonging to what Hans Joachim Berbig calls 'die Reichsfeiergemeinschaft' (the festive community of the *Reich*), was particularly strong in the Imperial Cities, whose survival was in so many ways fundamentally dependent upon the vigilance of the Emperor.[33] The *Reich* protected them against the expansionist ambitions of the princes, and also guaranteed their internal stability. The histories of many such cities after 1648 – Frankfurt and Hamburg were prominent examples – demonstrated clearly their reliance on the protection and guidance of their overlord in Vienna.[34]

Cities like Nuremberg celebrated many more occasions than Hamburg, since they also included the Emperor's family in their devotions. But the festivities at Hamburg, limited though they were to the life-cycle of the Emperor himself, illuminate the functions and implications of such public rituals with exceptional force.[35] A variety of external and internal factors accounted for this. Until 1768 Hamburg's status in the *Reich* was insecure, and the celebrations staged there were clearly conceived as part of a strenuous and protracted campaign to gain formal recognition of the city's Imperial status. For although the city paid all Imperial taxes after 1618, its former Danish overlords never officially recognised Hamburg's translation to the *Reich*. Until 1686 the Danes were prepared to pursue their claims with military force; thereafter they aimed to extract a sizeable tribute from the city in return for recognition, and periodically attempted to assert their privileges by creating difficulties over currency and tariffs.[36] In the

---

[32] The two best studies are those by Hans Joachim Berbig: 'Krönungsritus im alten Reich' and 'Kaisertum und Reichsstadt'.

[33] Ibid., pp. 219–20, 276–80. On the relationship between the Hanseatic cities and the *Reich*, see Frensdorff, 'Das Reich und die Hansestädte'.

[34] See Brunner, 'Souveranitätsproblem'; Hildebrandt, 'Rat contra Bürgerschaft'; Schilfert, 'Bürgerliche Revolutionen'. On the power and status of Imperial Residents, see Bog, 'Reichsverfassung und reichsstädtische Gesellschaft'. See also Conrad, 'Verfassungsrechtliche Bedeutung der Reichsstädte'.

[35] This contradicts the view of Rainer Ramcke, the only other historian who has mentioned them; he dismissed them as mere 'Randerscheinungen': Ramcke, *Beziehungen*, p. 14.

[36] Reincke, *Betrachtungen*, pp. 9–13; Wohlwill, 'Gottorper Vergleich', *passim*.

meantime, the Senate behaved as if its objective had already been achieved, and repeatedly made use of the Emperor's help in trying to find a solution to the internal conflicts which all but paralysed the city before 1712.[37] Here the function of elaborate acts of homage was twofold: firstly, to encourage such intervention, and, secondly, to reinforce the authority of the Senate in the eyes of the citizens.

The ambiguity of Hamburg's position in the *Reich* accounted for the limits placed on the number of Imperial festivities observed there. The births of Imperial archdukes, the marriages and deaths of other members of the Imperial family were not marked there until after 1768. Before then the Senate sent letters of congratulation or condolence, as it did with regard to the Emperor himself or his widow. But otherwise no formal arrangements were made, nor was any official announcement made from the pulpits.[38]

On the other hand, that same legal uncertainty, combined with the city's dependence on Imperial intervention on the domestic front, made those occasions which were celebrated unusually extravagant. Three particularly crucial phases in the diplomatic or the domestic spheres coincided with three potentially rich periods of celebration or commemoration.

During the 1690s the first purposeful attempts were conceived to negate the Danish claims to sovereignty once and for all. The desire for Imperial support in this aim of elevating Hamburg into a neutral free-trade port was reflected and, in a significant way, embodied in the celebration of the coronation of Joseph I as king of the Romans in 1690, and of his marriage in 1699. The next significant Imperial events (the deaths of Leopold I and Joseph I, the coronation of Charles VI, and the birth of the Archduke Leopold in 1716) all coincided with the period of the city's greatest reliance upon the Emperor, as his commissioner set about restoring order and promulgating the new constitution – all of which was achieved without damage to the city's independence and prosperity. These events were marked more elaborately than those which preceded them, and were surpassed only by the staggering splendour of the celebrations of the next period, the 1740s. Here again, lavish celebration reflected more than just years of general prosperity. For these years saw the inception of the last great diplomatic initiative against Denmark. The ultimate aim of forcing Denmark to relinquish her claims was not achieved then, but the pro-Austrian stance developed and reinforced during the 1740s prepared the

---

[37] See Hübbe, *Kaiserliche Kommissionen*, *passim*.
[38] StAH, Senat, Cl.VII Lit.Ra3 No.1 Vol.1 Fasc.6, 7 April 1762, note made by Senator Cornelius Poppe. Letters of congratulation and condolence are scattered throughout the files: StAH, Senat, Cl.VII Lit.Ra3 No.1, Vol.1 Fasc.1–37.

way towards the Treaty of Gottorp in 1768, by which Hamburg was finally recognised as a Free and Imperial City.[39]

The occasions themselves all followed a similar basic pattern laid down in the seventeenth century and later embellished as circumstances demanded. The most simple throughout was the mourning procedure, apparently already used in 1657 on the death of Ferdinand III. The announcement of an Emperor's death inaugurated four weeks of public mourning: the bells of all churches were tolled daily from 11 a.m. to 12 a.m.; all music, both secular and ecclesiastical, was banned; after the last week of mourning, special sermons devoted to the subject of the Imperial bereavement were read; and if no immediate successor had already been chosen, prayers were then read for a speedy election.[40] Such prayers continued for two years during the interregnum which followed the death of Charles VI.[41] This formula was extended in 1711 to include playing songs of mourning on the bells of all churches and the performance of special music on the last Sunday of the mourning period.[42] In 1740 and 1745 these arrangements were further elaborated by the addition of an oratorio by Telemann, a feature which was retained for the mourning of 1790 and 1792.[43]

A similar pattern of growing complexity and splendour can be established in the other main group of Imperial festivities – those concerned with celebration rather than commemoration. The elections of Ferdinand IV (as king of the Romans in 1654) and Leopold I (as Emperor in 1658) were attended by special church services, *Te Deums* and festive bell-ringing.[44] In 1690, on the election of Joseph I as king of the Romans, the *Te Deum* was complemented by a festive secular oration in the old monastery Church of St John and a specially-commissioned opera paid for by the city.[45] On that occasion a firework display on the Alster was financed by the Imperial Resident, but in 1699, in celebration of Joseph's marriage, the Senate paid for this too.[46]

[39] Ramcke, *Beziehungen*, pp. 151–62; Wohlwill, 'Gottorper Vergleich', *passim*.

[40] StAH, Ministerium, II 2, p. 210. On the death of Leopold I (1705) see ibid., II 5, p. 8; ibid., III A1s, no. 464; ibid., A1k, no. 454.

[41] Klefeker, *Verfassungen*, 8, p. 549; Blank, *Mandate*, 3, pp. 1391–3.

[42] Blank, *Mandate*, 2, pp. 708–9; StAH, Ministerium, II 5, p. 274; ibid., III A1k, nos. 446–50, 452.

[43] Blank, *Mandate*, 3, pp. 1369–70, 1479, 1484–93; Klefeker, *Verfassungen*, 8, pp. 548–9, 551; Fabricius, *Memoriae hamburgenses*, 8, pp. 275–308. For the ceremonies of 1790 and 1792, see Anderson, *Verordnungen*, 3, pp. 109–16, 269–74; StAH, Ministerium, II 8, pp. 570–1, 587; StAH, Senat, Cl.VII Lit.Ra3 No.1 Vol.1 Fasc.20b and Fasc.21b.

[44] StAH, Ministerium, II, 5, pp. 194, 210.

[45] Blank, *Mandate*, 1, p. 397; Klefeker, *Verfassungen*, 8, p. 410; Steltzner, *Versuch*, 4, pp. 12–13; Fabricius, *Memoriae hamburgenses*, 4, pp. 199–232.

[46] Blank, *Mandate*, 1, pp. 534–5; Klefeker, *Verfassungen*, 8, p. 410; Fabricius, *Memoriae hamburgenses*, 4, pp. 233–61; Steltzner, *Versuch*, 4, p. 356.

Joseph's elevation to the Imperial throne in 1705 was not celebrated in Hamburg, although the usual financial offerings were made – both bribes to key ministers in Vienna and the financial tributes to the Emperor which became a mutually agreeable substitute for formal acts of homage in the *Reich*.[47] But in 1712 the coronation of Charles VI was celebrated with unprecedented lavishness, all the more splendid because of the presence of the Imperial Commissioner, Count Schönborn. A *Te Deum* was sung in all the major churches; Professor Fabricius addressed the urban elite and numerous outside guests in a Latin oration; a special medal was minted.[48] The highlight of the celebration was undoubtedly the most splendid firework display yet mounted on the inner basin of the Alster. It lasted for about two hours and consisted of three acts, each representing a symbolic tableau, and involving the illumination of structures and machines floating on the water. First came Mercury bearing the arms of the city of Hamburg flanked by two castles, one bearing the letter V (*Vivat*), the other the letter C (*Carolus*). Then two pyramids appeared displaying the names of Charles V and Charles VI – a tableau which underlined the felicitous reunion of the Austrian and Spanish crowns. Finally, a gate of honour was illuminated. Inside it, Atlas held up the skies which contained ten stars representing the *Reichskreise*; on top of the archway stood the motto: *Carolo VI. Rom. Imperatori, O[rbis] P[acificatori] U[rbis] P[rotectori]*. Each act was preceded by cannon salvos and accompanied by the trumpets, french horns, and drums of the city musicians. The scene was completed by the presence of thousands of spectators, so many that a child was drowned in the crush.[49]

With one exception, the next three decades were devoid of Imperial celebrations. The only occasion was the birth of the Archduke Leopold in 1716, which was marked in Hamburg by a special day of thanksgiving with bell-ringing and *Te Deums*. The main festivities were, however, organised and paid for by the Imperial Resident (including an opera and the illumination of his own house as a temple of honour). In this case, Hamburg's facilities were thus used as a vehicle for Imperial propaganda rather than as a vehicle for the promotion of the city's interests.[50]

47 On payments to the Emperor in general, including those of 1705, see StAH, Senat, Cl.VII Lit. Ra3 No.1 Vol.1 Fasc.1 and Fasc.4 (esp. Fasc.4, 29 November 1745, Von der Donation der Stadt an die neu-erwählten Römische Kaiser).

48 Blank, *Mandate*, 2, pp. 747–9, 752; Klefeker, *Verfassungen*, 8, p. 521; Fabricius, *Memoriae hamburgenses*, 4, pp. 262–87; Langermann, *Medaillen-Vergnügen*, pp. 105–6; StAH, Ministerium, II 5, p. 285; ibid., III A1k, nos. 530, 623–5.

49 Steltzner, *Versuch*, 5, pp. 230–2; Finder, *Hamburgisches Bürgertum*, pp. 405–7; Langermann, *Medaillen-Vergnügen*, pp. 105–11. The best account of the display is a contemporary pamphlet: *Beschreibung des solennen Freuden-Festins...de Anno 1712*. The costs are recorded in StAH, Kämmerei I, No. 13, Bd. 31, pp. 71, 115 and ibid., No. 23 Bd. 9, nos. 103, 107.

50 Blank, *Mandate*, 2, p. 862; Klefeker, *Verfassungen*, 8, pp. 545–6; Steltzner, *Versuch*, 5, pp. 412–22;

Those interests were, however, pursued with renewed vigour during the 1740s, and the opportunities presented by the coronations of 1742 and 1745 were exploited to the full. In 1742 a dazzling firework display was organised. Telemann was commissioned to compose oratorios to follow the *Te Deum*, and music to follow the fireworks. Huge quantities of food and drink were ordered to feast the Senate and its guests at the display, including no less than 136 barrels of wine.[51]

The first *Te Deum* was sung on 3 February when the news of the election was announced. But the main festivities were postponed until 24 April, the feast of the monarch's second-name patron, Albert. In the early afternoon the Senate and its guests gathered to hear a festive oration and to enjoy Telemann's music. In the evening they reassembled in the wealthiest houses on the Jungfernstieg to watch the fireworks on the Alster, an elaborate affair involving complex machines supported by 136 stakes driven into the bed of the lake.[52]

This public rejoicing was surpassed in grandeur three years later, on the election of Francis I. It was decided that the firework display would be even bigger than that of 1742.[53] In addition, Syndic Klefeker and Senator Brockes, the two men responsible for organising the festivity, felt that it would be appropriate to commission an opera to mark the coronation. In 1742 there had been no opportunity to do this, but now a highly successful troupe directed by Pietro Mingotti was staying in the city and had offered its services. The financial officials, representatives of the *Bürgerschaft*, had severe misgivings about such an extravagant proposal. But the Senate brushed aside their objections and insisted that the opera, Metastasio's *La Clemenza di Tito*, be performed on the evening of 8 December after the festive oration and Telemann's oratorio.[54] The firework display, the usual three acts accompanied by Telemann's 'warlike' music, was then held in the following week.[55]

Throughout the festive period (lasting from the announcement of the election on 26 September to the firework display on 15 December), the

Gaedechens, *Münzen und Medaillen*, 2, p. 33; StAH, Ministerium, III Aɪm, no. 73; ibid., II 5, pp. 394–5, 402. The fireworks were described in an illustrated pamphlet: Jungckheim, *Ausführliche Nachricht von dem herzlichen Freuden-Festin...wegen der Gebuhrt des Ertz-Hertzogs und Printzen von Asturien*.

51 Blank, *Mandate*, 3, pp. 1391–3; Klefeker, *Verfassungen*, 8, pp. 549–50; StAH, Kämmerei I, No. 23, Bd. 86, 11 June 1742, bill submitted by Peter Greve.

52 For a text of the oratorio, see Blank, *Mandate*, 3, pp. 1393–401. The firework display and the preparations for it are described in StAH, Baudeputation, A 3, Bd. 1, pp. 393–5, 415. See also Melhop, *Alster*, p. 634 and *Neue Europäische Fama*, 83 (1742), pp. 937–40.

53 StAH, Baudeputation, A 3, Bd. 2, pp. 77, 79–86.

54 Schütze, *Hamburgische Theater-Geschichte*, pp. 199–200; StAH, Kämmerei I, No. 13, Bd. 49, pp. 408–10, 429–31, 473–8, 483–6; StAH, Senat, Cl.VII Lit.Fl No.2 Vol.4f.

55 StAH, Baudeputation, A 3, Bd. 2, pp. 99–101; Langermann, *Medaillen-Vergnügen*, pp. 134–6.

Senate ensured that maximum publicity was given to its activities. Official announcements were inserted in the *Hamburgischer Correspondent*.[56] Copies of a commemorative volume, containing an exact description of the festivities, were ordered to be sent to Vienna. The Emperor himself requested an engraving of the firework display. His request caused some initial embarrassment, for the pictures were not yet ready. The reason for this delay was revealing: the etcher had omitted to include the masses of spectators, and had thus failed to capture the true sense of public excitement and commotion; his draft had been returned for revision.[57] But even without this revealing manipulation of the pictorial record, Hamburg's celebrations received their due recognition. Indeed, the editor of the *Neue Europäische Fama* paid special tribute to the work of Klefeker and Brockes: their efforts had carried on a great tradition, 'for this city has never failed to display all the characteristics of a special patriotic devotion on occasions like this, and to distinguish itself from others by good performances'.[58]

The following decades saw significant modifications of the celebrations and commemorations of the 1740s, although there is no evidence to suggest that they resulted from a decline of interest. The election of Joseph II as king of the Romans in 1764, and his marriage in 1765, both fell in the worst phase of the post-war crisis. Firework displays and operas were thus considered too expensive. Thereafter they were a thing of the past: firework displays became old-fashioned, and in 1775 the city disposed of all of the old machinery and ceremonial cannon; the opera also finally collapsed after Mingotti's departure in 1754. What remained of the formula of the 1740s was the festive oration, the bell-ringing, *Te Deums* and oratorios.[59] As Hamburg's status became more regular with the annulment of all Danish claims in 1768, so her celebration of the Emperor became less extraordinary and more like all other Imperial Cities.

The fact that the city continued to observe Imperial occasions until the dissolution of the *Reich* does not detract from the unusual nature of the festivities in the period 1690–1745. The celebrations of those decades were endowed with a more explicit function than any previously. For in every sense they served to create and to reinforce an image of the city which was by no means universally accepted in the seventeenth century. Danish claims to sovereignty were still pursued by military force until 1686, and they were

---

[56] Blank, *Mandate*, 3, pp. 1537–45; *Staats- und Gelehrte Zeitung des hamburgischen Correspondenten*, 1745, nos. 198, 201–2 (10, 17, 18 December).
[57] StAH, Senat, Cl.VII Lit.Ra3 No.1 Vol.1 Fasc.1, ? 1746, Klefeker to Imperial Chancellor.
[58] *Neue Europäische Fama*, 129 (1746), p. 797.
[59] StAH, Senat, Cl.VII Lit.Ra3 No.1 Vol.1 Fasc.11; Blank, *Mandate*, 5, pp. 2416–20, 2424–37; ibid., 6, pp. 7–20; Klefeker, *Verfassungen*, 8, pp. 561–4. On the coronation festivities of 1790 and 1792, see Anderson, *Verordnungen*, 3, pp. 143–62, 330–8; StAH, Senat, Cl.VII Lit.Ra3 No.1 Vol.1 Fasc.20b and 21b.

very nearly established. Some elements of the *Bürgerschaft* in Hamburg itself apparently supported those claims for some time, even if only because to do so implied opposition to the Senate.[60] Thus, to the world at large, the Senate's elaborate public celebration of Imperial occasions served as a powerful polemical vehicle for the articulation of its claim to Imperial rather than Danish overlordship. To the citizenry at home, such high-level 'discourse' with the Emperor reinforced the Senate's own authority and the view of the polity enshrined in the constitution of 1712.

Both policies were ultimately successful. Hamburg's Imperial status was recognised in 1768, and the Senate's authority went unchallenged after 1712. But there was a price to be paid. For by claiming membership of the *Reich*, the Senate was obliged to accept its laws. And that meant accepting a doctrine of limited toleration which could be exploited by liberals and reactionaries alike. On the one hand, the Senate could insist on its view that non-Lutherans should not be expelled. On the other hand, the clergy could insist that they be forced to live without the public privileges which defined the liberty of the Lutherans.

These Imperial festivities most obviously point to the political pressures which constrained the Senate from taking harsh measures against Catholics. Equally they imply why there was so little incentive to change the law, and why the Catholics were treated in the same way as the Calvinists, despite their exalted patron. For the law of the *Reich* was one which Hamburg alone could not change, and whose existence overshadowed any local regulations the Senate might aspire to make.

Precisely during the period when the non-Lutheran minorities were being established in Hamburg, pressures were thus being built up which infinitely complicated and ultimately hindered their full acceptance. These pressures are as difficult to pin down today as they were important in the minds of contemporaries. For the clauses of the laws which they strove to extend, or behind which they sheltered, were but the visible elements of complex mental or cultural structures which confined as well as defined. Hamburg's repeated acts of public homage to the Emperor in Vienna reveal how profoundly the city was committed to the *Reich*. They also show how fundamentally that commitment became part of the self-image of the city, a self-image which created the mental and legal framework for all policy. Yet the Imperial dimension was only a part of that self-image. Other dimensions, which focussed the contemporary mind on religious and domestic political traditions, were equally important.

[60] Wiskemann, *Welthandelspolitik*, pp. 101–13; Wohlwill, 'Gottorper Vergleich', pp. 9–10.

III

Hamburg's status as an Imperial City was dubious, but her credentials as a stronghold of Lutheran Orthodoxy were impeccable. There could be no doubt about her right to belong to another group within the festive community of the *Reich*, a group defined by religion. Its identity and survival was commemorated in the celebration of the religious anniversaries of the Reformation. For Protestant states all over Germany, the dates 1517, 1530 and 1555 came to symbolise the origins of their present constitutions; while in Hamburg the year 1528–9 marked the introduction of the local Reformation by Luther's disciple, Johannes Bugenhagen.

The significance of the year 1517 has always been recognised. Similarly, many historians have studied the way in which images of Luther changed over the centuries.[61] But few have realised the equal significance of the later anniversaries.[62] In the eighteenth century, the centenary of the Peace of Westphalia was added to this festive canon. For the Peace both ended a war and reaffirmed the religious freedom granted to Lutherans in 1555; it marked the end of the religious struggle begun during the Reformation, and it shaped the constitution of the *Reich* until 1806.

For German Protestants such days of commemoration were rare days of unity and solidarity. The Catholic Church of Rome had many points of historical reference. United under the Pope, it was relatively easy to demonstrate the cohesion of Catholicism: its calendar, full of saints' days and holy days, provided perennial reminders of its historical unity and legitimacy. The problem of unity was much more acute for the Protestant Churches. The Lutherans, for example, even apart from their differences with other Protestants, were themselves physically divided by the concept of the *Landeskirche* (territorial Church), which tended to encourage the consolidation of differing tendencies within the Church. In a sense, only the celebration of the great centenaries provided a common iconography. The life and works of Luther formed a corpus of thematic images and traditions, both visual and literary, as vital to the Lutheran Church as the Acts of the Apostles were to the Roman Church.[63]

Although they drew on the same source, the celebrations of each century were shaped by contemporary events, as secular rulers and clergy alike reacted to what they perceived as the current threat to their position. The celebrations of 1617 took place in the midst of the confessional struggles

---

[61] See, for example, Bornkamm, *Luther im Spiegel der deutschen Geistesgeschichte* and Zeeden, *Luther und die Reformation*.

[62] A notable exception is Ernstberger, 'Nürnberger Reformationsjubiläen', which deals with the celebrations in 1617, 1630 and 1655. See also: François, 'De l'uniformité à la tolérance', pp. 788–9.

[63] See Schönstädt, *Antichrist, Weltheilsgeschehen und Gottes Werkzeug*, pp. 1–7, 304–21.

which preceded the Thirty Years War.[64] Those of 1717 coincided with disputes within the Lutheran Church over Pietism, and over the current projects for a union of Calvinism and Lutheranism; in North Germany they were also marked by the hysterical reaction of the clergy to the Jesuit missionary activity which followed the establishment of the Mission of the North in the 1680s.[65] By 1817, Luther had been transformed into a German citizen and patriot who would lead his country to nationhood, similar to the kind of Teutonic warrior resurrected in 1917.[66]

In Hamburg, as elsewhere, more specifically local factors were also important. On one level, the celebrations of the eighteenth century can be seen as an attempt to stress internal peace and unity after decades of conflict. The new political *status quo* was thereby placed in historical perspective and shown to derive its legitimacy from the religious and moral revival of the Reformation. On another level, the clergy aimed to stress the image of an Orthodox Lutheran city. This frequently led to clashes with the Senate, which was anxious to moderate their extremism. Both Senate and clergy saw the great importance of such commemorative festivities, and both participated with equal enthusiasm. But their motives for doing so often appeared to be very different.

The one thing which was never questioned in the eighteenth century was the desirability of celebrating at all. That issue had been decided in 1617 when the clergy prevailed over the Senate's reluctance to enter potentially dangerous waters. There was little evidence to support the clergy's claim that some commemoration of the life and work of Luther had always been held either on St Martin's Day or on All Saints' Day. On the contrary, it was quite clear that they took their general inspiration from the Heilbronn decision of the Protestant Union to celebrate the centenary on 2 November, and their specific cue from the Elector of Saxony who decided to celebrate on 31 October. The latter date was a weekday and would thus make a greater impression on the young and on ordinary people than a Sunday.[67]

The celebrations were announced on 26 October. They began on Thursday, 30 October with special sermons, a *Te Deum* and festive music in St Peter's, followed by bell-ringing in all churches in the afternoon. On the next day, commemorative sermons were again delivered in all churches; *Te Deums* were sung, together with especially selected hymns from the Lutheran repertoire, including Luther's own hymn, *Eine feste Burg ist unser*

---

[64] Ibid., p. 4.

[65] Rode, *Hamburg und die Reformationsjubiläen*, pp. 8–9.

[66] On 1817, see Winckler, *Luther als Bürger und Patriot*. On 1917, see Mehnert, *Evangelische Kirche und Politik*, pp. 48–56.

[67] Schönstädt, *Antichrist, Weltheilsgeschehen und Gottes Werkzeug*, pp. 10–12, 33–5; Rode, *Hamburg und die Reformationsjubiläen*, pp. 1–4.

Gott, the marching song of militant Protestants everywhere.[68] In the afternoon, a further commemoration was held in the Gymnasium, where Professor Bernhard Wehrenberg assessed the historical development of the Reformation, and the proceedings were concluded by the declamation of Latin poems in praise of Luther and his work.[69]

One theme predominated throughout the mandates, prayers, sermons and speeches which accompanied the celebrations. All were aggressively anti-Papal, particularly concerned with the threat posed by the Jesuits to German Protestants. References abound to the darkness of medieval Catholicism, to the corruption and paganism of the Church in Rome. The Senate's mandate of 26 October and the special prayer read out five days later both stressed the local significance of the Reformation, and pointed out the causal relationship between the new religion and the city's political stability and commercial prosperity. Luther, the modern Elijah who had led the German people out of the 'Egyptian captivity' of Rome, was presented as the source of light and moral regeneration.[70]

The sermon delivered by Nicholas Hardkopf of St Nicholas' was typical. It had three main objectives: to expose the corruption of the teachings of the Roman Church; to sketch the history of the Reformation; and to show how an understanding of these themes in the light of the Bible might lead to a new interpretation of the Christian message. Hardkopf concluded with the pious hope that his successors might celebrate the second centenary with equal zest, and with a final blast against the Pope and the pernicious Jesuits. A plea for Protestant solidarity against the common enemy; an analysis of the historical legitimacy of Luther's revolution; an exhortation to obey the magistrates and to heed the guidance of the clergy – all were combined in this rousing invective. The identity of the local community was reinforced by, but not subsumed within, the image of the militant Lutheran diaspora.[71]

The next centenaries were celebrated relatively modestly. The first centenary of the Augsburg Confession in 1630 was inevitably overshadowed by the Thirty Years War; and in Hamburg, the proximity of Tilly's Catholic army enjoined caution to even the most impetuous minds. Thus on 26 June, the clergy were permitted to 'give thanks and offer prayers in their sermons', but no other special arrangements were made.[72] In 1655,

---

[68] Blank, *Mandate*, 1, p. 21; Klefeker, *Verfassungen*, 8, p. 363. The printed sources are collected in Fabricius, *Memoriae hamburgenses*, 5, pp. 1–94. On the significance of Luther's hymn, see Grisar, *Luthers Trutzlied*.

[69] Rode, *Hamburg und die Reformationsjubiläen*, pp. 4–7; Fabricius, *Memoriae hamburgenses*, 5, pp. 17–94. [70] Ibid., pp. 2–12.

[71] The sermon is printed ibid., 2, pp. 809–39.

[72] Blank, *Mandate*, 2, p. 1106; Klefeker, *Verfassungen*, 8, pp. 363–4. See also StAH, Senat, Cl.VII Lit.Ha No.4 Vol.1c1, 3 March 1730, report by Archivist von Som.

on the centenary of the Peace of Augsburg, the celebrations were more elaborate. They included festive bell-ringing, *Te Deums*, commemorative sermons and special biblical readings. But little further evidence has survived, and a later report stressed that, regardless of circumstances, contemporaries thought that neither 1630 nor 1655 was as significant as 1617.[73]

Indeed, it was only in the eighteenth century that, untroubled by war or any other external restraint, the Lutheran festival really came into its own. Pastor Hardkopf's pious wish, that later generations might equal if not surpass his own in commemorating their religious heritage, was more than realised. The second centenary of the Reformation was much more elaborate than the first, and it was followed by similar celebrations in 1730, 1748 and 1755.

To some extent this renewed consciousness of the city's Lutheran heritage can be related to the more general themes of Hamburg's 'festive renascence'. The Lutheran centenaries proved an ideal vehicle for the transmission of images of stability and solidarity. For Hamburg's whole political system was itself a product of the Reformation, so that these occasions demonstrated Hamburg's unique destiny as vividly as the Imperial celebrations of the same era.

At the same time, however, the disputes which arose regarding these centenaries showed signs that there was now more than one interpretation of that destiny. In 1617, neither clergy nor Senate were restrained by anything more than a basic instinct for self-preservation, an awareness of the price one might have to pay for expressing too strident a hatred of non-Lutherans. By 1717, both were explicitly constrained by the Peace of Westphalia, and by an Imperial decree of 1715, from outright inflammatory denunciation of any Christian religion.[74] Increasingly, members of the Senate, especially those who were to become Patriots in the 1720s, were inclined to take a more liberal attitude to the non-Lutheran minorities for a variety of political, economic and religious reasons which have been discussed at length above. This new attitude did not involve any formal concessions, but the clergy regarded it as a major threat all the same. As a result, they attempted to exploit the centenaries as a means of reasserting the exclusive solidarity of Lutheran Orthodoxy in Hamburg. In 1717 this meant strident and anti-Catholicism; in 1730, it meant an attack on the Calvinists, and on those who did not rush to condemn the idea of a union of Calvinists and Lutherans. On both occasions, the Senate rightly felt that it had been misunderstood: it opposed the clergy not because it now wanted

---

[73] Blank, *Mandate*, 1, p. 141; Klefeker, *Verfassungen*, 8, pp. 406–7; Steltzner, *Versuch*, 3, p. 709; Fabricius, *Memoriae hamburgenses*, 6, p. 1; StAH, Ministerium, II 2, pp. 153–4.

[74] Klefeker, *Verfassungen*, 8, pp. 529–30.

open toleration, but because it was becoming increasingly clear that the old polemical intolerance no longer served the city's best interests.

The preparations for the second centenary of the Reformation began in August 1717. As in 1617, the formal stimulus came from the Elector of Saxony; the only difference was that his letter now stressed moderation in the organisation of the festivities. The Elector himself had a strong personal interest in this, since his succession to the Polish throne had necessitated his conversion to Catholicism; but he also based his case on the Peace of Westphalia, which only excluded heretics, enthusiasts and separatists.[75] The Hamburg clergy deliberated on 6 August, and then proposed that the feast be organised on the lines of the first centenary. Despite overwhelmingly heavy pastoral duties, they declared to the Senate, they were more than willing to assume the burden of organising this additional feast, which they thought should last for three days starting on 31 October.[76]

Having consulted the *Rat* of Lübeck, the Senate notified the *Oberalten* of its plans: on 23 October the feast was to be announced in all churches the *Senior* should choose special biblical texts; church bells were to be rung as on all other high feast days; and *Te Deums* would be sung at all services. *Cantor* Gerstenbüttel was to compose special music to be played before and after the sermon in St Peter's; the Professor of Eloquence, J. A Fabricius, should deliver a solemn oration in the Gymnasium; and, finally, a medal was to be minted to mark the occasion. With the approval of the *Oberalten*, all this was commissioned on 1 September and complemented later by the offer of the *Rector* of the Johanneum to hold a further public commemoration in his school on 2 September.[77]

Fundamentally, everything had been the same in 1617, even if now the celebrations were considerably more elaborate. The only new departure was the fact that the Senate had drafted a new public prayer of thanksgiving. This had been approved by both the *Oberalten* and the Sixty. But the clergy were not slow to challenge the innovation. They protested that they could not bring themselves to read out a prayer written by a politician: 'preaching and offering public prayers on behalf of God's community in church go together. If politicians were to begin to write church prayers, they would in time even wish to compose sermons and send them to the preachers, who would learn them by rote and recite them, or simply read them out.'[78]

The crux of the argument, however, lay elsewhere. Whether or not politicians had the legal right to formulate or to revise public prayers was a matter for dispute. The real point was that the contents of the new prayer

[75] Rode, *Hamburg und die Reformationsjubiläen*, pp. 9–10.
[76] StAH, Senat, Cl.VII Lit.Ha No.4 Vol.1a, 12 August 1717, clergy to Senate.
[77] Ibid., 30 August and 1 September 1717, EPS.
[78] Ibid., 1 October 1717, clergy to Senate.

differed markedly from that of 1617. As the clergy pointed out, the moderation of the Senate's text would radically undermine the Lutheran Church's credibility. Lutherans elsewhere would be forced to conclude that, on the instructions of the Senate, they had become 'syncretists, indifferentists, libertinists and hypocrites... who halt between two opinions'. The new prayer did mention 'the powerful and proud Papacy', but it said nothing 'of the idolatries, of the papal Anti-Christ, and his false teachings'. Its sole aim was to placate the Catholics; its sole result would be to undermine Lutheranism.

In reality, the dispute was thus as much about toleration as anything else. The Senate insisted that it must obey the dictates of the Peace of Westphalia. Recognising this, the clergy based their arguments not only on the Peace but on the fundamental laws of the city and on the Bible. So violent a reaction was obviously unexpected. The Senate attempted vainly to mollify the clergy by assuring them that there was no intention of censoring their sermons.[79] But the pastors insisted that the issue of the prayer be sent to the Sixty. Once it became clear to the Sixty that the Senate had in fact tried to bypass the clergy, they changed their minds, and some of them even proposed spreading the church services over two days. That proposal was defeated; but the Sixty insisted on the retention of the old prayer.[80]

The result was a resounding defeat for the Senate. The attempt to steer a diplomatic course based on prudence and humanitarian moderation had foundered on the opposition of the clergy supported by the citizenry. With great satisfaction, *Senior* Seelmann noted in the minutes of the Ministry: 'Praise be to God for this victory which the Ministry has gained against half-heartedness in religious matters and against the papacy; I make a note of this for the benefit of posterity, and with an eye to the Calvinists.'[81]

The centenary itself was thus transformed into an eloquent expression of militant Lutheranism. On 31 October each *Hauptpastor* preached a sermon on the history of the Reformation with particular emphasis on the evils of popery. *Senior* Seelmann dealt particularly with the relationship between secular and ecclesiastical authority before the Reformation, drawing obvious morals for the present. Pastor Neumeister preached against the Pope as a religious leader, while praying for his soul as a terrestrial monarch. Pastor Wolf enjoined the city's rulers to remember that their power derived not only from God, but from the Reformation too: toleration of Catholics, he argued, would lead both to the decline of the

---

[79] Ibid., 6 October 1717, EPS.
[80] StAH, Bürgerliche Kollegien, B1, Bd. 7, pp. 360–1, 366–71, 373–8.
[81] Quoted by Rode, *Hamburg und die Reformationsjubiläen*, pp. 12–13.

Church and to the decay of secular authority. Pastor Heinson spoke without any restraint at all, as if the recent dispute had never happened. Only Pastor Johann Winckler made an obvious effort to appear moderate and conciliatory.[82]

On the following day, the Senate then presided over a secular ceremony in the Gymnasium. After a musical prelude at 9 a.m., Professor Fabricius delivered an oration on the fruits of the Reformation.[83] Then ten scholars gave Latin speeches on doctrinal issues. A midday break was followed by twelve further speeches on various aspects of ecclesiastical history since the Reformation, after which the ceremony was concluded with more music.[84] On Tuesday, 2 November a similar ceremony was held in the Johanneum school. A festive oration by *Rector* Hübner introduced eleven Latin speeches on the superiority of Lutheranism; while in the afternoon twenty-two pupils spoke in German on the history of the Reformation. These performances were continued on the following day with more speeches on the history of the Lutheran Church, culminating in a disquisition by Johann Friedrich Scheutt of Glückstadt who spoke 'Of the decline of Lutheranism'.[85]

The second centenary was thus both more elaborate and no less zealous than the first. The citizenry participated with great enthusiasm and several private houses were illuminated with festive displays.[86] Even the Senate did not let its bitter defeat in the matter of the prayer stand in the way of a dignified and solemn occasion. Yet the determination to moderate such intolerant and potentially harmful outbursts of militant Lutheran zeal remained undiminished. Indeed, the anti-Catholic riot of 1719 and its aftermath, together with the anti-Calvinist agitation of the 1720s, made such restraint appear all the more essential. The clergy stood their ground, but the emergence of the Patriotic Society in 1724 gave more force to the arguments in favour of prudence.

The centenaries of 1728 and 1730 provided the first test for the new balance of power. In March 1728, prior to the second centenary of Bugenhagen's reforms in Hamburg in April, the clergy proposed a repetition of the festivities of 1717. But the Senate managed to avoid another confrontation by persuading the Sixty that this was a purely local anniversary.[87] It followed, therefore, that no special arrangements should be made apart from festive bell-ringing and *Te Deums*.[88]

In public, the clergy accepted this ruling; but the Orthodox case was made forcefully by Professor Sebastian Edzardi who accused the Senate

---

[82] Ibid., pp. 13–17.   [83] Fabricius, *Memoriae hamburgenses*, 5, p. 133.
[84] Ibid., pp. 133–5.   [85] Ibid., pp. 145–50.   [86] Steltzner, *Versuch*, 5, p. 479.
[87] StAH, Senat, Cl.VII Lit.Ha No.4 Vol.1b, 12 March 1728, EPS.
[88] Klefeker, *Verfassungen*, 8, p. 537; Blank, *Mandate*, 5, pp. 2538–41.

of indifference. His action merely strengthened the Senate's resolve: his pamphlet was publicly burned, and he himself was prosecuted and later heavily fined.[89] The centenary was marked only by a commemorative medal and, in October, by an oration on the history of the Reformation in Hamburg from 1529 to the present by Professor Michael Richey.[90]

In 1730, by contrast, it was clear that some form of special church celebration to mark the second centenary of the Augsburg Confession was inevitable. But again the Senate initially resolved that it should be relatively modest. The Archivist von Som reported that he could find no mention of any special festivities in 1630. He added wrily that the clergy would in any case find ample inspiration in the reading concerning the lost sheep, which appeared on the ordinary calendar on 25 June 1730.[91]

The Civic Colleges, however, had other notions. The *Oberalten* insisted that the festivities of 1717 be used as a model, in particular that a special prayer of thanksgiving be used. The Sixty wanted cannons fired from the city walls on 25 June, and trumpets and drums played on the tower of St Nicholas', too. These were unprecedented proposals, but the Senate agreed all the same.[92] Its acquiescence was motivated by the hope that the Civic Colleges might help fend off the inevitable clerical objections to the prayer drafted by Syndic Klefeker. The clergy duly reiterated their arguments of 1717, and, despite a revision of the prayer and the pleas of the *Oberalten* and the Sixty, they stood firm in their rejection of a text written by a politician (especially one who belonged to the Patriotic Society). Ultimately, the Sixty again gave way and the clergy were allowed to submit their own text, which in fact differed little from Klefeker's original proposal.[93] Once more the will of the clergy prevailed; but the Senate had obtained a text which was considerably more moderate in tone than that of 1717. It confined itself to thanking God for His bounty provided through Lutheranism, and did not explicitly damn those who sought salvation by other paths.[94]

In every other respect, the festivities of 25–27 June were more splendid than ever before. Bell-ringing music from the tower of St Nicholas', cannon salvos from the city walls – all this was complemented by festive music in all five major churches, and not just in St Peter's as before. The music commissioned for the secular ceremonies in the Gymnasium and the Johanneum was also more elaborate, no longer merely instrumental overtures and finales, but whole oratorios. All the music was composed by

---

[89] Cf. p. 134 above. See also Mutzenbecher, 'Sebastian Edzardi', pp. 214–17.

[90] Blank, *Mandate*, 5, pp. 2538–41; Klefeker, *Verfassungen*, 8, p. 8; Fabricius, *Memoriae hamburgenses*, 6, pp. 2–86.   [91] StAH, Senat, Cl.VII Lit.Ha No.4 Vol.ici, no. 1, 3 March 1730.

[92] Ibid., nos. 1, 4, 8, 10, 11.   [93] Ibid., nos. 21–5, 49, 53.

[94] The prayer is printed in Fabricius, *Memoriae hamburgenses*, 7, pp. 7–13.

Telemann, who also organised its performance. With this rich fanfare, the city fittingly commemorated the Augsburg Confession in church services, secular orations by Fabricius and Hübner, and speeches by young scholars. Throughout, the proceedings were marked by a spirit of moderation, and a concentration on civic pride, which even Pastor Neumeister's anti-Calvinist sermons could not dispel.[95]

The common interest of both State and Church in celebrating the Lutheran tradition was most satisfactorily established in 1730. That interest again manifested itself in 1748 and 1755, and now the friction which accompanied earlier occasions was entirely absent. In 1728 and 1730, the Senate had attempted to play down the need to celebrate; in September 1748, it insisted on commemorating the Peace of Westphalia, even though it was uncertain whether other Protestant states would do so.[96] It was proposed to hold special services in all churches and an oratorio by Telemann in St Peter's on 27 October. But since the feast was not universally recognised, there were to be no subsequent secular ceremonies.[97]

The really significant fact, however, was that an early agreement was reached with the clergy. *Senior* Wagner promised that he would ensure that his colleagues' sermons were moderate, in particular that they would avoid offence to any foreign powers.[98] Most important of all, the Senate was able to accept his draft of a special prayer with only one minor alteration – the omission of a reference to 'the darkness of the Papacy'. For the rest, the prayer was a model of restraint. It celebrated the Peace of Westphalia as the end of religious conflict and as the foundation of Hamburg's peace and prosperity. For the first time it included a plea that God might have mercy on all Christians and that he might defend them all against those 'terrible wolves' and 'heretics' who threatened to lead them astray. The preservation of 'our Hamburg Zion' came first; but the clergy also prayed for the redemption of all Christians, and the damnation of none but heretics.[99]

This theme of magnanimity in strength and unity was also underlined in the commemoration of the Peace of Augsburg in 1755. The celebrations were more elaborate on this occasion since this centenary was an established

95 Blank, *Mandate*, 2, pp. 1105–6; Klefeker, *Verfassungen*, 8, pp. 547–8; Steltzner, *Versuch*, 6, pp. 201–5. The printed sources are collected in Fabricius, *Memoriae hamburgenses*, 7, pp. 1–133.

96 StAH, Senat, Cl.VII Lit.Ha No.4 Vol.1d. In fact many other Protestant cities and principalities celebrated the centenary. See *Acta historico-ecclesiastica*, 12, pp. 880–950 and 13, pp. 727–88. See also: François, 'De l'uniformité à la tolérance', pp. 788–9.

97 Blank, *Mandate*, 3, pp. 1655–72; ibid., 5, pp. 2545–6; Langermann, *Medaillen-Vergnügen*, pp. 297, 299; Klefeker, *Verfassungen*, 8, pp. 553–4. Melhop, *Alster*, p. 635 claims that a firework display was held on this occasion. There is, however, no evidence for this.

98 StAH, Senat, ClVII Lit.Ha No.4 Vol.1d, 8 October 1748, Wagner to Senate.

99 Blank, *Mandate*, 3, pp. 1655–63.

part of the Lutheran tradition: in addition to an oratorio on Sunday, 5 October, a secular ceremony was decreed for the Gymnasium on 7 October.[100] The preparations and the occasion itself passed without friction. Again the special prayer was highly important. Indeed, as Klefeker later emphasised, Wagner's text of 1755 was exemplary.[101] His prayer combined patriotic pride and a concern for Hamburg's prosperity with the genuine hope that all religions might live in peace, harmony and freedom in the *Reich*. The Lutheran message was still firm and clear: like his predecessors, Wagner stressed that 'our Protestant Hamburg Zion' was paramount in his mind; but the old aggressive militance was gone. The contrast with the prayers and sermons of 1717 could not have been greater.[102]

The centenary of 1755 was the last major Lutheran centenary of the eighteenth century. Although, in itself, the fact that the centenaries fell in a period of just forty years was fortuitous, it had important repercussions. For the recurrence of such events in quick succession kept the city locked in the celebration of an exclusive religious tradition; they provided constant reminders to those who may have felt that changing times might permit a more relaxed and tolerant policy.

It is easy to see why the clergy were so eager to exploit these particular centenaries and why they were able to do so. Extraordinary church services focussed the urban mind and the eyes of the populace on the pulpits. On such occasions, the clergy vindicated their claims to be leaders of the people, spiritual colleagues of the magistrates. The effect on the Senate is perhaps less obvious but no less important. For while strenuous efforts were made to moderate the tone of what was said in 1717 and 1730, there was ultimately no debate about the fact that these centenaries should be commemorated with anything but whole-hearted enthusiasm, a fact underlined by the Senate's behaviour in 1748 and 1755. Certainly, the evidence clearly suggests that the Senate was concerned to avoid aggressive and intolerant statements at all costs. But this did not mean a denial of the ideals of the tradition which the clergy sought to promote – merely that diplomacy and public relations dictated that one shrouded references to Catholics, heathens and heretics in language which did not implicate patrons, allies or trading partners of the city.

The Senate might thus effect a change in tone, but apart from that there was little room for manoeuvre if one wanted to celebrate such events at all. In this sense, the Lutheran centenaries became a kind of self-fulfilling

---

[100] Ibid., 4, pp. 2000–33; Klefeker, *Verfassungen*, 8, pp. 556–7; StAH, Senat, Cl.VII Lit.Ha No. 4 Vol.1e.   [101] Klefeker, *Verfassungen*, 12, p. 741.
[102] The prayer is printed in Blank, *Mandate*, 4, pp. 2005–12.

ideology: they reflected the minds of their organisers, but also, in time, influenced and constrained those minds. After all, how could they begin to challenge the intolerant arguments of the clergy while they themselves subscribed wholeheartedly and publicly to the religious values on which those arguments were founded?

IV

The great Lutheran centenaries provided both an image of the city in the present and a vision of its past. In this past, the Reformation was the most important milestone. For although, like many places, Hamburg's origins lay shrouded in the mists of time, its historians in the eighteenth century did not dwell on the legitimacy provided either by Roman antiquity or by medieval charters. For them, Hamburg's history began in 1529: the constitution of 1712 was the apotheosis of the reforms of that year, and most of Hamburg's institutions were infused with the ideals and aspirations which derived from them.[103] The celebration of the centenaries of those bodies in the period 1713–65 underlined the continuing vitality of the structure of urban government, a theme of immense importance immediately after the restoration of peace and harmony in 1712.

At the same time, these celebrations also served to elaborate the sense of identity which formed the theme of the church festivities. The Lutheran tradition projected a broad vision of the urban community within its regional and Imperial context; the civic tradition focussed on more specific features of the community itself. There were seven centenaries in all: the Gymnasium (1713), the civic Militia (1719), the Bank (1719), the Admiralty (1723), the *Oberalten* (1728), the *Kämmerei* (1763) and the *Kommerzdeputation* (1765). Like the Lutheran festivals, they spanned the crucial decades following the promulgation of the constitution of 1712. And they also spanned exactly the years of the first Patriotic Society. The first centenary of the *Kommerzdeputation* in 1765 was the last to be organised by men associated with the first Patriots. The occasion was no less magnificent than those which preceded it. But it was symbolic nonetheless that on this occasion the first public step was taken towards the foundation of the second Patriotic Society – and that marked the emergence of a new sense of purpose and direction, concerned less with the past than with the present and the future.

Partly because these centenaries were entirely new to the eighteenth century, they were the most eloquent expression of the ideals of those who created them. In the case of both Imperial festivities and Lutheran

---

[103] [Richey], 'Kurze Anleitung zum studio hamburgenses'. This concentration on the period after 1529 is underlined by Klefeker, *Verfassungen*, 8, pp. 3–4.

centenaries, there had been precedents, which precipitated celebration after 1700, and which largely determined the form of celebration. All that really happened was that the occasion became more elaborate. The centenaries of urban institutions were new – even for institutions which celebrated a second centenary – and their celebration reflected a conscious choice of occasion and of message. They can also be clearly identified as the inspiration of two men who formed the core of the first Patriotic Society: J. A. Fabricius and Michael Richey. Their efforts were aided by friends like Johann Hübner (close to the Patriots, but not one of them) and Telemann after 1721.

It seems likely that the celebration of the first centenary of the Gymnasium was conceived by J. A. Fabricius, Hamburg's leading intellectual after about 1700. The event fell in the midst of the last great urban crisis: the constitution had just been promulgated in 1712, but the city was still threatened by plague and war. For the first time, an intellectual stepped out in public to offer leadership; not political guidance, but an historical perspective which might anchor the uncertain present.[104]

On Sunday, 20 August a prayer of thanks was read out in all churches which drew attention to the coming centenary. It gave thanks for the survival of the Gymnasium, in which so many distinguished citizens had been educated. Divine foresight had preserved it and ensured that the Protestant faith continued to be taught there. The congregations were enjoined to give thanks for the preservation of this pillar of urban life which was as crucial for the prosperity of the city as good merchants and international peace.[105]

Four days later the *Rector* invited the Senate and the clergy to commemorate the centenary itself. Fabricius opened the proceedings by giving a history of the Gymnasium. He stressed that those who enhanced the position of the city by trade were not always those who governed it: the lessons of traditional scholarship were useful for all men, but particularly for those who governed republics. Above all, education ensures stability and moderation in troubled times. The threat of war and plague, he argued, made it doubly important to commemorate the glorious past in the hope of resurgence and renewal.[106] This theme was then elaborated by Hübner, who wrote a festive ode, and by several scholars of the Gymnasium who also read out essays or papers. Hübner especially stressed that the Gymnasium should be seen as an institution which embodied the living ideals of the Reformation in Hamburg, 'this beautiful city of God, of which

---

[104] On Fabricius, see Schröder, *Lexikon*, 2, pp. 238–59 and Möller, 'Fabricius'. On the crisis as the context for the centenary, see Wohlwill, 'Pestjahre', pp. 397–406.
[105] Klefeker, *Verfassungen*, 6, pp. 51–2; Fabricius, *Memoriae hamburgenses*, 4, pp. 21–2.
[106] Ibid., pp. 1–20.

one may truly say that it early embraced the pure teachings and has adhered to them'. The history of the Gymnasium proved 'that Minerva can stand side by side with Mercury, and that Eusebie [mother of godliness] can be content with this'. Schools, Hübner argued, were a form of capital which paid interest as long as they were cherished and supported. Other orators made the same point and blessed the Gymnasium's patrons: the Senate, the clergy who ward off all heretics and preserve purity of dogma, the *Oberalten* who promote harmony between Church and State.[107] Only thus, declared Christian Eustachius Köten, 'will this Athens blossom in the grace of God, and her praise be sung throughout all Germany...'[108]

The images used by Fabricius and his scholars were carefully chosen. In 1717 Hamburg was to be praised as Zion with images derived from the Old Testament. In 1713, Athens was the model. Christian piety was mingled with Classical wisdom in the first expression of the ideology of *Der Patriot* later vilified by the Orthodox clergy. In 1713 these ideals won much applause and no opposition. The same was true on subsequent occasions of a similar nature. For it was only when they were taken out of a clearly defined festive context that the ideals of the Patriots hinted at heterodoxy, or at least at the eventual autonomy of the secular powers over the Church.

As in the case of the Lutheran centenaries, the ideology was both reinforced and elaborated by frequent reiteration. Little is known about the centenary of the Bank in 1719, except that two medals were minted.[109] But the first centenary of the Society of Colonels and Captains of the Militia in August 1719 took up many of the themes of 1713.[110] The decision to celebrate was made by the Captains in February, and the Colonels readily agreed with their plan to postpone the annual *convivium* of the Captains until 1 September and to devote several days to a general celebration of the Militia's role in maintaining peace and continuity in civic life. The organisers omitted 'nothing which might be conducive not only to the honour of the city and its worthy society [of captains], but also to the splendour of this feast which we now celebrate for the first time'.[111] The city Drillhaus was taken, and renovated by the *Bauhof* (the public works department); the Artillery provided cannon and illuminations; the music was composed by Matthias Christoph Wideburg, and Michael Richey prepared the libretto for an oratorio.[112]

The preparations themselves attracted considerable attention: some 2,000 people attended a rehearsal of the oratorio.[113] And such popular

---

[107] Ibid., pp. 81–8 (quotations from pp. 83–4, 84–5, 87).   [108] Ibid., p. 98.

[109] The medals are described: ibid., 5, pp. 247–52; Langermann, *Medaillen-Vergnügen*, pp. 161–3, 265–7; Klefeker, *Verfassungen*, 1, pp. 618–19.

[110] Steltzner, *Versuch*, 5, pp. 504–5. A detailed account is printed in Fabricius, *Memoriae hamburgenses*, 5, pp. 199–246.   [111] Ibid., p. 203.   [112] Ibid., p. 205.   [113] Ibid.

excitement was a fitting prelude to the great feast laid out in the Drillhaus on 31 August. The festivities opened with an oratorio which incorporated many church hymns accompanied by cannon salvos outside the hall. Then a splendid meal was served during which endless toasts were drunk, each toast again accompanied by cannon salvos signalled to the Artillery by a trumpeter at an open window in the gallery. Both inside and outside the hall, spectators crowded around: inside the hall they apparently watched the company eat only a few steps away.[114]

As darkness fell and the meal drew to a close, the whole hall was illuminated – with particular emphasis on the fifty-seven flags of the militia companies and the images of their patron saints. Another nine-fold salvo announced the performance of Richey's final serenade entitled *Mars und Irene in vergnüglichster Verbindung* (The most blissful union of Mars and Irene), a copy of which was given to each guest, together with a gold medal especially commissioned for the occasion.[115]

The serenade was a moving expression of the Patriotic ideology. The cast of Mars, Irene, Hammonia (Hamburg), Eris (goddess of strife), together with the choruses of the 'Heroes in the suite of Mars', 'The Graces, or companions of Irene' and the 'Citizens of Hamburg' ('Die Kinder der Hammonia'), summed up the fruits of a civic tradition which had survived despite internal and external obstacles. Hammonia and her children valiantly withstand Eris' attempt to break the solid chains of unity. They receive the blessing of Irene, goddess of peace and harmony, while Mercury lends his support and Mars exhorts the officers of the militia to use their weapons to preserve peace and liberty.

The triumph of civic virtue is at last announced by Irene who proclaims:

You Hammonia, treasure of the banks of the Elbe, / shall with my aid stand as the very crown of Germany. / Your town hall shall be a safe abode / of justice and wisdom, / founded on the marble stone of harmony. / Your church services shall be a true diamond hoard / never polluted by anything false. / Your Exchange shall be a meeting place / where profits throng just as citizens do. / The ships which so often and so freely / sweep through your waters this way and that / ensure with their bursting wombs / that your commerce will bear blessed fruit. / My gentle steps, under which only balsam melts, / will never leave your sweet meadows, / where one sees a joyous elysium, / filled with a hundred pleasures of paradise.[116]

A final hymn, sung by Joy, Gratitude, Humility, Harmony and Time, reinforces Irene's blessing by assuring:

[114] Ibid., pp. 206–9.   [115] Ibid., pp. 220–1; the text is printed ibid., pp. 226–38.
[116] Ibid., p. 237.

Dear Hamburg, do not despair, / you will remain robust. / God is the guardian of your battlements, / God himself is with you there. / The early morning light of his help / will dispel all the cares of night.[117]

Richey had indeed captured the aspirations of his contemporaries: the mercantile metropolis as rural idyll; its rulers, the shepherds of a peace-loving flock; the militia, their faithful watchdogs.

This vision also set the tone for Richey's next great public festivity, the centenary of the Admiralty in April 1723. Again a highly-important civic body was involved, an institution concerned with the protection and promotion of the city's most important economic interests. Richey once more sought to place its functions in their broadest historical and civic context. His efforts were aided this time by Telemann, who composed music to accompany the serenade and also composed an orchestral suite entitled the *Wasser-Ouvertur* or *Hamburg Ebb' und Fluht* (the Hamburg tides).[118]

The feast was held in the hall of the Nieder Baum Haus at the harbour gates. The Admiralty flag ship, the *Wapen von Hamburg*, lay at anchor close by, its cannon firing repeatedly as toasts were drunk during the meal. All other ships in the harbour were also specially decorated with flags. Thirty-seven people, including the four *Bürgermeister*, the officials of the Admiralty and various other dignitaries, sat down to a great feast which lasted well into the early hours. As usual, hundreds of spectators gathered to watch the proceedings.[119] Indeed, many were apparently encouraged to come and watch: about 900 copies of Richey's serenade were printed and distributed amongst the city elite; some were also sent to friends and allies abroad in Amsterdam, Sweden and Leipzig (where two copies were sent to the *Teutschliebende Societät*).[120]

Contemporary newspaper accounts devoted considerable attention to the musical entertainment. The most unusual feature was thought to be Telemann's *Wasser-Ouvertur*, an instrumental overture in ten movements played during the meal. It was the first such piece of programme music to be played in Hamburg, and it became immensely popular at public concerts during the next decade or so.[121] A saraband describing 'Die schlafende Thetis' (the sleeping Thetis) led on to other episodes, such as a gavotte entitled 'Die spielenden Najaden' (the playing Naiads), and the piece concluded with a *canarie* (a popular dance) of 'Die lustigen Boots-Leute' (the merry sailors).[122]

---

[117] Ibid., p. 245. The hymn is printed as a separate piece ibid., pp. 239–46.
[118] Maertens, 'Telemanns "Admiralitätsmusik"', *passim*.
[119] Steltzner, *Versuch*, 5, p. 631; Klefeker, *Verfassungen*, 1, pp. 4–5; Langermann, *Medaillen-Vergnügen*, pp. 313–15, 319–20.
[120] StAH, Senat, Cl.VII Lit.Ca No.2 Vol.1b, no. 64, Richey's list of copies received and distributed.
[121] Maertens, 'Telemanns "Admiralitätsmusik"', p. 114.
[122] Fabricius, *Memoriae hamburgenses*, 5, p. 272.

Richey's serenade developed these images in a more conventional manner. The characters of Hammonia (Hamburg), Albis (the Elbe), Neptune, Mercury and Mars, accompanied by the choirs of citizens, Tritons and Nymphs, all combined in florid praise of the city's 'incomparable constitution'. All promised to remain faithful to the eternal values of Hamburg's past, values of which the Admiralty was at once a repository and a vigilant guardian. The progression from the maritime idyll which formed the subject of the opening movement of the *Wasser-Ouvertur* to the mercantile bacchanalia with which it concluded was mirrored and elaborated in Richey's text.[123]

Five years later, Telemann's music again provided the framework for another great civic centenary, this time accompanying words written by Johann Hübner. The second centenary of the *Oberalten* in May 1728 represented a celebration of the whole urban constitution through the congratulation of one of its central institutions, the body which mediated between Senate and *Bürgerschaft*, and which acted as a watchdog over the laws of the city.

The Senate gave 200 *taler* and provided a guard of honour for the evening of 27 May in the old monastery of St Mary Magdalene.[124] The *Oberalten* and their guests assembled at midday, and before, during and after their meal they were edified and entertained by Telemann and his musicians.[125] First came an oratorio by Hübner in which 'Die drey Land-Verderber' ('Die Heucheley, der Missbrauch, die Zwietracht') competed with 'Die drey Schutz-Engel' ('Die Frommigkeit, die Weisheit, der Frieden') for the favours of 'Die Zeit' and of 'Hamburg mit seinen Bürgern'. Wisely, they rejected the former and embraced the latter: the efforts made by Hypocrisy, Abuse and Discord to destroy the city were thwarted by its citizens. They took courage from the words of Time, who warned that the three Evils would return even though they had been expelled. All the same, the threat which they posed might be lessened if the citizens resolved to embrace the Virtues, who in turn promised to remain steadfast by the courageous citizens.[126]

More music was played during the meal, and the festivity was concluded with a serenade which harked back to the pastoral themes of previous centenaries.[127] Flora, Mercury and Eusebie (mother of godliness) all pride themselves on their achievement in Hamburg, while Irene proclaims her worthy presence in the city. Irene's claims expressed a common theme in the civic festivities of this period; but they are less credible than most made

---

[123] Printed ibid., pp. 253–71.
[124] StAH, Senat, Cl.VII Lit.Ba No.2 Vol.8, nos. 1, 4: 14 April and 26 May 1728, EPS.
[125] Steltzner, *Versuch*, 5, pp. 112–14.
[126] Fabricius, *Memoriae hamburgenses*, 6, pp. 87–101.   [127] Ibid., pp. 102–8.

on such occasions. Since the foundation of the *Oberalten*, she claimed, justice and peace had embraced each other despite the cunning of all enemies.[128] The memory of the bitter internal conflicts of the decades before 1712 was obliterated. The stability which had prevailed since then was projected onto the past as well. The celebration of tradition was not only important for that which was remembered: what was forgotten was just as significant. The strategic use of amnesia was as important to the festive life of the city as the mobilisation of the collective memory.

More than three decades elapsed after the second centenary of the *Oberalten* before another similar occasion arose with the second centenary of the *Kämmerei* in 1763. As a result of the problems accompanying the Seven Years War, the occasion was marked without pomp, 'in discreet silence'.[129] But another opportunity soon arose with the first centenary of the *Kommerzdeputation* on 19 January 1765.

The preparations for the celebration were similar to those on previous occasions: a medal was designed by H. S. Reimarus: Telemann composed festive music to texts by Archdeacon Zimmermann of St Catherine's; meals were ordered, cannon fire arranged on ships in the harbour and distinguished guests invited. The costs, at a total of over 9,000 mark, were high, and the day itself was a splendid celebration, no less grand than any other similar centenary.[130]

Yet it marked the end of a festive era. The reasons for this are complex. On the one hand, there were – quite simply – no fitting opportunities for such centennial celebrations during the next decades. Secondly, those who had organised the celebrations of the period before 1765 gradually died: Telemann (d. 1767) and Klefeker (d. 1775) were the last survivors of the first Patriotic generation. But their deaths and the lack of opportunities also coincided with a less fortuitous transition. For it was no accident that at the centenary of the *Kommerzdeputation* on 19 January 1765, Johann Ulrich Pauli distributed to the assembled guests his pamphlet proposing a new Patriotic Society – 'a society for the promotion of the useful arts and manufactures'.[131]

The idea for a new society was eagerly taken up, and, as numerous scholars have pointed out, its ideals and its activities dominated the public life of the city well into the nineteenth century. It did not reject tradition, but it did seek to be active in ways which the first Patriots would not have thought possible. The first Patriots saw the very celebration of tradition as a form of positive action – indeed, almost the only form of positive action. The second Patriots, by contrast, thought in terms which transcended the

128 Ibid., p. 107. 129 Klefeker, *Verfassungen*, 2, pp. 409, 459–60.
130 Baasch, *Handelskammer*, 1, pp. 668–74; Klefeker, *Verfassungen*, 6, pp. 438–41.
131 Baasch, *Handelskammer*, 1, p. 671.

worship of tradition without rejecting it; they thought in terms of useful projects, of the manipulation of an environment which their predecessors had thought of as God-given and immutable.

This shift in emphasis again underlines those factors which facilitated all kinds of change in Hamburg after the 1760s. Until then, the celebration of the civic centenaries helped bind the city more closely to an exclusive tradition which precluded change out of respect for the past. Their prime functions were to generate respect for the constitution and to reinforce a domestic *status quo* which had frequently been upset by bitter conflicts. But that positive intention also had a negative dimension: what many applauded as stability could also manifest itself as intransigence and immobility. The fortuitous cessation of such celebrations thus created a felicitous vacuum within which the new Patriots could pursue their ideal of the resurgence and renewal of the polity.

V

The three types of secular and ecclesiastical occasion analysed above reveal a very similar pattern. The attempts to define the community and to impress that definition on the world at large were particularly intensive during the century or so before the 1760s. Thus, at precisely the time when Hamburg was becoming a more complex and apparently more heterodox society, the prevailing tendency amongst both the magistrates and the clergy was the assertion of a more strident orthodoxy, whether religious or political. Of course there were important disagreements about how rigidly the exclusiveness of Lutheranism was to be interpreted in practice. But these repeated public celebrations both restricted liberal interpretations and inhibited any attempt to find a lasting solution to the problem of religious worship for the non-Lutheran minorities.

The importance of this period before the 1760s can also be established in many other areas. An examination of funeral legislation, for example, shows that laws confining public burial to Lutherans were firmly established after 1650, and were repeatedly reinforced until the 1760s, when changes in the place of burial, from the city churches to rural cemeteries, gradually undermined their significance.[132] The same pattern is also evident in the celebration of days of penance. The annual *Busstag*, instituted in 1686 and celebrated consistently after 1700, was another perennial reminder of the exclusiveness of the Lutheran community in Hamburg. During the services on that day, the city gates were closed and Lutherans assembled for prayers which enjoined God to unleash his wrath on the heathens who did not recognise his name. Although the service was modified in 1747, the central

---

[132] See Whaley, 'Symbolism for the survivors', pp. 85–6.

prayer remained unaltered until 1771. Then several clergymen refused to read out a text which they thought aggressively intolerant and offensive. The debate over a proposed change was bitter and public, eagerly exploited by the intransigent *Senior* Goeze's numerous secular and clerical enemies. The conflict was only resolved when Goeze resigned as *Senior*; this facilitated an emendation of the prayer which now only condemned atheists and blasphemers, and left uncondemned Catholics and Calvinists, and even, by implication, the Jews.[133]

This particular debate was an important indicator of changing attitudes to the problem of toleration, as I argued in Chapter 5 above.[134] But it assumes a more general significance in the context of the festivities analysed here. For it was but one of many areas where the public assertion of exclusive Lutheran values seemed to become less important after the 1760s.

The economic crisis after 1763 was crucial in this shift. But the new Patriots and those who broadly supported their views displayed more than just a simple reaction to economic pressures, however profound they were. In complex ways, the crisis stimulated them to search for solutions to problems which had frustrated their predecessors. The need to accommodate non-Lutheran aliens was prime among those problems – pressing because of the obvious economic and humanitarian arguments, yet intractable because of the equally obvious political and religious objections. It was only after the crisis of the 1760s that the new Patriots found ways of reconciling in their own minds the public primacy of Lutheranism with the recognised existence of Calvinism, Catholicism and even, though to a much more limited degree, Judaism. The crisis undermined old preconceptions and old certainties; it forced men to look for new ways of stimulating growth, new ways of ordering human affairs more rationally. In Hamburg that meant – among other things – an attempt to resolve the central problem of the economically important religious minorities.

The process of resolving this problem did not involve a rejection either of Lutheranism or of the urban past. The polity was still dominated by Lutheranism until the separation of Church and State in 1860. The city also remained highly conscious of its history. Indeed, the foundation of the *Verein für hamburgische Geschichte*, the local historical society, in 1839 marked the beginning of a new and lasting preoccupation, almost an obsession, with the city's past which has endured to the present.[135] And while the Imperial celebrations inevitably ceased after 1806, the celebration of Lutheran and urban centenaries continued.

---

[133] Klefeker, *Verfassungen*, 8, pp. 408–10, 538–40; Röpe, *Goeze*, pp. 103–23; Oehlke, *Lessing*, 2, pp. 314–17.   [134] See pp. 152–3 above.
[135] On the foundation of the *Verein*, see Postel, *Lappenberg*, pp. 165–74.

But there was a difference – the difference between the living statement and the reiteration of tradition. In the former, the infrastructure of the Lutheran polity was being built. In the latter, its completed façade was being paraded; and behind it even non-Lutherans could take their stand, live their lives, and exercise their religion. Ironically, an important part of that façade was the myth of the tolerant society in Hamburg, the ambivalent search for which had in fact dominated the city's history until the late eighteenth century.

7

The aftermath

In the late sixteenth century, Hamburg provided an attractive haven for many whose livelihood was threatened in Western Europe by the turmoil and persecution which accompanied the Reformation and the Religious Wars. From the 1580s, Catholics, Calvinists and Jews began to settle there. Later exiles, such as the Huguenots, also gravitated to the city, which had become the most prosperous and dynamic commercial centre in Germany by 1700.

Collectively, the immigrants had a substantial impact on the development of the city's economy. Their importance was recognised from the start. But the process of acceptance and establishment was both long and difficult. For the liberal policies of the mercantile Senate repeatedly came up against the opposition of the clergy, who for two centuries struggled to maintain the exclusive position of the Lutheran Church in Hamburg.

The fortunes of the original immigrant groups differed markedly. The Sephardim were replaced by the poorer Ashkenazim within sixty or seventy years. But although the latter also provided valuable economic skills, the Jews were exceptional from beginning to end. They were thoroughly alien in terms of both race and religion, and although a significant attempt was made to give them religious freedom in the 1740s, they were not included in the toleration debate after 1760.

The Catholic community also changed, losing its original mercantile character. By 1700 at the latest, it was composed largely of poor people, labourers and servants. Only the Calvinists maintained their wealth and prestige: both Dutch and French communities remained prosperous and influential until modern times. It was this which made them central to the toleration debate which began in earnest after the economic crisis of 1763.

From the start, the city did more than merely accept passively the bounty provided by the *Fremde*. At first, contracts were drawn up with the various communities, which defined their relationship with the city and granted them considerable economic liberties. The Christians were also encouraged to become *Bürger* rather than just remain *Einwohner*. They were allowed civil liberties and permitted to serve in certain urban institutions like the *Bürgerwache* and the garrison. But they were denied full political freedom: they were excluded from the *Bürgerschaft* and from all public offices until 1819.

The crucial factor which divided civil from political liberty was religion. For the constitutions of 1529 and 1603 were based on the Lutheran Church. While first political and mercantile prudence and later the Peace of Westphalia guaranteed all groups against outright persecution, it proved impossible to grant even limited religious freedom under the protection of the Senate until 1785.

Until then, two factors ensured that the economic advantages of staying in Hamburg were not outweighed by religious restrictions. The first was that the nearby Danish town of Altona pursued perhaps more liberal religious policies than any other town in Germany. Founded and promoted in an attempt to draw trade away from its powerful neighbour, Altona offered religious freedom to all groups, from Jews to sectarians, Catholics and Calvinists. But it failed to attract as settlers those for whom it provided chapels and preachers. On the contrary, Hamburg benefited from Danish tolerance since it alleviated the pressures on the Senate to adopt a more liberal view.

Inside Hamburg itself, foreign diplomats performed a similar function. Especially after 1648, when permanent foreign Residents became established, the Imperial, Dutch and Prussian governments strove to extend diplomatic immunity to the religious worship of Catholics and Calvinists in their chapels. In the case of the Calvinists, this led to a formal secession of the Hamburg communities from their Altona consistories in the eighteenth century.

Although Altona and the diplomats thus facilitated a *modus vivendi* regarding the religious issue, it was an uneasy one. The Senate was increasingly concerned about competition from Altona: a succession of profound economic crises from the 1690s threatened that Altona might indeed reap the economic fruits of its religious diplomacy. At the same time, the patronage of the diplomats detracted from the sovereignty of the city and brought unwelcome foreign intervention in its domestic affairs.

The opposition to a more liberal policy in Hamburg itself was twofold. Unlike neighbouring princes, the Senate did not enjoy exclusive sovereignty over the city. The *Bürgerschaft* and the Civic Colleges were in every sense *Mitregenten* (co-regents), and they repeatedly frustrated the Senate's efforts to give greater religious freedom to groups whom they regarded as economic competitors and potential political rivals.

Their opposition was compounded by that of the Lutheran clergy. Although their intervention was not sanctioned by the constitution itself, the clergy managed to manipulate the decision-making system by alerting the Civic Colleges to the dangers inherent in toleration. Self-consciously Orthodox in dogmatic terms, their implacable resistance to the Senate's initiatives was based both on theological grounds and on fears about the future of the established Church in an heterodox world. They feared that the Lutheran community, the power and prestige of its pastors as well as their incomes, would be eroded if *Gewissensfreiheit* were translated into public freedom of worship.

The intransigence of the *Bürgerschaft* and the clergy explains why it took so long to reach the compromise of 1785. But it does not explain the limitations of the mandate. It was never merely a question of a simple juxtaposition of liberal and tolerant magistrates on the one hand and conservative citizens and Orthodox Lutheran clerics on the other. The decline in power of the clergy enabled a compromise. But the compromise itself was moulded by legal preconceptions deeply rooted in the constitution and the ambiguous legal framework of the Treaty of Osnabrück. The Senate was as faithful as the clergy to this legal tradition, and the concession of 1785 only marked the victory of a liberal interpretation of its restrictions rather than its outright rejection.

As the celebration of religious and civic centenaries and Imperial occasions showed, the magistrates were always as concerned to conserve and perpetuate the city's religious and political heritage as the citizenry or the clergy. Where they differed, and often appeared to be progressive and indifferent as a result, was in their definition of the degree of latitude which this heritage allowed with regard to the aliens. Indeed, it is significant that the most elaborate celebration of civic occasions occurred in the first half of the eighteenth century, at precisely the same time as the Senate struggled to formulate a coherent religious policy.

Until 1650, official policy was dominated by the idea of the contract or official treaty binding foreign merchants to the city by oath. In the case of the Jews, this policy continued up to the nineteenth century. But before 1700 no serious attempt was made to find a lasting solution to the contentious issue of religious worship, even for the Christian groups. Only the impact of war, plague and severe economic depression in the period 1700 to 1730 stimulated the magistrates to attempt to establish a more satisfactory *Toleranz-System* after the promulgation of the new constitution in 1712. This initiative also reflected the increasing predominance of lawyers in the Senate. Inspired by the legal philosophies of Thomasius and Wolff, they sought to reconcile the existence of an established Church with the religious liberties theoretically guaranteed to minorities by the Treaty of Osnabrück.

These efforts were frustrated by the opposition of the clergy and the citizenry. The spectre of a theologically-indifferent state, the fear of an overbearing Senate arrogating to itself the rights of the *jus patronatus* which, according to the constitution, it shared with the *Bürgerschaft*, placed insuperable obstacles in the way of those who espoused moderation.

Only in the context of the economic crisis of 1763 did a second generation of Patriots succeed in pushing through a concession which in every respect bore the imprint of their Thomasian and Wolffian predecessors. The proposed *Toleranz-System* was not markedly changed by the *Aufklärung*. New insights into the nature of economic growth, more radical theological demands for toleration, made its establishment in Hamburg more urgent, and ultimately facilitated its acceptance by a *Bürgerschaft* now willing to oppose a divided clergy. But *Aufklärung* worked within an inherited legal and institutional tradition. It might rationalise some of its elements, and effect sensible reforms; but it did not either reject the past, or fundamentally undermine the deep-rooted loyalty of even the enlightened elite to the historically-determined religious, legal and institutional framework of its environment. Jews and sectarians, even the economically-powerful Mennonites, were still denied even the *exercitium religionis privatum*. Effectively, all that the 'party of humanity' achieved in Hamburg, as elsewhere in Germany, was the clarification and limited implementation of the guidelines laid down in 1648. For that was all that trade and commerce, and Christian charity, demanded of magistrates who were neither philosophers nor utopian reformers.

In 1744, *Freiherr* von Bielfeld voiced the sentiment which best summed up the ambivalence of the proponents of toleration in Hamburg when he wrote that 'En tolerant on est charmé de pouvoir sauver les apparences'.[1] At the beginning of the nineteenth century, Goethe expressed the aspirations of a new age, aspirations which were fuelled by the French Revolution, and which remain fundamental and largely unrealised to this day, when he wrote: 'Toleration should really only be a transitory attitude. It must lead to recognition. To tolerate is to insult.'[2]

Such statements as Goethe's were common in the first decade of the nineteenth century. The reforming euphoria generated by events in France after 1789 and, more immediately, by the Napoleonic period in Germany itself, seemed to herald new beginnings in virtually all areas of human experience. The Holy Roman Empire was dissolved in 1806, and with it disappeared the complex legal and institutional paraphernalia which had made inertia seem like a Teutonic condition. At last, many German intellectuals believed, there was room for movement: progress guided by

---

[1] StAH, Senat, Cl.VII Lit.Hf No.2a Vol.6b, 10 April 1744, Bielfeld to Chaunel.
[2] Quoted by Schultze, *Lessings Toleranzbegriff*, p. 11.

the precepts of reason, and by restrained Teutonic sense which would avoid the horrors of the French way of the 1790s. Of course, not even all intellectuals regarded the events of this time with anything like the equanimity of the late *Aufklärer*. Already, powerful currents of political and social reaction, propelled and moulded by a resurgent religiosity, were becoming apparent, and in some areas, like Prussia, even almost dominant. Indeed, in most of Germany the position of the rationalist was bolstered not so much by reason as by the reality of occupation by, or involuntary alliance with, the French.

For all that, however, the years between 1806 and 1815 marked a caesura rather than a clean break. After 1815 continuity appeared both more desirable and more real than change. The Holy Roman Empire was not revived, but most of the Napoleonic constitutions were abolished. The German Confederation may have been more 'modern' than the old Empire, but in a sense that was merely because its constitution was couched in the language of the nineteenth century. Just how far its modernity extended beyond its linguistic form was not entirely apparent. The contradiction between the legislation of the Napoleonic and early Restoration eras only gradually became clear. The discussion of and resolution of these contradictions preoccupied German governments for much of the nineteenth century. It is only in the light of the resolution of successive points that the Federal Act of 1815 appears retrospectively to assume the status of a modern legal framework.

The issue of religious rights in the nineteenth century exemplified the complexity of this process. The question is overshadowed in most modern accounts of the development of Germany since 1815 by the analysis of the evolution of legal systems and constitutions: but religious liberties and their implications for civil and political rights, and the wider question of the relationship between Church and State, remained one of the central problems of the day. In the long-term view, the developments in these areas are subsumed under slogans like secularisation or dechristianisation. In the short term, however, neither secularisation nor dechristianisation appeared either inevitable or desirable.

It is thus important not to be misled by the irenicist or universalist rationalism implicit in Goethe's statement. The differences between religious faiths were not dissolved by the humanitarian solvent of French revolutionary ideals. Indeed, the first half of the nineteenth century saw a marked revival of the claims of the various Churches. Both Catholicism and Protestantism were characterised by a revival of confidence in the universal validity of their respective beliefs.[3] Powerful forces in both camps

---

[3] Nipperdey, *Deutsche Geschichte*, pp. 403–6.

saw such a revival as an urgent response to the corrosive influence of the ideas of 1789. By the 1840s it seemed that a new confessionalism had emerged, no less combative than that of the immediate post-Reformation era.

Yet there was no revival of violent religious conflict. There were, of course, some major disputes involving religious issues during the nineteenth century. Between 1835 and 1840 the Prussian government was in bitter conflict with its Catholic subjects in the Rhineland over the question of mixed marriages and civil registration. In the 1870s Bismarck's *Kulturkampf* again exploded into a struggle between the Protestant state and the Catholic Church. However, both of these episodes were fundamentally different from the confrontations of the early modern era. The first arose out of the pursuit of liberal constitutional principles to their logical conclusions. Bismarck's later campaign was motivated by political considerations which had little to do with traditional confessionalism and more to do with the mobilisation of bias to reinforce the legitimacy of the new *Reich*.

After 1815 the discussion of religious freedom and the relationship between Church and State was never again characterised by the violent physical confrontations of the early modern era. The dominant preoccupations of the Restoration Churches provide an important insight into the reasons for this. They also indicate the extent to which the political and social framework within which the Churches existed had changed.

Two characteristics were particularly important. The first was the emergence in both the Catholic and Protestant Churches of the so-called 'internal missions' during the 1830s – most notably that of Johann Hinrich Wichern in the Lutheran world and that of Adam Kolping in the Catholic Church. Both demonstrated a preoccupation with the position of the Churches with regard to the mass of the population, hinting at a perceived crisis in the relationship between traditional religious institutions and their congregations. To a large degree, this was in turn a reaction to social change common to Churches all over Western Europe. The rapid growth of population, and the particularly intense growth of cities, placed unprecedented strains on traditional ecclesiastical structures, which had evolved in essentially agrarian societies. Even in urban centres like Hamburg, where Wichern began his mission, the Churches were ill-equipped to cope with a dramatic increase in the size of the population. The major problem was no longer that of converting 'heretics' to the true faith, but of ensuring that Christianity remained capable of ministering to the needs of people who might otherwise reject it or remain indifferent to it by default.[4]

The second characteristic of the development of the Churches reveals

[4] Ibid., pp. 406–40.

a rather different but complementary crisis. The increasing involvement of the Churches in politics, culminating in the emergence of religious parties in the middle decades of the century, showed a similar sense of insecurity with regard to their position within the political system. In a sense this development marked the first involuntary recognition of what later became the pluralistic state. The Churches were forced to respond to the powerful arguments of secularist critics of the age-old marriage of the political and ecclesiastical regimes, arguments largely put forward by radical atheists, but often supported by liberal Christian politicians.[5]

This second phenomenon points to the way in which the nature of the legal framework of the religious issue changed as a result of the upheavals of the Napoleonic period and the Restoration settlement. Even before 1806 the restrictions of the Peace of Westphalia were being undermined in some states. In Prussia, for example (albeit a state not affected by Napoleonic reforms after 1806), the *Allgemeines Landrecht* of 1794 had already established a radically different system.[6] All subjects were granted freedom of conscience. The three Churches recognised by the Peace of Westphalia were granted equal status as public corporations. Other sects were allowed the possibility of becoming 'religious societies'. They were permitted to function in private (to hold services without public rights or bell-ringing) as long as they undertook to provide Christian education and guaranteed their loyalty to the state. Similar moves were made in Bavaria after 1800. But here, as well as elsewhere, the major changes came after 1806. In varying degrees and combinations all of the states in the new Confederation of the Rhine, and those outside it which were allied to France, granted equality to individuals of all faiths and parity within the state to the three Churches privileged in 1648. The two types of measure were complementary, but they contained a contradiction which was only resolved in a minority of states. In Westphalia, for example, all Churches were granted public equality. Similarly, in Hamburg, incorporated into the French Empire in 1810, full political rights for individuals of all denominations including the Jews were accompanied by the abolition of the privileged status of the Lutheran Church in accordance with the stipulations of the Code Napoleon.[7]

Such legislation was inevitably piecemeal, and not often taken to its logical conclusion by the time the Napoleonic regime collapsed. In the majority of states the pre-1815 legislation was either rescinded or held in abeyance while new legal and constitutional principles were negotiated. Above all, the situation in Germany as a whole was crucially determined

[5] Ibid. See also: Heckel, 'Säkularisierung', p. 28.
[6] Birtsch, 'Religions- und Gewissensfreiheit in Preussen', *passim*; Fürstenau, *Grundrecht der Religionsfreiheit*, p. 83.   [7] Ibid., pp. 86–96.

for the next few decades by the provisions of the Federal Act of 1815, the first general statute on the subject since the Peace of Westphalia.[8]

In some ways the Act merely perpetuated old concepts. When it spoke of 'Christian faiths', for example, it meant the three faiths recognised in 1648, though this was not spelled out because it was thought anachronistic. Anachronistic or not, however, the old assumption still prevailed: rights in religious matters were only firm and fundamental in so far as they pertained to Catholics, Lutherans or Calvinists.[9]

At the same time, however, the Act included provisions whose implications ultimately undermined and destroyed this limitation. The Peace of Westphalia had spoken exclusively about the freedom of Churches: freedom accrued to the individual only in so far as he was a member of a recognised Church, and it pertained only to his activities within that Church. Hence men such as Pastor Goeze could both declare their adherence to the principle of religious freedom and at the same time bitterly oppose public worship (and the political rights which that implied) for any but Lutherans. The Federal Act of 1815, by contrast, spoke almost exclusively of the freedom of individuals. In Article 16 it declared that differences in religious beliefs must not be the cause of any civil or political disability. All Christians were to enjoy civil and political liberties without prejudice. The Jews were explicitly excluded from this provision: the clause merely added that an attempt would be made to formulate some more satisfactory general principle to apply to the Jews at a later date.[10]

Even in the case of the Christians, however, there was no immediate change in all states. To a large extent the provisions of Article 16 were dependent on the prior implementation of Article 13, which enjoined the members of the Confederation to introduce constitutions. Only as this was done in the majority of states in the decade or so after 1815 was the principle of full civil and political rights gradually extended. The Federal Act still permitted rulers to maintain an established religion of state. Similarly, a ruler might still impose restrictions upon Churches other than the Catholic, Lutheran or Calvinist; but the crucial breakthrough was the explicit assertion of the right of all Christians to 'political liberty' – a concept translated directly from the French *droits politiques*, and novel to the German legal system.[11]

Like the Peace of Westphalia, the Federal Act established a series of guidelines rather than a precise set of mandatory regulations. The result was the emergence after 1815 of a regional diversity in confessional legislation as complex as that which prevailed after 1648. Certain fundamental individual rights had ostensibly been recognised: but their inter-

---

[8] Ibid., pp. 97–119.   [9] Ibid., pp. 101–2.   [10] Ibid., pp. 99–102.
[11] Ibid., pp. 111–12.

pretation was often a contentious issue. The majority of states confined those rights to the members of the three major Churches. There was also vociferous debate over the question of whether freedom of public worship was in fact a civil right at all. The conclusion most often reached, that Article 16 merely guaranteed the right to family worship in private without the guidance of ministers or priests, in a sense cast dissenting Christians back into the situation they had been in during the eighteenth century. The only major innovation in practice was that now the German princes for the most part gave up their old right to enforce religious uniformity by obliging such dissenters to emigrate. The old *jus reformandi* was now limited with regard to the three major Christian Churches, but remained with regard to dissenters, whom a prince might still exclude from political participation.[12]

The position of the Jews was even less clearly defined in this period. The commission proposed by the Federal Act to discuss their situation met, but it never produced a report. No general guidelines were formulated, and in many states the Jews continued to be dealt with under eighteenth-century statutes complemented by minor legislation from time to time. In Prussia, for example, the Jews had been granted citizenship in 1812, but in the 1820s and 1830s their privileges were gradually eroded once more. Finally in 1847 a new general decree was promulgated which both reaffirmed the original grant of citizenship and incorporated the subsequent limitations and qualifications.[13] In Hamburg, the emancipation which logically followed the introduction of the French constitution in 1810–11 was fully abrogated in 1814. Thereafter the Jewish question was discussed by a variety of Senatorial committees and public pressure groups; but various initiatives were thwarted by outbreaks of antisemitic violence. A more continuous and fruitful discussion began again in 1842, but no real progress was made before 1848.[14]

In the special case of the Jews, as in the more general case of the various Christian Churches and sects, the most radical break with the past came in 1848. The legislation of the revolutionary interlude was more radical than that of the Napoleonic period. For now the principles formerly implemented only briefly in territories under direct French rule were implemented in all the German states; and they were also embodied in the Fundamental Rights of the German People and in the German Constitution drawn up by the Frankfurt Parliament. For the first time, the principle that no individual should suffer limitation of his civil and political liberties was extended unequivocally to all Christians. It was extended even to the Jews,

[12] Ibid., pp. 113–19.
[13] Ibid., pp. 160–70. See also: Nipperdey, *Deutsche Geschichte*, pp. 248–55; Toury, *Geschichte der Juden*, pp. 277–92.   [14] Ibid., pp. 279, 282, 285.

without any restriction or qualification. More crucial still was the fact that this principle was now complemented by a declaration of the separation of Church and State.[15]

In the most obvious sense the laws promulgated by the Frankfurt Parliament and by the liberal state governments in 1848 and 1849 were a failure. They were just as much casualties of the reaction as the Frankfurt Parliament itself. In August 1851 a new Federal law declared all legislation of the revolutionary period null and void, and the *status quo* was restored.[16] However, these measures did have an important impact on the legislation drawn up in the German states during the next two decades. It was this legislation which regulated the position of the Churches in Germany until 1918. Again, the result was a complex patchwork of varying legal systems; but overall it is possible to discern a two-fold general pattern. On the one hand there was an increasing tendency towards explicit affirmation of the principle of liberty of conscience coupled with political rights, a principle finally enshrined in the constitution of the *Reich* in 1871. This in effect meant an unqualified denial of the ruler's *jus reformandi* with regard to the individual. By 1871, furthermore, this principle had also been extended to the Jews throughout Germany. On the other hand many states now tended to recognise the right of all religious congregations to worship freely in public. The old distinction between *publicum* and *privatum* was not abolished, nor was that between corporations and societies. It was, however, no longer manifest in the purely external signs which had obsessed early modern policy makers – the bells, the spires and other symbols of state recognition and public freedom. Now also the list of 'corporations' also generally included the Jewish communities; they were defined as larger bodies which were given the right to levy internal taxes, and over whose ecclesiastical appointments the state retained some control. A 'society' was generally defined as a small sect on which the state made no claims, and whose legal status did not permit it to make legally-valid financial claims on its own members either.[17]

The precise number and relative status of corporations and societies varied from state to state. The constitution of the *Reich* merely guaranteed the rights of the individual and left the issue of the Churches to the state governments. In most states, notably in Prussia, established Churches survived as especially privileged corporations: Protestantism was the state religion and the Kaiser was the *summus episcopus* of the Church. Hamburg again was exceptional in that it had introduced the separation of Church and State in 1860, in a new constitution which finally replaced the old

---

[15] Fürstenau, *Grundrecht der Religionsfreiheit*, pp. 179–94.
[16] Ibid., p. 179.   [17] Ibid., pp. 226–58.

system of 1712 – an arrangement which only became characteristic of the whole of Germany with the constitution of the Weimar Republic.[18]

The evolution of the issue of religious toleration during the nineteenth century was thus protracted. It was characterised by the same bewildering complexity of regional variations which had prevailed under the Holy Roman Empire. The general tendency was an emphasis on problems thrown up by eighteenth-century toleration edicts like that passed in Hamburg in 1785.

The extension of the notion of freedom of conscience to embrace full civil and political liberties involved an often painful dissolution of the bonds between Church and State. To most late eighteenth-century politicians the notion of an indifferentist state would have been unthinkable. Some two or three generations later, it was not only thinkable but, in the eyes of many, desirable. The statement of the principle of religious freedom for the individual in 1815 was thus in many ways a symbolic milestone in the process whereby the bonds between Church and State, strengthened and formalised by the Reformation, were eroded. The statement summed up the changes wrought as a result of the struggles of the early modern era. Its ambiguities, and the limitations placed upon its implementation in practice, set the context for the subsequent debate and determined its themes.

Ultimately, the secularised state became regarded as one of the essential preconditions of a just and free society. However, the inception and growth of that conviction itself gave rise to debates and conflicts of conscience and belief which still preoccupy many democratic societies today. For the separation of Church and State in Germany in 1918, as elsewhere at other times, has rarely been a clear-cut or straightforward business. The state may have shed its confessional identity, but numerous aspects of the politico-ecclesiastical regime still survived. In Germany, for example, the religious oath and the issue of religious education, two of the most important pillars of the early modern state, are still debated today.[19] Only the nature of that debate is now different. For the issue is no longer primarily that of the relationship between Christianity and the state; ecclesiastical law has been transformed from a core discipline into an arcane, antiquarian and little understood backwater. Now the state provides a framework within which Christianity and indeed all other faiths are obliged to seek to define their relationship with society.

---

[18] Bergemann, *Staat und Kirche*, pp. 61–88.
[19] Heckel, 'Säkularisierung', pp. 7–18.

Bibliography

I. MANUSCRIPT SOURCES

Unless otherwise stated, all the primary sources listed below are to be found in the *Staatsarchiv der Freien und Hansestadt Hamburg*. Two collections are of particular importance and deserve some comment: the archive of the Senate and the archive of the *Ministerium*.

The Senate archive is organised according to a complex subject-classification system devised in 1710 and substantially unaltered to this day. The content of the files is, however, often considerably less coherent than their titles might suggest. The main reason for this lies in the hurried reconstruction of the archive after the great fire of Hamburg in 1842. Many parts of the Senate's collections were destroyed outright. Others, particularly those dealing with internal affairs, survived relatively unscathed, but were often unsystematically bundled together under the old headings. As a result, continuous series of letters within individual files are relatively rare, and papers relating to specific issues are often scattered throughout several files. Similarly, files are only rarely paginated; in most, the documents are numbered, again unsystematically, with individual documents often bearing a bewildering variety of numbers. This seems to be especially true of many of the files used for this book: their relevance to current affairs after 1842 was extremely limited and thus little attention was paid to the way in which they were reconstructed. In citing documents, I have used that form most likely to guide the reader to the relevant place in the file.

One significant gap in the Senate collection is the total lack of minutes for Senate meetings before 1742. This is compensated for, however, by the fact that extracts of the relevant passages were inserted in the files containing correspondence.

Despite its lacunae and disorganisation, the collection is extremely rich. It contains most of the correspondence of the Senate with the Lutheran clergy, the non-Lutheran minorities, and with foreign powers regarding them.

The papers of the Senate are complemented by the archive of the *Ministerium*. This consists of minute books, and of internal and external correspondence. The minute books run almost continuously from the early seventeenth century and are an invaluable guide to the issues which preoccupied the Lutheran clergy from week to week. The correspondence, together with large quantities of miscellaneous papers, was bound in huge volumes by *Senior* Wagner in 1743. The use of both series is facilitated by a detailed subject index together with an itemised list of papers compiled by *Senior* Goeze 1760–1 (StAH, Bestandsverzeichnis Ministerium, 511–1, Bd. 2–4). For documents in this collection, I have used Goeze's pagination and numeration throughout, even though it is not always wholly consistent.

Some of the material in this collection duplicates that found in the Senate archive. But it is invaluable in two ways. Firstly, it contains a considerable amount of Senatorial correspondence, copies of originals which were lost in 1842. Secondly, it contains a vast mass of material produced by the clergy themselves. It is particularly rich in information concerning the non-Lutheran minorities.

StAH, Senat

Cl.I	Lit.Hc	No.1–24	Imperial Resident's chapel 1712–90
Cl.VII	Lit.Aa	No.2 Vol.8a	Senate rules of procedure
Cl.VII	Lit.Ba	No.2 Vol.8	*Oberalten* bicentenary 1728
Cl.VII	Lit.Ca	No.2 Vol.1b	*Admiralität* centenary 1723
Cl.VII	Lit.Cc	No.2 Vol.1 Fasc.1	*Fremdenkontrakt* 1731
Cl.VII	Lit.Dd	No.4 Vol.3	F. N. Lütjens, Cammer-Meditationes 1768
Cl.VII	Lit.Fl	No.2 Vol.4f	Pietro Mingotti 1744–55
Cl.VII	Lit.Ha	No.4 Vol.1a–e	Religious centenaries 1717–55
Cl.VII	Lit.Hb	No.3 Vol.2b	Pastor Schultz, Diary 1686–99
		Vol.6	Miscellaneous correspondence 1725–6
		Vol.8	Miscellaneous correspondence 1730–9
		Vol.13	Miscellaneous correspondence 1760–5
		Vol.18a	Clerical oath 1784
Cl.VII	Lit.Hb	No.5 Vol.4	Goeze and Friderici 1776
Cl.VII	Lit.He	No.1 Vol.3	*ephorus gymansii* 1743
Cl.VII	Lit.Hf	No.1 Vol.1–3g	Non-Lutheran religious worship 1713–85
Cl.VII	Lit.Hf	No.2a Vol.1–17	Calvinist communities *c.* 1603–1786
Cl.VII	Lit.Hf	No.3 Vol.2–23	Catholic community *c.* 1604–1777
Cl.VII	Lit.Hf	No.4 Vol.5	Oppenheimer and Bennewitz 1750
Cl.VII	Lit.Hf	No.5 Vol.1–7	Jewish communities *c.* 1600–1789
Cl.VII	Lit. Ja	No.1 Vol.5–7	Correspondence with Austrian Residents in Hamburg 1717–23
Cl.VII	Lit.Ja	No.3 Vol.2	Ditto miscellaneous
Cl.VII	Lit.Jb	No.1 Vol.1b	Foreign diplomats
Cl.VII	Lit.Ka	No.4 Vol.5	Report on Hamburg's trade *c.* 1726
Cl.VII	Lit.La	No.3 Vol.9d	Goeze complaint against Klefeker 1773
Cl.VII	Lit.Lb	No.16 Vol.6a2	'Anstössige Schriften in theologicis'
Cl.VII	Lit.Lb	No.18 Vol.1–4	Jewish communities (civil legislation) 1619–*c.* 1790
Cl.VII	Lit.Ra3	No.1 Vol.1 Fasc.1–37	Imperial festivities *c.* 1650–1806
Cl.VIII		No.Xa 1742ff	Senate minutes
Cl.XI	Generalia	No.1 Vol.13	Catholic artisans 1760–81

I. Manuscript sources

StAH, *Ministerium*
Bestandsverzeichnis 511–1, Bd.2–4   Index to minutes and papers
II 2–8   Minute books 1648–1794
III A1d–w   Miscellaneous papers 1553–1767
III A2b   Imperial chapel 1716–20
III A2c   Calvinists and Jews 1746–59
III A2g   Miscellaneous papers 1737–60
III B (1778), (1779), (1785   Miscellaneous papers

StAH, *Akademisches Gymnasium*
C 1   Michael Richey's collection 1612–1760

StAH, *Baudeputation*
A 3, Bd.1–2   Minute books *c.* 1630–1820

StAH, *Bürgerliche Kollegien*
B 1, Bd.7   Minutes of the Sixty 1716–17

StAH, *Deutsch-evangelisch-reformierte Gemeinde (DRG)*
I A 13   Correspondence with Prussia 1684–7
    21   Miscellaneous pamphlets
    23   Miscellaneous pamphlets
    25   Miscellaneous pamphlets
I C 34   Correspondence 1709
II Aa Bd.12   Consistory minutes 1715–52
      Bd.13   Consistory minutes 1752–74

StAH, *Edzardische Proselyten-Anstalt*
B 1   Donation book 1667–1728
B 2   Donation book 1761–83
B 3   Report book 1761–1941

StAH, *Erbgesessene Bürgerschaft (EB)*
No.1 Bd.12–15   Minute books 1713–30
     Bd.24   Minute books 1774
     Bd.27   Minute books 1785

StAH, *Handschriftensammlung (Hss)*
No.273   Michael Richey, Anmerckungen über
                                     die bey Rengern in Halle herausgekom-
                                     mene Nachricht von Hamburg nebst
                                     einer Anleitung zur Hamburgischen
                                     Historie, 1758
No.304   Bericht und historische Erzählung von
                                     der Zerstörung der Catholischen Cap-
                                     elle in Hamburg den 16 Sept. 1719

Bibliography

No.305   Erträge der Hamb. Kirchen Collecten 1694–1772

No.381   Johann Ernst Friedrich Westphalen, Der Zustand des Handels in Hamburg während der letzten 50 Jahre. Hamburg Juli 1806

StAH, Kämmerei I
No.13 Bd.31   Minute book 1712
       Bd.49   Minute book 1745
No.23 Bd.9   Receipts and invoices 1712
       Bd.86   Receipts and invoices 1745

Commerzbibliothek, Hamburg (CBH)
S/984   Anti-Catholic riot 1719

Public Record Office, London (PRO)
SP 82/36   Correspondence from Hamburg 1719
    82/45   Correspondence from Hamburg 1728
    82/99   Correspondence from Hamburg 1718
SP 101/39–40   Newsletters from Hamburg 1663–1720

II. PRINTED SOURCES

Acta historico-ecclesiastica. Oder gesamlete Nachrichten von den neuesten Kirchen-Geschichten, 20 vols., Weimar, 1734–56.

Allgemeine Deutsche Bibliothek, ed. Friedrich Nicolai and C. E. Bohn, 117 vols. in 195, Berlin/Stettin, 1765–92, Kiel, 1792–4.

Anderson, Christian Daniel (ed.), *Sammlung hamburgischer Verordnungen*, 8 vols., Hamburg, 1783–1811.

Arckenholtz, Johann, *Mémoires concernant Christine, reine de Suède*, 4 vols., Amsterdam/Leipzig, 1751–60.

Ausführliche und recht gründliche Nachricht / Von denen bisshero in Hamburg passirten Religions-Affairen wie Selbige angefangen / continuiret / und endlich durch grossen Aufflauf der Jugend und Matrosen / mit Niederreissung der daselbst neu-erbauten Catholischen Capelle, sich geendiget; Welches ein Passagier, in einem Schreiben an einen vornehmen Minister, in nachfolgenden kürzlich berichtet, n.p., 1720.

Bartels, Johann Heinrich, *Neuer Abdruck der Vier Haupt-Grundgesetze der Hamburgischen Verfassung*, Hamburg, 1823.

[Basedow, J. B.], *Ernst Freimuths Exemplarischer Gebrauch des höchstunbedachtsamen Hamburgischen Ministerial-Zeugnisses wider die Reformirten*, Berlin. 1766.

Beschreibung des solennen Freuden-Festins, so die Stadt Hamburg wegen der Crönung Kaysers Caroli VI gehalten, de Anno 1712, Hamburg, 1712.

II. Printed sources

Ein Beytrag zur Geschichte der Toleranz in der protestantischen Kirche in der letzten Hälfte des XVIII. Jahrhunderts. E.E. Ministeriums Vorstellung gegen die den Holländisch-Teutschen Reformirten in Hamburg zu verstattende freye Privat-Religions-Uebung, unter dem Schutze und der Aufsicht E. Hochedl. und Hochweisen Raths. Mit hinzugefügten Anmerkungen, n.p., 1774.

Blank, J. F. (ed.), *Sammlung der von E. Hochedlen Rathe der Stadt Hamburg so wol zur Handhabung der Gesetze und Verfassungen als bey besonderen Eräugnissen im Bürger- und Kirchlichen, als auch Cammer-, Handlungs- und übrigen Policey-Angelegenheiten und Geschäften vom Anfange des siebzehnten Jahrhunderts bis auf die itzige Zeit ausgegangenen Mandate, bestimmte Befehle und Bescheide, auch beliebten Aufträge und verkündigten Anordnungen*, 6 vols. Hamburg, 1763–74.

Bolten, Johann Adrian, *Historische Kirchen-Nachrichten von der Stadt Altona und deren verschiedenen Religions-Partheyen, von der Herrschaft Pinneberg und der Grafschaft Ranzau*, 2 vols. Altona, 1790–1.

Büsch, Johann Georg. *Zum Andenken meiner Freunde Dorner und Sieveking*, Hamburg, 1799.

Versuch einer Geschichte der Hamburgischen Handlung, nebst zwei kleineren Schriften eines verwandten Inhalts, Hamburg, 1797.

Copia des Schreibens / Welches Ihro Hochmögenden Die Hn. Staaten General derer Vereinigten Niederlande / Wegen der Reformirten in Hamburg an den Magistrat daselbst / abgehen lassen, Altona, 1722.

Copia des Schreibens / Welches Ihro Königl. Majestät in Preussen / u. Wegen der Reformirten in Hamburg, An dasigen Magistrat abgehen lassen, Altona, 1722.

Denkwürdigkeiten der Glückel von Hameln, ed. Alfred Feilchenfeld, 4th edn., Berlin, 1923.

Dohm, Christian Wilhelm, *Über die bürgerliche Verbesserung der Juden*, Berlin/Stettin, 1781.

Dreves, Lebrecht (ed.), *Annuae missionis hamburgensis a MDLXXXIX ad MDCCLXXXI*, Freiburg im Breisgau, 1867.

Edzardi, Sebastian, *Kurtze Anzeige / dass sein Sohn Esdras Henricus Edzardus die gantz neulich herausgekommene Läster-Charteque, und alle noch etwa künftige Pasquillen keiner Antwort würdigen werde*, Hamburg, 1721.

Pelagianismus Calvinianorum commonstratus, Wittenberg, 1705.

Verzeichniss Allerhand Pietistischer Intrigen und Unordnungen / in Litthauen / vielen Städten Teutschlands / Hungarn / und America, Wittenberg/Altona, 1729.

Erörterung der Frage: Ob denen Calvinisten eine Kirchenversammlung in der Stadt Hamburg zu vergönnen? Hamburg, 1671.

Erwägung der Gründe für und wider die Bestätigung des Reformirten Gottesdienstes in Hamburg, n.p., 1775.

Fabricius, Johann Albert, *Memoriae hamburgenses, sive Hamburgi et virorum de ecclesia, reque publica et scholastica hamburgensi bene meritorum elogia et vitae*, 8 vols., Hamburg, 1710–45.

Fahrenkrüger, Johann Anton, 'Versuch eines Sittengemäldes von Hamburg (aus dem Jahre 1811)', in *Aus Hamburgs Vergangenheit*, ed. Karl Koppmann, 2 vols., Hamburg, 1886, 2, pp. 84–148.

Goethe, Johann Wolfgang von, *Werke. Hamburger Ausgabe*, 14 vols., Hamburg, 1961–5.

Goeze, Johann Melchior, *Beweiss dass der Satz: Ein Sandkorn, ein Wassertropf, ein Blumenbach, ein Würmchen ist weit grösser, als der aufgeklärtester Verstand der geübtesten Weltweisen, wahr u. vernünftig sei*, Hamburg, 1774.
    Die gerechte Sache der evangelisch-lutherischen Kirche, Hamburg, 1771.
    Pflichtmässiges und auf unbeweglichen Gründen beruhendes Zeugniss der Wahrheit, Hamburg, 1766.
    Vertheidigung seiner am 24 Sont. nach Trinitatis 1774 gehaltenen Predigt: gegen die ungegründeten und schmähenden Anmerkungen eines sogenannten Betrachters, Hamburg, 1774.

Graupe, Heinz Mosche (ed.), *Die Statuten der drei Gemeinden Altona, Hamburg und Wandsbek. Quellen zur jüdischen Gemeindeorganisation im 17. und 18. Jahrhundert*, Hamburger Beiträge zur Geschichte der deutschen Juden, vols. 3/1 and 3/2, 2 vols., Hamburg, 1973.

Griesheim, Christian Ludwig von, *Verbesserte und vermehrte Auflage des Tractats: Die Stadt Hamburg in ihrem politischen, ökonomischen und sittlichen Zustande, nebst Nachträgen zu diesem Tractate u. Beiträge zu der Abhandlung: Anmerkungen und Zugaben über den Tractat: Die Stadt Hamburg, welche selbigen ebenfalls verbessern u. gewisser machen*, Hamburg, 1760.
    Gründlicher Bericht von dem ehemals von der Hochansehnlichen Kaiserlichen Gesandtschaft in Hamburg bewohnten Stadt-Hause, und der, nach Absterben Weiland Ihro Allerglorwürdigsten Kaiserl. Majst. Herrn Carls des Sechsten dessfalls von einem Hoch-Edlen Rath daselbt anjetzo gemachten Verfügung, Hamburg, n.d.

Günther, Johann Arnold, 'Proben einer Bildergallerie Hamburgischer Männer des achtzehnten Jahrhunderts', *Hanseatisches Magazin*, ed. J. Schmidt, vol. 5, Bremen, 1801, pp. 115–72.
    Ueber das Verhältnis der jüdischen Einwohner in Hamburg, Hamburg, 1800.

Guthke, Karl S., 'Hamburg im Jahre 1753 von Christlob Mylius', *HGH*, 9 (1974), 157–66.

Hanway, Jonas, *An historical account of the British trade over the Caspian Sea*, 4 vols. in 3, London, 1753.

Hess, Jonas Ludwig von, *Hamburg topographisch, politisch und historisch beschrieben*, 3 vols., Hamburg, 1787–92.
    Hamburg topographisch, politisch und historisch beschrieben. Zweite Auflage, umgearbeitet und vermehrt, 3 vols., Hamburg, 1810–11.

Hess, Ludwig von, *Gesezliche und Statistische Betrachtungen über die Toleranz und insbesondere über den freien Gottesdienst der Holländisch-Deutschen Reformirten welche in Hamburg wohnen*, Berlin/Leipzig, 1780.
    Unwiederrufliches Fundamental-Gesetz, Regimentsform oder Haupt-Recess der Stadt Hamburg, n.p., 1781.

Hintzsche, E. (ed.), *Albrecht von Hallers Tagebücher seiner Reisen nach Deutschland*,

II. Printed sources

Holland und England (1723–1727). In vollständiger Fassung neu herausgegeben, St Gallen, 1948.

Hoffmann, Johann Adolf, *Politische Anmerckungen über die wahre und falsche Staats-kunst, worin aus den Geschichten aller Zeit bemercket wird, was einem Lande zuträglich oder schädlich sey*, Hamburg, 1725.

Jungckheim, Georg Heinrich, *Ausführliche Nachricht von dem herzlichen Freuden-Festin, seine Reichs-Hochgräfl. Excellence Herr Graf Fuchs wegen der Gebuhrt des Ertz-Hertzogs und Printzen von Asturien, in Hamburg gegeben*, Hamburg, 1716.

Keetmann, Peter, 'Lebenserinnerungen', *Hamburger Wirtschaftschronik. Forschungen und Berichte aus dem Hanseatischen Lebensraum*, 1 (1952), 129–229.

Klefeker, Johann, *Sammlung der Hamburgischen Gesetze und Verfassungen in Bürger- und Kirchlichen, auch Cammer- Handlungs- und übrigen Policey-Angelegenheiten und Geschäften samt historischen Einleitungen*, 12 vols., Hamburg, 1765–73.

Kleine Charakteristik von Hamburg. Von einem Kosmopoliten drey Treppen hoch, Hamburg/Leipzig, 1783.

Kühl, Heinrich, *Hamburgische Raths- und Bürger-Schlüsse vom Jahre 1700 bis zum Ende des Jahres 1800*, Hamburg, 1803.

Langermann, J. P., *Hamburgisches Münz- und Medaillen-Vergnügen*, Hamburg, 1753.

Lediard, Thomas, *Eine Collection curieuser Vorstellungen in Illuminationen und Feuer-Wercken, so in den Jahren 1724 biss 1728 inclusive, bey Gelegenheit einiger Publiquen Festins und Rejouissances in Hamburg, und mehrentheils auf dem Schauplatze daselbst, unter der Direction und von der Invention Thomas Lediards – sind vorgestellet worden. In sechzehn grossen Kupfer-Platten*, Hamburg, 1730.

The German spy, London, 1738.

Loen, Johann Michael von, *Kleine Schrifften von Kirchen- und Religions-Sachen*, Frankfurt/Leipzig, 1751.

Marwedel, Günter (ed.), *Die Privilegien der Juden in Altona*, Hamburger Beiträge zur Geschichte der deutschen Juden, vol. 5, Hamburg, 1976.

Ministerium, *Vorläuffige Erklärung*
R. Ministerii Hamburgensis Vorläuffige Erklärung und Erinnerung / Wegen des bissher so wohl in Schrifften als Predigten von Ihm gegen Reformirte Lehre / geführten Elenchi, Hamburg, 1722.

Ministerium, *Vorstellung*
Eines hochwürdigen hamburgischen Ministerii Vorstellung an Einen hochedlen Rath der kaiserl. freyen Reichsstadt Hamburg d.d. 7 Juni 1777 das Gesuch der Deutsch-Reformirten in Hamburg wegen freyer Religions-Uebung unter dem Schutze der hamburgischen Obrigkeit betreffend, Altona, n.d.

Die neue Europäische Fama, Welche den gegenwärtigen Zustand der vornehmsten Höfe entdecket, pts. 1–192, Leipzig, 1735–56.

Neumeister, Erdmann, *Kurtzer Beweis / Dass das itzige Vereinigungs-Wesen mit den sogenannten Reformirten oder Calvinisten / allen Zehen Gebothen / allen Articuln des Apostolischen Glaubens-Bekänntnisses / allen Bitten des Vater-Unsers / der Lehre von der heiligen Tauffe / den Schlüsseln des Himmelreichs /*

Bibliography

und dem heiligen Abendmahle / und als dem gantzen Catechismo / schnurstracks zuwieder lauffe, Hamburg, 1721.

Nugent, Thomas, *The grand tour*, 4 vols., London, 1756.

Travels through Germany, 2 vols., London, 1768.

Olearius, Johann, *Die gute Sache der Holländisch-Deutschen Reformirten in Hamburg, erwiesen und wider ihre Gegner vertheidiget*, Hamburg, 1775.

Otruba, Gustav (ed.), 'Bericht über eine im im Auftrag der mährischen Lehnsbank durchgeführte Kommerzialreise: Eine zeitgenössische Bestandsaufnahme zur Wirtschaftslage mitteleuropäischer Städte um die Mitte des 18. Jahrhunderts (Teil III)', *Jahrbuch für Wirtschaftsgeschichte* (1976/2), 253–78.

Der Patriot. Nach der Originalausgabe Hamburg 1724–26 in drei Textbänden und einem Kommentarband kritisch herausgegeben von Wolfgang Martens, 3 vols., Berlin, 1969– .

Patriotische Vorstellung des Gesuchs der hiesigen deutschen Reformirten um einen freyen Gottesdienst, worinn dasselbe nach Handlungsgrundsätzen geprüft, und dem hiesigen Publikum zur Beurtheilung vorgelegt, auch wider die wichtigsten Einwürfe, die man dagegen gemacht hat, gerettet wird, Hamburg, 1765.

Pauli, Johann Ulrich, *An alle wahre Patrioten Hamburgs gerichtete Ermahnung, zur Aufrichtung einer ähnlichen Patriotischen Gesellschaft, zur Aufnahme der Handlung, der Künste, der Manufacturen und des Ackerbaues, wie die zu London und Paris ist*, Hamburg, 1765.

The picture of Hamburg, or the Englishman's guide to that Free, Imperial City, London, n.d.

Rediger, Andreas, *Bestättigte Unschuld der Reformirten Kirchen und besonders der Evangelisch Reformirten Gemeinde in der Freyen Reichs-Stadt Worms gegen die unglimpfliche Beschuldigungen des Herrn Senior Goetzens zu Hamburg*, Frankfurt/Leipzig, 1768.

Rettung der Unschuld der Evangelisch Reformirten Gemeinde in der freyen Reichs-Stadt Worms, gegen die ungleichen Absichten welche ihr in dem ohnlängst divulgirten sogenannten Pflichtmässigen Zeugnis der Wahrheit des Evangelisch Lutherischen Ministerii zu Hamburg aufgebürdet werden wollen, Düsseldorf/Frankfurt, 1767.

[Richey, Michael], 'Eines ungenannten gelehrten Patrioten kurze Anleitung zum studio historiae hamburgenses', in A. Dathe, *Versuch einer Geschichte von Hamburg*, Hamburg, 1767, appendix pp. I–XXXVI.

[Sack, August Friedrich Wilhelm], *Ein Wort zu seiner Zeit, von einem Christlichen Juristen. Bey Gelegenheit des Zeugnisses der Wahrheit E. Hochehrwürdigen Hamburgischen Ministerii, und desselben Aktenmässigen Vertheidigung*, Cölln, 1768.

Schlüter, Matthias, *Historisch- und Rechts-begründeter Tractat von denen Erben in Hamburg*, 2 vols., Hamburg, 1698.

Schmid, Ludolf Heinrich, *Versuch einer historischen Beschreibung der an der Elbe belegenen Stadt Altona*, Altona/Flensburg, 1747.

Schütze, J. F., *Hamburgische Theater-Geschichte*, Hamburg, 1794.

Staats- und Gelehrte Zeitung des Hamburgischen Unpartheyischen Correspondenten, Hamburg, 1731–1811.

III. Secondary literature

Steltzner, Michael Gottlieb, *Versuch einer zuverlässigen Nachricht von dem kirch-lichen und politischen Zustande der Stadt Hamburg*, 6 vols., Hamburg, 1731–9.

Über die Wahlen der Hauptpastoren in Hamburg, Hamburg, 1801.

Uffenbach, Z. K. von, *Merkwürdige Reisen durch Nieder-Sachsen, Holland und Engelland*, 3 vols., Ulm, 1753.

Vernon, James, *Travels to Denmark in 1702*, London, 1707.

Voltaire, François-Marie Arouet de, *Dictionnaire philosophique*, ed. René Pomeau, Paris, 1964.

Ein wichtiges Document zur Erläuterung der neuesten Hamburgischen Kirchen-geschichte, oder letzte Vorstellung des Hamburgischen Ministeriums an den Rath der Stadt Hamburg, betreffend das Gesuch der Reformirten um die Vergünstigung eines öffentlichen Religions-Exercitii in besagter Stadt, n.p., 1775.

Willebrandt, J. P., *Abrégé de la police accompagné des réflexions sur l'accroissement des villes*, Hamburg, 1765.

Grundriss einer schönen Stadt, in Absicht ihrer Anlage und Einrichtung zu Bequemlichkeiten, zum Vergnügen, zum Anwachs und zur Erhaltung ihrer Einwohner, nach bekannten Mustern entworffen, 2 vols., Hamburg/Leipzig, 1775–6.

Hamburgs Annehmlichkeiten von einem Ausländer beschrieben, Hamburg/Leipzig, 1772.

Vermehrte Nachrichten von den Annehmlichkeiten in und um Hamburg, mit freundschaftlichen Erinnerungen für Fremde und Reisende, Hamburg, 1783.

Winckler, J. D., *Nachrichten von Niedersächsischen berühmten Leuten und Familien*, 2 vols., Hamburg, 1768–9.

Wotschke, Theodor (ed.), 'Erdmann Neumeisters Briefe an Ernst Salomo Cyp-rian', *ZVHG*, 26 (1925), 106–46.

'Erdmann Neumeisters Briefe an Ernst Salomo Cyprian', *ZVHG*, 30 (1929), 136–61.

'Erdmann Neumeisters Briefe an Ernst Salomo Cyprian', *ZVHG*, 31 (1930), 161–97.

'Johann Dietrich Wincklers Briefe an Joh. Christian Bartholomäi und Christian Wilhelm Schneider. Ein Beitrag zur Geistesgeschichte Hamburgs in der Aufklärungszeit', *ZVHG*, 37 (1938), 35–99.

Ziegra, Christian, *Sammlung von Urkunden, theologischen und juristischen Bedenken, Verordnungen, Memoralien, Suppliken, Dekreten, Briefen, Lebensbeschreibungen, kleinen Tractaten u.d.g.m. als eine Grundlage zur Hamburgischen Kirchen Historie neuerer Zeiten*, 4 vols., Hamburg, 1764–70.

III. SECONDARY LITERATURE

There is an exhaustive and indispensable bibliography of works relating to the history of Hamburg published 1900–70: *Bücherkunde zur hamburgischen Geschichte*, ed. Kurt Detlev Müller and Anneliese Tecke, 3 vols., Hamburg, 1939–71. The literature since 1970 has been reviewed annually in *Zeitschrift des Vereins für Hamburgische Geschichte*.

Bibliography

Adair, E. R., *The exterritoriality of ambassadors in the sixteenth and seventeenth centuries*, London/New York/Toronto, 1929.

Albrecht, Peter, *Die Förderung des Landesausbaues im Herzogtum Braunschweig-Wolfenbüttel im Spiegel der Verwaltungsakten des 18. Jahrhunderts (1671–1806)*, Braunschweiger Werkstücke (Reihe A). Veröffentlichungen aus dem Stadtarchiv und der Stadtbibliothek, vol. 16, Braunschweig, 1980.

Allgemeine Deutsche Biographie, 56 vols., Leipzig, 1875–1912.

Baasch, Ernst, 'Hamburg und Holland im 17. und 18. Jahrhundert', *Hansische Geschichtsblätter*, 16 (1910), 45–102.

Hamburgs Convoy-Schiffahrt und Convoywesen, Hamburg, 1896.

Die Handelskammer zu Hamburg, 3 vols., Hamburg, 1915.

Barrelet, Theodore, 'Zur Geschichte der französisch-reformirten Gemeinde in Hamburg', *GDHV*, 12 (1904), 5–37.

'Das Liebeswesen der Diakonie in der franz.-reformirten Gemeinde zu Hamburg 1686–1750', *GDHV*, 13 (1906), 1–24.

Bartels, Johann Heinrich, *Einige Abhandlungen über Gegenstände der Hamburgischen Verfassung*, Hamburg, 1835.

Nachtrag zum neuen Abdrucke der Vier Haupt-Grundgesetze der Hamburgischen Verfassung, Hamburg, 1825.

Beneke, Otto, 'Die eingewanderten Reformirten in Hamburg und Stade nach ihren Gewerben', *MVHG*, 6 (1883), 33–8.

'Zur Geschichte der nichtlutherischen Christen in Hamburg 1575 bis 1589', *ZVHG*, 6 (1875), 318–44.

Hamburgische Geschichten und Sagen, 3rd edn, 2 vols., Berlin, 1886.

Berbig, Hans Joachim, 'Kaisertum und Reichsstadt. Eine Studie zum dynastischen Patriotismus der Reichsstädte nach dem Westfälischen Frieden bis zum Untergang des Reiches', *Mitteilungen des Vereins für Geschichte der Stadt Nürnberg*, 58 (1971), 211–86.

'Der Krönungsritus im alten Reich (1648–1806)', *Zeitschrift für bayerische Landesgeschichte*, 88 (1975), 639–700.

Bergemann, Hans Georg, *Staat und Kirche in Hamburg während des 19. Jahrhunderts*, Arbeiten zur Kirchengeschichte Hamburgs, vol. 1, Hamburg, 1958.

Beuleke, Wilhelm, 'Die landsmannschaftliche Gliederung der drei hansestädtischen Réfugiésgemeinden', in *Huguenotten in Hamburg, Stade, Altona, Tagungsschrift zum Deutschen Huguenottentag. Hamburg, 23–26 April 1976*, ed. H. W. Wagner, Obersickle/Braunschweig, 1976, pp. 22–8.

Birtsch, Günter, 'Religions- und Gewissensfreiheit in Preussen von 1780 bis 1817', *Zeitschrift für historische Forschung*, 11 (1984), 177–204.

Bog, Ingomar, 'Reichsverfassung und reichsstädtische Gesellschaft. Sozialgeschichtliche Forschungen über reichsständische Residenten in den Freien Städten, insbesondere in Nürnberg', *Jahrbuch für fränkische Landesforschung*, 18 (1958), 325–40.

Bolland, Gustav, *Hamburg wie es einmal war. An Hand eines Kupferstiches von Arnoldus Pitersen aus dem Jahre 1644*, 2nd edn., Hamburg, 1953.

Bolland, Jürgen, *Senat und Bürgerschaft: Über das Verhältnis zwischen Bürger und*

III. Secondary literature

Stadtregiment im alten Hamburg, Vorträge und Aufsätze herausgegeben vom Verein für Hamburgische Geschichte, vol. 7, 2nd edn., Hamburg, 1977.

Borgmann, Karl, *Der deutsche Religionsstreit der Jahre 1719/20*, Abhandlungen zur Mittleren und Neueren Geschichte, vol. 80, Berlin, 1937.

Bornkamm, Heinrich, *Luther im Spiegel der deutschen Geistesgeschichte*, Heidelberg, 1965.

Boué, Peter, 'Abriss der Geschichte der französisch-reformirten Gemeinde in Hamburg bis zum Jahre 1976', in *Huguenotten in Hamburg, Stade, Altona. Tagungsschrift zum Deutschen Huguenottentag. Hamburg, 23–26 April 1976*, ed. H. W. Wagner, Obersickle/Braunschweig, 1976, pp. 14–21.

Bracker, Jürgen, *Die 'Wapen von Hamburg' (III) – ein schwimmender Barockpalast*, Hamburg Porträt 1/1976, Hamburg, 1976.

Brandes, Friedrich, *Geschichte der kirchlichen Politik des Hauses Brandenburg*, 2 vols., Gotha, 1872–3.

Braubach, Max, 'Johann Christoph Bartensteins Herkunft und Anfänge', *Mitteilungen des Instituts für Österreichische Geschichtsforschung*, 61 (1953), 99–149.

Braun, Hans Joachim, *Technologische Beziehungen zwischen Deutschland und England von der Mitte des 17. bis zum Ausgang des 18. Jahrhunderts*, Düsseldorf, 1974.

Brilling, Bernhard, 'Das erste Gedicht auf einen deutschen Rabbiner aus dem Jahre 1752. Ein Beitrag zum Emden-Eibenschütz-Streit', *Bulletin des Leo Baeck Instituts*, 11 (1968), 38–47.

'Der hamburger Rabbinerstreit im 18. Jahrhundert', *ZVHG*, 55 (1969), 219–44.

Bruhn, Hans, *Die Kandidaten der hamburgischen Kirche von 1654 bis 1825. Album Candidatorum = Die hamburgische Kirche und ihre Geistlichen seit der Reformation*, ed. Wilhelm Jensen, vol. 3, Hamburg, 1963.

Brunner, Otto, 'Die Patriotische Gesellschaft in Hamburg im Wandel von Staat und Gesellschaft', in *idem, Neue Wege der Verfassungs- und Sozialgeschichte*, 2nd edn., Göttingen, 1968, pp. 335–44.

'Souveranitätsproblem und Sozialstruktur in den deutschen Reichsstädten der frühen Neuzeit', in *idem, Neue Wege der Verfassungs- und Sozialgeschichte*, 2nd edn., Göttingen, 1968, pp. 294–321.

Buek, F. G., *Genealogische und biographische Notizen über die seit der Reformation verstorbenen hamburgischen Bürgermeister*, Hamburg, 1840.

Die Hamburgischen Oberalten, ihre bürgerliche Wirksamkeit und ihre Familien, Hamburg, 1857.

Butterfield, Herbert, 'Toleration in early modern times', *Journal of the History of Ideas*, 38 (1977), 573–84.

Colshorn, Hermann, 'Hamburgs Buchhandel im 18. Jahrhundert. I: Die grossen Firmen', *Börsenblatt für den Deutschen Buchhandel. Frankfurter Ausgabe*, No. 34, 30 April 1971, 185–91.

Conrad, Hermann, *Deutsche Rechtsgeschichte. Bd. 2: Neuzeit bis 1806*, Karlsruhe, 1966.

'Religionsbann, Toleranz und Parität am Ende des alten Reiches', *Römische Quartalschrift für christliche Altertumskunde und Kirchengeschichte*, 56 (1961), 167–99.

Bibliography

'Die verfassungsrechtliche Bedeutung der Reichsstädte im Deutschen Reich (etwa 1500 bis 1806)', *Studium Generale. Zeitschrift für die Einheit der Wissenschaften im Zusammenhang ihrer Begriffsbildungen und Forschungsmethoden*, 16 (1963), 493–500.

Daur, Georg, *Von Predigern und Bürgern. Eine hamburgische Kirchengeschichte von der Reformation bis zur Gegenwart*, Hamburg, 1970.

Deckelmann, Wilhelm, 'Das Glaubensbekenntnis des Barthold Henrich Brockes', *ZVHG*, 36 (1937), 146–61.

Denzler, Georg, *Die Propagandakongregation in Rom und die Kirche in Deutschland im ersten Jahrzehnt nach dem Westfälischen Frieden*, Paderborn, 1969.

Dickmann, Fritz, 'Das Problem der Gleichberechtigung der Konfessionen im Reich im 16. und 17. Jahrhundert', in *Zur Geschichte der Toleranz und Religionsfreiheit*, ed. Heinrich Lutz, Wege der Forschung, vol. 246, Darmstadt, 1977, pp. 203–51.

Dietrich, Richard, 'Landeskirchenrecht und Gewissensfreiheit in den Verhandlungen des Westphälischen Friedenskongresses', *Historische Zeitschrift*, 166 (1963), 563–83.

Dingedahl, Carl Heinz, 'Johann Carl Daniel Curio: Lehrer, Schriftsteller und Redakteur', *HGH*, 10 (1977), 1–17.

Dollinger, Philippe, *The German Hansa*, transl. and ed. D. S. Ault and S. H. Steinberg, London, 1970.

Dominguez Ortiz, Antonio, *The Golden Age of Spain 1516–1659*, transl. James Casey, London, 1971.

Dreves, Lebrecht, *Die Geschichte der Katholischen Gemeinden zu Hamburg und Altona: Ein Beitrag zur Geschichte der nordischen Missionen*, 2nd edn., Schaffshausen, 1866.

Dreyfus, François G., 'Die deutsche Wirtschaft um 1815', in *Deutschland zwischen Revolution und Restauration*, ed. Helmut Berding and Hans-Peter Ullmann, Königstein/Düsseldorf, 1981, pp. 353–82.

Duhr, Bernhard, *Geschichte der Jesuiten in den Ländern deutscher Zunge*, 7 pts. in 4 vols., Freiburg im Breisgau, 1907, Munich/Regensburg, 1921–8.

Ehlers, Joachim, *Die Wehrverfassung der Stadt Hamburg im 17. und 18. Jahrhundert*, Militärgeschichtliche Studien herausgegeben vom Militärgeschichtlichen Forschungsamt, vol. 1, Boppard am Rhein, 1966.

Ehrard, Jean, 'Les Lumières et la fête', *Annales historiques de la révolution française*, 47 (1975), 356–74.

Ehrenberg, Richard, 'Hamburgs Handel und Schiffahrt', in *Hamburg vor 200 Jahren*, ed. T. Schrader, Hamburg, 1892, pp. 261–97.

Eisenhardt, Ulrich, *Die kaiserliche Aufsicht über Buchdruck, Buchhandel und Presse im Heiligen Römischen Reich Deutscher Nation (1406–1806). Ein Beitrag zur Geschichte der Bücher- und Pressezensur*, Studien und Quellen zur Geschichte des Deutschen Verfassungsrechts, Reihe A: vol. 3, Karlsruhe, 1870.

Erbe, Helmut, *Die Hugenotten in Deutschland*, Essen, 1937.

Ernstberger, A., 'Drei Nürnberger Reformationsjubiläen', *Lutherjahrbuch*, 31 (1964), 9–28.

III. Secondary literature

Evans, R. J. W., *The making of the Habsburg monarchy 1550–1700*, Oxford, 1979.

Ewald, Martin, 'Das Archiv und die gedruckten Sammlungen hamburgischer Rechtsvorschriften im 18. und 19. Jahrhundert', in *Beiträge zur Geschichte des Staatsarchivs der Freien und Hansestadt Hamburg*, Veröffentlichungen aus dem Staatsarchiv der Freien und Hansestadt Hamburg, vol. 5, Hamburg, 1960, pp. 169–82.

Der Hamburgische Senatssyndicus. Eine verwaltungsgeschichtliche Studie, Universität Hamburg. Abhandlungen aus dem Seminar für Offentliches Recht, Hamburg, 1954.

Fähler, Eberhard, *Feuerwerke des Barock. Studien zum öffentlichen Fest und seiner literarischen Deutung vom 16. bis 18. Jahrhundert*, Stuttgart, 1968.

Fehring, M., *Sitte und Brauch der Tischler: Unter besonderer Berücksichtigung hamburgischer Quellen*, Hamburg, 1929.

Feilchenfeld, A., 'Anfang und Blüthezeit der Portugiesengemeinde in Hamburg', *ZVHG*, 10 (1899), 199–240.

Feine, Hans Erich, 'Zur Verfassungsentwicklung des Heil. Röm. Reiches seit dem Westphälischen Frieden', *Zeitschrift der Savigny-Stiftung für Rechtsgeschichte*, 52 (1952), Germanistische Abteilung, 65–133.

Finder, Ernst, *Hamburgisches Bürgertum in der Vergangenheit*, Hamburg, 1930.

François, Étienne, 'De l'uniformité à la tolérance: confession et société en Allemagne, 1650–1800', *Annales, E.S.C.*, 37 (1982), 783–800.

Freimark, Peter, 'Zum Verhältnis von Juden und Christen in Altona im 17./18. Jahrhundert', *Theokratia. Jahrbuch des Institutum Judaicum Delitzschianum*, 2 (1970–2), 253–72.

Frensdorff, F., 'Das Reich und die Hansestädte', *Zeitschrift der Savigny-Stiftung für Rechtsgeschichte*, 20 (1899), Germanistische Abteilung, 115–63.

Fürstenau, Hermann, *Das Grundrecht der Religionsfreiheit nach seiner geschichtlichen Entwickelung und heutigen Geltung in Deutschland*, Leipzig, 1891.

Gaedechens, D. C. and C. F., *Hamburgische Münzen und Medaillen*, 3 vols., Hamburg, 1850–76.

Gay, Peter, *The Enlightenment: an interpretation*, 2 vols., London, 1967–70.

Geffcken, Johannes, *Johann Winckler und die hamburgische Kirche seiner Zeit*, Hamburg, 1861.

'Ueber die theologischen Responsa und deren Bedeutung im siebzehnten Jahrhundert', *ZVHG*, 1 (1841), 249–80.

Gerber, W., *Die Bauzünfte im alten Hamburg. Entwicklung und Wesen des vaterstädtischen Maurer- und Zimmergewerbes während der Zunftzeit*, Hamburg, 1933.

Gericke, Wolfgang, *Glaubenszeugnisse und Konfessionspolitik der Brandenburgischen Herrscher bis zur Preussischen Union, 1540 bis 1815*, Unio und confessio, vol. 6, Bielefeld, 1977.

Gleiss, W., *Esdras Edzardus. Ein alter Hamburger Judenfreund*, 2nd edn., Hamburg, 1871.

Gonsiorowski, Herbert, 'Die Berufe der Juden Hamburgs von der Einwanderung bis zur Emanzipation', unpublished dissertation, Hamburg, 1927.

Bibliography

Grab, Walter, *Demokratische Strömungen in Hamburg und Schleswig-Holstein zur Zeit der ersten französischen Republik*, Veröffentlichungen des Vereins für hamburgische Geschichte, vol. 21, Hamburg, 1966.

Graupe, Heinz Mosche, *Die Entstehung des modernen Judentums. Geistesgeschichte der deutschen Juden 1650–1942*, Hamburger Beiträge zur Geschichte der deutschen Juden, vol. 1, Hamburg, 1969.

Greschat, Martin, *Zwischen Tradition und neuem Anfang. Valentin Ernst Löscher und der Ausgang der lutherischen Orthodoxie*, Untersuchungen zur Kirchengeschichte, vol. 5, Witten, 1971.

Grisar, H., *Luthers Trutzlied 'Eine Feste Burg' in Vergangenheit und Gegenwart*, Luther Studien, vol. 4, Freiburg, 1922.

Grossmann, Walter, 'Edelmann und das "öffentliche Schweigen" des Reimarus und Lessing: Toleranz und Politik des Geistes', *Zeitschrift für Kirchengeschichte*, 85 (1974), 358–82.

'Religious toleration in Germany, 1648–1750', *Studies on Voltaire and the Eighteenth Century*, 201 (1982), 115–41.

'Toleration – *exercitium religionis privatum*', *Journal of the History of Ideas*, 40 (1979), 129–34.

Gruber, A. C., *Les grandes fêtes et leurs décors à l'époque de Louis XVI*, Geneva, 1972.

Grunwald, Max, 'Der Hamburger Judentumult im Jahre 1730', *MVHG*, 7 (1901), 587–95.

Aus dem Hamburger Staatsarchiv. Beiträge zur Geschichte der Juden in Hamburg, Berlin, 1902.

Hamburgs deutsche Juden bis zur Auflösung der Dreigemeinden 1811, Hamburg, 1904.

'Hochzeits- und Kleiderordnung der Hamburger Juden von 1715 und 1731', *MVHG*, 8 (1905), 33–44.

Guggisberg, Hans R., 'Wandel der Argumente für religiöse Toleranz und Glaubensfreiheit im 16. und 17. Jahrhundert', in *Zur Geschichte der Toleranz und Religionsfreiheit*, ed. Heinrich Lutz, Wege der Forschung, vol. 246, Darmstadt, 1977, pp. 455–81.

Hassinger, Erich, 'Wirtschaftliche Motive und Argumente für religiöse Duldsamkeit im 16. und 17. Jahrhundert', *Archiv für Reformationsgeschichte*, 49 (1958), 226–45.

Hauschild-Thiessen, Renate, 'Johann Berenberg (1674–1749) und seine "Genealogien"', *HGH*, 10 (1979), 183–6.

Die Niederländische Armen-Casse: 'Hamburgs stille Wohlthäterin'. Ihre Geschichte von 1585 bis zur Gegenwart, Hamburg, 1974.

Healey, Robert M., 'The Jew in seventeenth-century Protestant thought', *Church History*, 46 (1977), 63–79.

Heckel, Martin, 'Säkularisierung. Staatskirchenrechtliche Aspekte einer umstrittenen Kategorie', *Zeitschrift der Savigny-Stiftung für Rechtsgeschichte*, 97 (1980), Kanonische Abteilung, 1–163.

III. Secondary literature

Staat und Kirche nach den Lehren der evangelischen Juristen in der ersten Hälfte des 17. Jahrhunderts, Jus ecclesiasticum, vol. 6, Munich, 1968.

Heinen, Ernst, 'Der Kölner Toleranzstreit (1787–1789)', *Jahrbuch des Kölnischen Geschichtsvereins*, 46 (1973), 67–86.

Hering, Carl Wilhelm, *Geschichte der kirchlichen Unionsversuche seit der Reformation bis auf unsere Zeit*, 2 vols., Leipzig, 1836–8.

Hermes, Rudolf, *Aus der Geschichte der Deutschen evangelisch-reformirten Gemeinde in Hamburg*, Hamburg, 1934.

Hildebrandt, Reinhard, 'Rat contra Bürgerschaft: Die Verfassungskonflikte in den Reichsstädten des 17. und 18. Jahrhunderts', *Zeitschrift für Stadtgeschichte, Stadtsoziologie und Denkmalpflege*, 2 (1975), 221–41.

Hiltebrandt, Philipp, *Die kirchlichen Reunionsverhandlungen in der zweiten Hälfte des 17. Jahrhunderts. Ernst August von Hannover und die katholische Kirche*, Bibliothek des Preussischen Historischen Instituts in Rom, vol. 14, Rome, 1922.

Hitzigrath, H., *Die Kompagnie der Merchants Adventurers und die englische Kirchengemeinde in Hamburg 1611–1835*, Hamburg, 1904.

Höck, J. H., *Bilder aus der Geschichte der Hamburgischen Kirche seit der Reformation*, Hamburg, 1900.

Hoffmann, P. T., 'Politik und Geistesleben in Altona vom 17. bis 19. Jahrhundert', *ZVHG*, 39 (1940), 41–85.

Hübbe, H., *Die kaiserlichen Kommissionen in Hamburg*, Hamburg, 1856.

Hubrig, Hans, *Die patriotischen Gesellschaften des 18. Jahrhunderts*, Weinheim, 1957.

Huhn, F-K., 'Die Handelsbeziehungen zwischen Frankreich und Hamburg im 18. Jahrhundert; unter besonderer Berücksichtigung der Handelsverträge von 1716 und 1769', 2 vols., unpublished dissertation, Hamburg, 1953.

Imme, Kurt, 'Bilddarstellungen des ersten deutschen Opernhauses in Hamburg aus dem 17. Jahrhundert', *HGH*, 6 (1961), 54–60.

Isler, M., 'Zur ältesten Geschichte der Juden in Hamburg', *ZVHG*, 6 (1875), 461–79.

Jaacks, Gisela, '"Engelgleiche Musik", "Elbschwäne" und "Salomos Tempel"': Hamburg als Zentrum geistiger und musikalischer Kultur im Barock', in *300 Jahre Oper in Hamburg*, Hamburg, 1977, pp. 36–49.

Festzüge in Hamburg 1696–1913, Hamburg, 1962.

Jeannin, Pierre, 'Die Hansestädte im europäischen Handel des 18. Jahrhunderts', *Hansische Geschichtsblätter*, 89 (1971), 41–73.

Jensen, Wilhelm, *Die hamburgische Kirche und ihre Geistlichen seit der Reformation*, vol. 1, Hamburg, 1958.

Jersch-Wenzel, Stefi, *Juden und 'Franzosen' in der Wirtschaft des Raumes Berlin/ Brandenburg zur Zeit des Merkantilismus*, Einzelveröffentlichungen der Historischen Kommission zu Berlin, vol. 23, Berlin, 1978.

Joachim, Hermann, *Historische Arbeiten aus seinem Nachlass*, Veröffentlichungen des Vereins für Hamburgische Geschichte, vol. 10, Hamburg, 1936.

Bibliography

Kantzenbach, Friedrich Wilhelm, *Protestantisches Christentum im Zeitalter der Aufklärung*, Evangelische Enzyklopädie, vol. 5/6, Gütersloh, 1965.

Karniel, Josef, 'Die Toleranzpolitik Kaiser Josephs II.', in *Deutsche Aufklärung und Judenemanzipation*, Jahrbuch des Instituts für Deutsche Geschichte Tel-Aviv, Beiheft 3, Tel-Aviv, 1980, 55–77.

Katz, David, *Philo-semitism and the readmission of the Jews to England 1603–1655*, Oxford, 1982.

Katz, Jacob, *Out of the ghetto: the social background of Jewish emancipation, 1770–1870*, Cambridge, Mass., 1973.

Kayser, Rudolf, 'Johannes a Lasco und die Londoner Flüchtlingsgemeinde in Hamburg', *ZVHG*, 37 (1938), 1–15.

Kayser, Werner, 'Drucker und Verleger in Hamburg 1491–1860', in *Buchhandel in Hamburg. Eine Festschrift anlässlich der Gründung des Hamburg-Altonaer Buchhändler Vereins vor hundert Jahren*, Hamburg, 1960, pp. 28–43.

(ed.), *Hamburger Bücher 1491–1850*, Mitteilungen aus der Staats- und Universitätsbibliothek Hamburg, vol. 7, Hamburg, 1973.

Kellenbenz, Hermann, 'Diego und Manoel Texeira und ihr Hamburger Unternehmen', *VSWG*, 42 (1955), 289–352.

Sephardim an der unteren Elbe. Ihre wirtschaftliche und politische Bedeutung vom Ende des 16. bis zum Beginn des 18. Jahrhunderts, *VSWG*, Beiheft 40, Wiesbaden, 1958.

Unternehmerkräfte im Hamburger Portugal- und Spanienhandel 1585–1625, Veröffentlichungen der Wirtschaftsgeschichtlichen Forschungsstelle e.V., vol. 10, Hamburg, 1954.

Kiefl, Franz Xaver, *Der Friedensplan des Leibniz zur Wiedervereinigung der getrennten christlichen Kirchen*, Paderborn, 1903.

Kiesel, Helmut, 'Problem und Begründung der Toleranz im 18. Jahrhundert', in *Festgabe für Ernst Walter Zeeden zum 60. Geburtstag am 14 Mai 1976*, Reformationsgeschichtliche Studien und Texte, vol. 2, Münster, pp. 370–85.

Klemenz, Dieter, *Der Religionsunterricht in Hamburg von der Kirchenordnung von 1529 bis zum staatlichen Unterrichtsgesetz von 1870*, Beiträge zur Geschichte Hamburgs herausgegeben vom Verein für Hamburgische Geschichte, vol. 5, Hamburg, 1971.

Kopitzsch, Franklin, 'Gotthold Ephraim Lessing und Hamburgs Gelehrte 1767–1781', in *Gelehrte in Hamburg im 18. und 19. Jahrhundert*, ed. Hans-Dieter Loose, Beiträge zur Geschichte Hamburgs herausgegeben vom Verein für Hamburgische Geschichte, vol. 12, Hamburg, 1976, pp. 9–55.

Grundzüge einer Sozialgeschichte der Aufklärung in Hamburg und Altona, Beiträge zur Geschichte Hamburgs herausgegeben vom Verein für Hamburgische Geschichte, vol. 21, Hamburg, 1982.

'Die Hamburgische Gesellschaft zur Beförderung der Künste und nützlichen Gewerbe (Patriotische Gesellschaft von 1765) im Zeitalter der Aufklärung: Ein Überblick', *Deutsche patriotische und gemeinnützige Gesellschaften*, ed. Rudolf Vierhaus, Wolfenbütteler Forschungen, vol. 8, Munich, 1980, pp. 71–118.

III. Secondary literature

'Die jüdischen Schüler des Christaneums im Zeitalter der Aufklärung – Ein Kapitel aus der Geschichte der Juden in Altona', *Christianeum. Mitteilungsblatt des Vereins der Freunde des Christianeums*, 33 (1978), 19–28.

'Lessing und seine Zeitgenossen im Spannungsfeld von Toleranz und Intoleranz', in *Deutsche Aufklärung und Judenemanzipation*, Jahrbuch des Instituts für Deutsche Geschichte Tel-Aviv, Beiheft 3, Tel-Aviv, 1980, pp. 29–85.

'Die Sozialgeschichte der Aufklärung als Forschungsaufgabe', in *Aufklärung, Absolutismus und Bürgertum in Deutschland*, ed. Franklin Kopitzsch, Nymphenburger Texte zur Wissenschaft: Modelluniversität, vol. 24, Munich, 1976, pp. 11–169.

Koppmann, Karl, 'Von den ältesten Spuren der Juden in Hamburg', *ZVHG*, 6 (1875), 256–8.

'Das Kollegium des Klingelbeutels an der Domkirche und dessen Konvivium', *ZVHG*, 7 (1883), 327–44.

Krabbe, P., 'Ueber das geistliche Strafamt Rev. Ministerii', *ZVHG*, (1841), 465–83.

Kraus, Antje, *Die Unterschichten Hamburgs in der ersten Hälfte des 19. Jahrhunderts. Entstehung, Struktur und Lebensverhältnisse. Eine historisch-statistische Untersuchung*, Sozialwissenschaftliche Studien, vol. 9, Stuttgart, 1965.

Krohn, Helga, *Die Juden in Hamburg 1800–1850. Ihre soziale, kulturelle und politische Entwicklung während der Emanzipationszeit*, Hamburger Studien zur neueren Geschichte, vol. 9, Frankfurt, 1967.

Krüger, Liselotte, *Die hamburgische Musikorganisation im 17. Jahrhundert*, Strassburg/Leipzig/Zurich, 1933.

Lappenberg, J. M., 'Von den ältesten Spuren der Juden in Hamburg', *ZVHG*, 1 (1841), 281–90.

'Von der Ansiedlung der Niederländer in Hamburg', *ZVHG*, 1 (1841), 241–8.

'Listen der in Hamburg residirenden, wie der dasselbe vertretenden Diplomaten und Consulen', *ZVHG*, 3 (1851), 414–534.

Laufenberg, H., *Hamburg und sein Proletariat im achtzehnten Jahrhundert. Eine welthistorische Vorstudie zur Geschichte der modernen Arbeiterbewegung im niederelbischen Stadtgebiet*, Hamburg, 1910.

Le Roi, J. F. A. de, *Die evangelische Christenheit und die Juden unter dem Gesichtspunkt der Mission geschichtlich betrachtet*, vol. 1, Karlsruhe/Leipzig, 1884.

Levis, R. Barry, 'The failure of the Anglo-Prussian ecumenical effort of 1710–1714', *Church History*, 47 (1978), 381–99.

Levy, Hartwig, *Die Entwicklung der Rechtsstellung der Hamburger Juden*, Hamburg, 1933.

Liebel, Helen, 'Der aufgeklärte Absolutismus und die Gesellschaftskrise in Deutschland im 18. Jahrhundert', in *Abolutismus*, ed. Walter Hubatsch, Wege der Forschung, vol. 314, Darmstadt, 1973, pp. 488–544.

'Laissez-faire vs. Mercantilism: the rise of Hamburg and the Hamburg bourgeoisie vs. Frederick the Great in the crisis of 1763', *VSWG*, 52 (1965), 207–38.

Bibliography

Linckemeyer, Carl, *Das katholische Hamburg in Vergangenheit und Gegenwart*, Hamburg, 1931.

Loose, Hans-Dieter, *Hamburg und Christian IV von Dänemark während des Dreissigjährigen Krieges. Ein Beitrag zur Geschichte der hamburgischen Reichsunmittelbarkeit*, Veröffentlichungen des Vereins für Hamburgische Geschichte, vol. 18, Hamburg, 1963.

'Das Zeitalter der Bürgerunruhen und der grossen europäischen Kriege 1618–1712', in *Hamburg. Geschichte der Stadt und ihrer Bewohner. Bd. 1 Von den Anfängen bis zur Reichsgründung*, ed. Hans-Dieter Loose, Hamburg, 1982.

Lorenz, Reinhold, 'Eine Hamburgische Residentschaft Kaiser Leopolds I. (Hans Dietrich von Rondeck 1679–1685)', in *Historische Studien, A. F. Pribaum zum 70. Geburtstag dargebracht*, Vienna, 1929, pp. 71–116.

Maertens, Willi, 'Georg Philipp Telemanns Hamburger "Admiralitätsmusik" 1723', in *Konferenzbericht der 3. Magdeburger Telemann-Festtage 1967*, Magdeburg, 1969, pp. 106–23.

Martens, Wolfgang, *Die Botschaft der Tugend. Die Aufklärung im Spiegel der moralischen Wochenschriften*, Stuttgart, 1968.

'Die Flugschriften gegen den "Patrioten" (1724). Zur Reaktion auf die Publizistik der frühen Aufklärung', in *Rezeption und Produktion zwischen 1570 und 1730. Festschrift für Günther Weydt zum 69. Geburtstag*, ed. Wolfdietrich Rasch, Hans Geulen and Klaus Haberkamm, Bern/Munich, 1972, pp. 515–36.

'Über Naturlyrik der frühen Aufklärung (B. H. Brockes)', in *Wege der Worte. Festschrift für Wolfgang Fleischhauer*, ed. Donald C. Riechel, Cologne/Vienna, 1978, pp. 263–76.

Marx, H. J., 'Geschichte der Hamburger Barockoper. Ein Forschungsbericht', *Hamburger Jahrbuch für Musikwissenschaft*, 3 (1978), 7–34.

Matthei, Henning, *Untersuchungen zur Frühgeschichte der deutschen Berufsschule dargestellt am Wirken der Patriotischen Gesellschaft zu Hamburg im 18. Jahrhundert*, Hamburg, 1967.

Mattingly, Garrett, *Renaissance diplomacy*, London, 1958.

Mauersberg, Hans, *Wirtschafts- und Sozialgeschichte zentraleuropäischer Städte in neuerer Zeit. Dargestellt an den Beispielen von Basel, Frankfurt a.M., Hamburg, Hannover und München*, Göttingen, 1960.

Mehnert, Gottfried, *Evangelische Kirche und Politik 1917–1919. Die politischen Strömungen im deutschen Protestantismus von der Julikrise 1917 bis zum Herbst 1919*, Beiträge zur Geschichte des Parlamentarismus und der politischen Parteien, vol. 6, Düsseldorf, 1959.

Meister, Alois, 'Der preussischer Residentenstreit in Köln. Ein Versuch zur Einführung des reformierten Gottesdienstes', *Annalen des Historischen Vereins für den Niederrhein*, 70 (1901), 1–30.

Mejer, Otto, *Die Propaganda, ihre Provinzen und ihr Recht. Mit besonderer Rücksicht auf Deutschland*, 2 vols., Leipzig/Göttingen, 1852–3.

Melhop, W., *Die Alster. Geschichtlich, ortskundlich und flussbautechnisch beschrieben*, Hamburg, 1932.

III. Secondary literature

Melle, W. von, *Die Entwicklung des öffentlichen Armenwesens in Hamburg*, Hamburg, 1883.

Metzler, Johannes, *Die Apostolischen Vikariate des Nordens. Ihre Entstehung, ihre Entwicklung und ihre Verwalter. Ein Beitrag zur Geschichte der nordischen Missionen*, Paderborn, 1919.

Mönckeberg, Carl, 'Die Ausweisung der Englischen Exulanten aus Hamburg im Jahre 1553', *ZVHG*, 3 (1851), 186–201.

'Die Geschichte des hamburgischen Catechismus', *ZVHG*, 4 (1858), 581–604.

Hermann Samuel Reimarus und Johann Christian Edelmann, Hamburg, 1867.

Muir, E., 'Images of power: art and pageantry in Renaissance Venice', *American Historical Review*, 84 (1979), 16–52.

Müsing, H. W., 'Hermann Samuel Reimarus (1694–1768) und seine Religionskritik anhand eines unveröffentlichten manuskriptes', *ZVHG*, 62 (1976), 49–80.

'Speners *Pia Desideria* und ihre Bezüge zur deutschen Aufklärung', *Pietismus und Neuzeit*, 3 (1976), 32–70.

Mutzenbecher, Johann Friedrich, 'Sebastian Edzardi', *ZVHG*, 5 (1866), 210–23.

Nahrstedt, Wolfgang, *Die Entstehung der Freizeit. Dargestellt am Beispiel Hamburgs. Ein Beitrag zur Strukturgeschichte und zur strukturgeschichtlichen Grundlegung der Freizeitspädagogik*, Göttingen, 1972.

Narr, Dieter, 'Fest und Feier im Kulturprogramm der Aufklärung', *Zeitschrift für Volkskunde*, 62 (1966), 184–302.

Neddermeyer, Franz Heinrich, *Topographie der Freien und Hansestadt Hamburg*, Hamburg, 1832.

Nipperdey, Thomas, *Deutsche Geschichte 1800–1866. Bürgerwelt und starker Staat*, Munich, 1983.

Nirrnheim, Hans, 'Die hamburgische Verfassungsfrage 1814 bis 1848', *ZVHG*, 25 (1924), 128–48.

O'Brien, Charles H., *Ideas of religious toleration at the time of Joseph II. A study of the Enlightenment among the Catholics of Austria*, Transactions of the American Philosophical Society, N.S. vol. 59, pt 7, Philadelphia, 1969.

Oehlke, Waldemar, *Lessing und seine Zeit*, 2 vols., Munich, 1919.

Oellrich, W., 'Der hamburgisch-dänische Währungsstreit 1717–1736', *ZVHG*, 52 (1966), 23–54.

Otto, F., *Die rechtlichen Verhältnisse des Domstifts zu Hamburg von 1719 bis 1802*, Arbeiten zur Kirchengeschichte Hamburgs, vol. 6, Hamburg, 1962.

Petersen, Christoph, 'Die Teutsch-übende Gesellschaft in Hamburg', *ZVHG*, 2 (1847), 533–64.

Petzoldt, Richard, *Georg Philipp Telemann*, transl. Horace Fitzpatrick, London, 1974.

Philipp, Wolfgang, *Das Werden der Aufklärung in theologiegeschichtlicher Sicht*, Forschungen zur systematischen Theologie und Religionsphilosophie, vol. 3, Göttingen, 1957.

Pieper, Anton, *Die Propaganda-Congregation und die nordischen Missionen im siebenzehnten Jahrhundert. Aus den Akten des Propaganda-Archivs und des Vatikanischen Geheimarchivs dargestellt*, Vereinsschrift der Görresgesellschaft, No. 11(2), Cologne, 1886.

Pohl, Hans, *Die Portugiesen in Antwerpen (1567–1648). Zur Geschichte einer Minderheit*, *VSWG*, Beiheft 63, Wiesbaden, 1977.

Postel, Rainer, *Johann Martin Lappenberg. Ein Beitrag zur Geschichte der Geschichtswissenschaft im 19. Jahrhundert*, Historische Studien, vol. 423, Lübeck/Hamburg, 1972.

'Reformation und bürgerliche Mitsprache in Hamburg', *ZVHG*, 65 (1979), 1–20.

'Reformation und Gegenreformation 1517–1618', in *Hamburg. Geschichte der Stadt und ihrer Bewohner. Bd. 1 Von den Anfängen bis zur Reichsgründung*, ed. Hans-Dieter Loose, Hamburg, 1982.

'Zur Bedeutung der Reformation für das religiöse und soziale Verhalten des Bürgertums in Hamburg', in *Stadt und Kirche im 16. Jahrhundert*, ed. Bernd Möller, Schriften des Vereins für Reformationsgeschichte, vol. 190, Gütersloh, 1978, pp. 168–76.

Prange, Carsten, *Die Zeitungen und Zeitschriften des 17. Jahrhunderts in Hamburg und Altona. Ein Beitrag zur Publizistik der Frühaufklärung*, Beiträge zur Geschichte Hamburgs herausgegeben vom Verein für Hamburgische Geschichte, vol. 13, Hamburg, 1978.

Preetz, M., 'Die Privilegien für die deutschen Hugenotten', *Der deutsche Hugenott*, 25 (1961), 76–85.

Preiss, W., 'Handwerkerunruhen in der 2. Hälfte des 18. Jahrhunderts in Hamburg', unpublished dissertation, Hamburg, 1960.

Pütz, Peter, *Die Deutsche Aufklärung*, Erträge der Forschung, vol. 81, Darmstadt, 1979.

Ramcke, Rainer, *Die Beziehungen zwischen Hamburg und Österreich im 18. Jahrhundert. Kaiserlich-reichsstädtisches Verhältnis im Zeichen von Handels- und Finanzinteressen*, Beiträge zur Geschichte Hamburgs herausgegeben vom Verein für Hamburgische Geschichte, vol. 3, Hamburg, 1969.

Rathje, Jürgen, '"Der Patriot". Eine hamburgische Zeitschrift der ersten Hälfte des 18. Jahrhunderts', *ZVHG*, 65 (1979), 123–43.

Reils, P. D. H., 'Beiträge zur ältesten Geschichte der Juden in Hamburg. Aus den Acten des Staats- und Ministerial-Archivs gesammelt und zusammengestellt', *ZVHG*, 2 (1847), 357–424.

'Von der ältesten Niederlassung der Juden in Hamburg', *ZVHG*, 2 (1847), 157–66.

Reincke, Heinrich, 'Hamburgs Aufstieg zur Reichsfreiheit', *ZVHG*, 47 (1961), 17–34.

'Hamburgs Bevölkerung', in *idem, Forschungen und Skizzen zur Geschichte Hamburgs*, Veröffentlichungen aus dem Staatsarchiv der Freien und Hansestadt Hamburg, vol. 3, Hamburg, 1951, pp. 167–200.

Historisch-politische Betrachtungen über die Reichsunmittelbarkeit der Freien und Hansestadt Hamburg, Hamburg, 1952.

Reissmann, Martin, *Die hamburgische Kaufmannschaft des 17. Jahrhunderts in sozialgeschichtlicher Sicht*, Beiträge zur Geschichte Hamburgs herausgegeben vom Verein für Hamburgische Geschichte, vol. 4, Hamburg, 1975.

III. Secondary literature

Die Religion in Geschichte und Gegenwart. Handwörterbuch für Theologie und Religionswissenschaft, ed. Kurt Galling, 3rd edn., 6 vols., Tübingen, 1957–62.

Rengstorf, Karl Heinrich, 'Judentum im Zeitalter der Aufklärung. Geschichtliche Voraussetzungen und einige zentrale Probleme', *Wolfenbütteler Studien zur Aufklärung*, 4 (1977), 11–37.

Rode, A., *Hamburg und die drei früheren Reformationsjubiläen 1617, 1717, 1817*, Hamburg, 1917.

Roosbroeck, Robert van, 'Die Niederlassung von Flamen und Wallonen in Hamburg (1567–1605)', *ZVHG*, 49/50 (1964), 53–76.

Roosen, B. C., 'Kurze Zusammenfassung der Geschichte der Hamburg-Altonaer Mennoniten-Gemeinde, von ihrer Entstehung bis zum Altonaer Brande', *ZVHG*, 3 (1851), 78–108.

Geschichte unseres Hauses, n.p., 1905.

Röpe, G. R., *Johann Melchior Goeze. Eine Rettung*, Hamburg, 1860.

Röthel, Hans, *Bürgerliche Kultur und Bildnismalerei in Hamburg während der ersten Hälfte des 18. Jahrhunderts*, Aus Hansischem Raum: Schriftenreihe der hansischen Gilde, vol. 10, Hamburg, 1938.

Rückleben, Hermann, *Die Niederwerfung der hamburgischen Ratsgewalt. Kirchliche Bewegungen und bürgerliche Unruhen im ausgehenden 17. Jahrhundert*, Beiträge zur Geschichte Hamburgs herausgegeben vom Verein für Hamburgische Geschichte, vol. 2, Hamburg, 1970.

Sägmüller, J. B., 'Der Begriff des *exercitium religionis publicum, exercitium religionis privatum* und der *devotio domestica* im Westfälischen Frieden', *Theologische Quartalschrift*, 90 (1908), 255–79.

Scheibe, Jörg, *Der 'Patriot' (1724–26) und sein Publikum. Untersuchungen über die Verfassergesellschaft und die Leserschaft einer Zeitschrift der frühen Aufklärung*, Göppinger Arbeiten zur Germanistik, vol. 109, Göppingen, 1973.

Schellenberg, Carl, *Hamburg und Holland. Kulturelle und wirtschaftliche Beziehungen*, Berlin, 1940.

Schepansky, Ernst W., 'Ein Beispiel zur Sozialgeschichte des Fremden. Mennoniten in Hamburg und Altona zur Zeit des Merkantilismus', *Hamburger Jahrbuch für Wirtschafts- und Gesellschaftspolitik*, 24 (1979), 219–34.

Scheuner, U., 'Die Auswanderungsfreiheit in der Verfassungsgeschichte und im Verfassungsrecht Deutschlands', in *Festschrift Richard Thoma zum 75. Geburtstag am 19.XII.1949. Dargebracht von Freunden, Schülern und Fachgenossen*, Tübingen, 1950, pp. 199–224.

Schieder, Theodor, 'Kirchenspaltungen und Kirchenunionspläne und ihre Rückwirkungen auf die politische Geschichte Europas', *Geschichte in Wissenschaft und Unterricht*, 3 (1952), 591–605.

Schilfert, G., 'Die welthistorische Stellung der bürgerlichen Revolutionen des 16. bis 18. Jahrhunderts und ihre Auswirkungen auf die deutschen Territorien', *Zeitschrift für Geschichtswissenschaft*, 21 (1973), 1443–63.

Schilling, Heinz, 'Calvinistische Presbyterien in Städten der Frühneuzeit – eine kirchliche Alternativform zur bürgerlichen Repräsentation? (Mit einer quantifizierenden Untersuchung zur holländischen Stadt Leiden)', in *Städtische*

Führungsgruppen und Gemeinde in der werdenden Neuzeit, ed. Wilfried Ehbrecht, Städteforschung: Veröffentlichungen des Instituts für vergleichende Städtegeschichte in Münster Reihe A: Darstellungen, vol. 9, Cologne/Vienna, 1980, pp. 385–444.

Niederländische Exulanten im 16. Jahrhundert. Ihre Stellung im Sozialgefüge und im religiösen Leben deutscher und englischer Städte, Schriften des Vereins für Reformationsgeschichte, vol. 187, Gütersloh, 1972.

'Religion und Gesellschaft in der Calvinistischen Republik der Vereinigten Niederlande', in *Kirche und gesellschaftlicher Wandel in deutschen und niederländischen Städten der werdenden Neuzeit*, ed. Franz Petri, Städteforschung: Veröffentlichungen des Instituts für vergleichende Städtegeschichte in Münster Reihe A: Darstellungen, vol. 10, Cologne/Vienna, 1980, pp. 197–250.

Schimanck, Hans, 'Stand und Entwicklung der Naturwissenschaften im Zeitalter der Aufklärung', in *Lessing und die Zeit der Aufklärung. Vorträge gehalten auf der Tagung der Joachim Jungius-Gesellschaft der Wissenschaften in Hamburg am 10. und 11. Oktober 1967*, Göttingen, 1968, pp. 30–76.

Schlaich, Klaus, 'Kirchenrecht und Vernunftrecht. Kirche und Staat in der Sicht der Kollegialtheorie', *Zeitschrift für evangelisches Kirchenrecht*, 14 (1968–9), 1–25.

Kollegialtheorie. Kirche, Recht und Staat in der Aufklärung, Jus ecclesiasticum, vol. 8, Munich, 1969.

Schmidt, Erich, *Lessing. Geschichte seines Lebens und seiner Schriften*, 3rd edn., 2 vols., Berlin, 1909.

Schoeps, Julius H., 'Aufklärung, Judentum und Emanzipation', *Wolfenbütteler Studien zur Aufklärung*, 4 (1977), 75–102.

Scholder, Klaus, 'Grundzüge der theologischen Aufklärung in Deutschland', in *Aufklärung, Absolutismus und Bürgertum in Deutschland*, ed. Franklin Kopitzsch, Nymphenburger Texte zur Wissenschaft: Modelluniversität, vol. 24, Munich, 1976, pp. 294–318.

Scholem, Gerschom, *Sabbatai Sevi: the mystical Messiah 1626–1676*, London, 1973.

Schönstädt, H. J., *Antichrist, Weltheilsgeschehen und Gottes Werkzeug. Römische Kirche, Reformation und Luther im Spiegel des Reformationsjubiläums 1617*, Veröffentlichungen des Instituts für Europäische Geschichte Mainz, vol. 88, Wiesbaden, 1978.

Schramm, Percy Ernst, *Hamburg. Ein Sonderfall in der Geschichte Deutschlands*, Vorträge und Aufsätze herausgegeben vom Verein für Hamburgische Geschichte, vol. 13, Hamburg, 1964.

'Hamburg und die Adelsfrage (Bis 1806)', *ZVHG*, 55 (1969), 81–93.

Neun Generationen. Dreihundert Jahre deutscher 'Kulturgeschichte' im Lichte der Schicksale einer Hamburger Bürgerfamilie (1648–1948), 2 vols., Göttingen, 1963–4.

'Zwei "Millionäre" aus Refugié-Familien', in *Huguenotten in Hamburg, Stade, Altona, Tagungsschrift zum Deutschen Huguenottentag. Hamburg, 23–26 April 1976*, ed. H. W. Wagner, Obersickle/Braunschweig, 1976, pp. 26–48.

III. Secondary literature

Schröder, Hans (ed.), *Lexikon der hamburgischen Schriftsteller bis zur Gegenwart*, 8 vols., Hamburg, 1851–83.

Schultze, Harald, *Lessings Toleranzbegriff. Eine theologische Studie*, Forschungen zur systematischen und ökumenischen Theologie, vol. 20, Göttingen, 1969.

'Toleranz und Orthodoxie. Johann Melchior Goeze in seiner Auseinandersetzung mit der Theologie der Aufklärung, *Neue Zeitschrift für systematische Theologie*, 4 (1962), 197–219.

Schwentner, B., *Die Rechtslage der katholischen Kirche in den Hansestädten Hamburg, Bremen, Lübeck*, Hamburg, 1931.

Schwering, Leo, 'Zur äusseren Lage des Protestantismus in Köln während des 18. Jahrhunderts', *Annalen des Historischen Vereins für den Niederrhein*, 89 (1910), 1–29.

'Die religiöse und wirtschaftliche Entwicklung des Protestantismus in Köln während des 17. Jahrhunderts', *Annalen des Historischen Vereins für den Niederrhein*, 85 (1908), 1–42.

Scoville, Warren C., *The persecution of Huguenots and French economic development 1680–1720*, Berkeley/Los Angeles, 1960.

Seffrin, R., *Die katholische Bevölkerungsgruppe im Staate Hamburg*, Quakenbrück, 1938.

Sieveking, Heinrich, 'Die Hamburger Bank 1619–1875', in *Festschrift der Hamburgischen Universität ihrem Ehrenrektor Herrn Bürgermeister Werner von Melle...zum 80. Geburtstag am 18. Oktober 1933 dargebracht*, Hamburg, 1933, pp. 20–110.

'J. G. Büsch und seine Abhandlung von dem Geldumlauf', *Jahrbuch für Gesetzgebung, Verwaltung und Volkswirtschaft im Deutschen Reich*, 28 (1904), 77–115, 559–98.

Sillem, C. H. W., 'Zur Geschichte der Niederländer in Hamburg von ihrer Ankunft bis zum Abschluss des Niederländischen Contracts 1605', *ZVHG*, 7 (1883), 481–598.

Die Matrikel des Akademischen Gymnasiums in Hamburg 1613–1883, Hamburg, 1891.

Soliday, Gerald Lyman, *A community in conflict: Frankfurt society in the seventeenth and early eighteenth centuries*, Hanover, New Hampshire, 1974.

Specht, Gerhard, 'Der Streit zwischen Dänemark and Hamburg aus Anlass der Erhebung Altonas zur Stadt', in *300 Jahre Altona. Beiträge zu seiner Geschichte*, ed. Martin Ewald, Veröfftenlichungen des Vereins für Hamburgische Geschichte, vol. 20, Hamburg, 1964, pp. 19–33.

Stoob, Heinz, 'Über frühneuzeitliche Städtetypen', in *Dauer und Wandel der Geschichte. Aspekte europäischer Vergangenheit. Festgabe für Kurt von Raumer zum 15. Dezember 1965*, ed. Rudolf Vierhaus and Manfred Botzenhart, Neue Münstersche Beiträge zur Geschichtsforschung, vol. 9, Munster, 1966, pp. 163–212.

Thadden, Rudolf von. *Die Brandenburgisch-Preussischen Hofprediger im 17. und 18. Jahrhundert. Ein Beitrag zur Geschichte der absolutistischen Staatsgesellschaft in Brandenburg-Preussen*, Arbeiten zur Kirchengeschichte, vol. 32, Berlin, 1959.

Bibliography

Toury, Jacob, 'Die Behandlung jüdischer Problematik in der Tagesliteratur der Aufklärung (bis 1783)', *Jahrbuch des Instituts für Deutsche Geschichte Tel-Aviv*, 5 (1976), 13–47.

Soziale und politische Geschichte der Juden in Deutschland 1847–1871. Zwischen Revolution, Reaktion und Emanzipation, Düsseldorf, 1977.

Valentin, Ernst, *Telemann in seiner Zeit. Versuch eines geistesgeschichtlichen Porträts*, Veröffentlichungen der Hamburger Telemann-Gesellschaft, vol. 1, Hamburg, 1960.

Venturi, Franco, 'La première crise de l'ancien régime (1768–1776)', *Études sur le XVIIIe siècle*, 7 (1980), 9–24.

Vierhaus, Rudolf, *Deutschland im Zeitalter des Absolutismus*, Deutsche Geschichte, ed. Joachim Leuschner, vol. 6, Göttingen, 1968.

Vocelka, Karl, 'Manier – Groteske – Fest – Triumph. Zur Geistesgeschichte der frühen Neuzeit', *Österreich in Geschichte und Literatur*, 21 (1977), 137–50.

Vogel, Walter, 'Handelskonjunkturen und Wirtschaftskrisen in ihrer Auswirkung auf den Seehandel der Hansestädte 1560–1806', *Hansische Geschichtsblätter*, 74 (1956), 50–64.

Voigt, J. F., 'Bedenken der Oberalten gegen Sätze im Teil II der Origines Hamburgenses Petri Lambecii, 1661', *ZVHG*, 12 (1971), 213–19.

Rückblick auf die Stellung der Juden in Hamburg, Hamburg, 1881.

Wächter, Leonhard, *Historischer Nachlass*, ed. Christian Friedrich Wurm, 2 vols., Hamburg, 1838–9.

Weintraub, Wiktor, 'Tolerance and intolerance in old Poland', *Canadian Slavonic Papers*, 13 (1971), 21–43.

Westphalen, N. A., *Geschichte der Haupt-Grundgesetze der hamburgischen Verfassung*, 3 vols., Hamburg, 1844–6.

Hamburgs Verfassung und Verwaltung in ihrer allmähligen Entwickelung bis auf die neueste Zeit, 2 vols., Hamburg, 1841.

Whaley, Joachim, 'New light on the circulation of early newspapers: the case of the *Hamburgischer Correspondent* in 1730', *Bulletin of the Institute of Historical Research*, 52 (1979), 178–87.

'The Protestant Enlightenment in Germany', in *The Enlightenment in national context*, ed. Roy Porter and Mikuláš Teich, Cambridge, 1981, pp. 106–17.

'Rediscovering the *Aufklärung*', *German Life and Letters*, N.S. 34 (1981), 183–95.

'Symbolism for the survivors: the disposal of the dead in Hamburg in the late seventeenth and eighteenth centuries', in *Mirrors of mortality: studies in the social history of death*, ed. Joachim Whaley, London, 1981, pp. 80–105.

Wild, Rainer, 'Freidenker in Deutschland', *Zeitschrift für historische Forschung*, 6 (1979), 253–85.

Winckler, Lutz, *Martin Luther als Bürger und Patriot. Das Reformationsjubiläum von 1817 und der politische Protestantismus des Wartburgfestes*, Historische Studien, vol. 408, Lübeck/Hamburg, 1969.

Wiskemann, Erwin, *Hamburg und die Welthandelspolitik von den Anfängen bis zur Gegenwart*, Hamburg, 1929.

III. Secondary literature

Wohlfeil, Rainer, *Einführung in die Geschichte der deutschen Reformation*, Munich, 1982.

Wohlwill, Adolf, *Aus drei Jahrhunderten der Hamburgischen Geschichte (1648–1888)*, Jahrbuch der Hamburgischen Wissenschaftlichen Anstalten, 14 (1896), Beiheft 5, Hamburg, 1897.

'Zur Geschichte des Gottorper Vergleichs vom 27. Mai 1768', *Jahrbuch der Hamburgischen Wissenschaftlichen Anstalten*, 13 (1895), 1–42.

'Hamburg während der Pestjahre', *Jahrbuch der Hamburgischen Wissenschaftlichen Anstalten*, 10/II (1892), 289–406.

Neuere Geschichte der Freien und Hansestadt Hamburg insbesondere von 1789 bis 1815, Gotha, 1914.

Wolff, Helmuth Christian, 'Ein Engländer als Direktor der alten Hamburger Oper', *Hamburger Jahrbuch für Musikwissenschaft*, 3 (1978), 75–83.

'Die Hamburger Oper 1678–1738', in *300 Jahre Oper in Hamburg*, Hamburg, 1977, pp. 72–91.

Wucher, Agathe, 'Die gewerbliche Entwicklung der Stadt Altona im Zeitalter des Merkantilismus 1664–1803', in *300 Jahre Altona. Beiträge zu seiner Geschichte*, ed. Martin Ewald, Veröffentlichungen des Vereins für Hamburgische Geschichte, vol. 20, Hamburg, 1964, pp. 49–101.

Wurm, Christian Friedrich, *Verfassungs-Skizzen der Freien und Hansestädte Lübeck, Bremen und Hamburg*, Hamburg, 1841.

Yerushalmi, Yosef Hayim, *From Spanish court to Italian ghetto. Isaac Cardoso: a study in seventeenth-century Marranism and Jewish apologetics*, London/New York, 1971.

Zeeden, Ernst Walter, *Martin Luther und die Reformation im Urteil des deutschen Luthertums. Studien zum Selbstverständnis des lutherischen Protestantismus von Luthers Tod bis zum Beginn der Goethezeit*, 2 vols., Freiburg, 1950–2.

Zimmels, Hirsch J., *Ashkenazim and Sephardim: their relations, differences and problems as reflected in the rabbinical responsa*, Jews' College Publications, N.S. vol. 2, London, 1958.

Zimmermann, Mosche, *Hamburgischer Patriotismus und deutscher Nationalismus. Die Emanzipation der Juden in Hamburg 1830–1865*, Hamburger Beiträge zur Geschichte der deutschen Juden, vol. 6, Hamburg, 1979.

Index